WAR II

Land, Sea & Air Battles 1939-1945

Christopher Chant
Brigadier Shelford Bidwell O.B.E.
Anthony Preston
Jenny Shaw

**Foreword by Admiral of the Fleet,
The Earl Mountbatten of Burma**

Sundial

First published 1977 by
Sundial Books Limited
59 Grosvenor Street
London W1

Fourth impression, 1979

© 1977 Hennerwood Publications Limited

ISBN 0 904230 30 9

Produced by Mandarin Publishers Limited
22A Westlands Road
Quarry Bay, Hong Kong

Printed in Hong Kong

WORLD

Contents

Foreword

by Admiral of the Fleet, the Earl Mountbatten of Burma, KG, PC, GCB, OM, GCSI, GCIE, GCVO, DSO, FRS.

More than three decades have passed since the end of World War II and to many of the rising generations that conflict is a period of history confined to books and films. Words and even pictures cannot always convey the horror, hardships and deprivation suffered but those of us who served or lived through World War II know it as a very real experience.

I have written about some of my own experiences to set the scene for this illustrated history of World War II and to emphasise the frightening realities of war. There are those who say it is ancient history and we should forget it. But it is only by remembering or learning of the sacrifices made by millions of men, women and even children during that terrible period that we can hope to strengthen the resolve of the world to avoid the mistake of plunging into a nuclear holocaust which will be the end of civilisation as we know it.

For the first 21 months of World War II, I was in command of the 5th Destroyer Flotilla and my own ship, the Flotilla Leader, was HMS *Kelly*. After many adventures and having survived being mined, torpedoed, bombed and repaired, the *Kelly* was finally sunk during the Battle of Crete.

I had been ordered to take three of my Flotilla, HMS *Kashmir* and HMS *Kipling* as well as the *Kelly* to give fire support to the New Zealand Brigade in their attack on Maleme Airfield. By a merciful providence, the *Kipling* developed steering trouble, and I ordered her to part company. That left just the two of us. We put down our barrage with our 4·7 inch guns to support the New Zealanders. Then, at about 8 o'clock, on the morning of May 23, 1941, 24 Junkers 87 Stukas (dive-bombers) appeared on the horizon.

I made a signal to the *Kashmir* to act independently and put the engine-room telegraph to 'Full Ahead'. We must have been making over 33 knots. The Stukas came down in waves of three. The first wave went down on to the *Kashmir*, the second made for the *Kelly*. The third wave of bombs hit the *Kashmir*, and I saw that she was finished.

The next wave came in on us and I ordered 'Hard a-starboard'. With the wheel hard over, the ship was listing heavily over to port. And then one Stuka came in lower than any others – so low that he was one of the three we shot into the sea; but his bomb was released so close to the ship that it couldn't miss. It hit square below 'X' gundeck and killed the crew of the twin 4·7 inch gun mounting.

I gave the order 'Midships' and then 'Hard a-port' but we only listed over more heavily.

I gave the order 'Stop engines' and the coxswain shouted up the voice-pipe 'Ship won't answer the helm, sir. No reply to the engine-room telegraphs'.

I shouted out 'Keep all guns firing' because I could see another wave coming in. It was an unnecessary order because all the guns were firing. As we went over I could see some of the gun-crews being washed away from their guns while still trying to keep them in action.

I realised the ship was rolling right over and water was coming up in a raging torrent. When she was right over I took a deep breath as the seas closed over my head. Somehow I managed to pull myself under the bridge-screens in the darkness. I was already beginning to need air, so I held one hand over my mouth and one over my nose, hoping I would have the strength to keep them there. I thought my lungs were going to burst but at last I came to the surface, without having taken in any sea-water.

I yelled to everybody to swim to the one Carley raft afloat. We put the wounded inside it and the rest of us clung to the outside or to each other. The Stukas came back again, firing at us, and a number of men were killed. And then the miracle happened: there was the *Kipling*. I don't think I've ever been so pleased to see any ship in my life.

After the *Kelly* and the majority of the rest of the flotilla had been sunk, I was appointed to command the Aircraft Carrier HMS *Illustrious*, then under repair in the USA following damage in action off Malta.

At the invitation of the Chief of US Naval Operations, I visited the US Pacific Fleet in Pearl Harbor and gave lectures on the war at sea to their officers.

It was during this visit to Pearl Harbor in October 1941 that I was recalled by the Prime Minister, Winston Churchill, to succeed Admiral of the Fleet Lord Keyes (on whose staff I had served as a young Lieutenant in 1927) in charge of Combined Operations.

I was instructed by Churchill to work out the philosophy of invasion – to land and advance against the enemy. New landing craft, appurtenances and appliances had to be designed and quickly constructed in large numbers, and the three services had to be trained to act together as a single force in combined operations. Winston said 'All other headquarters in England are engaged on defensive measures; your headquarters must think offensively. The south coast of England is a bastion of defence against Hitler's invasion; you must turn it into a springboard to launch our attack.' This was most inspiring talk at a time when most people thought we had our backs to the wall.

At the Combined Operations Head-quarters, I found only 26 persons all told and not a single regular active-service officer or man among them. Before I left, this number had increased twenty-fold all working at full pressure. The actual sailors, soldiers and airmen in the Combined Operations Command increased to 50,000 trained experts.

At the beginning of 1942 I was ordered, in conjunction with the Commander-in-Chief of Home Forces, to prepare invasion plans. Other senior officers, British, American and Canadian became associated with us and we became known as the 'Combined Commanders'.

From the start, the Allied Generals and Air Marshals wanted the invasion to take place from the Dover area across the straits to Calais and the surrounding district. I resolutely and ceaselessly opposed them. I pointed out that the German Generals had come to the same conclusion and were rapidly building up reinforcements in the Calais area. These reached a force of no less than 25 Divisions before we landed in France. Our intelligence showed the Germans had developed a really powerful coast defence system, which could dominate our ships and had established strong defence in depth behind Calais.

So I insisted we should land in the Baie de la Seine area just to the eastward of Cherbourg mainly at Arromanches. I put my case to Churchill and our Chiefs of Staff direct, for I was a member of their Committee. I won through and in due course we landed successfully in Normandy.

In the autumn of 1943, I was sent out to set up the Supreme Allied Command in South East Asia and so was many thousands of miles away on D-day.

When I took over operational command in South East Asia the situation was not encouraging. The Japanese were in firm possession of the whole perimeter; from Northern Burma to New Guinea through Malaya and the Netherlands East Indies. Their forces dominated the Bay of Bengal; our Forces were clinging precariously to the north-eastern approaches to India, with lines of communication that were barely adequate for purposes of defence, let alone attack.

For two years we had been continuously defeated at sea, on land, and in the air, and it would have been a miracle if the morale of our troops had not been seriously affected. I feel I can pay no greater tribute to all the men in my Command, than to say that they recovered their spirit, and it was this factor, more than any other, which brought about the defeat of the Japanese in Burma. Without the highest morale, the campaign itself could never have been undertaken; for the troops were asked to invade Burma from the north-west, and to fight over country which had previously only been crossed by the most intrepid explorers.

By the time I arrived a great amphibious fleet had been collected in South East Asia, ready to seize an advanced base in the Andamans, which would have enabled us to go on to Rangoon or some other suitable objective. But soon after my arrival, this fleet was recalled for operations in the European theatre, and we were forced to re-conquer Burma 'against the grain', a feat which had until then been regarded as out of the question. This invasion took place over mountain ranges, in places more than 2,743 metres (9,000 feet) high, covered with an almost impenetrable jungle through parts of which – in the 'creeper country' of the Huk-awng valley, for instance – it was impossible, even without enemy opposition, to advance more than 3 to 4 km (2 to 2½ miles) in 24 hours.

Even this terrible terrain might have been manageable but for the monsoon. For five months in every year the monsoon beats down on the jungle, in a monthly rainfall ten times that of London. For five consecutive months men remained almost permanently soaked to the skin; since a heavy mackintosh would make the tropical heat unbearable. Their few possessions were permanently damp; the roads they built were almost at once washed away. Flying conditions were truly terrifying. I know of no case of an aeroplane entering one of the dreaded cumulo-nimbus thunder clouds and coming un-damaged out of it again.

Custom and local military opinion, both Allied and Japanese, had until the end of 1943, regarded the south-west monsoon as a close season for operations. But as this would have limited serious campaigning to six or seven months in the year, from 1944 on-wards the Allies fought on as hard in the monsoon as in the dry weather and gained the advantage which comes to the side that fights on, when the other is expecting both sides to stop.

More serious than the monsoon, however, was the incidence of tropical disease with which the jungles of Burma were infested. These presented a more redoubtable enemy than the Japanese army itself. In 1943, for every man who was admitted to hospital with wounds, there had been 120 who were casualties from these tropical diseases. Through the brilliant activities of our tropical disease specialists these 120 men had been reduced during 1944 to 20. During the first half of 1945 the rate halved and during the

last six weeks of the war we only had ten men down with disease for every one battle casualty.

The Allies in South East Asia overcame all obstacles: the mountain ranges, the jungle, the monsoon and the ravages of malaria. Perhaps the most disheartening factor, how-ever, with which the theatre had to contend, was that it continued to be lowest on the priority list. Outward and visible signs of this became evident to the troops. In the midst of the Burma Campaign the order was received to send back artillery ammunition to the European theatre.

We had just sufficient transport aircraft to make the recapture of Burma 'the wrong way round' by air-supplied soldiers possible. The number of additional aircraft we got however, when added to those we already had, met only half our real requirements; we made up the other half by flying double the hours normally allowed for sustained operations. Working an entire Air Force at double normal hours had hitherto been con-sidered permissible only for a day or two, or in an extreme emergency for a week or two; but these gallant men, British and American alike, worked at this rate day after day, week after week, month after month and produced the greatest air lift ever known.

In order to keep our forward air-supply bases within reach of the central thrust south-wards, parallel to the coast, it became necessary to seize bases and create landing strips along the enemy held Arakan coast. There was still a great dearth of landing craft, which were only beginning to arrive back from Europe as our advance proceeded. In response to my appeal, however, the Royal Navy collected and prepared all the old crocks which we had been allowed to keep back for training; and this scratch amphibious force pushed its way up uncharted 'chaungs' leap-frogging the 15th Army Corps forward, and keeping it supplied and supported.

At the time of the Japanese Surrender, the enemy in South East Asia were in full retreat at sea, on land and in the air; and over 190,000 Japanese dead had been counted in the Burma Campaign alone, though we could never discover the full scale of their casual-ties. A quarter-of-a million of our soldiers fully armed and equipped were being loaded into ships and craft for the great assault on Malaya and Singapore – an assault that we now know, from General Itagaki's own plans, could not have failed to be quickly and overwhelmingly successful. The Japanese had only 139,000 troops in Malaya; they did not know when or where our attacks would come; they only knew that the tide of war had long turned against them every-where; the Atomic Bomb afforded their Emperor the excuse to accept an Uncon-ditional Surrender, which had become in-evitable.

The myth of the invincible Japanese had been exploded in the Pacific and in Burma – this had been achieved by the courage, en-durance and superior fighting skill of the Allied soldiers, sailors and airmen.

In October 1976, I was in Singapore and visited the waxworks Surrender Tableau which the Singapore Government have put on show. I then revisited the City Hall in Singapore where this historic event had taken place, and it was a very moving ex-perience to recall that moment on Wednesday, September 12, 1945 when I received the un-conditional surrender of two-thirds of a million enemy soldiers, sailors and airmen.

There was an electrifying feeling through-out the ceremony and I shall never forget the amazing experience of driving through two miles of densely packed crowds to one never-ending thunderous roar of cheers.

Mountbatten of Burma

9

Introduction

HISTORIANS are still arguing about the causes of World War II. In the meantime, the view of the average man-in-the-street that it was Hitler's fault seems to come quite close to the truth, even though it does not answer that more important question, whose fault was Hitler? The man-in-the-street well knows that Hitler was possessed by a passionate desire to expand Germany, and that in the German army and air force he had the ideal tools for his ambition, and that his election as German chancellor in January 1933 marked the start of an accelerating progression towards world war. But this does not explain how far personal ambition, how far desire for German glory, and how far the quest for additional German territory interacted to produce September 1939. Nor does it explain whether Hitler really wanted war, or was simply more prepared than others to risk war. It does not, moreover, explain how far German public opinion (and especially the army) was behind Hitler. Nor does it pass judgement on the other protagonists who at one stage or another encouraged Hitler when they could have stopped him; men like Mussolini, who by invading Abyssinia made a promising Italian alliance with Britain impossible, or Stalin, who ordered the German communists to fight the anti-Hitler German socialists, or Chamberlain, who at Munich allowed Hitler to exploit his hatred of war. And what, too, of the so-called statesmen who imposed the grossly unfair Treaty of Versailles on an anti-war and democratic German government after World War I, a treaty whose real and imagined consequences persuaded a normally cautious German public to give their votes to a man like Hitler because he promised them release from its terms? And what, finally, of Bismarck, whose calculated and humiliating aggression against France in 1870 ignited a French hatred of Germany which led directly to the vengeful Treaty of Versailles?

At the core of Adolf Hitler's grand strategy was the need for more *Lebensraum* (living space) for Germany. The concept of *Lebensraum* was not new for it had arisen when Germany, its industry and population growing rapidly, noticed that it had been left behind by France and Britain in the quest for colonies. German dependence on foreign food and raw materials had been lethally demonstrated in World War I, when the British blockade and hostilities with Russia created famine and industrial shortages. A Germany expanded to incorporate not distant colonies, but neighbouring territory, seemed to many Germans a viable solution to this worrying problem.

Probably this problem of *Lebensraum* dominated Hitler's military-political thinking: the space must be had, and if Germany could not secure it by peaceful means, then war would have to be employed. Of course it was not all as simple as that, for Hitler's racial and political convictions also played a major part in shaping his policies. In the great plains to the east of Germany lived only Slavs, Hitler said, and they were sub-humans (*Untermenschen*), to be despised. And in Russia, there was the arch-enemy of all, communism, the antithesis of all that Hitler believed to be important in western civilization.

The securing of *Lebensraum* and the fulfilling of the associated concepts were therefore Hitler's prime aims from an early stage in his political career. The other factors in his campaigns were subsidiary, window-dressing to raise him to the position in which he could start on his real ambitions.

Was Hitler set on securing his ambitions by means of war? The difficult question to answer here is concerned with the *Führer's* psychological make-up. He was an aggressive person, liable to fly into the most appalling tantrums at the least provocation. Yet this does not necessarily mean that Hitler felt an inner compulsion to secure his desires through war. In fact, he was usually very cautious about his approach to a situation involving a war risk. An astute, even a brilliant, exponent of the art of brinkmanship, Hitler in his early days could judge matters to a niceness that entirely escaped his entourage, political or military. Time and

Below : **Forbidden by the Treaty of Versailles from possessing tanks, the German Army gained experience with mock-ups.** *Right :* **Von Papen, General von Blomberg, Hitler and Goebbels at a youth demonstration.**

time again his generals, fearful lest the German armed forces be drawn into a conflict for which they were not ready, awaited the inevitable disaster – which, of course, eventually came. During Hitler's re-occupation of the Rhineland (demilitarized by the Versailles Treaty) in 1936, for example, the German general staff was naturally worried that the French might react with considerable strength, which the German forces would be unable to contain. Yet Hitler's judgement proved correct, the French making no overt military moves.

In 1938, Hitler decided to give the armed forces an exercise during the 'invasion' of Austria that prefaced the *Anschluss* (annexation). Luckily for Germany there was no opposition, for the army's showing was not spectacular, especially that of the armoured forces, whose tanks showed an alarming tendency to break down. Nevertheless, so far Hitler's plans had worked out well, and his army and air force had gained useful experience while fighting on the side of General Francisco Franco's nationalists in the Spanish Civil War (1936–39).

When Hitler announced to his general staff in late 1937 that he had a considerable programme of annexations, starting with the German-speaking Sudetenland of Czechoslovakia in the following year, the generals began to have second thoughts again. General Ludwig Beck, chief of the general staff, thought that France and Great Britain would inevitably come to Czechoslovakia's aid. The general staff sent a memorandum about their fears to Hitler, and when he ignored it, Beck resigned. Some generals started to plot for Hitler's removal, but then the British and French agreement to Hitler's demands, at the celebrated Munich meeting, cut the ground out from under their feet.

Why did France and Great Britain agree to

Above : **SA men march into the arena at one of Hitler's Nuremberg rallies.**
Below right : **Men of** *Leibstandarte-SS, Adolf Hitler*, **Himmler's para-military élite and Hitler's bodyguards.**

allow Hitler to take Czechoslovakia's rich and strategically vital border regions? The reason seems quite simply that it was the easier solution. The British and French governments hoped that Hitler had limited ambitions, and that it was better to humour him with these than to risk another war that might be bloodier still than World War I. Right from the beginning of Hitler's leadership this compliant attitude had been apparent, and possibly contributed to Hitler's assurance in his brinkmanship. Hitler's confidence that France and Great Britain would do nothing to frustrate his ambitions in eastern Europe received a fillip in November 1937 when Lord Halifax, Lord President of the Council and Chamberlain's right-hand man, seemed to hint to him that this was the case.

Shortly after Halifax's visit, the British ambassador in Berlin, Sir Neville Henderson, reinforced Halifax's words, and Hitler not unnaturally thought that Britain, at least, regarded his territorial ambitions in eastern Europe as only reasonable. Much has been made of the fact that Germany was only poorly prepared for war in 1939, and that Hitler had frequently told his senior commanders that 1943 was the earliest year in which they might expect a major war. Indeed, he had told his naval commanders that 1945 was the likely date. That war came in 1939 may well have been the result of the assumptions which Hitler made in the light of the Halifax and Henderson interviews.

Russia, by this time, had come to distrust Hitler's ambitions, and made it known that she would certainly join France and Great

Left : **Chamberlain waves the piece of paper which he piously believed gave a guarantee of 'peace in our time'.**
Above : **Overjoyed Austrians in Salzburg greet Hitler after the** *Anschluss* **of 1938.** *Below left :* **The Hitler Youth were to ensure a solidly Nazi future for Germany.**

Britain in any efforts to maintain the *status quo*, by force if necessary. Yet Britain seemed cool towards Russian offers, and this must have encouraged Hitler further. The matter came to a head in September 1938, with Hitler's demands for the Sudetenland; again Russia had offered to help, but had then not been given a place at the Munich conference. Having gained the Sudetenland, Hitler seemed to moderate his ideas – he now merely wanted from Poland access across the Danzig Corridor to East Prussia, isolated from the rest of Germany by Polish territory. Poland and Hungary, it should be noted, had helped Germany in the Czech crisis by threatening Czechoslovakia's rear from two directions.

Then on March 15, 1939, Hitler (who had been planning to move for some time) used the excuse of a separatist declaration of independence in Slovakia to take over the rest of Czechoslovakia. Although at first Chamberlain claimed that this was not a breach of the Munich Agreement, he soon changed his mind, and on the 29 March, Chamberlain made Poland an offer of support in the event of anyone threatening her independence. This guarantee to Poland was like a red flag to a bull as far as Hitler was concerned: how dare Britain make, and Poland accept, so ridiculous an offer, which was nothing more than a slur on Germany's intentions into the bargain. Salt was rubbed in Hitler's wound by the fact that Britain hitherto had seemed so compliant.

The key to the whole problem, however, was Russia, the only country which could offer Poland any material aid. The Poles, sceptical of such aid, which might turn out to be an invasion in disguise, did not help with their anti-Russian attitudes. Britain and France realized that Russia was essential to their plans, but made no great efforts to secure Russia's commitment.

This left the field open for Hitler. Russia, still feeling slighted by the British and French attitudes in the last few years, was ready to listen to Hitler's blandishments, especially after the foreign minister, the anti-Nazi Litvinov, was replaced by the cold, practical Molotov. Hitler moved fast, and on 23 August a non-aggression pact was signed, incorporating a secret clause by which both Germany and Russia were to invade and partition Poland.

War was now almost inevitable. Hitler felt free to invade Poland, because of the secret clause in the Russo-German pact. He also believed that the British and French would see the futility of declaring war on Germany as a result of this invasion. Meanwhile, Mussolini was out in the wings, waiting like a hyena for some of the spoils from the top table to fall his way; and the United States was hoping that war would not come, or if it did would not involve her. She was nevertheless rearming herself. Finally, on the other side of the world, Japan was involved in her great war with China, thinking of how she might profit from the squabbles of the Europeans by seizing some weakened colonies or protectorates.

Hitler now wanted all of western Poland, and using the Poles' intransigence over the corridor issue as an excuse, Germany was well advanced with her plans for the opening campaign of what was to become World War II.

GERMANY T

With her forces better prepared than those of her enemies, Germany seemed invincible in the heady days of her triumph between 1939 and 1941: Poland fell in less than a month, Denmark and Norway in a few weeks, and the Low Countries in six weeks. By the end of June 1940 only Great Britain was left in the fight against Germany, though the Battle of Britain seemed to offer hope for the future. Then Hitler turned on Soviet Russia in June 1941. And though his forces had crushed resistance in the Balkans swiftly, the delay was to prove fatal to his plans in Russia . . .

RIUMPHANT

Preis: 20 Pfennig

JB
Illustrierter
Beobachter

DONNERSTAG, 6. JUNI 1940
15. JAHRGANG · FOLGE 23

AUS DEM INHALT:

VERLAG FRANZ EHER NACHF. · MÜNCHEN 22

Poland

DESPITE the existence of a non-aggression treaty between Poland and Germany, Hitler was determined to give the German people *Lebensraum* (living room) by conquering Poland. Detailed planning of the campaign started in April 1939, and on 23 August, the Russo-German non-aggression pact was signed which set out demarcation lines for the future partition of Poland.

One of Hitler's main concerns was to delay Britain's mobilization of her armed forces for as long as possible, particularly as Britain had reiterated her pledge to assist Poland be invaded. To this end, Hitler put on a show of sham diplomacy to convince the world of his peaceful intent. He even postponed the start of the offensive and continued his diplomatic appearances to ensure that Poland's potential allies were as ill-prepared as possible before his attack. By the end of August he could wait no longer; he issued Directive Number One for the Conduct of War and on September 1, 1939 the assault was launched.

Poland could not easily be defended against German aggression, being open to attack on three sides: from East Prussia, Pomerania and Slovakia. The Polish frontier contained a huge salient stretching from the East Prussian and Lithuanian border to the Carpathian passes, a distance of 2,000 km (1,250 miles), not including the defence requirements of the Danzig 'Corridor' linking the port of Danzig with the rest of Poland. The Poles had been advised by the French to base their defences along the line of the Niemen, Bobr, Narew, Vistula and San rivers, thus creating a strong river barrier and a front line of only 675 km (420 miles). However, they were loth to give up the important industrial areas and fertile agricultural lands that would consequently lie to the west of their front line.

The Polish troops could not defend 2,000 km effectively, and their commander-in-chief, Marshal Edward Rydz-Smigly, made matters worse by deploying many of his troops in Danzig and around Poznan, although he had received accurate intelligence reports on the forces massing against him. On 1 September, this huge front was defended by only 17 divisions, 3 infantry brigades and 6 cavalry brigades. There was no adequate command structure between Rydz-Smigly and his eight commanders of the Pomeranian, Modlin, Poznan, Lodz, Krakow, Carpathian, Prussian and Narew armies. There were two reserve army groups, the Pyskor and the Wyskov, the former including Poland's only tank unit, the Armoured Brigade Warsaw. The Polish Air Force had 433 (mostly obsolete) operational aircraft, the majority of them PZL P-7 and P-11 fighters and PZL P-23 bombers.

Hitler's objective was the swift destruction of the Polish armed forces, using crushing, surprise blows. Converging attacks on Warsaw would come from Silesia, Pomerania and East Prussia, and the German forces would execute two pincer movements – one on Warsaw and the second further east to trap any retreating forces. The German Army had 13 armoured and motorized divisions to launch the attack, plus 31 infantry divisions.

The forces were deployed in two main army groups, North and South. Army Group North, commanded by Colonel-General Fedor von Bock, comprised on its left flank the 3rd Army under General Georg von Küchler, and on its right flank the 4th Army under General Günther-Hans von Kluge. Army Group North would attack from East Prussia and Pomerania, its left flank taking on the Polish forces in the Danzig Corridor and then driving south towards Warsaw, while its right flank was to attack from Pomerania and defeat any Polish troops guarding the Danzig Corridor. Army Group South, commanded by Colonel-General Gerd von Rundstedt, had the 8th Army as its left flank under General Johannes Blaskowitz; the 14th Army as its right flank under General Wilhelm List; and the 10th Army in the centre under General Walther von Reichenau. Army Group South was to attack from Silesia and Slovakia. The 8th Army would engage Polish forces in the region of Poznan–Kutno, the 10th Army would drive north-east, towards Lodz and on to Warsaw, and the 14th Army would strike across the Carpathians and pin down the Poles around Krakow and Przemysl.

Each army group was supported by an air fleet. *Luftflotte* 1, commanded by General Albert Kesselring, would operate with Army Group North, and *Luftflotte* 4, commanded by General Alexander Löhr, would support Army Group South. Together, the air fleets comprised 897 bombers, dive-bombers and ground-attack aircraft, plus 210 fighters and 474 reconnaissance and transport machines.

Poland did not begin general mobilization until 1100 on 31 August and was thus caught with 13 of her 40 divisions still moving towards their concentration points, and a further 9 not yet mobilized, when the Germans struck on 1 September.

Ahead of the armies, the *Luftwaffe* prepared the way. Its mission was firstly to destroy the Polish Air Force on the ground, then to assist the ground forces, attack military installations and terrorize the civilian population. The Polish Air Force was practically annihilated by day three, although Polish pilots kept up sporadic attacks until 17 September, flying with great determination and skill. However, the *Luftwaffe* was supreme. Its dive-bomber units, consisting of Junkers Ju 87 Stukas, delivered pinpoint attacks at crucial moments in the offensive, and the Germans' ability to coordinate their air forces with the motorized and armoured formations was something new in warfare, giving great flexibility to these units without traditional artillery support.

Within a week, the *Wehrmacht* (German armed forces) had struck deep into Poland, armoured units pushing on ahead of the infantry. If the German equipment was modern, so were the tactics, and generals such as Guderian, Hoepner, Hoth, von Kleist and von Wietersheim quickly displayed their

Below: **From west and east. Germany and Russia crushed Poland with great ease.** *Right:* **Polish prisoners start the march into captivity and often death.**

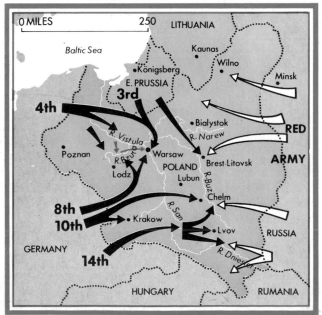

German advance 1-14 Sept 1939

Polish counterattack and retreat 9 Sept

Red Army invades from the East 17 Sept

Polish Poznan Army surrendered 19 Sept

skill in commanding and manoeuvring *Panzer* divisions. Against them, the Poles, having only one armoured brigade, could do little. The 12 brigades of Polish cavalry charged valiantly against the German *blitzkrieg*, but their swords and lances were worse than useless. All the Polish armies on the frontiers were quickly driven back by the fierce German offensive. Rydz-Smigly ordered his forces to withdraw eastwards on 6 September, but this was too late to save the frontier armies.

The German 10th Army rapidly approached Warsaw, its two armoured divisions reached the city but failed to take it on 8 September due to lack of infantry support. The rest of the 10th Army reached the Vistula on 10 September and defeated the Lodz Army. Further north, the German 4th Army reached and crossed the Vistula, and began its march on Warsaw.

Poland's Pomeranian and Poznan Armies, falling back on Warsaw, met the German 8th Army, which tried to block its retreat north of Lodz. Although virtually surrounded by Germans, the commander of the Poznan Army, General Kutrzeba, resolved to strike south against the flank of the main German eastward drive. This courageous move resulted in the Battle of the Bzura, in which the Poles succeeded in capturing bridgeheads across the Bzura river near Lowicz and driving back the German 30th Division. This crisis drew into the battle motorized and *Panzer* Corps, and even a corps from the 4th Army in the north.

These reinforcements, and the persistent, unresisted attacks by Stukas, forced the 170,000 Poles eventually to surrender after a hard battle fought at Lowicz on 19 September.

To the south, the German 14th Army drove on and reached the San river. Meanwhile, the inner pincers were closing around Warsaw as the 3rd Army encircled the city from the east and the 8th Army from the west. At the same time, a start was made on the outer pincer manoeuvre as the 3rd Army's left column struck out for Brest-Litovsk, 160 km (100 miles) behind the battle front. General Heinz Guderian who, with XIX *Panzer* Corps, had had great success earlier in the campaign in the Danzig area, was instrumental in the second pincer movement. On 9 September the *Panzers* crossed the Narew river upstream of Lomza, reaching Brest-Litovsk on 15 September. The 3rd *Panzer* Division pressed ahead and made contact with elements of the 10th and 14th Armies approaching from the south. The 14th Army had reached Lvov in the east and swung northwards to meet Guderian. The pincers met and snapped shut, trapping thousands with no hope of escape.

The Russians were surprised at the speed of the German advance. In spite of the Russo-Polish non-aggression pact, Russia could not stand by and see the Germans in control of Poland so, on 17 September, the Soviets announced that Poland and its government had now ceased to exist and that Russia must intervene to protect her own spheres of interest, the lands to the east of the Narew, Vistula and San rivers. The Russian armies swarmed across the virtually undefended eastern frontier of Poland, ending any further

Above left : **Ju 87 dive-bombers, 'flying artillery' for the ground forces, helped open a new era in warfare.** *Above :* **Polish cavalry stood no chance against German mechanised strength.** *Below left :* **Germans pour into Poland.**

hopes the Poles may have had of resisting. The Russian motorized columns rolled westward on a broad front. On 18 September they occupied Vilna and met the Germans at Brest-Litovsk.

The ruin and subjugation of Poland was nearly complete. On 18 September, the Polish government fled to Romania. Warsaw and Modlin were still holding out against the Germans, an heroic though futile struggle. Warsaw was violently bombarded daily by air and by heavy artillery. On 27 September, it capitulated in flames. Warsaw radio ceased to play the Polish national anthem and Hitler himself went to the great city. Modlin held out valiantly for one further day.

Thus in one month, the nation of Poland, with its 35,000,000 people, was wiped off the map. The geographical area was divided into two by the Treaty of Delimitation and Friendship signed on 28 September by Russia and Germany. In central Poland, the demarcation line connected the Bug and Vistula rivers, and was marked by the San river in Galicia. Lithuania was incorporated into the Soviet sphere in return for German sovereignty over parts of the province of Warsaw and the whole of Lublin. Poland had lost 694,000 prisoners to Germany and 217,000 to Russia. One hundred thousand Poles escaped to the west by way of Romania.

The Winter War

FINLAND, a country of dense forest and lakes with a sparse population of about 4,500,000 people scattered over 337,000 square kilometres (130,000 square miles), was the scene of one of the most amazing conflicts in history. Her tiny army held out against the might of Russia and, at the beginning of a campaign that lasted 105 days, inflicted severe casualties on the aggressor.

The Russo-Finnish Non-Aggression Pact was signed in 1934. On October 14, 1939 Stalin made various territorial demands on Finland in return for a considerable border adjustment in Karelia. Finland, wishing to retain its neutrality, offered to compromise on these demands, but Russia would not. The Russians had already prepared for their offensive. They had photographed the Karelian isthmus and Finland's ports, roads, industrial areas and fortifications, and considered that the Finns were hopelessly ill-equipped to defend themselves.

On 30 November, without any formal declaration of war, the Soviet land, sea and air *blitzkrieg* began. Helsinki suffered terrible air bombardment, with many dead. The Finns had begun calling up their reserves, but when the onslaught started the commander-in-chief, Marshal Carl Gustaf von Mannerheim, had only nine divisions at his disposal.

II and III Corps were deployed in the Karelian Isthmus with five divisions, commanded by Lieutenant-General Hugo Ostermann. IV Corps was on the east shore of Lake Ladoga with two divisions, under Major-General Hägglund. The Central Finland Group comprised V Corps (nine frontier battalions) under Major-General Vilpo Tuompo. In the Lapland Group were four independent battalions commanded by Major-General Kurt Wallenius. Two incomplete divisions (I Corps) and a cavalry brigade formed the reserve.

The Red Army invaders were grouped as follows: in the Karelian isthmus, the 7th Army with eight divisions, a tank corps and two independent tank brigades was to force the Mannerheim Line, take Viipuri and push on to Helsinki; deployed on the east shore of Lake Ladoga, the 8th Army with six divisions was to assist the 7th Army by drawing off the Finnish defence; the 9th Army with four divisions was to launch two columns, of which the left was to make for Oulu and the right for Kemi in central Finland; and in Lapland, the 14th Army with two divisions was to take Petsamo and sever Finnish links with Norway.

Mannerheim knew that the good roads and easy communications lay only in the centre of Finland and that the Finns must prevent the Russians reaching them. He was familiar with Russian tactics and military manuals and was able to predict Russian moves. In the event, manuals were useless in the winter conditions of Finland. The Russians fell immediate victims to the cruel weather; heavy snow blocked their advance and grounded their planes; the Finns proved to be masters of irregular and guerrilla warfare. They struck hard at the Russians in the dark, or during snowstorms; they would suddenly appear on skis, dressed in white, attack and disappear: to the Russians, the Finns seemed to be everywhere. Many booby-trap devices were employed to slow down the invader; minefields guarded all approaches and the Finns were expert at destroying tanks with 'Molotov cocktails' – bottles filled with a mixture of crude kerosene, tar and petrol.

Mannerheim's reservists mostly wore their own clothes, with perhaps a cap or belt for identification. Their marching was sloppy, but their skiing superb. Finnish soldiers would approach the Russian infantry on skis from the flanks, and sharpshooters then picked off the tightly clustered Red soldiers by the hundred.

The Finns were amazed as masses of heavy tanks bore down on them, but the Russians did not seem confident of how to use their *matériel* superiority to the greatest effect. However, the tanks became bogged down in the snow. The Russian troops were inexperienced and uncoordinated, and lacked ski training. Also, Stalin's purge of 1937 and 1938 had robbed the Red Army of its best leaders.

At first, the Russian soldiers bore up quite well, but as the temperature sank below zero, morale flagged. They froze and their weapons froze. Indeed, many thousands just froze to death. The Finns were better clothed and able to get their weapons working smoothly; they were at home in sub-zero temperatures, and were operating on home ground.

The Russians were beaten on almost all fronts. On their extreme right, they did take Petsamo in the middle of December by overwhelming its defenders with the superior fire power of a large force based on Murmansk. In the Karelian isthmus, however, the Mannerheim Line, with its anti-tank obstacles, extending 145 km (90 miles) and consisting of regular field fortifications, ditches and trenches, stopped the Russians. Open fields lay in front of the line, but the Finns chose not to venture out. The Russians were obliged to try breaking a line they knew little about. There was almost continuous fighting, the Russians constantly put in fresh divisions, and were constantly beaten back.

The Russian 7th Army's 139th and 75th Divisions reached Tolvajärvi on 12 December where their 45,000 men, 335 artillery pieces, 140 tanks and heavy mortars were ambushed and annihilated by seven Finnish battalions under Colonel Talvela, with 9,000 Finns and 20 pieces of artillery.

In central Finland, the column of the Soviet 9th Army was counterattacked at Suomussalmi on its way to Oulu. Colonel Siilasvuo led the Finns in this furious battle. The Russian 163rd Division was cut off after a Finnish attack lasting 17 days and the 44th Division was also eliminated as it too tried to retreat. Eight hundred Russians from the 44th Division dug in and the Finns attacked them at will, at the same time capturing an assortment of their weapons.

On all fronts, a pattern emerged of attack and counterattack, and both sides rapidly became exhausted. The Finns pushed the enemy back towards Russia, and by this time the Russians had lost approximately 27,500 dead. Stalin was frantic at this news, and on 12 December the League of Nations condemned Russia's aggression in Finland. Hitler remained neutral and refused to allow

Left : **Well equipped Finnish infantry in a prepared position near Ilomantsi wait for the Russian onslaught.**
Right : **Tactically naive, the Russians were decimated by well controlled Finnish fire in the early part of the war.**

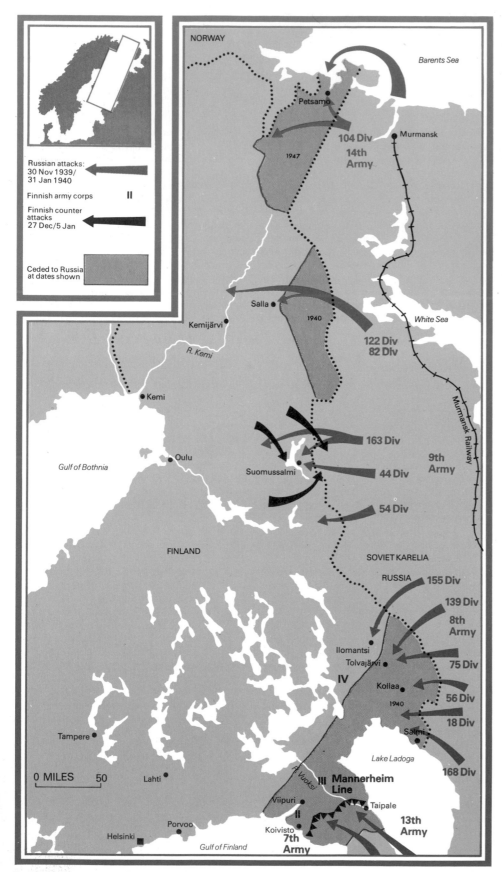

Map labels:
NORWAY
Barents Sea
Petsamo
Murmansk
104 Div
14th Army
1947
Salla
1940
Kemijärvi
White Sea
R. Kemi
122 Div
82 Div
Kemi
Murmansk Railway
163 Div
Gulf of Bothnia
Oulu
Suomussalmi
44 Div
9th Army
54 Div
FINLAND
SOVIET KARELIA
RUSSIA
155 Div
139 Div
8th Army
Ilomantsi
Tolvajärvi
75 Div
IV
Koilaa
56 Div
1940
18 Div
Salmi
Tampere
Lake Ladoga
0 MILES 50
Lahti
168 Div
R. Vuoksi
III Mannerheim Line
Viipuri
Taipale
Porvoo
II
13th Army
Koivisto
Helsinki
7th Army
Gulf of Finland

Legend:
Russian attacks:
30 Nov 1939/
31 Jan 1940
Finnish army corps II
Finnish counter attacks
27 Dec/5 Jan
Ceded to Russia
at dates shown

Left : **Although they fought magnificently, in their hearts the Finns knew that their position was hopeless against the great strength deployed by Russia.** *Above :* **Finnish ski troops proved a constant thorn in the Russians' side.** *Above right :* **The Finns used reindeer transport in the northern Petsamo region.** *Right :* **The Finns had to use improvised weapons such as explosive charges and Molotov cocktails.**

24 infantry divisions with 3 more in reserve, backed up by 20 artillery regiments and 7 armoured brigades. The ground forces had the support of 450 aircraft.

Mannerheim rightly predicted that the Russians would attack east of Summa village to the west of the Karelian isthmus, where the open fields would facilitate concentrations of tank and infantry. The offensive began on February 1, 1940 with the temperature 30 degrees below freezing. The Russians had learnt vital lessons since November, and they were now a coordinated force, often directed from observation balloons. They used trains of armoured sledges drawn by tanks to convey infantry, and employed flame-throwing tanks.

Heavy artillery constantly pounded the Finns, wearing them down. Blanket bombing of Finnish rear areas from 1 February marked the beginning of the end. The Russians attacked in massive waves with tremendous losses as the Finns machine-gunned them.

On 6 February, the final assault began. Three divisions with 150 tanks attacked an 8-km (5-mile) front, supported by 200 aircraft. On 7 February, they penetrated the region of Muolaa and struck at Summa. Timoshenko then moved the main thrust of his attack further east and by 11 February the Russians had broken through the Mannerheim Line. The Finns withdrew in perfect order, counterattacking all the while, and took up a new defensive line which, being longer than the Mannerheim Line, stretched

Italian aid to Finland to pass through Germany.

Russia therefore determined to beat the Finns at all costs. She threw in approximately 45 divisions, or 40 per cent of her land forces stationed in European Russia. Stalin rearranged the leadership of his armies; Marshal Semyon Timoshenko became com-

mander of the Finnish campaign; his most urgent task was to mastermind the Karelian isthmus breakthrough.

The Soviet 7th Army, having failed to break through the Mannerheim Line, was moved to the Gulf of Finland, and the 13th Army took its place with its right flank on Lake Ladoga. Timoshenko's force comprised

their resources thinly. They continued to harass the Russians. Between 20 and 22 February 800 Russians were killed and tank losses ranged from 10 to 30 per day.

On 24 February, the Russians seized Koivisto island in the frozen Gulf of Finland and the 7th Army was ordered to cross the ice to the mainland and take Viipuri. Soon after, the main road from Viipuri to Helsinki was in Russian hands.

The Finns, having lost 25,000 killed and 43,000 wounded, were battle-weary. Further resistance seemed impossible because of the shortage of manpower and ammunition. Mannerheim therefore told the Finnish government that peace was essential.

On March 12, 1940 the Russo-Finnish Treaty was signed, ceding 41,400 square kilometres (16,000 square miles) to Russia. The new frontier left Finland naked to any aggressor, and the Russians in control of most of Karelia. Their losses had been staggering: some 200,000 dead and 400,000 wounded.

The Seizure of Denmark & Norway

ON December 14, 1939 the leader of the small Norwegian Party of National Union, Vidkun Quisling, alleged that British intervention in Scandinavia was imminent. Hitler immediately ordered preliminary studies for a possible expedition to Norway and Denmark.

Germany obtained two-thirds of her iron-ore from Scandinavia, exported through Luleå in Sweden, and Narvik in Norway. If the Allies could cut these supply lines, Germany's ability to wage war would be severely curtailed. Various means of achieving this end were considered, including the mining of the Leads, the sea corridor between Norway's offshore islands and the mainland down which the German merchant ships sailed. Finally it was the Russo–Finnish war which, in November 1939, afforded the Allies the opportunity of sending troops to Scandinavia for intervention on Finland's behalf.

On February 16, 1940 the German supply ship *Altmark* was seen in Norwegian territorial waters. The British, believing she was carrying Allied prisoners, intercepted her and freed 299 captive merchant seamen. This incident convinced Hitler that the Allies might act first in Scandinavia, and he immediately appointed Lieutenant-General Nikolaus von Falkenhorst commander of the projected conquest of Norway and Denmark.

Left : **German paratroopers in Norway.**

Below : **German troops use a mortar against Norwegian mountain troops.**

D-day was to be 20 March, but was later put back to 9 April.

Meanwhile the Finnish surrender had spoilt Allied plans for intervention on her behalf; they decided to lay mines and only to land troops in response to German aggression, naïvely believing that there would be ample time to deploy in strength in the main Norwegian ports before the Germans arrived.

For Operation Weser – the invasion of Denmark and Norway – Hitler's forces comprised two corps: for Norway XXI Corps with two mountain divisions and five infantry divisions; and for Denmark XXXI Corps with two divisions, the 170th and 198th. They would be supported by all available warships and 41 troop transports; and by the *Luftwaffe* with 290 bombers, 40 Stukas and 100 fighters.

The element of surprise was necessary for success, yet most of the troops and their supplies had to be transported by sea. Hitler's plan was thus for a lightning attack on vital objectives using fewer than 9,000 assault troops in the spearhead. Nowhere did an initial landing force exceed 2,000 men.

At about the same time, Allied troops destined for Scandinavia also embarked, and the British fleet put to sea.

The German preparations were in fact noticed, but the Norwegian government did not call for general mobilization. Thus, when the German invasion force slipped past the British fleet, it met no organized resistance on landing.

As expected, Denmark succumbed within 24 hours on 9 April. At most of the principal Norwegian ports the assault troops landed

punctually or were merely delayed by brave but largely ineffectual resistance.

In Norway, the Germans landed at Kristiansand, Stavanger, Bergen, Trondheim, Narvik and Oslo. In the process, two Norwegian coastal defence vessels were blown out of the water at Narvik; at Trondheim, the heavy cruiser *Hipper* and four destroyers forced the fjord entrance; at Bergen the cruiser *Königsberg* was damaged but landed enough troops to capture the town promptly; and in the long Oslofjord, Rear-Admiral Oskar Kummetz's force came under heavy fire, and *Blücher*, Germany's most modern cruiser, was sunk while the pocket battleship *Lützow* was damaged and had to pull out. Consequently, half the force intended for Oslo were lost, but the city was taken by airborne troops. The sea-route to Oslo was temporarily blocked and German supplies and reinforcements could not be landed. Sola airfield and Stavanger were taken by paratroops.

At Narvik, the German 3rd Mountain Division disembarked successfully from ten destroyers, but its equipment and supplies failed to arrive, and also one of two tankers intended to refuel the destroyers for their homeward journey. These were thus delayed in Vestfjord, leading to Narvik, and were found there at dawn on 10 April by Captain B A W Warburton-Lee, commanding the British 2nd Destroyer Flotilla, who had taken the initiative by sweeping into the fjord. In the resulting battle, during which Warburton-Lee was killed, half the German destroyers were disabled or destroyed, and the other half were accounted for three days later when another flotilla entered, led by the battleship *Warspite*. Some 2,600 German survivors joined their compatriots ashore, being supplied with weapons from a nearby Norwegian depot.

The assault phase left Denmark a conquered country, and German garrisons established in the major towns of Norway. The Allies had completely failed to prevent the landings, although they did achieve some success at sea. The battlecruiser *Renown* damaged the German battlecruiser *Gneisenau* on 9 April; a British submarine sank the light cruiser *Karlsruhe*; and *Königsberg*, damaged at Bergen, was later finished off by naval aircraft.

The Germans at Narvik would have been unable to withstand an immediate Allied assault, and the Allied naval commander, Admiral of the Fleet Lord Cork and Orrery, favoured such action. However, the land commander, Major-General P J Mackesy,

disagreed, arguing that the harbour was strongly fortified with machine-gun posts. Mackesy wanted to take two unoccupied positions on the approaches to Narvik and to wait there until the snow melted. The two commanders were deadlocked while the Germans profited by the delay, and claimed that the Allies had been brought to a standstill in front of Narvik.

The Norwegian commander-in-chief, General Otto Ruge, had the unenviable task of holding on to the vast areas of Norway not occupied by the Germans, and of winning back what Norway had lost. Ruge believed he could hold out until Allied reinforcements arrived, and decided to retain as much as possible of the open country around Oslo where Allied troops, unaccustomed to mountain warfare and lacking the equipment for it, might be successful. But the Germans quickly brought in reinforcements and equipment once the way to Oslo was reopened, and Ruge's forces were threatened at too many points for him to concentrate more than a small proportion in any one sector. By mid-April, he could no longer defend the region of Oslo, and made a stand to the south of Lillehammer. Here he hoped to wait for reinforcements, and to prevent the Germans in the south linking up with their compatriots at Trondheim.

The Allies now realized that the key to the reconquest of Norway was Trondheim, the main link between the north and south of the country. It therefore became, with Narvik, an Allied objective, and they planned for a frontal assault on Trondheim from the sea (Operation Hammer), and for two subsidiary landings – one at Namsos, 130 km (80 miles) to the north of Trondheim, and another at Andalsnes, 240 km (150 miles) to the south. Major-General A Carton de Wiart commanded the Namsos force, comprising the 146th Infantry Brigade and a *demi-brigade* of French *Chasseurs Alpins*. Brigadier H de R Morgan led the Andalsnes landing with the 148th Brigade. Both landings were a success, but the British chiefs-of-staff then recommended that Operation Hammer itself be cancelled since they did not wish to put the fleet at risk. Instead, a pincer movement would close in on Trondheim from Andalsnes and Namsos, and the troops already landed would receive reinforcements.

This course of action was decided upon, but by now the Germans had also received reinforcements. The *Luftwaffe* had complete mastery of the air and the Allies were subjected to continual air attack. Namsos in particular afforded no protection. However, the Namsos force advanced to Verdal on the head of the fjord, 80 km (50 miles) from Trondheim, but the Germans sent a stronger force to the attack on 21 April, and the Allies withdrew in heavy snow. De Wiart recommended that his force be evacuated, which it was on 3 May under heavy air attack.

In response to Ruge's request for reinforcements, Morgan and his 148th Brigade had hastened from Andalsnes to Lillehammer and joined up with the exhausted Norwegians. On 24 April, Major-General B T C

Paget and the 15th Brigade reinforced them, Paget assuming command. They faced the Germans with great determination, a series of bitter battles being fought. On 1 May, the Allies were evacuated from Andalsnes.

Forces were then withdrawn from the Trondheim area – the Inter-Allied Supreme War Council had decided on 26 April to concentrate on Narvik. Norwegians were greatly disappointed at the abandonment of central Norway.

The superiority of the Germans was obvious. The Allies had failed at Trondheim; and at Narvik a mixed and improvised force of 6,000 Germans had so far held 20,000 Allied troops at bay.

Lieutenant-General Claude Auchinleck now became commander of the Narvik land forces, and the withdrawal from central Norway meant that the Narvik sector could be built up, although some British troops were deployed to check any German attempt to advance overland from Trondheim.

Reinforcements included General Marie Emile Béthouart's 1st *Chasseur* (Light) Division, two battalions of the French Foreign Legion, four Polish battalions and 3,500 Norwegians.

The German commander at Narvik, Lieutenant-General Eduard Dietl, had also been reinforced, and on paper, 13 Allied battalions faced 10 German battalions. Dietl and Béthouart were both experts at mountain warfare.

At midnight on 27 May, Béthouart led a force supported by an all-British naval bombardment in an assault southwards across the mile wide Rombaksfjord. Simultaneously, two Polish battalions attacked eastward on the south bank of the fjord. By 1700, the German garrison had retreated inland and Béthouart's forces were on the outskirts of Narvik. He then stood aside to let the Norwegian 6th Division enter the town.

On 7 June, the Germans found the Allies gone and the port installations demolished. The Allies had slipped quietly and secretly away between 4 and 8 June, a move necessitated by the deteriorating situation in France. They departed unhindered in four convoys.

However, *Scharnhorst*, *Gneisenau* and *Hipper* were at sea and on 8 June, a British tanker and armed trawler were sunk. Then the troopship *Orama* was hit. Later, the British aircraft carrier *Glorious* was sighted. *Scharnhorst* and *Gneisenau* set her ablaze, and also sank the destroyer *Ardent*. But another destroyer, *Acasta*, launched a torpedo which severely damaged *Scharnhorst*.

Thus ended the last action of the Norwegian campaign. On 10 June, General Ruge signed the treaty of capitulation for the Norwegian Army. The Germans lost 5,636 men killed; Norway lost 1,335, Britain 1,869, France and Poland some 530.

Although Allied action did not achieve its objective in cutting the iron route, or in reconquering Denmark and Norway, the action at sea meant that the German navy suffered losses which ultimately resulted in there being too few ships for the proposed invasion of England.

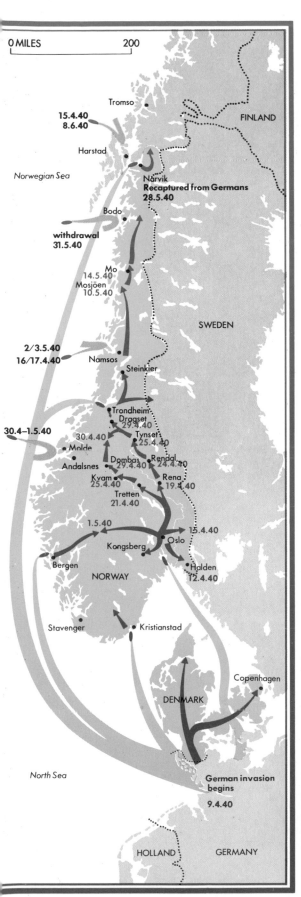

0 MILES 200

Tromso

15.4.40
8.6.40

Harstad

FINLAND

Norwegian Sea

Nárvik
Recaptured from Germans
28.5.40

Bodo

withdrawal
31.5.40

Mo
14.5.40
Mosjöen
10.5.40

SWEDEN

2/3.5.40
16/17.4.40

Namsos

Steinkier

Trondheim
Dragset
29.4.40

30.4–1.5.40

30.4.40
Molde

Tynset
25.4.40

Dombas
29.4.40
Andalsnes

Rendal
24.4.40

Kvam
25.4.40

Rena
19.4.40

Tretten
21.4.40

1.5.40

Oslo
15.4.40

Kongsberg

Bergen

Halden
12.4.40

NORWAY

Stavenger

Kristianstad

Copenhagen

DENMARK

North Sea

**German invasion
begins**

9.4.40

HOLLAND

GERMANY

German invasion of Denmark
and Norway, started
9 April 1940

14.5.40

German advance and dates
of capture

15.4.40
8.6.40

Allied landings, (top date) and
later withdrawals, (bottom date)

Above left : **A German AA machine-gun.**
Top right : **German infantry fight their
way forward in Norway.** *Centre right :*
**Dornier 217 bombers fly in towards
their target area.** *Right :* **Ju 87 dive-
bombers skim over the waters of a
Norwegian fjord.**

The Fall of the West

IN May and June 1940 Hitler unleashed his forces against the West. In one week, Holland surrendered and the French were talking of defeat. The attack was not unexpected, and both sides were roughly equal in numbers and equipment.

Until the beginning of 1940, the French commander-in-chief, General Maurice Gamelin, was broadly correct in his conception of German strategy, and his defensive measures stood a chance of success. It was reckoned that the Germans would try for a lightning victory, based on the Schlieffen Plan of 1914, with the main attack coming through Belgium. Belgium had expressed its neutrality in 1936 but, unlike Holland, co-operated to some extent with the Allies in planning the defence of its eastern border. Gamelin prepared alternative plans for the Allies to advance the British Expeditionary

Force (BEF), under General Lord Gort, and the 1st French Army Group, under General Gaston Billotte, to either the Dyle or Escaut river when the invasion occurred. The French 9th Army (General André Corap) would move up on the right to the Meuse river, whilst the mechanized 7th Army under General Henri Giraud moved up the coast on the left flank to secure the Scheldt estuary. Gamelin hoped that the Belgian Army would delay the Germans on the German–Belgian border in the region of Fort Eben-Emaël, reputedly the strongest fortress in the world.

The French thought the Maginot Line was strong enough a barrier on their own border with Germany, and they were confident that no surprise attack could be launched through the Ardennes. Most of the remaining Allied field formations were deployed behind the Maginot Line in case of a breakthrough. The

Allies were thus deployed with two strong flanks and a weak centre, with their armour committed to the north.

The assumption that the Germans' main attack would be on Belgium was correct until Lieutenant-General Erich von Manstein, chief-of-staff of German Army Group A, suggested that the bulk of the armoured units, and thus the principal thrust, should be transferred from the north to the centre; and that a surprise attack should be made through the Ardennes, against the weakest part of the French defences; whilst the Allied armies were drawn into north-east France and Belgium.

After discussion at Army High Command (OKH), von Manstein's plan found favour with Hitler, with the result that the Germans were deployed as follows: Army Group A, commanded by Colonel-General Gerd von

Rundstedt, was poised to sweep through the Ardennes and now included General Günther von Kluge's 4th Army from Army Group B; in total, Army Group A numbered 45½ divisions, including 7 *Panzer* and 3 motorized. The armour was organized as *Panzergruppe* von Kleist, which contained XIX *Panzer* Corps (General Heinz Guderian), XLI *Panzer* Corps (General Georg-Hans Reinhardt) and XIV Motorized Corps (Lieutenant-General Gustav von Wietersheim). In addition, the 5th and 7th *Panzer* Divisions formed XV *Panzer* Corps, under General Hermann Hoth, attached to the 4th Army. The armour was to act as a battering ram to thrust through the Allied lines in the Charleville–Sedan area and push quickly to the coast.

Army Group B, to attack Belgium and Holland, was commanded by Colonel-General Fedor von Bock. He had 29½ divisions, including 3 armoured and 2 motorized. After von Manstein's plan was accepted, von Bock's forces were reduced in strength, and von Bock was naturally concerned whether his two remaining armies would now be equal to their missions – the 6th Army to force and cross the Albert Canal, the 18th to capture Holland. Army Group C, commanded by Colonel-General Wilhelm von Leeb, was to attack from south Germany towards the Maginot Line with 19 divisions.

The German forces totalled 134 divisions, including reserves; the Allies had 130. The French had as many tanks as the Germans; but the German *Panzers* were superior in quality, and the Germans were also much better organized for armoured, mobile warfare, their *Panzers* being capable of existing and fighting independently. The French still believed in defensive warfare; the Germans had a brilliant and superbly executed plan.

Far left : **Well camouflaged German troops paddle across a Dutch river.**
Left : **An anti-tank gun clears the way.**
Below left : **The old quarter of Rotterdam was burned out on 14 May.**
Below : **Belgians welcome British troops moving towards the fighting.**

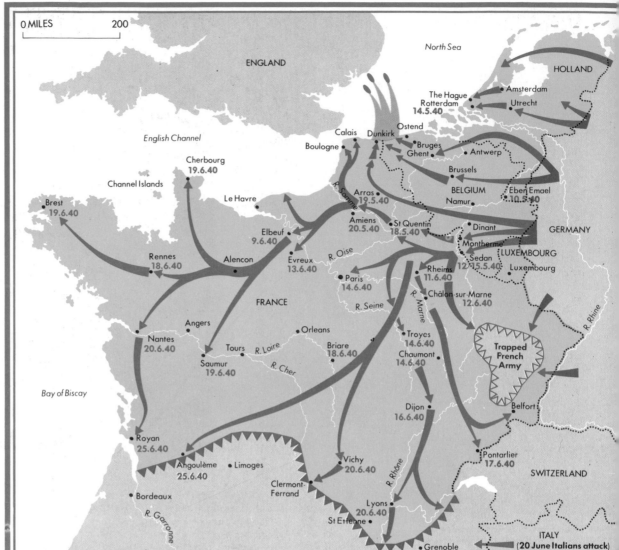

On 9 May Hitler ordered his forces to cross the frontiers of Holland, Belgium and Luxembourg at dawn the following day. They achieved total surprise with their airborne attack in Belgium and southern Holland, and for the first time paratroops won a decisive victory more or less unaided. Allied troops were not brought to the alert until after the assault had begun, and by daylight on 10 May, German paratroops had captured bridges around the Hague and Rotterdam in Holland, and had captured the main airfields. The first of von Bock's three armoured divisions advanced across the lower Maas (Meuse): the Dutch were unable to resist for long. France's 7th Army, attempting to link up with the Dutch Army near Breda, found the Germans already there and withdrew behind the Scheldt. The German 18th Army under General Georg von Küchler quickly overran the country and on 15 May the Dutch government capitulated after a devastating bombing attack on Rotterdam.

Simultaneously with the attack on Holland, the Germans pierced the Belgian frontier defences on 10 May with General Walther von Reichenau's 6th Army attacking along the Meuse and the Albert Canal; and airborne troops captured three of the main bridges

along the Albert Canal immediately west of Maastricht. On the same day, in a brilliantly executed manoeuvre, German gliders landed on top of Fort Eben-Emaël and the Belgian garrison surrendered. The Belgian Army retreated to the line of the Dyle river as the Allies put their Dyle Plan into operation. The BEF advanced to the Louvain–Wavre position and the French 1st Army moved forward to Namur. One third of the French first-line armoured vehicles were now on or behind this 35-km (22-mile) line linking Wavre with Namur.

But to the south, between Namur and Longuyon, a stretch of 155 km (95 miles), the French had only 12 infantry divisions; moreover, when the Germans arrived only 4 cavalry divisions and 2 cavalry brigades were in position. The French were short of anti-tank and anti-aircraft guns, and ground defences were lacking, especially around Sedan, the junction point of the French 2nd and 9th Armies. Reserves were few and far between. It was on these forces that the German *blitzkrieg* fell.

British and French forces were still advancing into Belgium as Guderian and Major-General Erwin Rommel (leading the 7th *Panzer* Division) spearheaded the armoured thrust through the Ardennes.

Using the full width of the roads, the advance was rapid and no effective resistance was met on the way through Luxembourg and the Belgian Ardennes. On 12 May both von Kleist's and Hoth's forces reached the Meuse, and the French cavalry, after a short delaying action, retreated over the Meuse, blowing up the bridges.

Hoth's XV *Panzer* Corps was on a more northerly route, heading for Dinant, and Rommel arrived there on 12 May. Von Kleist's *Panzergruppe* advanced towards Sedan, which fell to Guderian's forces while its defenders were subjected to Stuka and bomber raids. Monthermé fell to Reinhardt's corps. The advance of Army Group A comprised the greatest concentration of tanks ever seen in war, the force being over 160 km (100 miles) deep from head to tail. The Germans possessed great offensive spirit and the French were bewildered by the pace and style of the German advance.

The Meuse was crossed near Sedan and Monthermé initially by infantry and motor-cycle regiments, and pontoon bridges were then thrown across by *Panzer* engineers for the tanks. The Germans had deliberately chosen to attack at the junction of the French 2nd and 9th Armies, where second-rate troops were deployed. On 14 May, the

Left : **After overrunning the Low Countries and driving to the Channel coast, the Germans turned south and west.** *Above :* **German armoured cars patrol a captured Channel port.** *Above right :* **British prisoners move inland from Dunkirk.**

9th Army retreated 16 km (10 miles) – a retreat which then turned into frightened flight. Guderian's bridgehead was now 50 km (31 miles) wide and 25 km (15 miles) deep. By 16 May, the Germans were moving forward at the incredible rate of 65 km (40 miles) per day. Guderian and XIX Corps surged forward towards Abbeville and the Channel, the tank commanders being told to keep going while they had sufficient fuel. Thus, in four days, *Panzergruppe* von Kleist and XV *Panzer* Corps had destroyed eight divisions from the French 2nd and 9th Armies and had opened a breach of 130 km (81 miles) in the French front.

The French had no real reserve to plug this gap, and the Allies did not fully understand the situation. This eliminated any chance of getting reinforcements to where they were needed. The available reserves were deployed piecemeal, their movements being hampered by *Luftwaffe* attacks. The Allies were often applying their minds to a situation which was at least several hours out of date, and relations between the powers were not ideal. Allied forces were under the overall control of Billotte, not an effective coordinator, and communications were extremely difficult. The BEF in particular suffered from lack of information.

Meanwhile, the Germans made good use of the Allied chaos to further their advance. But then, surprisingly, the *Panzers* were called to a halt. The German high command was surprised at the ease with which the Meuse had been crossed, and daily expected a French counterattack. Hitler wanted the armour to wait until a large number of infantry units had been brought up to provide flank cover along the Aisne river. Von Kleist therefore ordered Guderian to halt on the night of 15 May. Guderian protested, and after considerable argument, the advance was resumed for a further 24 hours. On 16 May, Rommel and the 7th *Panzer* Division forced the Franco-Belgian border, quickly advancing to surprise Le Cateau at dawn the following day, thus achieving an advance of 50 km (31 miles), during which units of the French 18th Division and 1st Armoured Division were scattered, and the rear areas of the 9th Army thrown into confusion.

Next, Guderian was most surprised to receive a further order to halt. This time, von Kleist adopted a hostile attitude towards Guderian, who offered his resignation. General Wilhelm List, commander of the 12th Army, mediated and ordered Guderian to obey the halt command, but said a 'reconnaissance in force' towards the west could be continued. In fact, Guderian's reconnaissance in force consisted of the entire 1st and 2nd *Panzer* Divisions which, on 17 May, pushed a bridgehead across the Oise river at Moy. By 19 May they had reached

Péronne, and by nightfall on 20 May they were in Abbeville at the mouth of the Somme. Von Wietersheim, with the motorized divisions, was hard on Guderian's heels and took over the defence of the sector along the Somme from Peronne to Abbeville, while Guderian turned north. He had already cut the BEF's lines of communication to its bases south of the Somme; next he aimed to cut its line of retreat to the sea.

Von Rundstedt was now in a position to wheel north and north-east to catch the Belgian Army, the BEF and the French 1st Army in a pocket between his and von Bock's army groups. However, von Rundstedt's southern flank, between the mouth of the Somme and Sedan, was very weak. This was noticed by the French, but they were preoccupied attempting to restore their battered centre. The speed of the advance gave scarce time to rally dispersed forces.

Gamelin ordered a combined attack from north and south of the Somme to isolate the *Panzers*, but General Maxime Weygand then took over as commander-in-chief, and he postponed the order while he assessed the situation. It was doubtful if the proposed attack would have succeeded since the *Luftwaffe* had control of the air.

On 19 May, the second of two local counterattacks by the incomplete 4th Armoured Division under Colonel Charles de Gaulle against the left flank of XIX *Panzer* Corps was successful in itself, but made little difference to the campaign as a whole.

Meanwhile the Allies were losing in

Left : **The victors of the French campaign take their ease on one of the excellent beaches of France's Channel coast.** *Above :* **Declared an open city by the French, Paris fell intact to the advancing Germans. Here the early morning victory parade moves down the city's Avenue Foch seen by only a few early risers.** *Right :* **General Heinz Guderian was one of the architects of Germany's armoured forces and also helped devise the tactics that made them so successful. He had a brilliant command career in Poland, France and the beginning of the Russian campaign.**

Flanders. Weygand visited the northern group of armies and directed the BEF and part of the French 1st Army to counter-attack towards Cambrai and Bapaume under cover of the retreat to the Yser river by the Belgian Army. Weygand's enthusiasm unfortunately created the impression that the Allies were succeeding, and Lord Gort, commander of the BEF, had to explain that his troops were under great pressure from von Bock's armies and could not break off to march in another direction. On 21 May Gort had some success in a local assault on Arras. Two British light infantry battalions, a motorcycle battalion and 74 tanks from the 4th and 7th Royal Tank Regiments, plus 70 French tanks, caught Rommel's 7th *Panzer* Division unawares and Rommel believed he had been attacked by very strong forces with hundreds of tanks. But there was no attack from the south to complement the British effort. Weygand ordered one on 22 May, but communications were bad – his supreme headquarters did not even have a radio. The commander in the south did not have the troops or the ammunition to do as Weygand ordered, and the divisions were no longer where Weygand thought they were.

However, at Arras, German confidence had been shaken and the high command was convinced now that the armoured units were taking too many risks.

Guderian's force was meanwhile striking north. He isolated Boulogne on 22 May and Calais on the next day, then drove on to the

Aa river at Gravelines, only 16 km (10 miles) from Dunkirk. Reinhardt's corps also reached the canal line from Aire to Gravelines via St Omer, which was sparsely defended. There was then nothing between the *Panzers* and Dunkirk, the last port of escape for the BEF, but at that moment, von Rundstedt ordered von Kleist to halt his armour: Hitler wanted to preserve it for the coming offensive south of the Somme, and the land around Dunkirk was thought too marshy for tanks. Guderian, as always, protested vehemently, but this time the order was quite definite.

While the Germans dithered and delayed, the BEF escaped from Dunkirk. With such a desperate situation in Flanders, Gort had decided that the BEF must be evacuated. The British government agreed, and the withdrawal into the Dunkirk perimeter began, the French XVI Corps taking over the defence of the perimeter from the British. Vice-Admiral Bertram Ramsey planned the operation, named Dynamo, in which 338,000 men, including 113,000 Frenchmen, were taken off the beaches at Dunkirk. Ships of all shapes and sizes made the two-way journey across the Channel time and time again, braving *Luftwaffe* strikes on the coast of France. For the most part, however, the RAF was able to keep the *Luftwaffe* in check and so prevent it from stopping or severely disrupting the evacuation.

Now it was the turn of the Germans to feel bewildered. Allied troops were also evacuated from Boulogne, Le Havre, Cherbourg, St Nazaire and Bordeaux. In all, some 500,000 men were rescued during the month ending 26 June. Operation Dynamo itself started on 26 May and finished on 4 June. The Belgians had surrendered on 28 May, having given the British time to withdraw to Dunkirk.

Operation Dynamo was a miracle for the Allies, but it also represented a considerable victory for the Germans. In their lightning campaign, they had suffered 60,000 casualties and had taken over 1,000,000 prisoners. The Belgian and the Dutch armies had been eliminated, and the French had lost the support of 12 British divisions, most of whose equipment fell into German hands after the evacuation.

Weygand, having lost 30 divisions, now had only 66 left, many of which were not at full strength, to defend the area from Abbeville to the Maginot Line, a hopeless task. Two British divisions were still in France south of the Somme, and two more were sent over later.

The Germans had had time to bring up the mass of their marching infantry and re-organize. On 5 June, with 140 divisions, they began their southerly assault. There were three aims: to advance between the Oise and the sea to the lower Seine below Paris; to advance in a south-easterly direction to defeat the French army in the Paris–Metz–Belfort triangle and thus render useless the Maginot Line defences; and to pierce the Maginot Line in the direction of Nancy–Luneville.

Weygand deployed most of his remaining strength on the Somme–Aisne line, his troops being posted in a series of strongpoints which

were theoretically linked together, but in fact had large gaps with no adequate artillery cover. Both minefields and mobile reinforcements were sadly lacking. Weygand's plan to stand and fight was extremely inflexible and resulted in his troops often being by-passed or encircled by the Germans.

Von Bock's Army Group B attacked and crossed the Somme on 5 June, while von Rundstedt attacked across the Aisne, where the French resisted stoutly, although largely ineffectually. The *Panzer* forces then fanned out in a southerly direction: Guderian turned south and east towards the Swiss frontier; some elements of *Panzergruppe* von Kleist struck out south-eastwards making for Dijon and Lyon and the Mediterranean beyond; and other units of *Panzergruppe* von Kleist turned south-west towards Bordeaux.

Von Kluge's 4th Army attacked on the extreme right flank between Amiens and the sea, with Rommel's 7th *Panzer* Division quickly reaching the Seine at Rouen. By now, the French armies were breaking up into uncoordinated fragments. On 14 June, von Leeb's Army Group C struck at the Maginot Line. The *Luftwaffe* supported the armoured formations, bombing defended positions prior to the armoured assault.

The arrival of the Germans before Paris set off a new flood of refugees, causing congestion on the roads and providing targets for the *Luftwaffe*. On 10 June, the French government left Paris for Tours, with Bordeaux as the ultimate destination. On 14 June, German troops entered Paris. On 16 June, at a meeting of the French Council of Ministers, Prime Minister Paul Reynaud argued that resistance must continue, if necessary from abroad. He was supported by Brigadier-General de Gaulle but by few others, and so he resigned and was succeeded by the aged Marshal Henri Pétain, who negotiated for an armistice.

The *Panzer* thrust continued, and by 22 June, the day of the French surrender, the Germans had overrun all but southern France. Rommel and the 7th *Panzer* Division had reached Cherbourg, and the 5th *Panzer* Division had driven on to Brest. XVI *Panzer* Corps (Höpner) had taken Lyon and Grenoble; XIX *Panzer* Corps (Guderian) had reached the Swiss frontier and had turned north-east to Belfort. The Maginot Line had finally crumbled.

With the fall of France a certainty, Mussolini declared war on France and on 21 June, 450,000 Italians attacked the French Alpine front. The 185,000 French troops deployed there successfully held off the Italians; nowhere was there a breach of the French defences. South-eastern France at least was saved from Axis occupation.

The armistice was signed at Compiègne on the same site as the 1918 armistice, when Germany was the vanquished power. Hitler allowed Mussolini to occupy Corsica, Savoy and parts of Provence. The Germans occupied northern, eastern, western and south-western France, thus gaining control over the entire Atlantic and northern coastlines of Europe.

Above left : **Heinkel 111 medium bombers, which proved quite easy prey for the British fighters, fly towards their target.** *Left :* **Staff of a civilian air-raid centre wait for attack reports to come in.** *Above :* **The radar network was essential for enemy detection during the battle.** *Above right :* **An AA machine-gunner scans the skies.**

The Battle of Britain

WITH the end of hostilities between France and Germany on June 25, 1940 the only active enemy the Third *Reich* had still to conquer was Great Britain. Hitler, all along convinced that Britain would either not go to war or make only a token gesture, was now finally convinced that something would have to be done about the recalcitrant British. No serious plans for an invasion had been considered, and now the army and navy were at loggerheads over plans for the proposed invasion, codenamed Operation Sealion, which had been made on 5 June. The army wanted a major effort across the Channel on a broad front, whereas the navy was loth to contemplate even a narrow-front assault across the Straits of Dover, so great had been its losses in the Norwegian campaign.

Yet the first requirement of Operation Sealion was command of the air, to prevent the Royal Navy cutting the invasion fleet to pieces and to give the assaulting forces the necessary air support against the Royal Air Force. Hermann Göring was convinced that his mighty *Luftwaffe* could fulfil this task, despite the losses suffered in the French campaign. In fact, Göring's ambitions for his air force went further: he was convinced that on its own the *Luftwaffe* could force Britain to sue for terms, by knocking out the RAF and dominating southern England so that the British would see the futility of continued resistance to German arms. But the *Luftwaffe* had been designed and built as a tactical air force, and Göring was now entertaining for it strategic ambitions in face of opposition from the best air force the Germans had yet to meet.

So while the planning for Sealion continued, the *Luftwaffe*'s three main formations were to start the battle: *Luftflotte* 5 (General Hans-Jürgen Stumpff) from bases in Norway, *Luftflotte* 2 (Field-Marshal Albert Kesselring) from bases in the Low Countries and north-eastern France, and *Luftflotte* 3 (Field-Marshal Hugo Sperrle) from bases to the west of the Seine river. Between them these three air fleets could muster an establishment strength of 3,600 aircraft, of which some 2,700 were serviceable on the first day of July.

To face this formidable and experienced German aerial armada were the forces of the Royal Air Force's Fighter Command, under the control of Air Chief-Marshal Sir Hugh Dowding: 10 Group (Air Vice-Marshal Sir Quintin Brand) in the west of England, 11 Group (Air Vice-Marshal Keith Park) in London and south-east England, 12 Group (Air Vice-Marshal Trafford Leigh-Mallory) in East Anglia and the Midlands, and 13 Group (Air Vice-Marshal R E Saul) in northern England and Scotland. At the beginning of July the squadrons of these four groups had an establishment strength of some 871 single-engined fighters, of which 644 were serviceable. Although the supply of aircraft from the factories and repair units often caused concern during the forthcoming battle, the real problem faced by Fighter Command was the acute shortage of pilots, despite the fact that other RAF commands and even the Fleet Air Arm had been combed for suitable replacements.

Although considerably outnumbered, Fighter Command had certain distinct advantages: firstly there was radar and its associated fighter control system, backed up by visual observers stationed round the coast to confirm or correct the radar's warning of raids building up off the coast of Britain. This system allowed fighters to be sent up in the right numbers and at the right time to intercept the most important German raids. *Luftwaffe* intelligence had underestimated the importance of this British control system, and the Germans thus failed to devote anything like sufficient attention to the elimination of the easily visible coastal radar stations.

Secondly, the British pilots were initially fresher than their opponents, and enjoyed the advantage of operating over their own country. Return flights to base with a damaged aircraft were relatively short, and pilots who had to bale out landed on friendly territory. The Germans, on the other hand, faced the gruelling flight back to the continent with damaged machines, or had to bale out over England or the Channel. From the latter they were usually fished out by the efficient British air-sea rescue service to become prisoners of war.

Thirdly, the key to domination of the skies over England lay with the fighters, and here again the RAF enjoyed an advantage: by the time the German fighters had reached southern England, the length of time they could stay in the combat zone was very strictly limited if they were to get back to base without running out of fuel.

Fourthly, there was the question of the aircraft involved. The *Luftwaffe's* air strength for the Battle of Britain was divided into four main types of aircraft: twin-engined bombers; single-engined dive-bombers; twin-engined heavy fighters; and single-engined fighters. The British relied mainly on Supermarine Spitfire and Hawker Hurricane single-engined fighters, which were slightly inferior to the Messerschmitt Bf 109 in terms of firepower but otherwise comparable in terms of performance. This latter factor was being improved as the battle began, with the widespread introduction of constant-speed propellers. And once battle had been joined, the British fighters proved markedly superior to the other three main classes of German aircraft.

There is no way of fixing a date for the definitive beginning of the Battle of Britain, but by 1 July it may fairly be said to have entered upon its first phase, with harassing attacks on British coastal shipping, ports and installations by *Luftflotten* 2 and 3. The German plan was simple: by attacking these easily reached targets with bombers, the British fighters would be drawn up into combat on terms favourable to the German fighters and decimated. Underestimating the real strength of Fighter Command, the Germans imagined that the British would quickly start to lose more aircraft than they could afford to replace, and would thus be easy meat for the second phase of the German attack. The German plan backfired badly. The British fighters, positioned with the aid of radar, concentrated their attacks on the bombers and tried wherever possible to avoid dog-fighting with the German fighters. This coastal phase of the battle raged through July and the first week of August, and resulted in a serious setback to the Germans. Fighter Command losses had been acceptable, but German bomber losses had been relatively heavy, and the Junkers Ju 87 dive-bomber, hitherto regarded as a war-winner, was revealed as the easy prey for single-engined fighters.

Hitler appealed to Britain to come to terms on 19 July, but with the British refusal three days later, the Germans began in earnest to prepare plans for the defeat of Britain. On 1 August Hitler set the scene for the next phase

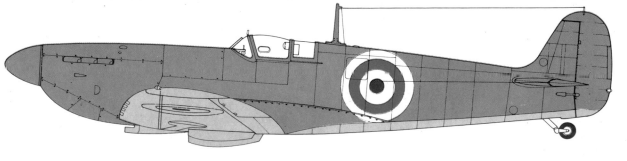

The Supermarine Spitfire, with a speed of some 350mph, was Britain's ablest match for German aircraft in fighter *versus* fighter combat.

Above left: **RAF fighter pilots wait for the order to get airborne.** *Above:* **The wreckage of a Messerschmitt 110 twin-engined fighter comes under interested examination near Dover.** *Top:* **Camera gun film reveals damage done to a Bf 110.**

of the battle by allowing German air attacks against Britain from 5 August onwards. The *Luftwaffe* was now to take the attack to the British forward fighter bases, coastal radar stations and other targets in southern England. Poor weather delayed the start of the German offensive until 8 August, and the second phase in fact lasted for only 16 days. Large numbers of relatively small forces roamed into southern England, strafing airfields and ports, to draw up the British fighter defences and engage them in close combat. The brunt of the defence was borne by Park's 11 Group, which because of the short warning available could only send up its squadrons individually or in pairs to meet the raids as they came in. Nevertheless, the British handled the German raids successfully, albeit at the price of quickly exhausting front-line squadrons.

Dowding's genius was well displayed at this time: he let his subordinate commanders get on with their jobs, and concentrated with remarkable skill on keeping up the flow of pilots and machines to the squadrons which needed them, and rotating new squadrons to the front at just the right moment, when current front-line units were on the verge of exhaustion. On the two main days of this second phase, 8 and 15 August, the Germans sent over 1,485 and 1,786 missions respectively but Fighter Command was able to contain them and also inflict severe losses on the Messerschmitt Bf 110 heavy fighters, as well as on the twin-engined bombers.

At this time, British fighter tactics were in the process of transition from the pre-war mass formations of 12 or more aircraft towards the German method of using units of 2 or 4 aircraft, which proved much more suitable. The more numerous, but slightly slower Hurricanes were given the most important task of dealing with the German bombers, while the Spitfires dealt with the German fighters. The combination of target allocation and the German type of tactics was to prove a winner in the weeks ahead. Ending on 23 August, the second phase of the battle left the British in command of the skies over southern England and the Germans in some disarray as a result of their heavy losses.

The *Luftwaffe* now stepped up its efforts by introducing mass bomber formations into what became the third phase of the battle

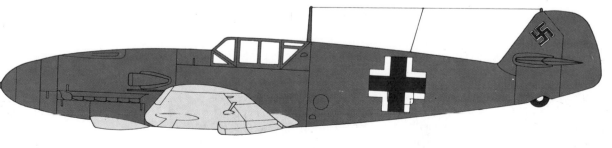

The Messerschmitt Bf 109 entered service in 1936, and was Germany's most numerous and successful fighter of the World War II period.

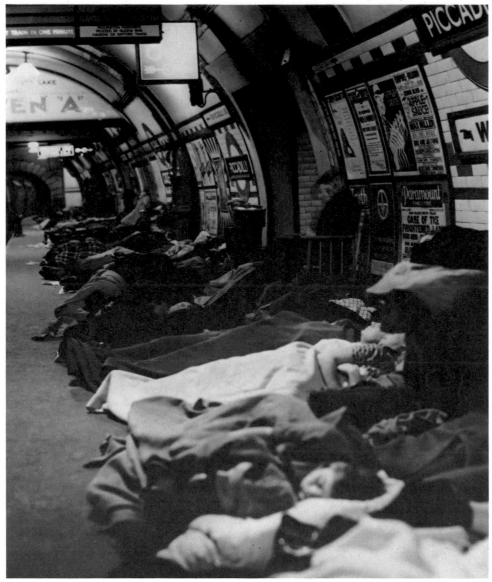

starting on 24 August. The idea was for 100 or more bombers in close formations and escorted by many fighters to beat their way through to the British fighter bases and destroy them. The fighters would deal with any British aircraft that rose to intercept, and any RAF machines that escaped would find their bases destroyed. This third phase, which lasted up to 5 September, was the closest that the Germans came to breaking Fighter Command, and the margin was very close indeed. Although the Germans again lost heavily, the British suffered the loss of over 450 aircraft and, more importantly, more

than 230 pilots killed or wounded. At the beginning of September, Fighter Command had very little left to throw into the fray: for the first time reserves were being used up faster than they could be replaced.

It was now that the Germans made their biggest blunder. Throughout this period, Bomber Command had been trying to carry the war to the Germans, attacking barge concentrations for the projected invasion by day, and targets in Germany by night. For the first time, on 24 August, Berlin was bombed. Hitler was so enraged that he ordered attacks on Fighter Command to cease, so that all

German efforts might be devoted to the destruction of London.

Just as the destruction of Fighter Command seemed imminent, the *Luftwaffe* switched to day-time bombardment of London. This, the fourth phase of the battle, began on 7 September. Up to the end of the month, German bomber formations wrought considerable havoc in London, but Fighter Command was given breathing time, with the result that both 11 and 12 Groups' squadrons could then concentrate on the massed German bombers and fighters. The destruction of these was great, and the supremely suc-

The Junkers Ju 88 was Germany's best medium bomber of the war, and also served as a day and night fighter, strike aircraft and reconnaissance machine.

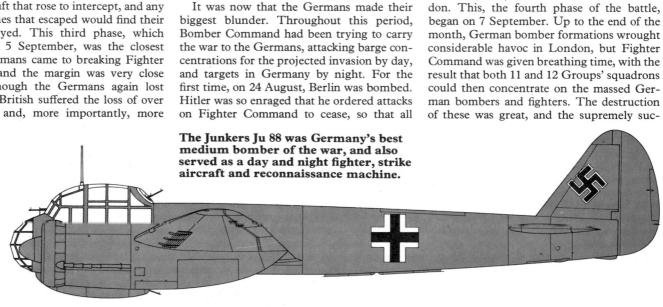

Above left : **Londoners shelter in Piccadilly Circus underground station.**
Above : **Searchlights crisscross the sky.**
Above right : **Although a useful deterrent, AA fire in 1940 was not very effective.** *Right :* **London children are evacuated in June 1940.**

cessful day of 15 September has since been celebrated as Battle of Britain Day.

Losses at this rate were too heavy for the *Luftwaffe* to support, and so on 1 October the last phase of the battle began. Fighter-bombers ranged over southern England by day, while bombers struck at London by night, but the tide was definitely against the *Luftwaffe*. Hitler cancelled his orders for Sealion on 12 October; the Battle of Britain had been won. There was, of course, the *Blitz* of London and other industrial centres from November onwards, but the Battle of Britain was over on 31 October. The British had lost 915 aircraft, but the Germans 1,733. In men, the Germans had fared even worse, for a large proportion of the losses had been multi-engine bombers.

Great Britain had won the first strategic air battle in history, and had driven off the German threat of invasion.

Naval War
1939-40

TO the newspapers it was the Phoney War, but it was not so to the U-boats, the Royal Navy or merchant seamen. From the morning of September 3, 1939, when the U-boats and surface ships already at their war stations received the signal from their high command telling them that war had been declared, the shooting war had started.

The British and French Admiralties had drawn up plans for cooperation, but inevitably it was the Royal Navy which took the lead in deciding policy. Although Hitler had endorsed the international protocol banning 'unrestricted' submarine warfare, or sinking merchantmen at sight, and had given strict instructions to Commodore Karl Dönitz and his U-boat arm to obey the Prize Regulations, the Admiralty assumed that the U-boats would not abide by the rules. This prediction seemed to be borne out when the unarmed liner *Athenia*, returning to England on the first day of the war, was torpedoed by *U-30* in the Western Approaches. Sadly, it was a genuine mistake on the part of *U-30*'s captain, who mistook the *Athenia* for a troopship, and a violation of Hitler's express orders. The British consequently put their full convoy-system into effect; within a matter of weeks U-boats were sinking merchant ships at sight and the dream of humanizing submarine warfare had vanished.

The U-boats had their biggest successes against warships, sinking the aircraft-carrier *Courageous* on 17 September and nearly destroying the new *Ark Royal*. On 14 October *U-47* penetrated the waters of the Home Fleet base at Scapa Flow and sank the old battleship *Royal Oak*, the propaganda value of which far outweighed the military value of the victim. It had another important strategic effect, for it forced the Home Fleet to abandon its main base until the defences of Scapa Flow could be overhauled. The linchpin of British naval strategy was to contain the German Navy in the North Sea, by minefields in the English Channel and by the Home Fleet holding the passage between the Orkneys and Norway. This policy of containment had worked superbly in World War I, and the Admiralty hoped to repeat its success while the resources of the British Empire were mustered to build up the country's strength. Conversely, if the German fleet should ever break out into the Atlantic its ships could disrupt the convoys bringing raw materials and munitions from Canada and the United States, and starve the British Isles into submission.

Left: **The British battleship** *Rodney*, **armed with nine 16-inch guns.** *Inset left*: **Grand-Admiral Erich Raeder (centre), C-in-C German Navy, lays his plans.** *Right*: **Merchant shipping formed Britain's lifeline to the world.**

Luckily for the British, the German Navy failed to exploit the temporary withdrawal of the Home fleet from October to December 1939. The two new battlecruisers *Scharnhorst* and *Gneisenau* made a sortie from Wilhelmshaven on 21 November passed north of the Shetlands and Faeroes without being sighted by British patrols, and attacked the armed liner (armed merchant cruiser) *Rawalpindi*, which was patrolling off Iceland. In a hopelessly unequal fight the liner lasted exactly 14 minutes and the German ships made their escape back to Germany. But the foray had achieved very little to break the British hold on the northern outlet to the North Sea and the Germans were lucky to escape the concentration of forces which were in the vicinity.

The Germans had recognized how tight the British blockade would be, and to avoid this they had made sure that two pocket battleships, *Admiral Graf Spee* and *Deutschland*, had put to sea in August, before the outbreak of war. Once the Polish campaign was over Hitler gave permission to attack British and French shipping, and soon the Admiralty was receiving reports of ships sunk by mysterious raiders all over the Atlantic. Eight hunting groups were formed, but only one of them had success, when on 13 December three cruisers caught *Graf Spee* off Montevideo. The German ship inflicted heavy damage on the biggest British ship, the heavy cruiser *Exeter*, but the combination of three opponents was too much for *Graf Spee* and she sought refuge in the River Plate. Skilful British propaganda suggested that a capital ship and an aircraft-carrier were close, whereas only one more cruiser was available. The *Graf Spee* was ordered by Hitler to avoid the indignity of being sunk and scuttled herself off Montevideo.

The Battle of the River Plate did much to

hearten the British and did little to encourage the Germans. *Deutschland* escaped back to Germany, but without sinking more than two ships. By the end of 1939 the first German challenge to the control of the sea had been checked, for the loss of only 15 merchant ships totalling 61,000 tons.

In home waters there was a new danger, the magnetic mine. The Germans, unaware that the British had their own magnetic mine, hoped to block British harbours with a mine to which there was no known countermeasure. Losses were severe, including not only merchant shipping but such important warships as the battleship *Nelson*, badly damaged while entering harbour; but the antidote was found. Ships were hurriedly equipped with degaussing gear to neutralize the hull's magnetism. As the British already had a magnetic mine of their own this first attempt to gain a tactical advantage with a supposedly secret weapon was not successful.

Patrols by shore-based aircraft belonging to RAF Coastal Command played an important part in defending shipping from U-boat attacks. But the lack of suitable aircraft, and much worse, the lack of a suitable weapon, robbed the RAF of much return for their efforts. The standard pre-war anti-submarine bomb was quite useless for its task, and in the spring of 1940 a modified naval depth-charge had to be introduced as an emergency measure. Fortunately for the British, this serious drawback was matched by a failure of German torpedoes.

Germany's invasion of Norway in April 1940 put a definite end to the Phoney War. It took the British and French navies by surprise, although the first contact was made between an Allied minelaying force on its way to lay mines in Norwegian waters and the German invasion forces. Many opportunities were lost by the Royal Navy through bad

planning and lack of coordination, and the devastating power of dive-bombers against warships came as an unpleasant shock. Nevertheless, it was the German Navy which suffered most in the Norwegian campaign. At the outset, the new heavy cruiser *Blücher* was blown out of the water by Norwegian coast defences, while Fleet Air Arm Skua dive-bombers sank the smaller cruiser *Königsberg* at Bergen. The two Battles of Narvik accounted for half of the total German destroyer-strength, a catastrophic loss which crippled subsequent German naval operations.

The battlecruiser *Renown* surprised the new battlecruisers *Scharnhorst* and *Gneisenau* in a snowstorm off Vestfjord and scored a damaging hit on one of the German ships before they escaped. The two German ships later scored an easy kill when they encountered the British aircraft carrier *Glorious* evacuating RAF personnel from northern Norway, but *Scharnhorst* was crippled by a torpedo from one of the escorting destroyers. *Gneisenau* did not escape either, for she was torpedoed by a submarine, and the active strength of the *Kriegsmarine* was badly depleted by June 1940.

The crisis in France in May and June 1940 meant an immediate end to the Anglo-French intervention in Norway, and soon the ships were involved in the enormous problem of evacuating troops from France. Operation Dynamo eventually rescued 338,000 British and French troops, but the cost was heavy in ships sunk and damaged. For a time, it looked as if Hitler really might invade the British Isles, and the entire resources of the Royal Navy were devoted to what many people saw as a last-ditch stand. Only afterwards did it become clear that the German Navy had suffered far too heavy casualties in Norway

Left : **The burning remains of the** *Graf Spee* **sit on the bottom off Montevideo after she had been scuttled to avoid ignominious defeat at the hands of a fictional British force waiting for her.**
Above : Graf Spee's **sistership** *Deutschland*, **also intended for long-range commerce raiding, was at sea in the Atlantic when World War II broke out, but had little success before returning home.**

The fall of France and the end of the Norwegian campaign mark the beginning of what was later known as the Battle of the Atlantic, a struggle which was to rage unabated for five years. It was not only the most vital sea campaign of the entire war but possibly the most important strategic area of all: for the Atlantic was the bridge between the United States and Great Britain. If the Atlantic lifeline had been cut, the industrial might of the United States could never have been brought to bear against Nazi Germany. In the long run, too, the Battle of the Atlantic was the link which connected the war against Japan with the war against Germany.

Fortunately, the British had taken timely steps before the war to remedy their weakness against U-boat attack. The existence of the ASDIC sonic underwater detector was suspected by the Germans but nothing actually known about it until the fall of France. A massive programme of cheap utility convoy escorts, the corvettes, had been started in 1939, and the first of these was ready in April 1940. In conjunction with the timely realization of how radar could be used, these countermeasures proved to be just in time to stave off disaster.

to be capable of supporting a sea-invasion, and when the *Luftwaffe* failed in its attempt to destroy the RAF, the nightmare of invasion gradually receded. It would have eased the minds of the British defenders if they had known that the strongest opponents of Hitler's Operation Sealion (invasion of England) were his naval staff.

The situation after Dunkirk was nonetheless extremely gloomy for the British. Not only were they now facing the Italians in the Mediterranean without the help of the French Navy, a vital component of the prewar strategy, but they also faced a hostile coastline occupied by German surface and subsurface forces, which stretched from Bordeaux to the Arctic Circle. The strategic position held by the Royal Navy in September 1939 had been completely outflanked, and had the Germans had a stronger navy with more understanding of the principles of sea power they could have forced the recalcitrant British to negotiate an armistice. The gravest consequence was that the U-boats could now operate from the Bay of Biscay. This left more fuel to get them to the convoy routes. As a result, a tremendous strain was brought to bear on the already hard-pressed escorts.

Wavell's 30,000

I
N June 1940 there were approximately 236,000 Italians under the overall command of Marshal Rodolfo Graziani in North Africa. The Italian 5th Army was in west Libya, and in the east was the Italian 10th Army, under General Berti, consisting of XXI and XXII Corps with three infantry divisions, one Blackshirt division and one Libyan native division. The Italians had 1,811 guns, 339 light tanks, 8,039 trucks and 151 first-line aircraft.

The British Commander-in-Chief, Middle East, General Sir Archibald Wavell, had five divisions (100,000 men), but of these only 36,000 men were in Egypt, formed into two incomplete divisions: Major-General M O'Moore Creagh's 7th Armoured Division with two brigades; Major-General P Neame's 4th Indian Division with two infantry brigades and part of its artillery. (In August Neame was replaced by Major-General N M de la P Beresford-Peirse.) The British

had 225 armoured vehicles. On 8 June Lieutenant-General Richard O'Connor assumed command of all troops in the Western Desert; this, the Western Desert Force, was later renamed XIII Corps.

The desert produced nothing for the support of armies. There were no roads, except along the coast, although there were a few recognizable tracks. Skilled driving could overcome the difficulties of desert terrain, but good navigation was essential in a practically featureless landscape. The British forces felt more at home than the Italians, and possessed some measure of vital desert sense.

The British kept the Italians off balance with daily motorized raids into Cyrenaica by the 7th Armoured Division. Graziani was under pressure from Mussolini to take the offensive, but felt his army was not ready. On 13 September, however, the 10th Army's offensive finally began. Two Italian columns advanced, one along the coast through

Sollum, and the other through the desert south of the escarpment parallel to the coastal strip, although it soon gave up this exposed route and moved through the Halfaya pass onto the coastal strip. The small British covering force fought an unhurried withdrawal battle for four days, firing on the Italian columns which presented excellent targets. On 16 September the Italians reached and occupied Sidi Barrani, where they halted. Graziani's main concern now was to build a new metalled road and a pipeline back to the border in order to receive water and supplies.

The British expected the Italians to push straight on towards Mersa Matruh, and planned to attack them when they moved. Meanwhile, Sidi Barrani was bombarded by the Royal Navy and bombed by the RAF.

In October the British situation in the desert was improved by the arrival of the 7th Royal Tank Regiment's Matilda I tanks, de-

Above : **Australian infantry stand guard over a batch of Axis prisoners awaiting transport to the rear.** *Above right :* **Pieces of artillery, of every conceivable calibre, were captured in great numbers during Wavell's classic offensive against the Italians.**

signed specially for the support of infantry, and having thick armour capable of withstanding Italian anti-tank guns. The 2nd Royal Tank Regiment and the 3rd Hussars also arrived at this time.

Wavell was now planning a short, swift raid against Sidi Barrani, and from this idea, the ambitious plan for Operation Compass developed. On 28 October, the Italians moved against Greece, and Wavell now had to manage without certain of his resources which were transferred to help there. He was therefore anxious for immediate action against Sidi Barrani. Operation Compass was a daring plan calling for the penetration of a 25-km (15-mile) gap in the defences of Sidi Barrani. The rocky terrain had prevented the Italians building an anti-tank ditch and they had few mines or anti-tank guns.

Operation Compass entailed detailed logistic and tactical planning. Some units would have to cross 120 km (75 miles) of open desert.

The Matilda I tanks would have to go through the Italian defences at night to avoid detection, and moonlight would be necessary if the forces were to get into formation after the trek across the desert. Dumps of ammunition and supplies were placed half way between Nibeiwa and Mersa Matruh. Secrecy was vital. Training of the troops was accomplished by exercises, the first being held on 26 November, which provided valuable experience. Only a few people knew that exercise number two on 9 December was the real attack.

While a force under Brigadier A R Selby attacked along the Maktila coast road, the British 7th Armoured Division and the 4th Indian Division struck through the gap in the Italian defences at dawn on 9 December. One battalion attacked near Nibeiwa at 0500 to divert attention, while the 11th Indian Brigade, 7th RTR with 48 tanks and the 4th Indian divisional artillery with 72 guns slipped through to form up beyond for the attack. Surprise was complete: at 0700 artillery bombarded the camp at Nibeiwa and the tanks approached the north-west entrance, destroying 20 unmanned Italian tanks before bursting into the camp followed by the infantry. The Italians fought sporadically, their artillery being the most resilient, but they gave up when unable to stop the advance of the Matilda I tanks. By 1040 it was all over. Two thousand Italians were taken prisoner and 35 tanks were in British hands.

The 7th Royal Tank Regiment wheeled north with the 5th Indian Infantry Brigade to attack Tummar West (held by the 2nd Libyan Division), which fell at 1600. The next day, the 4th Indian Division cleared Tummar East after spirited Italian resistance. On the evening of 9 December the 7th Armoured Division reached the sea, isolating the survivors of Tummar, and cut the road

between Sidi Barrani and Buqbuq. The Italian pocket at Maktila, too, had been cleared. Sidi Barrani itself fell in the evening of 10 December, having also been subjected to naval bombardment.

On 11 December the 4th Indian Division crushed the remaining resistance east of Sidi Barrani and the 7th Armoured Brigade cut off the 64th Catanzaro Division, caught on the move between Buqbuq and Sollum. The British, for 624 casualties, had bagged 38,300 prisoners, 237 guns and 73 tanks.

The 4th Indian Division was then transferred to the Sudan, much to O'Connor's dismay. It was replaced on 18 December by Major-General I G Mackay's 6th Australian Division, but without waiting for the new formation's arrival, O'Connor went in pursuit of the disorganized Italians. On 16 December the Italians evacuated Sollum and all posts on the Egyptian frontier, falling back to Bardia. Creagh's 7th Armoured Division and the British 16th Brigade followed up and cut the Tobruk–Bardia road. The Italian XXIII Corps, under Lieutenant-General Bergonzoli, was ordered to hold Bardia with 45,000 troops. The defences of Bardia were new and complete, having a 29-km (18-mile) perimeter, with small forts every 750 m (820 yards) or so. An anti-tank ditch 4 m (13 feet) wide and 1.25 m (4 feet) deep, a dense barbed wire network and also minefields were in evidence.

O'Connor had only 23 tanks left, the result of a shortage of spare parts. For the attack on Bardia, therefore, he decided that the infantry must cross the anti-tank ditch over a special assault bridge and clear the mines with the aid of sappers to allow the Matilda Is to exploit the breach. At dawn on 3 January the attack was launched, with 120 guns, and naval and air bombardment in support, as planned, the 6th Australian

Left : **The burned wreckage of an Italian Fiat CR 42 fighter. This type was Italy's most important fighter in the early stages of the war, despite being a biplane.** *Above :* **An Italian anti-aircraft gun, on a mobile mounting, fires at a British aircraft somewhere in the North African theatre.**

Infantry Division entered the ditch and the tanks rolled across the bridges into Bardia, meeting only ineffectual resistance. The Italian Air Force was eliminated, and on 4 January the Allies reached the sea having cut the Italian garrison in two. The Italians capitulated to XIII Corps, surrendering 45,000 prisoners, 460 guns, 131 tanks and 700 trucks.

The next objective was Tobruk, which possessed a deep-water port, and El Adem airfield, and which therefore had to be captured intact. The Tobruk defences were not yet completed and had a perimeter of about 65 km (40 miles). The Italian defenders, XXII Corps, consisting mainly of the 61st Sirte Division, had 25,000 men.

Tobruk was already surrounded after an unopposed advance by the 7th Armoured Division. The 6th Australian Division joined it and the attack began at dawn on 21 January. Mackay's infantry broke into the perimeter south of Tobruk and the Matilda I tanks then entered the bridgehead, taking the Italians by surprise. Despite a few ener-

getic counterattacks, the battle was over by nightfall. There was little damage to the harbour, and the seawater distilling plant remained intact. Some 25,000 Italians and their weapons passed into captivity.

Creagh's 7th Armoured Division then advanced towards Mechili and on 24 January the 4th Armoured Brigade engaged the Italian tanks, knocking out nine whilst the others escaped. On the same day, the 6th Australian Division appeared before Derna.

The Allies had done remarkably well to advance so far. Logistic problems of maintaining the advance were tremendous, but O'Connor wanted to keep the Italians on the run.

On 29 January the Italians evacuated Derna. O'Connor ordered the 6th Division to continue exerting pressure in the coastal region whilst the 7th Armoured Division advanced towards Msus. But the Allies had only 50 cruiser tanks left, most of which needed a good overhaul. O'Connor wanted to wait for two regiments of the British 2nd Armoured Division scheduled to arrive any time, but air reconnaissance showed signs of the Italian evacuation from Cyrenaica and if this was to be intercepted, immediate action was needed. Graziani had lost heart with the disappointment of seeing his tanks beaten at Mechili.

The retreating Italians used the coast road, while the Allies, cutting across from Mechili to Beda Fomm, had to cross rough desert.

Creagh's advance was headed by a wheeled column of all arms. The 80-km (50-mile) trek was slow going: the rocks and rough desert slowed down the light tanks. Lieutenant-Colonel J F B Combe's 11th Hussars with armoured cars reached Msus on 4 February. On the next day, they and the 2nd Battalion, the Rifle Brigade, arrived south of Beda Fomm, and positioned themselves astride the road down which the first Italian column came marching from Benghazi. Confused fighting raged throughout the following day, and burning tanks littered the site. The Allies were helped by the fact that the Italian tanks came along in bunches, thus presenting easy targets. The British tanks manoeuvred into good firing positions, using the lie of the land to their advantage, while The Italians were unable to coordinate an effective counterattack. Another 20,000 were captured.

Finally, the British reached El Agheila. O'Connor's XIII Corps, with two understrength Commonwealth divisions, overcame the severe logistical problems of advancing 900 km (560 miles) and destroyed the nine divisions of the Italian 10th Army.

Enter Rommel

LIEUTENANT-GENERAL Erwin Rommel arrived in Tripoli on February 12, 1941 to set up Operation *Sonnenblume* (Sunflower). Its objective was to save the Italians. O'Connor planned immediately to advance from El Agheila to Sirte and on to Tripoli, but General Sir Archibald Wavell was instructed that Cyrenaica must be secured with the smallest possible force, since all available manpower was urgently needed in the Balkans. Wavell saw no danger from the Germans before the summer, and deployed the 2nd Armoured Division, the 3rd Indian Motorized Brigade and the 9th Australian Division in Cyrenaica.

Rommel found the Italians preparing for a stand at Sirte with one incomplete armoured division and four infantry divisions, mostly without artillery. As his *Deutsches Afrika Korps* arrived, Rommel moved elements of its 5th Light Division forward to about 32 km (20 miles) west of El Agheila. He wanted to attack early in May, but was ordered to wait until the 15th *Panzer* Division arrived.

By the end of March, 15 convoys of Axis ships had been able to land 25,000 men, 8,500 vehicles and 26,000 tons of supplies in Tripoli, despite harassment by the Royal Navy and the RAF. Rommel was a commander of great charisma, and he persuaded the Italians that Tripoli could be held with German help.

At dawn on 24 March, the reconnaissance group of the 5th Light Division and the Italian Ariete Division attacked El Agheila. The British defenders pulled back without a fight, and took up new positions at Mersa Brega, which Rommel attacked on 31 March supported by some 50 German dive-bombers. Rommel encountered some resistance but the British retreated, with disorganized columns streaming back towards Benghazi and Mechili. Many armoured vehicles broke down and the British could not prevent a substantial body of German and Italian troops advancing up the coast of the Gulf of Sidra and fanning out to the northeast, towards Tmimi. For days Rommel exploited his success without informing his superiors and, in less than a fortnight, forced the British to give up most of Cyrenaica with the exception of Tobruk. In the process, the Germans also bagged some impressive prisoners, including the luckless O'Connor, who was found hopelessly off course, *en route* by car to Tmimi.

Wavell decided that Tobruk must be held: Major-General L J Morshead and the 9th Australian Division, plus other elements, withstood several attacks by Rommel. On the night of 13 April the Germans cleared a way through the anti-tank ditch and the 5th Light Division's tanks rumbled forward, conveying the infantry. The latter, however, was annihilated by the Australian artillery and 250 German prisoners taken. Rommel was furious and on 16 to 17 April personally directed the Italian Ariete Division in another attempt, again unsuccessful. A further attack in early May was also a failure.

Meanwhile the 15th *Panzer* Division took Bardia, which was unoccupied, along with Forts Capuzzo and Sollum, but then found its path to Egypt blocked by Brigadier W H E Gott.

With his forces thus dispersed, Rommel was instructed to await reinforcements before again attacking Tobruk. Meanwhile, the British were pouring in approximately 100 tons of supplies per day into Tobruk.

The arrival of 15th *Panzer* Division worried Wavell, but British reinforcements arrived via the Tiger convoy of fast merchant ships: on 12 May 43 Hawker Hurricane fighters and 238 tanks (135 Matilda Is, 82 cruisers and 21 Mark VIs) were unloaded at Alexandria, vital equipment for Operation Battleaxe to relieve Tobruk. Wavell's force consisted of the Western Desert Force, commanded by Lieutenant-General Sir Noel Beresford-Peirse, including the 4th Indian Division, the 7th Armoured Division and the 22nd Guards Brigade.

In the second half of May, Operation Brevity, the first of several operations, was mounted in the Halfaya–Sollum–Capuzzo–Bardia area. Although not a success, it provided useful experience.

The Battleaxe plan was for an advance on a 32-km (20-mile) front between Sollum and Sidi Omar, with infantry and a brigade of infantry tanks on the right, and a brigade of cruiser tanks plus support groups on the left. It was hoped to secure the Halfaya–Sollum–Capuzzo–Bardia area, defeat the Axis troops surrounding Tobruk and finally perhaps to drive on to the Derna–Mechili area.

Tobruk was guarded mostly by Italian troops; the 15th *Panzer* Division guarded the Egyptian frontier and the 5th Light Division was deployed on the coast between Tobruk and the border. The number of men, guns and tanks on each side was approximately

Far left: **German armour comes ashore in North Africa.** *Left*: **The Germans race towards Egypt.** *Below*: **Lieutenant-General Erwin Rommel.**

equal. Rommel, however, was well supplied with anti-tank weapons including about 12 88-mm anti-aircraft guns which could stop any British tank at a distance of 1,500 m (nearly a mile).

Battleaxe commenced on 15 June, with the RAF pounding the Germans. The British advanced, but Rommel committed only a small part of his armour, while making excellent use of his guns to inflict substantial losses on the British flanks. The 7th Armoured Brigade took Capuzzo, and then things started to go wrong. The 11th Indian Brigade and the Guards Brigade failed to take Halfaya, and in the evening the 7th Armoured Brigade clashed with the 5th Light Division and was reduced to 37 fit tanks. Rommel knew of most British movements as a result of the continued laxness in British radio security.

16 June was a day of rapid movement and hard fighting during which Rommel launched two counterattacks. Heavy fighting occurred around Halfaya, and the 7th Armoured Brigade fought a running battle with the 5th Light Division down to Sidi Omar. Rommel then struck east, hoping to surround the Western Desert Force.

He thus prevented the British from uniting their forces and crippled a good many tanks. On 17 June the British called off the offensive with only 22 cruiser and 17 infantry tanks available. They withdrew before their last line of communication was cut by Rommel, having lost 1,000 men, plus 22 cruiser and 64 I tanks.

Wavell was then succeeded by General Sir Claude Auchinleck, who arrived on 1 July. The date for Auchinleck's first offensive was 18 November: his objective was the relief of Tobruk and the operation was codenamed Crusader. Auchinleck organized his forces into the 8th Army, commanded by Lieutenant-General Sir Alan Cunningham. The British believed the key to the relief of Tobruk lay in the destruction of the two *Panzer* divisions, but Cunningham was uncertain of how to seek a decisive armoured battle.

By mid-November, Cunningham's army of six divisions and six independent brigade groups contained the largest body of armour as yet assembled by the British, with 724 front-line tanks and 200 in reserve. On the right flank was XIII Corps, latterly the Western Desert Force, commanded by Lieutenant-General A R Godwin-Austen with the New Zealand Division, the 4th Indian Division and the 1st Army Tank Brigade. On the left flank was XXX Corps, commanded by Lieutenant-General C W M Norrie, with the 7th Armoured Division (the 'Desert Rats') with 473 tanks, the 4th Armoured Brigade Group, the 1st South African Division and the 22nd Guards Brigade Group. The force was supported by the RAF and the Navy.

The Axis troops comprised the Italian XX (Mobile) Corps with two divisions; the *DAK* with the 15th *Panzer* Division, the 21st *Panzer* Division (formerly 5th Light Division), the *Afrika* Division and the Italian Savona Division; and the Italian XXI

Corps with four divisions. The Axis forces had approximately 400 tanks.

The *Afrika* Division and four Italian armoured divisions were surrounding Tobruk, with the 15th *Panzer* Division in their rear and to the east of them. One Italian division was deployed in the frontier area with the 21st *Panzer* Division astride and to the south of the Trigh Capuzzo.

Cunningham's plan was to use XIII Corps, consisting mostly of infantry and a tank brigade, to pin the enemy in the forward area while the highly mobile XXX Corps crossed the undefended frontier south of Sidi Omar from where it could move towards Tobruk or Bardia.

The British attack began at dawn on 18 November in torrential rain, and XXX Corps advanced to Gabr Saleh. However, Rommel thought this was only a reconnaissance in force and kept his armour back at Gambut, thus denying Cunningham his armoured clash.

The 7th Armoured Division then pushed on to Sidi Rezegh, where it was counterattacked by the 21st *Panzer* Division. Meanwhile, the 4th Armoured Brigade Group remained at Gabr Saleh to guard Godwin-Austen's flank.

Plans went ahead for the breakout from Tobruk on 21 November, where Major-General R M Scobie was now in command of the British and Polish garrison. Rommel rushed his armour to the Sidi Rezegh area to prevent the breakout.

So began a most confusing battle. For three days, tanks, infantry, guns and armoured cars coming south from Tobruk were opposed by German and Italian forces watching the perimeter, which were in turn counterattacked by the British 7th Armoured

Brigade supporting the breakout. German armour attacked in turn, having rushed from Gabr Saleh. The battlefield extended for 32 km (20 miles) and was often covered by clouds of dust. Both sides used tanks captured from the other.

Rommel became impatient with the slowness of the battle and on 24 November set off at the head of the 21st *Panzer* Division with 100 tanks to reach the Mediterranean by way of Sidi Omar and to strike the British in the rear. But he had no significant success and overextended his lines, with the 21st *Panzer* Division strung out along the Trigh el Abd with its forward units at Sidi Suleiman. The action declined into a series of sporadic bouts, inspired by Rommel's presence. On 26 November the *Panzers* withdrew into Bardia.

Meanwhile, the British set about reorganizing themselves, collecting and repairing numbers of knocked-out tanks. On 26 November, Cunningham was replaced by Lieutenant-General N M Ritchie, but Auchinleck directed the battle personally, and the British forces south of Tobruk made good progress. Rommel was forced to bring his tanks back.

The Germans and Italians were now becoming exhausted and after some confused engagements south of Tobruk, Rommel retreated because no further supplies could be delivered to him before the end of December. On 5 December he withdrew his forces east of Tobruk and a general retreat began the next day. Rommel's rearguards fought methodical delaying actions, which XIII Corps failed to overcome. The British reached Benghazi on 25 December and the Germans fought vigorously at Agedabia before withdrawing to El Agheila. XXX Corps reduced the Axis garrisons near the Egyptian

Above left : **British infantry move up through a barbed-wire entanglement.** *Top :* **Although not yet available, Sherman tanks helped turn the tide against Rommel.** *Above :* **Matilda tanks were well armoured but poorly armed.** *Right :* **With a long-barrelled 7.5-cm the PzKpfw IV was too good for British tanks.**

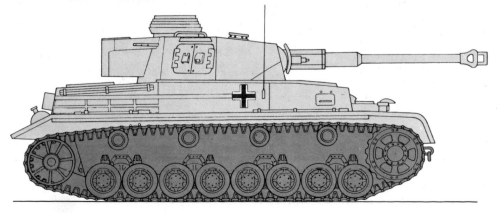

border and 15,000 prisoners were taken at Bardia on 17 January.

For a loss of 17,700 men, the British had bought some valuable battle experience, and had thrown the German and Italian armies out of Cyrenaica, inflicting 38,000 casualties.

Balkan Interlude

THE Balkan campaign was elaborately planned by Hitler as a direct response to Italy's inability to keep control of Greece, which Mussolini had invaded in October 1940. Hitler aimed to attack Greece in April 1941.

German troops had entered Bulgaria and the Athens government, having guessed correctly that Germany would invade Greece, requested help from Britain. On February 14, 1941, General Sir John Dill, the Chief of the Imperial General Staff, and Anthony Eden, the Foreign Secretary, flew to Cairo, their mission being to assess the situation with local commanders. A conference was held in Athens on 22 February with Greek political and military representatives. The bleak fact was that Britain did not have enough strength both to help Greece and to ensure victory in Africa. Nevertheless the British government, and Churchill in particular, were aware that an offensive against Hitler was necessary to prevent him from crushing Greece and then persuading Turkey to join the Axis powers.

The essence of British involvement in the strategy for the defence of Greece was twofold: firstly that a British Expeditionary Force (BEF) consisting of 58,000 British, Australian and New Zealand troops, with 100 tanks, should be sent to the Greek mainland; and secondly that a combined British and Greek defensive guard, consisting of some seven divisions, should form a line stretching from the river Aliakmon north of Mount Olympus to the Yugoslav frontier near Florina. These troops would be under the command of Lieutenant-General Sir Henry Maitland Wilson. Greek troops were also to be deployed in a line north of Serrai to delay any German thrust towards Salonika. A further 13 divisions would maintain the Greco-Italian front in Albania north of Erseke.

These positions left the extreme southern border between Yugoslavia and Greece – the Monastir gap – exposed to any German advance, a fact which caused dispute at the conference. Lack of manpower prevented this gap being effectively plugged and the conference's decision was to telegraph the British ambassador in Yugoslavia so that he might assess the position with the Belgrade authorities and ask them to protect the frontier and keep the Germans at bay. The only contingency plan available, should the Yugoslavs fail, was to hold the Olympus mountains and withdraw south-westwards towards Grevena to block the Monastir–Florina valley route.

As it happened, events moved too quickly for effective planning of Allied defences for the Monastir gap. German pressure on Yugoslavia to become an ally proved sufficient, and a tripartite pact was signed on 25 March. Nevertheless, a coup by a small band of Yugoslav officers led by a former chief of the air staff, General Simovitch, gave the Allies some hope.

But this hope was short-lived. Hitler was determined to destroy Yugoslavia. So superior were the German forces that Hitler declared war on Yugoslavia and Greece simultaneously on April 6, 1941 – only one week behind his original schedule. The defeat of Yugoslavia took just 12 days. German troops swept through the country and then into north-eastern Greece before Wilson's forces had completed their defences along the Aliakmon line.

The German forces in Yugoslavia comprised two armies and General Ewald von Kleist's 1st *Panzergruppe*. Armed with obsolete weapons, the Yugoslavs themselves were in indefensible positions. On 6 April Belgrade was heavily bombed and a *blitzkrieg* began. LXIV Motorized Corps covered 500 km (312 miles) in seven days along the Morava valley. By 8 April the Germans had taken Skopje; the next day they went on to Prilep and armoured units entered Salonika on 10 April. The 14th *Panzer* Division rushed through Zagreb and sped towards Sarajevo, which it occupied on 15 April. The morale of the Yugoslavs was very low and the capitulation of the country took place on April 17, 1941. Many Serbs, however, continued to fight against the Germans under the command of Colonel Draja Mihailovic.

Greece resisted more stubbornly. The Army of Macedonia took on the German XXX Corps and XVIII Mountain Corps, which entered northern Greece from southern Bulgaria on 6 April. There was bitter fighting in the region of Kelkayia and Istibey. German forces also approached through Yugoslavia: the 2nd *Panzer* Division crossed the Greek frontier at dawn on 8 April and sped on to Salonika the same day. The SS division *Leibstandarte* Adolf Hitler bore down on the Monastir gap, and the collapse of the Yugoslavs brought the right wing of the German 12th Army (Field-Marshal Wilhelm List) up to the Aliakmon line. Wilson was compelled to withdraw the BEF from the coast near Mount Olympus through Kozani up to the Siatista pass and on to Lake Prespa. The left flank of this arc was weak with large gaps.

This new position could not be held either, and as the Germans pushed through the Aliakmon valley Wilson fell back on 16 April

to Thermopylae, on the instructions of the Allied commander-in-chief, General Alexandros Papagos. The German XVIII Mountain Corps crossed the Aliakmon line, bypassed Mount Olympus, and reached Larissa by 18 April. At the same time, XL Corps forced a breach between the left of the British forces and the right of the Greek armies retreating from the Albanian front. The *Leibstandarte* Adolf Hitler captured Grevena on 21 April and went on to take Yannina.

This was a hopeless situation. On 19 April British and Greek generals agreed that in the best interests of both countries, the BEF should be evacuated from the Greek mainland. Rear-Admiral H T Baillie-Grohman made the arrangements for the withdrawal, and despite the fact that the *Luftwaffe* had control of the air, and all embarkations had to be made at night, the operation was successful. Four-fifths of the British troops – over 50,000 men including some Greeks and Yugoslavs – were taken off. Again, as at Dunkirk, heavy equipment had to be left behind. The majority of the evacuees were taken straight to Alexandria, but some went to Crete to swell the Allied garrison on the island.

On 24 April, 16 Greek divisions surrendered to the Germans at Salonika.

Crete was strategically significant in the Mediterranean in that Suda Bay was an ideal fuelling base for the Royal Navy between Malta and Alexandria. The airfields at Maleme, Retimo and Heraklion also provided a supply link with Tobruk, the focus of British resistance in the Middle East.

Hitler realized the island's importance, and on April 25, 1941 issued a directive for Operation *Merkur* (Mercury). Crete was to be taken by a colossal airborne assault led by Lieutenant-General Kurt Student, the man who initially developed this type of tactic. He commanded the newly-created *Fliegerkorps* XI, which included the 7th Paratroop Division with three infantry regiments. The air support needed for the operations was com-

Right: **German paratroops looked cheerful on their way to Crete.** *Far right:* **A stick of German paratroops floats down towards the bloody battle for the island of Crete.** *Opposite page:* **The Greek pre-dreadnought battleship** *Kilkis,* **lies on the bottom in Salamis harbour after being sunk by German dive-bombers.**

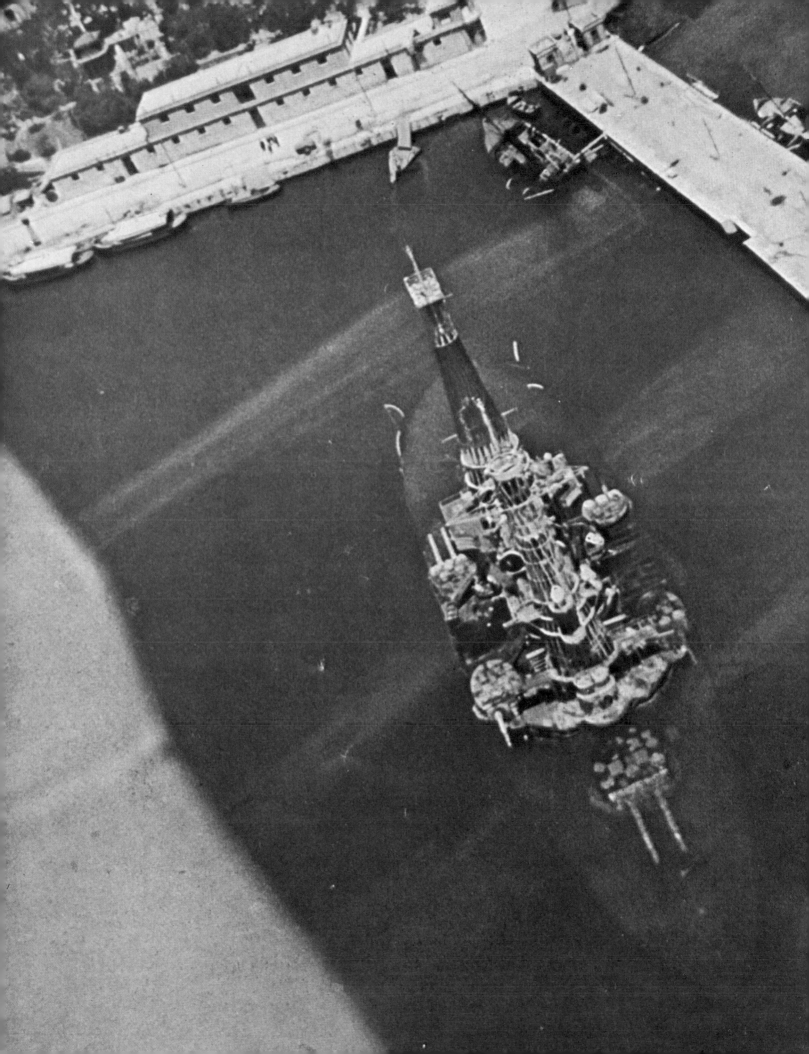

manded by General Wolfram von Richthofen. The forces available for *Merkur* included 500 bombers and fighters, a similar number of transport planes and 72 gliders. The primary objectives were the three airstrips.

Crete's defences rested mainly on the shoulders of one British infantry brigade, albeit swelled in numbers by Greeks, Australians and New Zealanders who had been evacuated from Greece. By the time the assault started, Allied forces numbered approximately 42,000 men. Nevertheless, even if the manpower was there, equipment was not. The Greek evacuees had brought some weapons with them – an adequate number of rifles, light automatics and a few machineguns – but there was a pitiful shortage of heavier supporting weapons: for example, only 68 AA guns on an island 260 km (162 miles) long. Tools and signalling equipment were also scarce. Air support for the ground forces was minimal: the RAF in the Middle East had suffered heavy losses in past months. By 19 May, after heavy bombardment from the Germans, there were only seven operational aircraft left on the island. This inadequate defence force was entrusted to Major-General B C Freyberg on 30 April, and he had little time to prepare.

Softening up attacks by bombers and fighters on the island's three airfields began on 20 May. Then, paratroops from the 7th *Fliegerdivision* were dropped on the approaches to the airstrips at Retimo, Heraklion and the town of Canea. The *Fliegerdivision* headquarters and most of its troops were dropped in Prison Valley. It was intended that the landings should take place where there were few defenders, but because of inadequate German intelligence, the paratroops found Allies waiting for them. Bitter fighting took place, especially in the Maleme vicinity where the Germans landed amongst the 22nd New Zealand Battalion. None of the three airfields was taken on the first day as planned, and the Germans were unable to back up the invasion with sufficient supplies. Their problem was exacerbated by the failure of two German convoys to land troops and stores on the island on 21 and 22 May, a result of the timely interception of three Allied cruisers and their accompanying de-

stroyers. These sank ten ships; the remainder of the German convoys fled in disorder without accomplishing their landings. The Royal Navy paid heavily for its successes: two destroyers, *Juno* and *Greyhound* and two cruisers, *Fiji* and *Gloucester*, were sunk. Other ships were badly damaged by incessant German bombing.

By 24 May the air attacks were making it impossible for the Royal Navy to continue its patrols near Crete in daylight. Admiral Sir Andrew Cunningham could no longer guarantee that German landings could be prevented. But Student was still faced with the problem of taking the Maleme airstrip. His orders were that the German Western Group was to be concentrated to take Maleme, and that the 5th Mountain Division was to land and join the troops at Prison Valley: together they should take Canea and Suda. Therefore on 21 May Student concentrated his forces at the perimeter of the airfield while Lieutenant-General Julius Ringel's mountain troops landed under heavy fire on the airfield itself. These troops managed to break out of Maleme and establish contact with forces in Canea. On 27 May the town was taken.

This final push by the invaders was sufficient for Freyberg to request aid in evacuating the island. This involved some 20,000 men – 4,000 from Heraklion and the remainder from Sphakia beach. On 28 May the troops were lifted from Heraklion. It took until 2 June to complete the evacuation, by which time the cruiser *Calcutta* and the destroyers *Hereward, Kashmir, Kelly* and *Imperial* had been sunk. Eight hundred evacuees and the ships carrying them failed to reach safety.

Fighting in Crete had been bitter and bloody. The Allies lost 1,800 killed, a similar number wounded, and 12,000 taken prisoner. Royal Navy casualties amounted to 1,828 killed and 183 wounded. Ships lost included three cruisers and six destroyers. One aircraft-carrier, three battleships, six cruisers and seven destroyers were damaged to a greater or lesser degree.

Yet the German victory was pyrrhic: they had lost nearly 7,000 paratroops out of an invasion force of 22,000, and 200 aircraft were destroyed. Invasion by air on this scale was

Above left : **With the Germans attacking from Bulgaria and Yugoslavia, the Italians were able to get under way again after their repulse by the Greeks in the previous year.** *Above :* **German paratroops pause for refreshment during the Crete operations. The battle for the island cost them heavy casualties, and persuaded Hitler never again to sanction such an attack.** *Above right :* **The Germans moved swiftly through Yugoslavia and Greece, and then airlanded on Crete.** *Right :* **Men of the German 1st Army arrive in Salonika, the first major city to fall into the hands of the Germans after the invasion, which had begun only three days earlier.**

novel and the results were awaited in Germany with keen interest. In the event, the heavy losses were sufficient to dissuade the Germans from trying the same type of operation again. Plans for an airborne invasion of Malta were abandoned by Hitler in June 1942: perhaps the memory of Crete weighed heavily in this decision.

The Greek campaign was if nothing else a political gesture, but it was a costly 56 days for the Allies. The Germans brought to bear superior weapons and technique while the Allies were unable to release the required number of men and material to achieve successful defence.

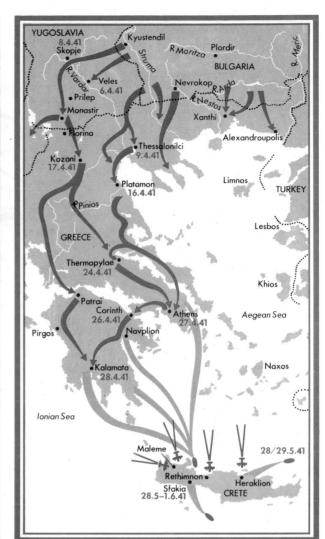

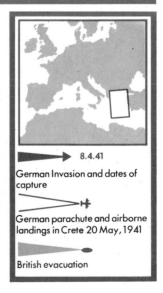

8.4.41

German Invasion and dates of capture

German parachute and airborne landings in Crete 20 May, 1941

British evacuation

Barbarossa

ON November 5, 1937 Hitler revealed in a secret interview with his military chiefs and Ribbentrop, the Foreign Minister, that his long-term ambitions in Europe were the seizure of *Lebensraum* (living room), if necessary by force. The needs of the German people in this respect were paramount, Hitler urged, and so it was vital that in the period between 1938 and 1943, Austria and Czechoslovakia be taken over by Germany, Poland be overrun, and finally that Russia be invaded and conquered. To say that his audience at this now celebrated meeting were thunderstruck would be to underestimate the effect Hitler had on these sober professional men. The German armed forces were unready for

even the smallest part of this grandiose scheme, they thought, and when it was considered that the intervention of France and Great Britain was probable, the dangers of the plan were multiplied considerably.

Yet at first, Hitler's plans succeeded, until by the end of 1940 only Russia was left, ignoring, that is, an apparently impotent Britain's refusal to give up the struggle. It should be noted, however, that although the desire for *Lebensraum* did play an important part in Hitler's thinking (the territories conquered or to be conquered were rich in resources of many kinds), a careful reading of the *Führer's* turgid but extraordinary *Mein Kampf* (My Struggle) reveals that back in the early 1920s he was thinking of the

war necessary against Russia not only in economic but also in political and emotional terms. Here lies the clue to the real reason why Hitler wished to crush Russia: the German onslaught was to serve the triple purpose of spearheading the western world's inevitable crusade against the 'disease' of Bolshevism, of the destruction of the racially inferior Slavs by the superior Teutons and of securing all Russia's resources for the German *Volk* (people). Complex indeed were the reasons, overt and covert, in Hitler's mind for this greatest of military steps taken in modern times. It is no overstatement to say that the outcome of World War II was decided in the vast spaces of Russia, where Germany deployed the

Above : **German infantry fight their way into the city of Zhitomir with the close support of a piece of artillery. Early in the campaign, the Russians could offer only sporadic resistance.**

majority of her forces against the great soviet war machine between 1941 and 1945.

Yet the history of Germany's careful approach to war with Russia shows Hitler's political cunning at its best. In 1939, he wished to have no distractions as he dealt with the rest of Europe, and so a Russo-German non-aggression treaty was signed in Moscow on August 23, 1939. Under its terms, the Russians were to invade hapless Poland shortly after the Germans had launched their own attack, and take over the eastern half of the country. At the same time, Germany was to provide Russia with technical assistance in return for raw materials and foodstuffs. With the possible threat to his east thus obviated, Hitler could then turn his undivided attention to the problem of France and Great Britain.

So Germany was able to launch her tremendous attack on the west in April and May 1940 with her eastern flank secure. But all this time, Hitler was still thinking of the great enemy that he must crush. His preoccupation with thinking and planning the Russian enterprise was not felt during the Battle of Britain, but since the war, it has become apparent that even if the *Luftwaffe* had crushed the RAF, Hitler would probably not have invaded Great Britain: he needed his forces elsewhere. Even before the formal abandonment of Operation Sealion, German land forces were being moved from the English Channel coast towards the east. Although not strictly germane to the present question, it should perhaps be mentioned that Hitler's decision not to close the issue with Great Britain ranks with the invasion of Russia as one of the two most important – and incorrect – strategic decisions taken by Hitler in the course of the conflict. The *Führer* was now condemning himself and his nation to a two-front war, the dangers of which he fully

knew. Yet his need to deal with the spectre of Bolshevism overrode his good sense in the matter, despite the fact that he had frequently spoken on the stupidity of fighting a two-front war.

Planning for what was to become Operation Barbarossa, the invasion of Russia, started in December 1940. German military planners, although taken aback by the magnitude of the task thrust upon them, worked industriously and produced a variety of plans. One by one these were examined and eliminated, their best features being gradually worked up into the definitive scheme. The date set for the initiation of the great crusade was May 5, 1941, which would give the German armies a good campaigning season before the arrival of the terrible Russian winter. All through the spring of 1941 the plans developed, the troops trained and all necessary for the campaign was massed in the greatest secrecy along the frontier with Russia. Everything was ready for the actual fighting, but one vital factor was left undecided.

Tactically and operationally, the German armies knew what they had to do, but strategically the high command was still in the dark: no strategic stopping line had been decided. The German field armies were to crash forward into the depths of Russia, while behind them their overall commanders hoped vaguely that the Russians would capitulate when their major cities in European Russia were overrun. No consideration had been given to Russia's implacable determination to survive, and Hitler had fixed no final objectives for his men. The nearest that the Germans came to establishing a strategic goal was the occasional mention of a vague line running from Archangel on the White Sea in the north to Astrakhan on the Caspian Sea in the south. The Germans thus entered into this great campaign with a clear political goal (the destruction of Russia and the seizure of her resources) but a totally unclear military objective. This was to bedevil the efforts of the troops in the field.

The German plan for the invasion was bold and massive. Three German army groups were to invade Russia proper. In the south, Field-Marshal Gerd von Rundstedt's Army Group South (three German armies, one Rumanian army and General Ewald von Kleist's 1st *Panzergruppe*) was to crush all Russian forces between the Black Sea and the Pripet marshes. In the centre, Field-Marshal Fedor von Bock's Army Group Centre (two German armies, General Heinz Guderian's 2nd *Panzergruppe* and General Hermann Hoth's 3rd *Panzergruppe*) was to advance on the axis Warsaw–Smolensk and then press on to take Moscow. In the north, Field-Marshal Wilhelm Ritter von Leeb's Army Group North (two German armies and General Erich Hoepner's 4th *Panzergruppe*) was to drive through the Baltic states to take Leningrad, the spiritual home of Bolshevism. Further north again, Finland, which fought as a co-belligerent, was to throw her forces, under the command of Marshal Carl Gustaf von Mannerheim, forward through the Karelian isthmus recently taken by Russia and threaten Leningrad from the north, as well as driving towards Lake Onega to cut railway communications with Murmansk in the far north. Here Colonel-General Nikolaus von Falkenhorst's Norway Army was to drive towards Murmansk. In all, the German plan envisaged the advance of some 3,000,000 men (250,000 of them from satellite countries) in 162 divisions along a 3,200-km (2,000-mile) front. As usual, the major tactical scheme to be used was the celebrated pincer, in which the armour broke through, trapping major enemy forces and then pressed on, leaving the trapped forces to be mopped up by the slower moving infantry, who still relied for the most part on horse transport. Four months were considered sufficient for this huge undertaking.

The Russians were heavily deployed along the same frontier for despite the non-aggression treaty, Stalin had few illusions about Hitler's long-term plans. In the south was Marshal Semyon Budyenny's South-West Front of six armies (52 infantry and 20 tank divisions) facing Army Group South. In the centre was Marshal Semyon Timoshenko's West Front of three armies (30 infantry and 8 tank divisions) facing Army Group Centre. And in the north was Colonel-General F I Kuznetsov's North-West Front of two armies (20 infantry and 4 tank divisions) facing Army Group North. Soon after the beginning of the fighting, Kuznetsov was replaced by Marshal Klimenti Voroshilov. Like the Germans, the Russians could field some 3,000,000 men, with a further 1,000,000 scattered over the rest of Russia. Once the war had started, mobilization began to increase this number rapidly. The main trouble with the Russian forces, however, was quality. Stalin's purges of the middle 1930s had robbed the armed forces of most of their best commanders. The Russian soldier was adequately trained and had a high capacity for endurance, but his weapons, with the exception of the artillery and the new T-34 tank, were inferior to their German counterparts. This was particularly the case with the Russian air forces.

Contrary to western practice, the Russian forces were massed along the frontier rather than deployed in depth, which greatly helped the German pincer tactics. Russian tactics, on the other hand, favoured mass attacks by very large numbers of troops, which made it virtually impossible to counter the German armoured pincer movement.

With preparations on the German side almost complete, there occurred one of those typically Hitlerian episodes which completely voided the overall plan. It was suddenly decided that Yugoslavia and Greece would have to be dealt with, and forces for Barbarossa were bled off to conquer these two nations. This inevitably meant that Barbarossa itself had to be postponed by five weeks, a delay that cut into the already short campaigning season with disastrous results. The invasion of Russia was now rescheduled for June 22, 1941.

Preceded by the normal artillery and aerial

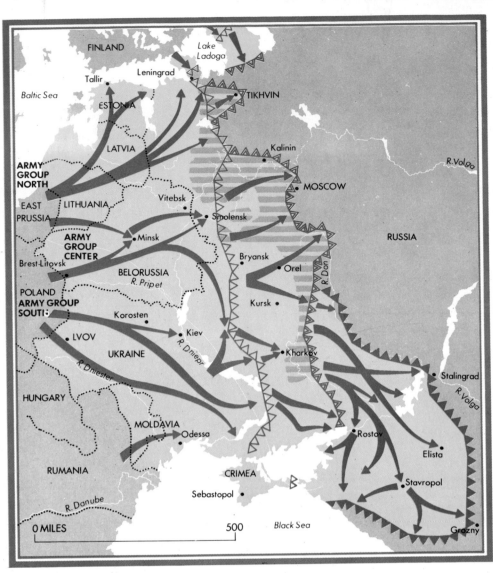

Axis Powers advance into Russia

22 June–1 Sept 1941

1 Sept–5 Dec 1941

Reoccupied by Russians during counterattack, 6 Dec 1941–April 1942

Further advance in the South 28 June–18 Nov 1942 (Regaining some of the ground lost in 41/42 winter campaign)

Above left : **Barbarossa was one of the greatest invasions of all time, and took the Germans deep into Russia.** *Left :* **German troops look for their next target during the savage battle for Smolensk.** *Above :* **The** *Panzers* **enjoyed superiority in equipment.**

bombardment of the Russian front lines, the German armies crashed forward at 0300 hours. Russian surprise, in the tactical sense, was complete, and nowhere did the Germans have more than nominal opposition to their initial breakthrough. Russian planes were caught on the ground in large numbers and destroyed by marauding fighters and bombers, while the few that managed to get into the air were swiftly disposed of by the superior German aircraft and pilots. On the ground, most of the Russian forces were caught completely unawares by the speed and power of the German advance and quickly overrun or bypassed. Cut off Russian forces, in groups up to an army in size, were contained by the German infantry and then destroyed. Hopeless though their prospects were, most of these Russian pockets along the front line fought with great determination, and did in fact contribute to the hindering of the German advance.

One of the major problems faced by the Germans was the complete disparity in the speeds of their forces: the mechanized supply echelon was much quicker than the infantry's, limited as it was by the speed at which the large number of horses used could bring up food, ammunition and other vital supplies. The problem was partially solved by allowing the armoured forces to press on as spearheads, leaving the infantry to mop up, but the determination of the Russian pockets further delayed the infantry, leading to dissension in the German camp. The *Panzer* commanders, convinced that speed was essential, wished to press on regardless of the infantry, but this the army group commanders often refused to allow. Inevitably, the slowness of the infantry hindered the rate of overall advance. Nevertheless, this rate was still very rapid by the standards of the time.

Understandably, the Russian camp was also in disarray. Had it not been for the extraordinary perseverance of the mass of Russian soldiers and the implacable resolution of the Russian dictator, Joseph Stalin, it is conceivable that the Russian armed forces might have dissolved in the face of this savage German attack. But the two factors just held the Russian armies together. Appalling as the losses were, Stalin was prepared to sacrifice almost any number of men to slow the German advance. His object was to gain time to dismantle the most important industrial facilities in the Germans' path and ship them off to new sites beyond the Ural mountains. It is almost impossible to give an idea of the efforts made by the Russian people, men, women and children, to save the industrial plant on which ultimately the survival of their nation depended. Yet most of it was saved, and that which proved impossible to remove was destroyed to prevent it falling into the hands of the enemy. The national effort at this time ultimately saved Russia. Stalin was prepared to sacrifice the lives of hundreds of thousands of his troops to make time; the time could then gradually be used in yielding space to the invaders. Should anyone doubt the nature of Stalin as revealed in the purges of the 1930s, his refusal to display any element of humanity at this time should dispel such doubts: commanders were shot or replaced wholesale, and losses were accepted to slow the German advance.

Although Stalin's plan worked, the speed of the Germans was nonetheless remarkable, especially that of Army Group Centre with its two *Panzergruppen*. (The *Panzergruppe* or Tank Group was a formation of armour and mechanized infantry, later upgraded in designation to *Panzerarmee* or Tank Army.) By the middle of July the 2nd and 3rd *Panzergruppen* had closed the trap on a huge Russian pocket just to the west of Minsk. Once the slower forces had arrived to seal off the pocket, the armour was then able to advance yet again. But so great were the numbers of Russian losses in this early stage of the campaign that they appear meaningless: at Minsk, for example, the Russians lost 330,000 men, 2,500 tanks and 1,500 pieces of artillery. Although there is still no complete agreement on the figures for such encirclements (some authorities claim the figures for Minsk were 290,000 men and 1,400 guns), there can be no doubt about the generally vast scale of Russian losses. By 5 August Army Group Centre, again in the form of its two *Panzergruppen*, had caught another great bag of Russians at Smolensk: 310,000 men, 3,200 tanks and 3,000 pieces of artillery. Army Group Centre was thus only some 320 km (200 miles) west of Moscow by this date, with virtually nothing to block its advance. Although making adequate progress to the north and south of Army Group Centre, von Leeb and von Rundstedt were facing problems that had not confronted von Bock. Army Group North was opposed by high-quality Russian forces, and also considerable difficulties in terrain; Army Group South was suffering from a lack of adequate armoured forces for the job entrusted to it.

Here the nature of the German preparations, and the shape of Russia herself, intervened. For as the German forces advanced eastwards, the 3,200-km (2,000-mile) front on which they had started was gradually widening, leaving the Germans with little alternative but to thin the troops at the front so as to be able to cover it completely. At the same time, the great length of the advance made supply increasingly difficult, especially as men, machines and horses were becoming rapidly exhausted by the heat and dust of the Russian summer and by the very distances involved. Inevitably, the lack of depth in the German Army, with its over-reliance on tooth formations at the expense of tail ones, made itself felt. At the same time Hitler stepped in, and the lack of proper strategic planning immediately became clear to all: Guderian's *Panzergruppe* and the 2nd Army were detached to aid Army Group South, while Hoth's *Panzergruppe* was similarly detached to aid Army Group North. Although the short-term results of this alteration in emphasis helped the two flanking army groups to catch up with Army Group Centre, the long-term result was that the central force lost its one real chance of taking Moscow easily and in good time.

In the south, the German forces had almost reached the great city of Kiev by 21 August. With the aid of Guderian's armour coming down from the north, Kiev was now turned into an enormous pocket. When the city finally fell on 20 September, some 665,000 Russians fell with it in the pocket just to the east. While this was happening, General Erich von Manstein's 11th Army had been making good progress down the Yuzhni Bug river towards Crimea.

In the north, Hoth's forces had also enabled Army Group North to speed up its advance, and real progress towards Leningrad was made. Although much of the momentum of the early days had been lost, October found the Germans handily placed. Von Leeb was able to take Leningrad under siege in October, von Bock was still pushing on from Smolensk with his infantry, and von Rundstedt reached the Don river on 15 October, posing a threat to the major industrial cities of Kharkov and Rostov. Only in the Finnish theatre was poor progress reported: von Mannerheim's forces were content just to retake the portions of Finland lost in the Winter War, and von Falkenhorst's army in the far north was stuck in very difficult terrain far short of its target.

In the air, the *Luftwaffe* continued to dominate, having destroyed over 4,500 front-line Russian aircraft for the loss of less than 2,000 of its own machines. But in the rear areas the problems of the Germans were increasing: troops which could have been used at the front now had to be detached to guard the lines of communication against the growing threat of Russian partisan groups. But worst of all, the weather was beginning to break. The autumn rains had begun, turning the unmetalled roads into mud sloughs and further hampering the German advance, and this was only a foretaste of the freezing winter that was to come. Time was running out on the Germans, and the delay occasioned by the Balkan foray was now having its effect.

Here, Hitler again changed his mind. Moscow was once more made the primary objective, and von Bock was given back the land and air forces lent to von Leeb and von Rundstedt. His Army Group Centre picked up speed, and between 30 September and 7 October created yet another great Russian pocket, this time at Vyazma. The haul here was more than 650,000 men. Just under a fortnight later Army Group Centre spearheads had reached Mozhaisk, only 64 km (40 miles) from Moscow. On the map, the German position looked good; at the front it looked poor, for all formations were down to less than 50 per cent strength of men and machines, and the turn in the weather had caught the Germans totally unprepared. As it was expected that the campaign would be over before the arrival of winter, no preparation had been made to provide the troops with winter combat clothing. Moreover, at the beginning of November, front line formations began to detect the arrival of fresh Russian reserves, just at the time they themselves were approaching the limits of their endurance. At the same time, the Russians had reorganized their command structure. Budyenny had been fired and replaced as commander-in-chief of the South-West Front by Timoshenko, whose place as head of the West Front had been taken by the greatest soldier Russia was to produce in World War II, Georgi Zhukov. Under Zhukov's driving direction, the defences before Moscow were strengthened, and try as they might during November and December, the Germans were unable to break through. There was desperate fighting in appalling winter conditions.

Above left : **The pace of the German Army's advance into Russia pushed men and machines to the limits of their physical endurance.** *Above :* **A German assault team makes good use of a flamethrower, one of the war's most dreaded weapons, in an attack on an improvised pillbox.**

Timoshenko's arrival in the south also firmed up the defence there, and on 15 November the Germans were driven out of Rostov – the first major reverse for German arms in the Russian campaign. The German command structure also altered at this time: by 5 December Field-Marshal Walther von Reichenau had replaced von Rundstedt, and Field-Marshal Günther-Hans von Kluge had succeeded von Bock. By this date the temperature had fallen to 40 degrees below freezing point, no winter clothing was available apart from that taken from Russian dead and prisoners, and the German armies were exhausted, only 40km (25 miles) from Moscow.

Then the Russians struck back. Fresh troops from Siberia, used to the cold, were carefully marshalled by Zhukov and un-leashed in a great counter-offensive around Moscow. The generals called for a strategic retreat in face of this Russian attack, but Hitler absolutely forbade it. In a feat of extra-ordinary military achievement, the Germans just about managed to hold on, whereas a retreat might very well have turned into a rout. Up to the end of the year, the great Russian offensives around Moscow and near Izyum in the Crimea slowly drove the Germans back, finally dashing any hopes of the Third *Reich* knocking out Soviet Russia in one devastating round. Hitler's decision to try to hold on at Moscow was typical of the German dictator; and in the context of the battle for Moscow it was a brilliant piece of insight. Unfortunately for the Germans, however, it further reinforced Hitler's high opinion of himself as a military genius, and convinced him also of the basic correctness of holding ground at no matter what cost. This latter conviction was to cause the German Army enormous and needless losses in the years to come.

The final results of the campaign infuriated Hitler, and in December he completely re-shuffled his high command to make himself actual as well as titular head of the German armed forces. Field-Marshal Walther von Brauchitsch lost his job as commander-in-chief of the army, to be replaced by Hitler, and Hitler took over as head both of OKH (Army High Command) with General Franz Halder as chief-of-staff, and of OKW (Armed Forces High Command) with Field-Marshal Wilhelm Keitel as chief-of-staff. OKH ran the war in Russia, OKW that in other theatres. Among other field commanders to lose their jobs were von Leeb and Hoepner.

Although they had failed (and the failure was to cost them the war), the Germans had performed a prodigious feat in purely military terms. So too, for that matter, had the Russians. The Germans had lost some 800,000 men, most of them veterans difficult to replace; the Russians had lost some 1,500,000 men killed and well over 2,000,000 prisoner, as well as millions of civilian dead. Yet in the long term, Stalin's policy proved strategically right, although the salvation of Russia's industries was bought by enormous losses of human life.

The Battle of the Atlantic

1940–41

AS the threat of the invasion of southern England receded, the Royal Navy turned its attention once more to the problem of the Atlantic convoys. In September 1940, the United States made an important declaration of sympathy by lending 50 old destroyers in exchange for a 99-year lease of bases around the world. These old destroyers were only fit for second-line duties, but they did release newer destroyers for fleet work and many were still in commission four years later.

Coastal escorts and air patrols proved successful against the U-boats, and so forced them to go out into the Western Approaches in search of targets. Here the new U-boat bases in the Bay of Biscay gave the Germans an important advantage, and the British were hard pressed to extend cover to convoys further out into the Atlantic. But Iceland had been occupied in July 1940 by British and Canadian troops – this was to prevent German occupation – and it provided airfields and a refuelling base which partly offset the U-boats' advantage.

Throughout 1941, the United States was benevolent in her neutrality, for President Roosevelt knew that US interests would not benefit from a German victory over Britain. In March 1941, the Lend-Lease Bill was passed, allowing more ships and equipment to be provided. In April the United States declared that the Defence Zone, in which American merchant ships were escorted by their own warships, would be extended to 26° west, regardless of whether they were carrying war material to Britain or not.

The worst problem for many convoy escorts was their lack of endurance. Destroyers were designed for high-speed attack, with slender hulls unsuited to North Atlantic weather, and their turbines were not economical. Many of the older destroyers were turned into long-range escorts by substituting an extra fuel bunker for one of the boilers, and the first of these was taken in hand in January 1941. The corvettes, which were now coming into service in large numbers from British and Canadian shipyards, had good endurance but lacked speed. This was inevitable, for the design had been framed to make the best use of available machinery, but by 1941 U-boats had taken to attacking convoys on the surface at night, and at top speed they could outdistance a corvette. Another problem was that convoy work demanded a great deal of loitering about to investigate a suspected underwater contact, or high speed dashes to find stragglers and herd them back to the convoy.

The answer was to design a proper North Atlantic escort capable of high endurance and carrying all the guns, depth-charges and sensors needed for submarine-hunting. The answer to the need was the River class frigate, which had twice the power of the corvette and ample space for the weapons needed. Unfortunately, none were ready until early in 1942. In the meantime, the existing escorts were given as much new equipment as possible to help them fight back. In May 1941, the first surface warning radar set went to sea in a corvette. Although the ASDIC detection device was very effective in locating submerged U-boats it had a weakness in that contact was lost during the final stages of a depth-charge attack. To remedy this, a new ahead-firing weapon had to be developed, and this promised to increase the rate of 'kills'. Known as 'Hedgehog', this was a spigot mortar firing a number of small contact fused bombs in a pattern, and the first ship was equipped with it by the end of 1941.

All these countermeasures were desperately needed for 1941 was a critical year, with shipping losses rising all the time and more and more U-boats coming into service. From 755,000 tonnes in 1939 losses rose to 3,991,000 tonnes, or 1,000 ships in 1940. But in 1941, despite rising output from the shipyards and ever-increasing skill in anti-submarine tactics the total rose to 1,300 ships, a staggering 4,328,000 tonnes. Such losses could not be sustained for long, and in August 1941 at the Atlantic Charter meeting the Americans agreed that American warships would henceforward be permitted to escort all merchant ships irrespective of nationality, while Canadian warships would similarly be allowed to escort US ships. The US Navy was already handing over its escorted ships to Anglo-Canadian escorts at a predetermined MOMP or Mid-Ocean Meeting Point, but in August 1941 this so-called 'Chop Line' was moved to 22°58 west to relieve the strain on British escorts.

While all this was happening on the convoy routes the German Navy was planning a bold stroke. The battleship *Bismarck* was ready for sea in the spring of 1941, and it was hoped to send her out into the Atlantic with the heavy cruiser *Prinz Eugen* to attack convoys. This could disrupt the whole delicate organization, even for a short time, and allow the

Right : **The Short Sunderland flying-boat was Britain's most important aerial weapon against the U-boats.**
Inset right : **A depth-charge exploding near a U-boat is seen from the belly turret of a patrol bomber.**

U-boats to slaughter unescorted ships. A further aim was to link up with the battle-cruisers *Scharnhorst* and *Gneisenau* which were at Brest. The prospect of three Nazi capital ships operating in the Atlantic appalled the Admiralty, and so they were prepared to do anything to stop the *Bismarck* breakout.

On May 21, 1941 the two German ships sailed from Bergen, heading for the Denmark Strait between Greenland and Iceland on their way to the Atlantic shipping-routes. The departure of the two German ships was reported to the Admiralty and two days later they were sighted by two British cruisers patrolling in the Denmark Strait. The battle-cruiser *Hood* and the new battleship *Prince of Wales* had been in Iceland and so they

were able to intercept the German ships next morning.

The British seemed about to frustrate the German plans, but disaster struck *Hood*: she blew up after firing only three salvoes, apparently as a result of a fire caused by a German shell. Although *Prince of Wales* was only slightly damaged she was so new that half her guns were not firing, and the admiral commanding the cruisers ordered her captain to break off the action. For two days the whereabouts of the German ships were unknown, but eventually a massive air- and sea-search located *Bismarck* (*Prinz Eugen* had already been detached to Brest) and the carrier *Ark Royal* was able to launch a torpedo-bomber strike. Two torpedoes wrecked the steering gear of the battleship,

and by nightfall on 26 May Vice-Admiral Günther Lütjens knew that his flagship was doomed.

Next morning the Home Fleet battleships *Rodney* and *King George V* hove into sight and opened fire at 16,000 yards. This time *Bismarck*'s gunnery was wild, and she failed to score a hit on either ship, apart from a single 'dud' medium shell. Under a hail of fire she turned rapidly into a flaming hulk, and in half an hour her guns were silent. She lay so low in the water that the shells could not penetrate her armoured deck, and after another hour of cannonading, the British commander-in-chief, Admiral Sir J C Tovey, ordered the cruiser *Dorsetshire* to sink her with torpedoes. *Bismarck*'s career had lasted three days and she left only 110 survivors.

Above : **A torpedo from a German U-boat strikes home on an Allied merchant ship. Lacking structural strength, the merchantman's best defence against submarine attack lay with the escort vessels and the size of the convoy.** *Above right :* **A German U-boat production yard. Although Allied bombers failed seriously to hinder such production, German production eventually could not match losses.**

In retrospect it was clear that the Germans had placed too much faith in *Bismarck*'s ability to withstand damage. She should have returned to Germany after the damage to her fuel tanks caused by *Prince of Wales*, and might well have eluded the Home Fleet in the poor visibility that prevailed. Instead she

chose to continue her Atlantic sortie with what amounted to major battle damage, and was later forced to make for Brest for lack of fuel. The German Navy was often accused of tactical timidity, but on this occasion it showed a degree of foolhardiness that is hard to understand.

With the destruction of *Bismarck* the German Navy virtually abandoned all ideas of using the surface fleet aggressively. Certainly it was never the same threat to the Atlantic convoys, and early the following year Hitler admitted as much by ordering *Scharnhorst* and *Gneisenau* back to Germany. *Tirpitz* was completed later in 1941 but she too spent an inactive life in Norway, content to tie down British ships by her mere presence rather than make any determined attack.

By the end of 1941 the Battle of the Atlantic had become nothing more than a grim struggle of attrition. The entry of the United States into the war was only a matter of time, but Admiral Dönitz tried to keep his U-boats from precipitating hostilities. Between September and December 1941 a series of incidents, including the torpedoing of three American destroyers off Iceland, strained relations to breaking point, but still the spirit of isolationism was strong enough to keep the United States from declaring war. Finally the knot was cut by the Japanese attack on Pearl Harbor, followed by Hitler's senseless declaration of war on the USA. The American entry into the war marked the end of the first phase of the Battle of the Atlantic, but in fact the grimmest part was yet to come.

THE ALLIED

By the end of 1942 the first glimpses of final victory were discernible in the Allied camp: Germany's North African adventure had been halted at El Alamein, the legend of the all-conquering German Army had been broken in the terrible siege of Stalingrad, and the great power of the United States had been drawn into the war by Japan's attack on Pearl Harbor. But though there was still to be dire fighting on all fronts, land, sea and air, Germany's and Japan's course of expansion through armed might was over. Now the Allies, with steadily growing strength, could regain what had been lost . . .

RECOVERY

East Africa & the Middle East

MUSSOLINI's empire in Africa included Eritrea, Italian Somaliland and Abyssinia. In Abyssinia, under command of the Italian Viceroy, the Duke of Aosta, were 250,000 troops, of whom 90,000 were metropolitan Italians. But these forces had only 24 medium and 39 light tanks. The air force's 34 Fiat CR42 fighters were outclassed by the RAF's Gloster Gladiator and Hawker Hurricane fighters. The Italians were also short of artillery, ammunition, fuel and basic foodstuffs.

General Sir Archibald Wavell considered them a threat to Kenya and Sudan: in July 1940 the Italians had captured Kassala, Gallabat and Kurmuk in the Sudan and the Moyale salient in Kenya. He further thought they could be defeated by an internal revolution of Abyssinian patriots, with the help of Allied forces, and that Haile Selassie might be restored to his throne. In Kenya and Sudan were thousands of Abyssinian refugees and Major Orde Wingate was entrusted with the task of organizing these partisans in Khartoum in his capacity as commander of Haile Selassie's forces and the emperor's adviser.

Meanwhile, British forces in Kenya and Sudan were adopting an aggressive defensive posture, although the 5th Indian Division failed to retake Gallabat in the Sudan during November 1940.

Wavell organized his forces into two commands, excluding Wingate's. An expeditionary force was to attack towards Eritrea from Sudan, commanded by Lieutenant-General W Platt, comprising the 4th and 5th Indian Divisions. In Kenya Lieutenant-General A G Cunningham's force comprised the 11th and 12th African Divisions, plus the 1st South African Division.

The Duke of Aosta saw that the British attack would be threefold, and organized his forces accordingly: General Frusci defended Eritrea with three colonial divisions and three brigades; Lieutenant-General Nasi, with four colonial brigades, was to stop Wingate and Major-General de Simone with ten colonial brigades had the task of defending southern Abyssinia and Italian Somaliland.

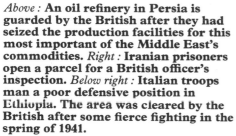

Above : **An oil refinery in Persia is guarded by the British after they had seized the production facilities for this most important of the Middle East's commodities.** *Right :* **Iranian prisoners open a parcel for a British officer's inspection.** *Below right :* **Italian troops man a poor defensive position in Ethiopia. The area was cleared by the British after some fierce fighting in the spring of 1941.**

In addition, each general had a variable number of irregular native forces. Two Italian divisions, the Savoia and Africa, were in reserve.

Platt opened his offensive from the Sudan on January 19, 1941. The German defeat at Sidi Barrani had demoralized the Italians, and the British were able to make some headway. The Italians under Frusci retreated from the Sudan frontier, where they considered the ground too flat to resist a British mechanized attack. On 18 January their garrisons at Kassala and Gallabat were abandoned as they withdrew to Agordat, Barentu, and to Chilga. Platt advanced quickly, reaching the Italian positions on 25 January. After five days of hard fighting, the Italians with-

drew again to the formidable Keren escarpment, where they reformed on 1 February. The Italians made a vigorous stand here, and the first battle of Keren was an Italian victory. Platt then mounted a full-scale offensive, backed up by strike aircraft. Although the Italians employed their reserve divisions, Keren finally fell on 27 March, and the British were able to reach Asmara on 1 April and then push on to Massawa by 8 April.

Cunningham meanwhile launched Operation Canvas, which achieved its objective, the port of Kismayu, on 14 February. The next obstacle was the Juba river, and here Cunningham found a weak spot in de Simone's defences. The river was crossed in two places and de Simone's forces disintegrated. On 22 February Jelib was cleared and the southern door to Abyssinia was open. Cunningham's forces drove on and reached the Somaliland capital, Mogadishu, on 25 February, and entered Addis Ababa on 6 April after a triumphant drive. Cunningham continued northwards to meet Platt who was coming down from Asmara.

Wingate's Gideon Force came eastwards from Khartoum, making for Mount Belaya, its supply train including 15,000 camels. Haile Selassie accompanied Wingate, and as they marched many local chiefs joined their emperor. The Italians thought that Gideon Force was larger than it was, and withdrew to Burye and Debra Markos, on the road to Addis Ababa. Gideon Force advanced to Burye where a force of 7,000 under Colonel Natale fell to Wingate's 450. Wingate's raids,

supported by the RAF, combined audacity, endurance and deception. The Italians, very demoralized, withdrew (losing 2,000 men) to Debra Markos, where Nasi was in command. Wingate continued to operate his well-planned raids, and deserters joined Gideon Force at the rate of over 100 each day. On 1 April the Italians withdrew up the valley of the Blue Nile, to join other forces at Dessie. Italian rule in Abyssinia had now collapsed. The Duke of Aosta left Addis Ababa to Haile Selassie and sought refuge in the Amba Alagi heights. Platt and Cunningham arrived in the foothills and, caught between these forces, Aosta – who was short of water and ammunition and subjected to heavy air bombardment – had little chance. He finally surrendered on 16 May, with 7,000 troops. Longer resistance was put up by Nasi, who eventually surrendered in the Gondar area on 27 November. Other British forces had crossed from Aden on 16 March to retake Berbera, the capital of British Somaliland, occupied earlier by the Italians. These forces cleared the Italians out of Somaliland and then linked up with Cunningham's men.

At the end of March 1941 the pro-British regent of Iraq was toppled by the Axis-backed premier, Rashid Ali, and by a mutiny in the army. British–Iraqi relations deteriorated rapidly, and when the British sent elements of the 10th Indian Division to Iraq, Rashid Ali decided to challenge the British before they became too strong. He therefore chose to attack the RAF Training School at Habbaniya, situated on the Euphrates river

west of Baghdad, and Iraqi troops moved to positions overlooking the airfield on 29 April. The British were worried as they had important oil interests in the area: were the rebels about to cut the oil pipeline between the Kirkuk fields and Haifa? On 30 April the Iraqis demanded that flying operations from Habbaniya should cease and that personnel should be restricted to base. The RAF commander, Air Vice-Marshal H G Smart, replied that any interference with flying would be regarded as an act of war. Whilst the diplomats sought a solution, Iraqi forces dug in and besieged Habbaniya. Smart prepared defences round the 11.25-km (7-mile) perimeter, using 1,000 RAF personnel, 1,200 locally-raised levies and as many of the 9,000 civilians on the station as were willing to help. Three hundred men from the Indian brigade at Basra were flown in, and eight Wellington bombers arrived from Egypt. The British ambassador demanded the withdrawal of Iraqi troops, and when Rashid Ali refused to comply, Smart was ordered to attack his besiegers.

Before dawn on 2 May all 33 available aircraft, plus the eight Wellingtons, took off and pounded the Iraqi positions. The Iraqis replied with artillery fire, but were unable to hit Habbaniya's power station or water tower. That first day, 200 sorties were flown and the pressure was kept up until 5 May. On 6 May a foot patrol found the Iraqis had abandoned their positions. They had withdrawn in two directions: to the east, they blocked the road to Baghdad at Falluja

Above left : **Indian troops further
enhanced their enviable fighting record
in the conquest of Eritrea.** *Above :*
**British infantry launch an assault
against an Italian position in Eritrea.
In this theatre the Italians did their
best fighting of the war.**

where it crosses the Euphrates; to the west,
they deployed at Ramadi where the Rutba
road passes between the Salt Lakes and the
Euphrates.

The British sent in the hastily assembled
Habforce, drawn from the 1st Cavalry
Division in Palestine. This force crossed the
Iraqi frontier on 13 May, traversed the
desert in a temperature of 49°C (120°F) and
then found the approach to Habbaniya
flooded by the Euphrates. It was additionally
harassed by German aircraft flying under
Iraqi colours.

Now the Germans were obliged to airlift
supplies destined for Iraq – the Axis had to
help Rashid Ali in order to keep Arab good
will. Not until 23 May, however, did Hitler
order a military mission to Baghdad. He was
too late: as the RAF bombed targets throughout Iraq, political opinion had swung away
from Rashid Ali.

Colonel Ouvry Roberts, commanding the
land forces, seized Falluja bridge on 19 May,
thus opening the road to Baghdad for
Habforce. Rashid Ali fled to Persia, and on
3 May the pro-British regent returned to
Baghdad.

Britain, suspecting that Hitler might also
have designs on Vichy French held Lebanon
and Syria, decided to act first. An expeditionary force, under Lieutenant-General Sir
Henry Maitland Wilson and composed of the
7th Australian Division, the 1st Cavalry
Division, the 5th Indian Brigade Group and
the Free French Legentilhomme Brigade,
entered Syria on 8 June. This force had no
tanks and few armoured cars. General Henri
Dentz, Vichy commander in Syria, had two
divisions.

The Australians crossed the frontier from
Palestine in two thrusts : one up the road towards Beirut and the other up the Litani
valley towards Rayak. Further inland, on the
desert flank, the 5th Indian Brigade advanced
ahead of the Free French towards Damascus.
The Vichy French put up spirited resistance
and were extremely bitter that the Free
French brigade should have been used
against them.

The Syrian campaign lasted for five weeks.
Vichy French resistance meant Britain had
to send reinforcements early, and two
brigades of the British 6th Division were
diverted to Syria from the Nile delta.
Damascus fell to the Allies on 21 June. After
Operation Battleaxe in the Western Desert,
aircraft were sent to Syria and promptly
neutralized the Vichy French air force which
had been harassing the Allied advance.

On 23 June, Wilson called for an all-out
offensive against Dentz, using four forces.
The Australian division was to continue its
northerly thrust up the coast towards Beirut,
and would now have the support of the Royal
Navy; the British 6th Division would cross

the mountains from Damascus to threaten
Beirut from the east; Habforce from Iraq
was to advance on Palmyra and Homs and
Major-General W J Slim's 10th Indian
Division was to advance from Basra, up the
lines of the Euphrates and the Baghdad–
Aleppo railway, into northern Syria.

The 6th Division's advance from Damascus made little progress in terrain ideally
suited to defence, and against stout resistance. Habforce was gallantly resisted by a
small Foreign Legion garrison at Palmyra
which did not capitulate until 13 July. The
10th Indian Division was hampered by
logistic difficulties, but made progress to
take Deir-ez-Zor on the Euphrates and then,
on 3 July, Tel Kotchek. Next, it advanced
towards Aleppo. On the coast, the Australians broke through Dentz's main defensive
position on the Damour river covering Beirut,
but it took five days of fierce fighting with the
support of 60 field guns ashore and 5 cruisers
and 8 destroyers off the coast, in addition to
heavy air bombardment. Dentz was not
reinforced, and lost 6,500 men, most of his
aircraft, a destroyer and a submarine. He
requested an armistice on 11 July and the surrender agreement was signed at Acre on 14
July. All Frenchmen were given the chance
of joining de Gaulle and the Free French,
but out of 38,000 only 5,700 did so.

Syria and Lebanon settled down to an
uneasy peace under British military occupation and Free French political control. Great
Britain's northern flank in the Middle East
was secure against German infiltration.

Naval War in the Mediterranean

IT has already been explained how the elimination of the French Navy altered the strategic balance in the Mediterranean, but this is not the full picture. Not only did the Italian Navy now outnumber the British, but their colonies in North Africa gave them air bases astride the main British supply-route through the central Mediterranean. The British were determined to hold the Suez Canal and to prevent the Axis powers from reaching the Middle Eastern oilfields: the common strategic weakness of both Italy and Germany was their lack of oil.

Fear that Mussolini and Hitler would not be able to resist the temptation to seize the remnants of the French Navy, which had gone to North African ports at the time of the French armistice in June 1940, led the British to take a drastic step. They gave the French an ultimatum to put their ships out of all possible reach of the Axis powers, and when the terms were rejected the British swiftly destroyed the French ships in their harbour at Mers-el-Kebir in Algeria. The price, French enmity, was heavy, but at least the Italian Navy now had no chance of suddenly doubling its strength.

One vital decision was made at the outset. Despite its closeness to Italian air bases and its lack of defences, the island of Malta was indispensable to the Royal Navy if the central Mediterranean was to be controlled. Malta had airfields and a large dockyard, which meant that it could act as a forward base for striking forces, both air and naval, operating against communications between Italy and North Africa. It would never be able to support a main fleet because of its proximity to the Sicilian airfields, and so two heavy forces were formed, one based on Gibraltar (Force H) and the other, the Mediterranean fleet, based on Alexandria.

Mussolini had called the Mediterranean *Mare Nostrum* or the Italian Lake, but his naval commanders were to find themselves opposed by a man who was almost a 20th-century equivalent of Nelson, Admiral Sir Andrew Cunningham. Their first shock came at the Battle of Calabria on July 9, 1940, when Cunningham's flagship *Warspite* pursued the Italian flagship to within sight of the Italian coastline and scored a hit at the great range of 15 miles. Eleven days later the Australian cruiser *Sydney* sank the Italian cruiser *Bartolomeo Colleoni* in a running fight off Crete. It became clear that the Royal Navy had established a moral ascendancy over the *Regia Navale* which more than offset the latter's superior numbers.

Cunningham was not content with skirmishing, and he planned a lethal blow against the Italian Fleet. On the night of November 11, 1940 the aircraft carrier *Illustrious* launched a strike of 21 torpedo-bombers against the main Italian base at Taranto. Within two hours, two battleships were badly damaged and a third was sunk outright, all for the loss of two aircraft. It was the first seaborne air strike against a defended base and it was studied with great interest by the Japanese.

British land forces from Egypt were also doing well against the Italian forces in North Africa, but in January 1941 the Germans stepped in to even the odds in favour of their hard-pressed partners. The specially trained *Fliegerkorps* X, an anti-shipping strike group, was sent to Sicily to deal with the British aircraft carriers which had caused so much damage. On 10 January *Illustrious* was very badly hit and just managed to crawl into Malta.

As soon as another carrier arrived, Cunningham returned to the offensive, and in March 1941 *Formidable*'s torpedo-bombers scored a hit on the new battleship *Vittorio Veneto*. During the night of 28 and 29 March Cunningham's three battleships pressed on, hoping to find the Italian ship. Instead, they ran into two heavy cruisers which had been sent back to look for a sister damaged earlier by a torpedo. The result was catastrophic, for the two cruisers had no idea that they were facing three battleships armed with 15-inch guns, ready for action. Within minutes *Fiume* and *Zara* were blazing wrecks, and shortly after *Pola* was also sinking after hits by destroyers' torpedoes.

The Battle of Cape Matapan ranks as one of the decisive sea battles of the war, not because of its rather meagre results but because it determined the future attitude of the Italian high command. Cunningham was furious at not getting *Vittorio Veneto* and withdrew next morning to avoid air attacks. But the full significance of the battle did not become clear until the following May during the evacuation of Crete, when the British suffered heavy casualties, but were not molested by the Italian fleet. Later still, when the battleship *Barham* and the carrier *Ark Royal* were torpedoed at sea and the *Queen Elizabeth* and *Valiant* were blown up by human torpedoes in Alexandria, the Italian fleet, mindful of Matapan, remained passive.

The position of Malta, so close to the Italian air bases, was always precarious, and the British always had to take care that the island was kept supplied with aircraft, fuel and supplies. In July 1941, a special fast convoy was run to Malta and in September the carriers *Ark Royal* and *Furious* ferried fighter aircraft. More submarines were sent and between June and September nearly 300,000 tons of scarce German and Italian shipping was sunk by the forces based on Malta. The German naval liaison staff in

Left : **Heavy cruisers of the Italian Navy patrol in the Mediterranean.**
Below : **The Fairey Swordfish was a constant threat to Italian shipping.**

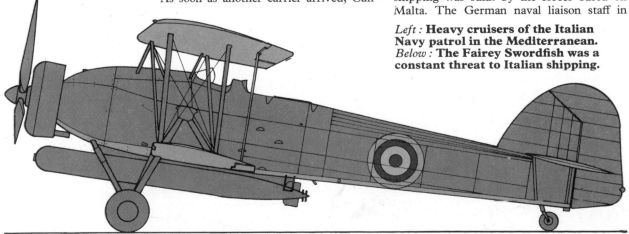

Above: **The British aircraft-carrier** *Formidable*, **which was part of the Mediterranean Fleet in 1941 and of Force H in 1943, prepares to enter port at Gibraltar, preceded by light units of her escort.** *Left:* **The British destroyer** *Kelly*, **first of the large 'K' class to be built, was launched in 1938, and was sunk in the battles off Crete in May 1941 while under the command of Lord Louis Mountbatten.**

Rome described the situation as 'catastrophic'; Italian troops in North Africa were being harried by the Empire forces in Egypt and were also running short of essential supplies. The Germans were forced to send the *Afrika Korps* under Lieutenant-General Erwin Rommel to help the Italians, but this merely exacerbated the supply problem. The only other assistance that the Germans could offer was half a dozen U-boats, and they more than justified their presence by sinking *Ark Royal* and *Barham*.

The reverses suffered by the Royal Navy

left Malta very vulnerable, particularly when in December 1941 the light forces based there ran into a minefield and lost a cruiser, a destroyer and two more cruisers damaged. The only ships which could run the gauntlet of constant air attack were submarines, and even they had to submerge in the harbour during daylight. Some daring trips were made by fast minelayers like *Manxman*, but the cost was high and supplies only the barest minimum to keep the Spitfires flying and the guns firing. Eventually, after the United States had entered the war and a joint amphibious landing in North Africa was proposed, the decision was taken to lift the siege. Some idea of the problem can be gathered from the size of the operation: 14 fast merchant ships escorted by 2 battleships, 3 carriers, 7 cruisers and 20 destroyers. Operation Pedestal was the biggest convoy battle of the war. Fought between August 10 and 13, 1942 it cost nine merchant ships, an aircraft-carrier and two cruisers. But the five ships which limped into Grand Harbour,

including the tanker *Ohio*, carried sufficient supplies to prevent the starvation of the civilian population.

The improving state of affairs in North Africa, marked by the Battle of El Alamein, was compounded by the Allied invasion in November 1942. With Axis forces cleared out of North Africa, the shipping route between Gibraltar and Alexandria could be reopened, and Allied forces soon regained the initiative. In July 1943, the Allies landed in Sicily, and only two months later the same forces were landed on the Italian mainland. The conquest of Italy was to prove harder than anyone had expected, but from the naval point of view, once the Allies gained a foothold in Italy the most important obstacle had been surmounted. The Mediterranean was now firmly under Allied control, and it could be used not only as a base from which the 'soft underbelly' (as Churchill termed it) of the Axis could be attacked, but also as a convenient supply-route to the Far East.

The last act of the naval war in the Mediter-

ranean was unexpectedly dramatic. The night before the landings at Salerno the Italians sued for an armistice. The landings went ahead as planned for the Germans clearly had no intention of surrendering, but the Italians were offered surrender terms. Under their conditions, the three modern battleships *Roma*, *Vittorio Veneto* and *Italia* (ex-*Littorio*) left La Spezia to be interned at Malta, but on 9 September they were attacked by German aircraft carrying radio-controlled bombs. *Roma* caught fire and blew up, leaving the two shaken survivors to meet *Valiant* and *Warspite* next morning. As they joined the rest of the once-proud Italian fleet in Malta, Admiral Cunningham signalled to the British Admiralty: 'The Italian Fleet now lies under the guns of Malta.' It was a mass-surrender only equalled by the surrender of the German High Seas fleet in 1918, and it was appropriate that Cunningham, in his famous flagship *Warspite*, should have been present, for they had both contributed greatly to the victory.

Stalingrad

FOR the exhausted men of the German armies in Russia, the first two months of 1942 seemed an interminable agony. The cold was more extreme than any of them could have conceived, and they lacked adequate winter clothing. The running of vehicles was almost impossible: oil froze solid unless the engines were kept running the whole time; and the Russians, whom the Germans imagined must be as near the limit of endurance as themselves, had sprung the great strategic surprise of General Georgi Zhukov's counter-offensive on December 6, 1941.

Denied permission to make great strategic withdrawals, the German generals tried to stand and fight during December. Divisions and corps were disposed in 'hedgehogs' for all-round defence, and in many cases were cut off. Slowly, the Russians drove the Germans back over the territory they had taken in November 1941. It should be noted, however, that without Hitler's refusal to allow ground to be yielded, the slow German retreat could have turned into a rout. Words can do scant justice to the trials, losses and hardships of both sides in the terrible winter of 1941 and 1942, but gradually the Russians won back much of the land lost at the end of the German offensive: the great salient between Lakes Ladoga and Ilmen, with its head at Tikhvin, was taken by the Volkhov Front; in the centre of the theatre, the Kalinin, West and South-West Fronts took back great areas between Staraya Russa and Kharkov; the South-West Front also drove a large salient into the German lines across the Donets river at Izyum; finally, in the far south, the Caucasus Front retook the Kerch peninsula in the Crimea, and as a reward was renamed the Crimean Front.

Heroic and determined as they were, the Germans could not halt the remorseless advance of the Russians, who used an increasing amount of material aid sent by the United States and Great Britain by means of the Arctic convoys to Murmansk and Archangel, and who seemed to have an inexhaustible supply of fresh troops from Siberia. At the same time, Stalin's wisdom and the Russian people's sacrifices in the previous summer were vindicated as plant from the factories evacuated from western Russia began production at new sites east of the Urals. However, the mud, which had slowed the German advance in the autumn of 1941, put an end to the Russian offensive in March. This *rasputitsa* is a feature of Russian conditions at the beginning and end of winter. At the end of autumn the prevalent rains turn roads and countryside into quagmires incapable of bearing motorized transport until winter conditions freeze the mud solid. At the end of winter, the process is reversed, the country again becoming impassable until the summer sun dries out the mud. As there were few metalled roads in Russia, the autumn and spring mud periods marked beginnings and ends of campaigns throughout the Russo-German war, as it had in previous wars.

March, April and May 1942 were marked by the relative absence of operations, with both sides pausing to rest, regroup and rehabilitate after the rigours of the winter campaign. Yet, as the weary front-line troops welcomed this interval, the planning staffs were busy preparing their next moves. First off the mark were the Germans, with many of their losses of the last few months replaced by the arrival of fresh German troops and some 51 divisions from Italy, Romania, Hungary and even a volunteer division from Spain. In a preliminary offensive between 8 May and 27 June, the Germans managed to straighten out their line by crushing the salients won by the Russian winter offensive. The most important was the great Izyum salient, crushed by Field-Marshal Fedor von Bock's Army Group South between 17 and 29 May. By the end of June, the Germans felt themselves ready to launch their major summer effort of 1942.

The campaign was codenamed *Blau* (Blue), and its history once again shows how competent German plans were destroyed by the vagaries of Hitler's strategic 'genius'. As first conceived, *Blau* was to secure for Germany the important oilfields near Maykop in the northern Caucasus: Army Group South was reorganized, with the 1st *Panzerarmee* and 17th Army of Field-Marshal Wilhelm List's Army Group A driving south-east and then south-west to take the fields. Meanwhile, the 4th *Panzerarmee* and 6th Army of Colonel-General Maximilian Weichs's Army Group B drove forward from the area of Kursk and Kharkov on the upper Donets to secure the line of the great bend of the Don river and so ensure the defence of the left flank of Army Group A.

Then Hitler's avid eye lit on the name Stalingrad, a major industrial city just beyond the objective of Army Group B. The plan was now changed, and Stalingrad, bearer of the ogre of communism's name, was now made a primary objective in itself. At the same time, Army Group A was given extra objectives: the Black Sea coast as far south as Batum, and all the Russian oilfields in the Caucasus as far south as Baku on the Caspian Sea. From a realistic campaign with one major objective and a strategic covering campaign, Hitler had altered his plans to overstretch the capabilities of Army Group A whilst denying it the cover it needed from Army Group B. The original plan had been possible but dangerous, as a Russian offensive from Stalingrad down the Don towards Rostov could have cut off Army Group A; but the revised plan was virtual suicide, for Army Group B could not now provide a flank guard for Army Group A. Yet again, Hitler's lack of a clear strategic goal, and the consequent dispersal of the German effort, was to lead to disaster.

The main effort by Army Group South, as it was still designated, had meanwhile started punctually on 28 June with the drive to the Don. The major city of Voronezh fell to the 4th *Panzerarmee* on 6 July, and von Bock's forces seemed well on the way to fulfilling Hitler's original intentions. Then on 9 July came the reshuffle of Army Group South into Army Groups A and B, with Bock commanding B until the arrival of Weichs on 13 July, the day on which Hitler finally decided to alter the original plan.

At first, all seemed to go relatively well. Army Group B continued to make steady progress in clearing the bend of the Don, with Colonel-General Friedrich Paulus's 6th Army of 18 divisions moving smoothly down the Donets corridor between the Don and Donets rivers to take all but the eastern end of the Don bend by 22 July. Colonel-General Hermann Hoth's 4th *Panzerarmee* was now detached from Weichs to aid Army Group A, which had been making only slow progress towards the line of the lower Don against stiff Russian resistance: Rostov, almost at the mouth of the river, had fallen only on 23 July. Coming into the line on List's left flank, the arrival of the 4th *Panzerarmee* helped to speed up the advance across the Don and south into the Caucasus, and also gave the Germans another line of approach towards Stalingrad from the south-west.

In the Crimea, meanwhile, success had crowned the efforts of Colonel-General Erich von Manstein's 11th Army. On 2 July the great bastion of Sevastopol had fallen, costing the Russians another 100,000 men. As the Kerch peninsula had been cleared once again in the middle of May, this left the Crimea wholly in German hands, which delighted Hitler so much that he promoted von Manstein to field-marshal.

By 1 August, the 1st and 4th *Panzerarmee* of Army Group A had made significant progress into the Caucasus. Further north, however, Army Group B had been slowing down, and Hitler now decided to switch the 4th *Panzerarmee* back to Weichs's forces. Army Group A continued to struggle forward, under the personal command of Hitler, some 2,000 km (1,250 miles) away in East Prussia. The 11th Army had been transferred north to reinforce the siege of Leningrad, and when List and Colonel-General Franz Halder, the

Right : **A Russian anti-German poster.**

ВОИНЫ КРАСНОЙ АРМИИ!
КРЕПЧЕ УДАРЫ ПО ВРАГУ! ИЗГОНИМ НЕМЕЦКО-
ФАШИСТСКИХ МЕРЗАВЦЕВ С НАШЕЙ РОДНОЙ ЗЕМЛИ!

OKH chief-of-staff, protested at these moves, they were both fired. Army Group A inched forward, eventually reaching points only 110 km (70 miles) from the Caspian Sea. Despite being almost entirely cut off from reinforcements and supplies, the North Caucasus and Trans-Caucasus Fronts fought with the utmost determination, yielding ground as slowly as they could.

Back to the north, Army Group B, with the aid of the 4th *Panzerarmee* and reinforced *Luftwaffe* strike units, had finally reached the Volga on 23 August. They now prepared for the attack on Stalingrad itself, whose defence was now in the hands of the Stalingrad Front, set up on 12 July and commanded by General A I Eremenko. The Russians were determined that Stalingrad should not fall, and supplies and men were rushed into the area whilst the armament factories in the city further stepped up their efforts. The scene was set for one of the climactic battles of the war. Dreadfully slow progress being made by Army Group A now meant that the southern Caucasian oilfields were out of Germany's reach, and so the major objective of Operation *Blau* became of necessity Stalingrad, a city of 500,000 inhabitants stretching for some 30 km (18½ miles) along the Volga river. Over a quarter of Russia's vehicles were built here, as well as tanks, guns and other weapons: the objective was important for both sides.

The assault on Stalingrad was undertaken from the north-west by the 6th Army and from the south-west by the 4th *Panzerarmee*, both of whom had reached Stalingrad's outer defence perimeter by 17 August. Defending

Stalingrad were the 66th, 4th Tank, 62nd, 1st Tank, 64th, 51st and 57th Armies, each about the equivalent of a German corps in strength. The 6th Army, which had started Operation *Blau* with only one *Panzer* division, now had two *Panzer* corps, and it was one of these, XIV *Panzer* Corps, which made the main break through the Russians' outer defences on 22 August. On the next day, the corps reached the Volga just to the north of Stalingrad, between Yerzovka and Rynok. By the end of the month the rest of the 6th Army and the 4th *Panzerarmee* had broken through the outer defences and closed up to the middle line, already breached by XIV *Panzer* Corps. The fighting, although already intense, now grew even fiercer as the Germans prepared to move into the city itself. Strangely enough, the 6th Army failed to make serious attempts to throw a bridgehead across the Volga to the north of the city. This would admittedly have been a very serious and costly undertaking as the river is wide and fast-flowing, but the arrival of the Germans on the east bank would have cut off the city from reinforcements from the north and east, as well as prevented the movement of Russian river traffic bringing in more troops and weapons. But here the diversion of the 4th *Panzerarmee* to Army Group A earlier in the campaign had its effect. The relatively slow progress made by the 6th Army on its own had given the Russians just enough time to strengthen their defences on the east bank to make any assault crossing virtually impossible.

By the end of August, Stalingrad was virtually cut off on three sides, with the Russians

78

Above left and right : **German armour, with infantry support, presses on into the Caucasus.** *Left :* **The fog of war starkly silhouettes a** *PzKpfw* **IV in the desperate fighting for Stalingrad.**

holding a perimeter some 50 km (30 miles) long by 30 km (18½ miles) wide. The Germans were now well placed to pursue their offensive by any one of several means, the least costly of which would have been a slow and methodical siege after a river crossing to invade the city from the east. Instead, they chose to assault the city frontally by direct assault. Given the Russians' determination to hold on at all costs, the result was inevitable: Stalingrad became the Verdun of World War II, with seemingly numberless troops being fed into a mincing machine geared to produce immense casualties.

The Germans continued to crash slowly forward during the first part of September, and by the 12th day of the month had reduced the Russian perimeter to a mere 50 km (30 miles). The Germans were now in the outskirts of the city itself, and the bloodiest part of the battle started. XIV and XXIV *Panzer* Corps of the 6th Army and XLVIII *Panzer* Corps of the 4th *Panzerarmee* had played their most important rôles in getting to and cutting off Stalingrad. It was now basically an infantry responsibility to reduce the final defences. The fierce fighting that followed was equalled by only a few other battles of World War II, but the combination of numbers and horror at Stalingrad was completely unequalled. Street by street, and house by house, the Germans pushed forward against fanatical resistance, taking and inflicting

great casualties. The main weapons of this phase of the battle were infantry weapons such as grenades, bayonets and sub-machine guns, supported by light artillery. Areas changed hands frequently, but the general trend still showed the Germans making slow progress.

By 13 October, Stalingrad was finally cut off on the west bank of the Volga when XLVIII *Panzer* Corps of the 4th *Panzerarmee* broke through the residential area in the south to reach the west bank of the Volga at Yelshanka. The most important part of the city, the industrial area in the north, remained in Russian hands, however, and the 62nd Army was determined as ever to hold on.

With his infantry exhausted, Paulus was forced to change his tactics. Frontal assaults were called off in favour of methodical artillery and air bombardment in an effort to flatten the factory complex and its defenders. Yet the change could hardly have suited the Russians more: as the Allies were to find at Cassino and at Caen in 1943 and 1944, the rubble caused by the bombardment provided excellent cover for the defence and made progress for the attackers almost impossible.

The struggle continued unabated right through to the middle of November. By the 18th day of that month, the 295th Infantry Division had reached the Volga in a couple of places, and had even managed to secure a bridgehead on the island opposite to the celebrated Tractor and Krasny Oktyabr factories, from which tanks were driven straight out into combat as soon as they came off the

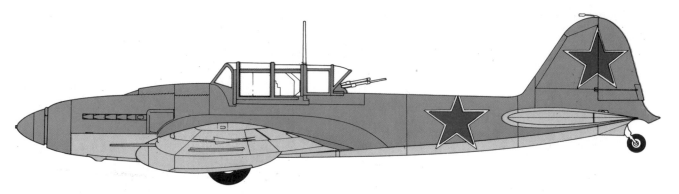

assembly lines.

As they had been just under a year before in front of Moscow, the Germans were now exhausted but still clawing forward slowly. Just as in the year before, the autumn rains played a considerable part in furthering this exhaustion, and once again the winter freeze came as a ghastly shock. The day of 18 November marked the high point of the German summer offensive of 1942, both of whose major objectives had not been reached.

The fall of the temperature below freezing point had long been awaited by the Russians, who had been planning carefully and precisely for their winter offensive. The success of this offensive showed clearly, had the Germans been looking for it, how much the rather ramshackle nature of Russian staff work during the previous year had changed. Stalingrad was at the head of a shallow salient into the Russian lines, with the first-class 6th Army and 4th *Panzerarmee* in the city. But to concentrate these German forces at the most important point, the German high command had been forced to place the defence of the shoulders of the salient on satellite armies of uncertain abilities: the Romanian 3rd Army to the north-west and the Romanian 4th Army to the south. Zhukov, in charge of planning the Russian counterstroke, saw that here was the Axis weak point in the area. At 0730 on 19 November, the South-West and Don Fronts, commanded by General N F Vatutin and General K K Rokossovsky respectively, crashed forward from the line of the Don through the weak defences of the Romanian 3rd Army. A day later, the forces of the Stalingrad Front to the south of the beleaguered city also launched a major offensive, against the Romanian 4th Army. Three days later the spearheads of the two Russian offensives met at Sovetskiy, 50 km (30 miles) to the rear of Paulus's desperate troops in Stalingrad. Weichs's Army Group B only just managed to extricate itself to the south-west, but five Romanian divisions were cut off just to the west of Kletskaya and surrendered on the 23rd. The 6th Army and part of the 4th *Panzerarmee* were cut off in Stalingrad. The besiegers had become the besieged.

Although precarious, the German position was still salvageable: the sensible thing would have been for Paulus to break out to the south-west and rejoin the rest of Army Group A before the Russians had had a chance to consolidate in his rear. This was

the course urged on the German commander by his immediate superior, Weichs. Yet again, however, Hitler's interference was to cost Germany dear: so involved was he with the whole Stalingrad operation that he had decided to assume personal command, and directed Paulus by radio, bypassing Weichs. Hitler, firmly convinced of the need to take Stalingrad and of the benefits of never pulling back, ordered Paulus to stand fast. Although he had at first been unsure in the matter, Hitler had been persuaded to come down on the side of a stand at Stalingrad by the promises of *Reichsmarschall* Hermann Göring. His *Luftwaffe*, Göring blithely assured Hitler, could supply the 400 tons of supplies needed by the 6th Army each day through a simple airlift. This convinced the *Führer*, who immediately ordered Paulus to hold out in 'Fortress Stalingrad' and await relief by Army Group Don, hastily formed from the 11th Army and other available units under the command of von Manstein, in whom Hitler placed great reliance.

Operation *Wintergewitter* (Winter storm) was not merely to effect the relief of the 6th Army, but also to restart the German offensive. Group Hoth, east of the Don, was to advance from the area of Kotelnikovo against the Stalingrad Front and link up with the 6th Army striking south-west from Stalingrad. Operational Group Hollidt, the half of Army Group Don on the west bank of the river, was meanwhile to press forward against the Don Front to keep this latter from interfering with Group Hoth's advance. After the relief of the 6th Army, all three components of von Manstein's force were to fall on the Don and South-West Fronts and restore the line as it was before 19 November.

Von Manstein's offensive started on 12 December, and for the first two days made good progress. But too much time had elapsed while Army Group Don was formed, and the Russians were able to halt the offensive with the forces they had rushed into the area since their own offensive, principally the 2nd Guards Army and VII Tank Corps. By 23 December, LVII *Panzer* Corps, Group Hoth's main striking force, had been halted, only 50 km (30 miles) from Stalingrad. Paulus was ordered by von Manstein to break out towards LVII *Panzer* Corps, but refused to do so after consulting Hitler. The 6th Army's last chance had just passed, and Army Group Don was now itself in great peril. On 24 December, the Russians launched yet another offensive, this time by the South-

West and Stalingrad Fronts against von Manstein's overextended and tired forces. Harried by superior Russian forces, von Manstein was pushed back towards Rostov, east of which he only just managed to hold open a corridor for Army Group A to escape from the Caucasus. The need for Army Group A to retreat had been made abundantly clear by the westward advance of the Stalingrad Front in December, and was hastened by the Trans-Caucasus Front's offensive of January 1, 1943. Only the 1st *Panzerarmee* managed to slip past Rostov to comparative safety, the rest of Army Group A falling back into the Taman peninsula opposite the Crimea.

The plight of the 6th Army in Stalingrad was now desperate. The *Luftwaffe* was able to fly in nothing like the quantities of food, fuel, ammunition and medicines required, and the winter cold was taking a heavy toll of both the fit and wounded. The reduction of the German pocket was in the capable hands of Rokossovsky and his Don Front, which now deployed seven armies against Paulus's formations, at first thought by the Russians to number only a few divisions. In fact some 200,000 men were trapped in the city. Rokossovsky called upon Paulus to surrender on 8 January, and when this demand was refused the Russians launched a major offensive two days later. Hitler refused to countenance any thought of surrender, and the Russian offensive slowly crushed the German pocket from the west. On 14 January the Germans lost their major airfield, Pitomnik, and on 25 January their only other airfield, Gumrak. The 6th Army was now totally cut off and collapsing fast. Hitler clutched at straws: no German field-marshal had ever surrendered, so Paulus was elevated to this rank. But all this was in vain, and by the end of January all the 6th Army, with the exception of XI Corps in the industrial area of the city, had surrendered. XI Corps finally surrendered on 2 February, and the German agony in Stalingrad was over. Some 100,000 men had died in the Don Front's offensive, and another 93,000 were taken prisoner. The summer campaign had cost Germany dear in more than lives and equipment, although these in themselves were bad enough.

However, of greater significance was the fact that the Russians had proved themselves capable of fighting the Germans on their own terms and beating them. The quality of Russian leadership and general military capability had risen sharply since the previous

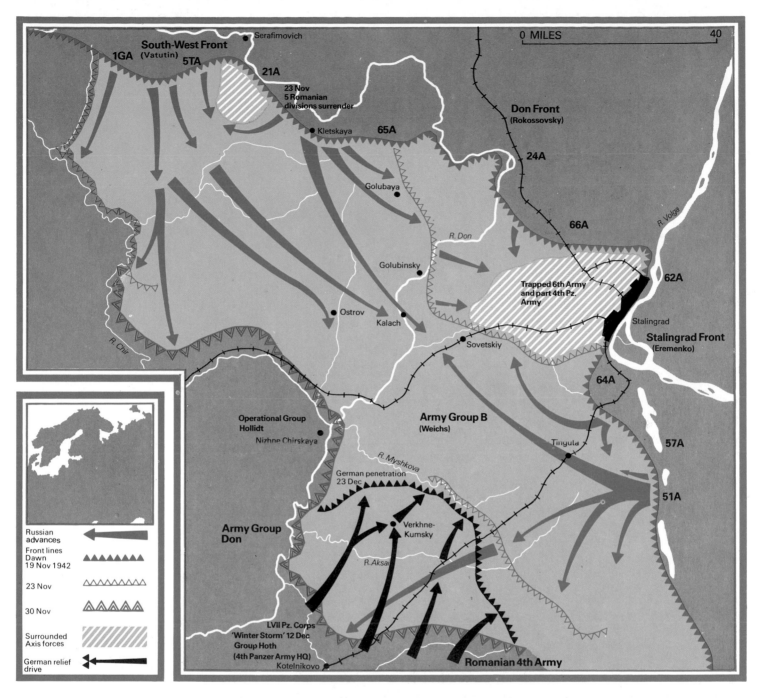

South-West Front (Vatutin)
1GA 5TA
21A
Serafimovich
23 Nov
5 Romanian
divisions surrender
Kletskaya 65A

Don Front (Rokossovsky)
24A
66A
R. Volga

Golubaya

R. Don
Golubinsky

Trapped 6th Army
and part 4th Pz.
Army
62A
Stalingrad

Ostrov Kalach
Sovetskiy
Stalingrad Front (Eremenko)
64A

R. Chir

Army Group B (Weichs)
Tingula
57A

Operational Group
Hollidt
Nizhne Chirskaya

R. Myshkova
German penetration
23 Dec

**Army Group
Don**
Verkhne-
Kumsky
51A

R. Aksai

LVII Pz. Corps
'Winter Storm' 12 Dec
Group Hoth
(4th Panzer Army HQ)
Kotelnikovo
Romanian 4th Army

0 MILES 40

Legend:
Russian advances
Front lines Dawn 19 Nov 1942
23 Nov
30 Nov
Surrounded Axis forces
German relief drive

year, and the Germans' ability to wage war had declined considerably. With a few exceptions, the satellite forces deployed by Hitler proved mediocre, and the burden of stemming the regular Russian offensives was now to fall ever more heavily on the German armies. It was to be a hopeless task.

The Russians were not yet through with their winter offensive. On 12 January, the Bryansk, Voronezh, South-West and South Fronts (the last was the renamed Stalingrad Front) flooded forward from the general line of the Don, between Orel in the north and Rostov in the south. Army Group B and Army Group Don, soon to be renamed Army Group South, resisted stubbornly but were driven steadily back by the remorseless Russian pressure of numbers. By 2 February, when the second stage of the offensive began, the Russian armies had reached a line from Taganrog in the south, up the Mius, Donets

and Oskol rivers to Livy in the north. Between 2 and 20 February, the Russians again swept forward, their most important conquest being Kharkov. There then occurred one of the most remarkable pieces of tactical genius seen in the war. Although outnumbered by seven to one, von Manstein restored his position in the south and retook Kharkov on 14 March. In an offensive between 18 February and 20 March, when the spring thaw put an end to operations, von Manstein used his forces brilliantly, switching his armour from place to place with consummate skill and determination to throw the Russians back to the line of the Donets. Yet even if this secures von Manstein's place amongst the great leaders of all time, the fact remains that the Russian winter offensive had pushed the Germans back still farther. They were in an awkward position for the summer campaign.

Opposite page : **The Ilyushin Il-2 Shturmovik, the best ground-attack aircraft of World War II.** *Above :* **Striking from east and west, the Russians cut off the 6th Army in Stalingrad.** *Below :* **The main protagonists in the relief attempt at Stalingrad were von Manstein (left) and Rokossovsky (right).**

El Alamein

IN January 1942, Lieutenant-General A R Godwin-Austen's XIII Corps was at the gateway to Tripoli, exactly where O'Connor's XIII Corps had been the year before. In 1942, however, over seven Axis divisions had escaped back into Tripoli. General Sir Claude Auchinleck was anxious to pursue them, but could not until Benghazi was operational as a supply base.

The British deployed the 200th Guards Brigade (which was in fact the 22nd, re-numbered) at Mersa Brega with the 1st Armoured Division's Support Group. The rest of the 1st Armoured Division was at Antelat and the 4th Indian Division was in the Benghazi area. Three British defensive positions were planned: the frontier area, using Axis defences between Sidi Omar and Halfaya; Mersa Matruh; and the El Alamein bottleneck between the Mediterranean and the Qattara depression. The offensive against Rommel was to continue on 15 February, with Tripoli the objective.

Rommel, however, struck first. At dawn on 21 January, having recently received 54 German tanks with crews and fuel, three columns advanced with strong air support. The *Deutsches Afrika Korps* came through the desert 32 km (20 miles) south of the Via Balbia, the Italian XX (Mobile) Corps came in the centre, and an *ad hoc* group led by Colonel Werner Marcks came along the Via Balbia. The British forward troops fell back as planned, the 200th Guards Brigade being swept along in front of the Germans who reached Agedabia on 22 January. Rommel had advanced 90 km (56 miles) in 48 hours. He then ordered his forces to move through Aged-abia and to turn eastwards towards Saunnu to prevent the 1st Armoured Division with-drawing to Msus, its supply base. However, the 1st Armoured Division escaped, thanks largely to the excellence of British artillery support. A running battle developed on 23 January. On 25 January, the *DAK* struck north, its two *Panzer* divisions advancing abreast, and captured Msus airfield. Rommel then moved north-west across country to Coefi on the coast to surprise and cut off Benghazi. At the same time, a German feint was made towards Mechili and it was not until Axis mobile formations approached Benghazi from the south that Lieutenant-General N M Ritchie finally agreed to evacu-ate Benghazi, although this had been pre-viously requested by Godwin-Austen. The 4th Indian Division at Benghazi managed to escape Rommel's encircling armies, but at a high cost in casualties.

On 3 February Rommel reached the Gulf

of Bomba, and was now 600 km (375 miles) from his base. He had disobeyed orders that he should only carry out limited operations. Meanwhile, the 8th Army retreated to a line from Gazala to Bir Hacheim, and Godwin-Austen resigned. He was replaced as com-mander of XIII Corps by Lieutenant-General W H E Gott.

Auchinleck maintained that a further British offensive would not be possible until June, and that Rommel wanted to forestall British preparations by taking Tobruk.

The Gazala line was a series of infantry brigade group defensive boxes, each sur-rounded by a perimeter of wire and mines. Each brigade group had its own artillery, en-gineer and logistic units. The armour was held in reserve, with XXX Corps responsible for manoeuvring it. Lieutenant-General C W M Norrie and XXX Corps were also responsible for the security of the southern half of the front, from the Trigh Capuzzo to the Trigh el Abd. The 1st Free French Brigade occupied Bir Hacheim, with the 3rd Indian Motorized Brigade extending from Bir Hacheim south-eastwards. The 1st and 7th Armoured Divisions were 14.5 km (9 miles) south of 'Knightsbridge', a crossroads of tracks leading to Sidi Muftah, Gazala and Bir Hacheim. The 29th Indian Brigade was at Bir el Gubi.

Gott's XIII Corps was deployed along the northern sector, with the 1st South African Division blocking the Via Balbia opposite Gazala, and the 50th Division blocking the track running parallel to the coast road further south. Gott was also responsible for the static positions in the rear, including Tobruk. The whole front was screened by a system of armoured car patrols. A few days before Rommel attacked Auchinleck advised Ritchie to place his two armoured divisions near El Adem expecting an attack in the centre, but Ritchie did not, being concerned that the Germans would fall on his desert flank.

Rommel's forces were divided into two. Under Lieutenant-General Ludwig Crüwell were the Italian XXI and X Corps, which would engage the 8th Army and prevent it from manoeuvring. Rommel would head his *Panzerarmee* consisting of the Italian XX Corps and the *DAK*. Ritchie had some 994 tanks and 190 aircraft. Rommel had 560 tanks and 497 aircraft.

On 26 May Crüwell started his frontal assault while Rommel commenced the great wheeling movement of the *DAK* to the south of Bir Hacheim. The next day both sides experienced some success and defeat. Crüwell's frontal attacks were not totally successful, and Rommel's force was severely mauled in its clashes with 1st and 7th Armoured Divisions. By the end of the day, XXX Corps was able to counterattack, and

the *Panzerarmee* became trapped in the mine-fields. Bir Hacheim held out and drove off the Italian Ariete Division. On 28 May, Rommel threw the mass of his armour against Got el Oualeb, held by the left flank of British 50th Division, and took 3,000 prisoners. The fall of Got el Oualeb allowed Rommel to make a gap through the minefields and con-centrate his armour in the 'Cauldron', west of Knightsbridge, where a battle of attrition was waged until 9 June. The Cauldron, too, was a defeat for the British, who fought valiantly but were unable to drive back the 15th *Panzer* and 90th Light Divisions, their attacks of 5 and 6 June being repulsed with heavy losses. The Germans took 4,000 prisoners and the British lost many tanks. The French fought a gallant but isolated battle at Bir Hacheim until 11 June, when Ritchie ordered them to withdraw.

Ritchie's forward defences as far south as the northern perimeter of the Cauldron were still intact, held by 1st South African and 50th Divisions. Ritchie still had 330 serviceable tanks and he reckoned that one more armoured battle might exhaust the enemy. But Rommel quickly seized the op-portunity to cut off the South African Division and the right flank of the British 50th Division, setting off quickly before Norrie could counterattack. In a fierce battle near Knightsbridge on 12 and 13 June, Rommel defeated Ritchie's armour, leaving him only 50 cruiser and 20 infantry tanks. The 8th Army then withdrew to the frontier, losing contact with Tobruk, where the 2nd South African Division was surrounded. Rommel launched his assault on Tobruk at dawn on 20 June after heavy air bombard-ment. A breach was made in the outer defences and by nightfall, the garrison had capitulated. The Axis forces took 33,000

prisoners and captured a great quantity of vehicles and supplies.

This great victory at Gazala illustrated all Rommel's tactical genius, and Hitler promoted him to field-marshal. Rommel now kept up his advance and quickly regrouped his forces. The *DAK* was despatched towards the frontier with the Italian Mobile Corps, where the British held only a delaying position. Ritchie ordered Gott's XIII Corps to delay the Axis armour while the rest of the 8th Army, reinforced by two fresh divisions, prepared to give battle at Mersa Matruh. Auchinleck at this stage decided to take over personal command of the 8th Army from the hesitant Ritchie. The Germans advanced and the British withdrew to El Alamein, where they were reinforced by the 9th Australian and 4th Indian Divisions.

The El Alamein line was a 65-km (40-mile) gap between the Mediterranean and the Qattara Depression, a salt marsh below sea level where outflanking was impossible. Norrie's XXX Corps was deployed in the northern sector with Gott's XIII Corps in the south, below the Ruweisat ridge.

Rommel's advance to El Alamein was so rapid that on 1 July he had only 6,400 men, 41 tanks and 71 guns. However, he ordered an immediate attack, which failed. Rommel had overstretched himself. He regrouped his forces and withdrew his German units behind a static front line of Italian divisions dug in with wire and mines. A deadly seesaw battle developed on the El Alamein line, with no significant headway being made by either side. After it had died down, major changes in the command structure took place. General Sir Harold Alexander replaced Auchinleck

as commander-in-chief and Lieutenant-General Bernard Montgomery took command of the 8th Army.

Montgomery arrived on 13 August. He rejuvenated the 8th Army and saw three tasks ahead: to restore the Army's confidence; to defeat Rommel's planned offensive and to launch Operation Lightfoot, which would drive Rommel from Egypt. Montgomery visited all units. He brought in two new corps commanders: Lieutenant-General B G Horrocks was now with XIII Corps, and Lieutenant-General Sir Oliver Leese commanded XXX Corps. Montgomery altered the troop deployments. He asked for and got reinforcements for XXX Corps, where the 9th Australian, 1st South African and 5th Indian Divisions were deployed in the northern sector. Regarding XIII Corps, Montgomery sent the newly arrived 44th Division to reinforce Alam el Halfa ridge. The New Zealand Division was deployed between the Ruweisat and Alam el Halfa ridges, and the remainder of the front was covered by the 7th Armoured Division. All defences were to be strengthened and no withdrawals were to be considered.

Rommel was now ill. He knew British supplies were flowing in and he planned to attack on 30 and 31 August, with all his mobile formations passing by night through the thinly held British front south of the Alam Nayil ridge and advancing 48 km (30 miles) through mined country to deploy south of the Alam el Halfa ridge. They would then drive to the north, reach the Alexandria road and cut off the 8th Army. Rommel had at his disposal 200 battleworthy German tanks and 240 Italian medium tanks in poor condition.

The 8th Army had well over 700 tanks, of which 164 were American M3 Grants, now fitted with powerful 6-pdr anti-tank guns. The British knew Rommel was coming, and his diversionary attacks against XXX Corps sector did not deceive Montgomery.

Rommel's initial advance on 30 August was hampered by minefields, and next day he changed his objective to a frontal assault by the *Panzers* on the 22nd Armoured Brigade south of Alam el Halfa. A furious battle ensued, and the *DAK*'s attack was repulsed. Air attacks by the RAF were continuous and the night of 1 and 2 September was the worst the *DAK* had ever experienced. On 3 September Rommel decided to withdraw. Montgomery was tempted to counterattack but not wanting to take risks did not press home.

The victory at Alam el Halfa was a psychological landmark for the British. Hitler promised Rommel all kinds of reinforcements – but the British were now receiving supplies in abundance, including American M4 Sherman tanks and many 105-mm guns.

The Axis forces dug in and laid 500,000 mines in two major fields, giving a honeycomb effect. Five infantry divisions faced the British, with battalions guarding sectors approximately 1.5 km (1 mile) wide by 3 to 4.5 km (2 to 3 miles) deep. The Ariete Armoured Division and 21st *Panzer* Division guarded the southern sector, while the 15th *Panzer* and Littorio Divisions held the north. In reserve, the 90th Light Division and the Trieste Motorized Division were deployed along the coast road. With Rommel on sick leave, General G Stumme was in command.

On the other side, troop training and rehearsals persuaded Montgomery to revise his

Opposite page, *top*: **British troops shelter behind a knocked-out German tank.** *Left*: **Lee tanks proved powerful weapons in the Western Desert.** *Top*: **A German tank crew surrenders.** *Above*: **Rommel ponders his next move.**

original plan for Lightfoot. He now aimed to contain the Axis armour while the infantry divisions were destroyed. His plan had three phases: the break-in by both corps, the dog-fight and the break-out. Montgomery made sure he had a reserve and when he had committed this where necessary, he formed another reserve from a quiet sector. He had also formed an armoured rival to the *Afrika Korps* – Lumsden's X Corps.

Montgomery planned to attack Rommel's northern sector, but successfully convinced the Axis forces that the attack would be on the southern defences. The 8th Army had 1,229 tanks and were superior in all equipment.

85

The Axis had 496 tanks.

At 2140 on 23 October, the 8th Army attack was launched and enjoyed complete surprise. The whole front at El Alamein lit up with a blaze of gunfire. British sappers led the advance and cleared the mines. The armour came next, with infantry behind. XIII Corps launched its diversionary attack and pinned down the 21st *Panzer* and Ariete Armoured Divisions in the south. In the north, XXX Corps made two inroads into the minefields with the 9th Australian Division on the right and the New Zealand Division on the left. While neither reached its planned objective, their action started the crumbling away of the Axis infantry, as envisaged by Montgomery. German armoured counterattacks were beaten off, and the Axis forces had to commit all their reserves. Montgomery urged his forces to carry on their attacks, and the battle became a conflict of fire-power. Rommel, now returned, came off the worse. Montgomery created a new strike force for the break-out stage, Operation Supercharge, which was to be spearheaded by the New Zealand Division. Meanwhile, the 9th Australian Division was doing well in the north and cut the coast road.

Air attacks causing major disruption in the enemy rear heralded the beginning of Supercharge, during which battles of great ferocity were fought between 2 and 4 November. The New Zealand Division, reinforced by two British infantry brigades, fought hard to force a breach for X Corps to pass through, losing many tanks in the process.

By now the Axis forces were totally outnumbered. Even to force a stalemate was no longer possible for them. They had only 187 tanks left, 155 of which were Italian and incapable of withstanding the fire of the Shermans. Rommel began to disengage on 3 November although Hitler issued a stand-fast order which was disregarded. Rommel succeeded under cover of a skilful rearguard

Top: **The Bf 109 gave the Axis forces powerful fighter protection.** *Above*: **German artillery was generally outclassed in the desert.** *Right*: **Axis reinforcements were largely prevented from reaching Rommel by the British stranglehold on the central Mediterranean.** *Far right*: *Afrika Korps* **troops rest briefly during their retreat.**

action in extricating many of his surviving troops, but had to leave behind a great deal of equipment, which the British picked up in addition to 30,000 prisoners. The Allies lost 13,560 men and 500 tanks.

Rommel began his long retreat to Tunis, followed steadfastly by Montomery's 8th Army, not even making a stand at Halfaya or El Agheila, so precarious was his position.

Air War in the Mediterranean

IN June 1940, Italy entered the war on the side of Germany and the Mediterranean theatre became active. The *Regia Aeronautica* or Italian Air Force was quite a large body, but lacked properly trained reserves of men or aircraft, especially in the fighter arm, and was short of truly modern combat aircraft. The majority of fighters were Fiat CR32 and 42 biplanes, appreciated by most Italian pilots for their manoeuvrability. The few monoplane fighters available had been designed to meet a similar outmoded concept of air fighting, with speed, rate of climb and armament sacrificed to agility. The best elements of the *Regia Aeronautica* were undoubtedly the bomber squadrons, equipped with Savoia-Marchetti SM79 three-engined monoplanes. These could be used for conventional bombing attacks or for torpedo-strike operations, in which the Italians were very skilled.

The British, on the other hand, had only a few aircraft in North Africa and Malta, most of them obsolete. But although reserves were small, the RAF had a distinct advantage in the calibre of its aircrew and ground organization. The mainstay of the British fighter arm in the Mediterranean was the Gloster Gladiator biplane, comparable in performance with the CR42. Apart from a moderate number of obsolete bomber types, the British also possessed some fairly modern Bristol Blenheim monoplane medium bombers. In the early stages of the campaign, therefore, the quality of the aircraft used by each side meant that the type of air warfare likely to be fought would be that which might have taken place over northern Europe in the mid-1930s. At the outset of the war with Italy, the British had some 300 aircraft in the Mediterranean and African theatres, and the Italians some 480 excluding those in metropolitan Italy.

The shortest route to and from the Far East, India and Australasia lay through the Suez Canal, and hence this area was of paramount importance to the British war effort. Yet without control of the Mediterranean, control of the Suez Canal was useless. And the key to the Mediterranean was the island of Malta, roughly equidistant from Gibraltar and the Suez Canal. Unfortunately, Malta lies only some 100 km (60 miles) south of the island of Sicily, well provided with air bases for the Italian fighters and bombers. Almost immediately after the Italian declaration of war, raids began to be dispatched against Malta from these bases.

Pre-war British plans had assumed that because of its location close to Italy and far from sources of reinforcement, Malta would be untenable. Thus, little thought had been given to practical measures for its preservation. Yet these first Italian raids were beaten off with some losses, and the island's defence seemed to be becoming more feasible. Its fighter force at first rested on the three survivors of four Sea Gladiators in reserve on the island, and these severely mauled the Italians until reinforcements, in the form of

Below: **Although obsolete, Fairey Swordfish torpedo-bombers scored a striking success against the Italian fleet in Taranto.** *Right*: **A** *Luftwaffe* **Junkers Ju 88 medium bomber prepares to take off on a strike.**

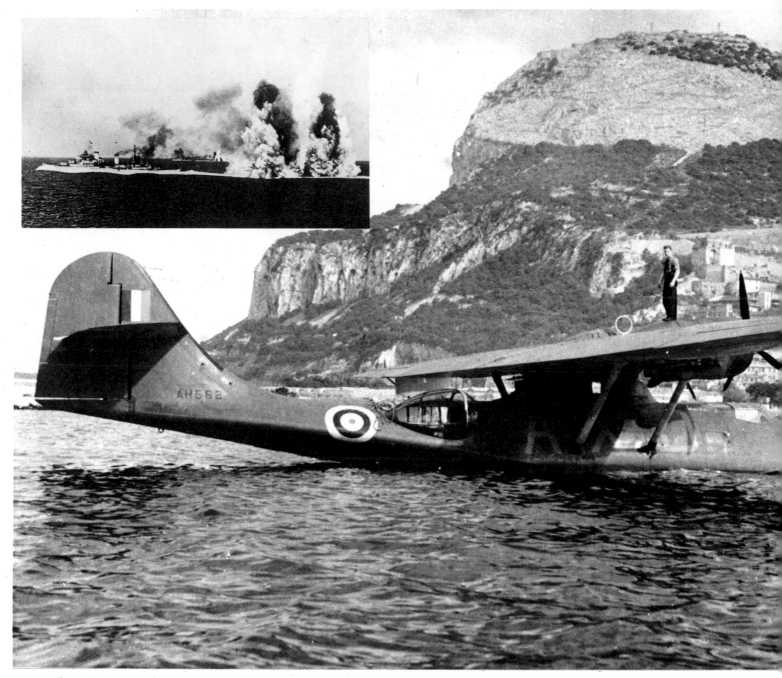

some Hawker Hurricanes, arrived at the end of June and the beginning of August. With the arrival of these aircraft, the Italian attacks gradually became ineffectual in strategic terms. The British realized that the island was indeed defensible, and so determined to hold out. There was to be very serious air fighting, but Malta was to survive Italian and German attacks, and eventually to go over to the offensive against Axis airfields and shipping; thus playing an important rôle in the final success of Allied arms in North Africa. In December 1940, the island's first proper force arrived, in the form of a squadron of Vickers Wellington twin-engined medium bombers. From then on the offensive strength of the island grew rapidly.

In North Africa, meanwhile, the RAF had played an important part in the rout of the Italian advance towards Cairo. Reinforced by aircraft flown in across the southern Sahara from the Gold Coast, the RAF had

shown itself to be superior in all important respects to the *Regia Aeronautica*. Yet the early successes in Malta and North Africa were to have unfortunate repercussions. With the Axis cause humiliated by the reverses suffered by the Italians, Hitler decided that he must bolster the efforts of his southern ally, and in December 1940 the first elements of *Fliegerkorps* X reached Sicily. The German formation's bombers were soon in action against Malta.

In January 1941, the German aircraft seriously damaged the carrier *Illustrious*, which had to lie at Malta whilst temporary repairs were carried out. With a target of this importance at the island, the Germans and Italians naturally enough stepped up their attacks very considerably for a period of one week in the middle of January. Furious battles raged over the island, but the defence held, and *Illustrious* was able to sail for proper repairs on 23 January. This miniature *blitz*

was a portent of what was to come.

During the same period, aircraft of Air Chief-Marshal Sir Arthur Longmore's Middle East air forces were operating with considerable success against the Italians in Greece, and provided the Greeks with much-needed tactical air support. Although at first no British land forces were involved, Longmore found the strain of the Greek campaign increasingly severe, yet was ordered to supply ever larger numbers of his aircraft to this theatre. Longmore's difficulties were further increased when the Germans invaded Greece in April 1941. The British forces put up a gallant but hopeless defence, and the RAF units in the area were able to do little more than slow the Germans at a great cost to themselves. If the obsolescence of biplanes had not been fully clear before the Greek campaign, it was amply demonstrated by the success of the *Luftwaffe*'s modern bombers and fighters, and from

Inset above left: **A British cruiser near Malta enjoys a narrow escape from bombs.** *Above:* **A Consolidated PBY Catalina patrol flying-boat lies at anchor at Gibraltar.** *Above right:* **An RAF Hurricane fighter stands guard over a wrecked Heinkel 111 bomber.**

henceforth biplanes disappeared from the RAF's front-line inventory.

Coming at the same time as Lieutenant-General Erwin Rommel's first offensive in North Africa, the Greek campaign proved too much for the already over-extended RAF units in the area, and meant that the British could hold neither Greece nor Cyrenaica. Longmore had been succeeded by Air-Marshal Arthur Tedder, and the latter decided to cut his losses and provide no air defence for the island of Crete which fell to German airborne assault in May 1941. Tedder was now free to concentrate on his prime areas, Malta and North Africa. By the middle of July, British successes in East Africa, Iraq and Syria had further reduced Tedder's worries, leaving only the two prime areas, in which most combat aircraft could now be concentrated.

This concentration was essential since by now elements of the *Luftwaffe* had arrived in North Africa.

For the rest of 1941 and 1942, the fortunes of the air war in North Africa closely reflected the pattern set by ground operations, the prevailing side generally enjoying a fair measure of air superiority. Although the Germans rarely deployed a great number of aircraft in this theatre, their performance in the air was of very high quality, epitomized by the great fighter ace, Hans-Joachim Marseille. In a short and spectacular career, Marseille shot down 158 Allied aircraft before his own death, which occurred just after he had been awarded Germany's highest military honour, the Oakleaves, Swords and Diamonds to the Knight's Cross of the Iron Cross. Marseille was one of only 27 recipients of this honour in the whole war. His career was quite exceptional, and included the shooting down of several aircraft in a single day on separate missions. His death was the result of an accident, rather than enemy action.

Nevertheless, throughout the period the RAF gradually improved its overall performance, and pioneered the widespread use of fighter-bombers operating in close support of the land forces. The Western Desert was an ideal place for such developments, which were to play an extremely important part in the Italian and north-western European campaigns later in the war. Large numbers of modern aircraft gradually found their way out to North Africa, and by the autumn of 1942 the Allies had secured almost total air supremacy over Libya. In the closing stages of the war, with the Allies gradually crushing the Axis forces into Tunisia from the east and west, their air superiority was total, and played a vital rôle in checking the last German offensives in the area. By May 1943, when the Axis forces in Tunisia capitulated and brought the North African war to an end, the Desert Air Force was a powerful tactical formation, possibly the most highly-trained and experienced force of its kind in the world.

During this period, Malta had suffered tremendous punishment, but had in turn played a significant part in the reversal of Axis fortunes in North Africa. Between June and October 1941, for example, Malta-based aircraft had sunk 115,000 tonnes of Axis shipping taking supplies to North Africa, action which was seriously affecting Rommel's efforts. Hitler decided in October 1941 that the problem of Malta must be cured by drastic measures. Field-Marshal Albert Kesselring was recalled from the Russian front to take command of air operations against the island. *Fliegerkorps* II joined *Fliegerkorps* X on Italian bases for the operation, which was launched three days before Christmas 1941. First the airfields, and then the towns themselves came under attack. The pattern and nature of the defence followed that set by London a year before, and both the civilians and troops behaved with great gallantry and fortitude. Despite the strength of the German and Italian offensive, the islanders never faltered, although frequently close to breaking point. The first stage of Kesselring's offensive lasted up to June 1942. By this time Malta was on the verge of starvation, and its aircraft almost out of fuel and ammunition. Convoys bringing in supplies of all kinds had suffered very heavily, but in June, just sufficient supplies arrived to revitalize the defence and cause Kesselring to call a temporary halt. In July, the German offensive restarted, but after one last desperate effort in October this too was overcome by the island's fighters. Meanwhile, Allied shipping based there had been striking at the Axis convoys to North Africa, action which finally starved Rommel of almost all essential supplies. By the beginning of 1943, Malta was firmly in control of the central Mediterranean sea lanes. The fate of the Axis forces in North Africa was sealed.

The End in Africa

OPERATION Torch was the Allies' plan to seize Morocco, Algeria and Tunisia. They faced a problem of where to land complicated by the threat of U-boats in the Atlantic and Mediterranean, the range of Axis aircraft and possible French opposition. Although there were no Axis forces in French North Africa, the proximity of Tunis to Sicily made it likely that the Germans and Italians would attempt to counter Allied landings there.

Operation Torch was the first large-scale amphibious operation to be launched over such long distances and the first Anglo-American combined operation. There were three landings: the Western Task Force landed at Casablanca, and was wholly American, conveyed from the United States in American ships; the Centre Task Force landed at Oran, with American ground troops (US II Corps) led by Major-General Lloyd R Fredendall, and came from Britain in British ships; the Eastern Task Force landed near Algiers and was predominantly British (1st Army) under Lieutenant-General K A N Anderson. Anderson's forces were to secure Tunis. (The ETF's nominal commander was the American Major-General Charles Ryder.)

Lieutenant-General Dwight Eisenhower was now Allied commander-in-chief, and it was envisaged that his forces would meet up with General Sir Bernard Montgomery's 8th Army to banish Axis forces from North Africa.

The landings took place before dawn on November 8, 1942 but not without opposition from the French. Their naval installations and ships at Mers el Kébir and Oran fired on the Allies, and there was fierce fighting at Oran itself. Admiral Jean Francois Darlan, commander-in-chief of the Vichy French forces, called for a ceasefire throughout French North Africa on 10 November, which saved Casablanca from Allied assault.

The Allies had landed safely, and the race for Tunis was on. Anderson immediately organized his 1st Army's movement eastwards. Between Algiers and Tunis were 650 km (400 miles) of mountainous, inhospitable terrain, and so his forces went by sea to Bône, then overland to approach Tunis.

By now, however, Hitler had decided to establish a bridgehead around Tunis and Bizerta: German and Italian troops originally intended as reinforcements for Rommel

Left : **Montgomery (seated centre) accepts the surrender of Messe (seated left) and von Liebenstein (seated right) in May 1943.**

arrived in growing numbers, and the *Luftwaffe* took over important airfields in Tunisia. By the end of November there were 15,000 Axis combat troops and over 50 tanks at Tunis, organized into XC Corps under General Walther Nehring. Nehring ordered General G Barré, French supreme commander of Tunisia, to clear the way for the Germans to Algeria, but Barré refused to co-operate. In mid-November, pro-Allied French ground troops formed a thin defensive line to keep the Germans at bay whilst the British 1st Army advanced.

Anderson's forces, the 78th Division and a detachment of the 6th Armoured Division, made good progress and came into contact with German battle-groups probing westwards on 17 November. On 18 November the 36th Brigade beat off a German attack at Djebel Abiod. The British attacked towards Tunis together with a few American units known as Blade Force, but were repulsed. The Germans carried out round-the-clock bombing. Anderson's line of communication was weak, and a depot system was lacking. However, Anderson had established contact with Barré and the French.

Anderson tried for another month, with American reinforcements, to crack the German defences, but torrential rain made movement difficult. On 24 December, Eisenhower abandoned the immediate attempt to capture Tunis and Bizerta. A stalemate ensued, and the Allies had lost the race for the time being.

Meanwhile, in two months Montgomery had advanced 2,400 km (1,500) miles from Egypt to Tunisia after his victory at El Alamein. On 23 November Field-Marshal Erwin Rommel withdrew into Mersa Brega. Montgomery decided to attack on 15 December, planning to pin Rommel by a frontal assault with two divisions, whilst the New Zealand Division carried out a 320-km (200-mile) outflanking march through the desert to block Rommel's withdrawal down the coastal road. Rommel's air reconnaissance spotted Lieutenant-General Sir Bernard Freyberg's New Zealanders approaching, and when they reached the coast road on the night of 15 December, they found that all Rommel's forces except the rearguards had already passed through.

Rommel was ordered to delay the 8th Army for at least two months before falling back to the Mareth Line, just over the Tunisian frontier, but his 21st *Panzer* Division was sent on ahead to Tunisia.

Tunisia's coastal plain contains the ports of Sousse, Sfax and Gabès, and there are two

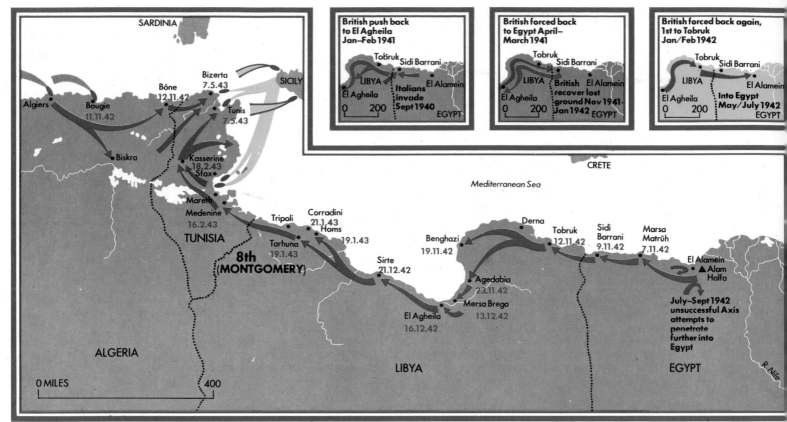

mountain ranges, the Eastern and Western Dorsales. French forces under Lieutenant-General Alphonse Juin occupied the passes in the Eastern Dorsale as far south as the Gulf of Gabès. The Anglo-American troops, as they arrived, were held in reserve along the Western Dorsale or in the plain between the two. The command system was complicated by the French refusal to take orders from the British, and Eisenhower assumed tactical control of the front. There was no dominant personality to lead the Allies. Anderson's 1st Army was in northern Tunisia and Fredendall's US II Corps was at Tebéssa with Major-General J E Welvet's French Constantine Division forward at the Faid pass and at Gafsa.

Operation Satin, devised by American planners, called for an advance of the American II Corps from Tebessa. The 1st Infantry and 1st Armoured Divisions, with the French Constantine Division, would push through to Sfax or Gabès and cut Axis communications between Tripoli and Tunis. The plan was vetoed, however, as the 1st Armoured Division was inexperienced.

The Axis had approximately 47,000 Germans and 18,000 Italians now formed into the 5th *Panzerarmee* under Colonel-General Jürgen von Arnim and comprising the 10th *Panzer* Division, 334th Infantry Division, Broich Division and 501st Tiger Tank Battalion. The Italians formed XXX Corps. The *Luftwaffe* had control of the air.

Operation *Eilbote* (Express Messenger) was launched to roll up Allied positions in the Eastern Dorsale from north to south. On January 18, 1943 a diversionary attack was made by the 10th *Panzer* Division against the British 6th Armoured Division at Bou Arada, where it was stopped by British artillery,

mines and the mud. Major-General Friedrich Weber's 334th Division struck further south along the Eastern Dorsale, cutting off and destroying the French garrisons. An effective, but late counterattack by Brigadier-General Paul Robinett's Command Combat B from the US II Corps put an end to *Eilbote*, but the Fondouk pass and 4,000 prisoners had fallen to the Germans.

On 30 January the 21st *Panzer* Division with approximately 150 tanks and strong air support attacked the Faid pass and 1,000 Frenchmen surrendered. Fredendall misjudged the situation and did not send enough help. All the passes were now in German possession, although their attempts to take Maknassy failed.

On 23 January, Rommel slipped out of Tripoli and started withdrawing to the Mareth Line, consisting of old French fortifications, which Rommel considered antiquated and too easily turned. Montgomery took Tripoli.

The Germans now planned to attack the Allied front by a north-westerly thrust from Faid to Fondouk, with the 10th *Panzer* Division attacking from Faid to Sidi Bou Zid whilst the 21st *Panzer* Division made a southerly detour to approach the American positions from Maknassy. The Americans were unaware of the scale of the German operation, launched on 14 February. The 10th *Panzer* Division occupied Sidi Bou Zid and Combat Command C bravely counterattacked the next day. In three days, the Germans destroyed two tank, two artillery and two infantry battalions of the US II Corps.

Anderson now realized that this was a major offensive and ordered prompt withdrawal of all forces to the Western Dorsale.

He sent units of the British 6th Armoured Division and 1st Guards Brigade to guard the Western Dorsale passes, including Sbiba and Kasserine.

The German *Panzers* pursued the Allied retreat, taking Sbeitla on 17 February. Rommel then ordered the *Afrika Korps* Assault Group to seize the Kasserine pass, through which he would then advance to Le Kef. The 21st *Panzer* Division was to break through Sbiba pass and also make for Le Kef, but the pass was heavily defended and the 21st *Panzer* Division was repulsed. The 10th *Panzer* Division went to the Kasserine pass, which was held by the US 26th Infantry Division and the 19th Combat Engineer Regiment. After being thrown back, the *Panzers* eventually forced their way through. The 10th *Panzer* Division struck out towards Thala and was repulsed by the British 6th Armoured Division and the guns of the American 9th Division. As a result the Germans withdrew from the Kasserine pass, and the Allies reoccupied it on 24 February, closing up on the Axis positions on the Eastern Dorsale.

There was now considerable tension and mistrust in the Allied command. Low morale and complacency were apparent, especially in the US II Corps. However, this changed after 15 February when General Sir Harold Alexander, as Eisenhower's deputy, set up his 18th Army Group headquarters to exercise tactical control over the land battle. Alexander, like Montgomery, insisted on training, discipline and no thoughts of withdrawal.

There were problems, too, on the Axis side. Von Arnim thought the Kasserine pass should be the final objective of a counterattack, while Rommel was convinced that a thrust from Tebéssa to Bône would cut the

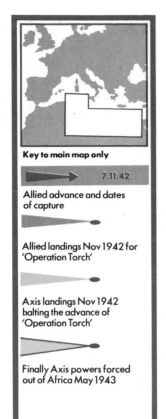

Above left : **The campaigns that sealed the fate of the Axis in North Africa.** *Above :* **French troops in the Tunis victory parade.**

Allied line of communications. Von Arnim was a difficult man with whom to deal. On 23 February, however, Rommel became commander of the new Army Group *Afrika*. General Giovanni Messe was now commander of the German-Italian 1st Army, including the *Afrika Korps*, which was to defend the Mareth Line.

Montgomery was now preparing to attack Rommel's main position south-east of Gabès and had pushed his advanced forces almost to the Mareth Line. But Rommel attacked first. On 6 March he threw the 10th, 15th and 21st *Panzer* Divisions against positions defended at Medenine by nearly 500 anti-tank guns, and they were repulsed with heavy losses. Rommel then returned to Germany on sick leave, handing over Army Group *Afrika* to von Arnim, reinforced by the Hermann Göring *Panzer* Division, Manteuffel Division and 999th Division. The rest of the Germans were now very tired.

On 6 March Alexander placed Lieutenant-General George Patton at the head of the US II Corps, a change for the better. Alexander's formula for success was to feint with one fist and hit with the other. He saw two stages to defeating the Axis: to pass the 8th Army through the Mareth Line and the Gabès gap to unite his two armies; and to tighten a land, sea and air noose around the Axis forces, to weaken them by blockade so that they would be unable to withstand the final blow. Alexander regrouped the forces into national units.

The Long Range Desert Group confirmed there was a way round the Mareth Line for the 8th Army through the desert west of the Matmata hills, and that the route back to the sea was through a narrow defile, the Tebaga gap. Lieutenant-General Sir Oliver Leese's

XXX Corps was to breach the Mareth Line in the coastal area, while the New Zealand Corps would make for the Tebaga gap. Montgomery kept X Corps and the 1st and 7th Armoured Divisions in reserve. The results of this Operation, codenamed Pugilist, were rather disappointing. XXX Corps advanced in heavy rain and reached Wadi Zigzaou where it was intercepted by the 15th *Panzer* Division. XXX Corps became bogged down in the mud and got no further. Freyberg's New Zealanders seized the entrance to the Tebaga gap on the night of 21 to 22 March, but next morning found the 21st *Panzer* Division blocking the way forward. Montgomery now sent X Corps and the 1st Armoured Division to Tebaga, where they arrived on 26 March and immediately attacked. The Desert Air Force ably supported the Allied drive which was highly successful, and stunned the enemy. But the breakthrough at El Hamma was too late to prevent Messe regrouping his forces along the Wadi Akarit, where he had only to defend the 13-km (8-mile) front between the Gulf of Gabès and the lake of Chott el Fedjadj.

Patton's II Corps had in the meantime captured Gafsa on 17 March. It was Patton's task to support Montgomery by drawing off Axis forces. On 28 March he attacked vigorously along the road from Gafsa towards Gabès and repulsed the 10th *Panzer* Division at El Guettar.

Montgomery's forces attacked the Wadi Akarit on 6 April. Three divisions of the 8th Army, supported by 450 guns, tore a gaping hole in the Axis position, and when X Corps' tanks entered the battle, von Arnim's forces retreated. The 8th Army passed through the Gabès gap and the two Allied armies finally met five months after the Torch landings.

The Allied build-up had been continual. Now they lacked for nothing, and had control of numerous airfields. Nevertheless, the Germans and Italians fought hard to hold Tunis and Bizerta. Hitler would not sanction evacuation, although von Arnim was left without proper communications, sufficient petrol or tank and gun replacements. He had 16 weary divisions to guard 220 km (135 miles) of front.

Alexander's Plan, Vulcan, gave the British 1st Army the task of capturing Tunis. The US II Corps (now led by Lieutenant-General Omar Bradley) was to capture Bizerta. The 8th Army was to draw the reserves away.

It took until 7 May for the Allies to succeed in taking Tunis and Bizerta. The Axis forces now had their backs to the sea. They received no further supplies – Hitler was thinking of Sicily. Each Allied attack was vigorously fought off. Montgomery and his 8th Army attacked Messe at Enfidaville twice and failed to break through. Alexander's *coup de grace* was Operation Strike on 6 May, when the British 4th and 4th Indian Divisions attacked side by side on a 2,743-m (3,000-yard) front astride the Medjez–Tunis road, supported by 650 guns and tactical aircraft. When the defences were breached, the 6th and 7th Armoured Divisions rushed through at speed heading for Tunis. Von Arnim knew they were coming, but was short of everything necessary to meet the attack. The way to Tunis was open at last, Tunis and Bizerta were captured, and it was truly the end for the Axis forces in Africa. Some 130,000 Germans and 118,000 Italians surrendered.

The U Boat War

January 1942 – May 1943

ANY hope that the entry of the United States into the war would lighten the burden on the British and Canadian navies was misplaced. Admiral Karl Dönitz had plans to move his U-boats across the Atlantic to dislocate American east coast shipping, and five days after Pearl Harbor he launched Operation *Paukenschlag* (Drumroll). It succeeded beyond anybody's wildest expectation, for the US Navy was caught with virtually no means of protecting its shipping.

The U-boats called it the return of the 'happy time', for merchant ships were unescorted, uncoded radio messages gave constant positions and all navigation lights were still lit. The US Navy had pinned its hopes on offensive patrolling by destroyers rather than on convoys, and so its considerable efforts were largely wasted. The U-boats gleefully noted the regularity with which destroyers passed at high speed, and surfaced as soon as the patrol had gone, secure in the knowledge that they could continue to sink shipping for another hour or two without interruption. The US Navy was woefully short of anti-submarine aircraft, and the US Army Air Force aircrews available were not well trained. All these problems were reflected in a massive rise in shipping losses. Between 1 January and 31 March a total of 60 tankers were sunk in the Caribbean alone, and losses along the whole of the east coast exceeded 1,000,000 tonnes during the same period.

The short-term answer was for the British to transfer 24 anti-submarine trawlers fitted with ASDIC and 10 Flower class corvettes to the US Navy. Even private aircraft were pressed into service, flying patrols along the coast in an effort to scare off the U-boats. In April, convoying was introduced, but this did not become universal until June. Significantly, the U-boats then returned to their main hunting ground in mid-Atlantic, where they were out of reach of shore-based aircraft.

Another heavy burden on the Allied escort forces was the commitment to carry equipment to Russia, following the German invasion of Russia in mid-1941. Losses were heavy as the convoy routes to Murmansk and Archangel went past German airfields and U-boat bases in Norway. The most unfortunate convoy of all was PQ17, which in July 1942 lost 23 out of 37 ships. Some idea of what this involved is conveyed by the fact that 99,000 tonnes of cargo, 3,350 vehicles, 430 tanks and 210 aircraft were lost in that single convoy action. The PQ17 disaster was caused by a premature report of the battleship *Tirpitz* putting to sea; she never made contact, but the convoy scattered and its ships were picked off singly by U-boats and aircraft.

By the autumn of 1942, however, British and American production was beginning to have its effect. Enough new escorts were now available to set up offensive support groups to carry the fight to the U-boats. A cure was found for the 'Black Gap' in mid-Atlantic, the area out of range of shore-based aircraft in which the U-boats scored their greatest successes. Four-engined Consolidated B-24 Liberator bombers with extra fuel tanks were introduced and finally it was decided to take aircraft to sea with the convoys. The first escort carrier, a merchant ship fitted with a small wooden flight deck, had been tried in the autumn of 1941, and although she had soon been sunk her success led to orders for more. These were now coming forward from American shipyards, and with the support groups they showed that the time had come to return to the offensive. Events in the Atlantic were moving towards a climax, for the U-boats were also coming forward from the shipyards in greater numbers. It remained to be seen if Dönitz could realize his ambition of sinking merchant ships faster than they could be built.

At this moment, the Allied leaders made what seems in retrospect a rash move. Goaded by demands from Stalin for a second front, but daunted by the obvious problems of landing in Europe, the Americans settled for an amphibious landing in North Africa at the end of 1942. While there were advantages to be gained by clearing Axis forces out of North Africa, particularly the elimination of the air bases which menaced the supply-route to Malta, the main motive behind the North African project was political. An important disadvantage to it was that the enormous convoys which would bring US troops and equipment straight across the Atlantic would need massive protection against U-boats. To achieve this, the new escort carriers and support groups were taken away from the Atlantic for the duration of Operation Torch.

It was too much to expect Dönitz to miss such a chance, and although his U-boats failed to stop the Torch convoys reaching North Africa, they were quick to exploit the reduced strength of Atlantic escort forces. Losses rose to 619,000 tonnes in October and to 729,000 tonnes in November. They fell again in December because of the severe weather, but at the end of that month Allied shipping losses for 1942 totalled 7,790,000 tonnes. Although U-boat construction was slower than Dönitz had hoped, there were now 312 boats in service as against 91 at the end of 1941.

As the new year opened, it became clear to the Allied leaders that they had reached the decisive moment of the war. If the U-boats continued to sink ships at such a rate Great Britain would be forced out of the war. Those who advocated stepping up the bombing offensive overlooked the fact that losses of oil tankers would soon cripple their efforts. Nor was it any use winning victories in North Africa if communications across the Atlantic were in jeopardy. In a running squabble between the British Air Ministry and the Admiralty, the strategic bombing lobby was far too successful in blocking the transfer of four-engined bombers to anti-submarine work. Even after January 1943, when the Casablanca Conference issued a directive to both British and American bomber chiefs to give top priority to defeating the U-boats, their response was to bomb U-boat building yards. Not until the end of the war did these raids destroy a single U-boat, but they did account for a large number of precious bombers which could have been put to better use in the Atlantic.

Meanwhile, the convoys were suffering appalling losses in a series of battles as ferocious as any yet seen. In the first two months of 1943 dreadful weather hampered the U-boats as much as it did the convoys,

Left: **The Type IXC class boat** *U-161* **sinks by the stern in 1943 after being depth-charged by US aircraft.** *Right:* **Other moments were happier for successful U-boats.**

but in March a massive four-day battle took place between 17 U-boats and a convoy, in which 13 ships, totalling some 60,000 tonnes, were lost. Two convoys bound for Halifax, one slow and one fast, were then attacked by 40 U-boats, and so fierce was the onslaught that the escort commanders combined both convoys to strengthen the escort. Before the U-boats' grip could be loosened by the arrival of shore-based aircraft, they had sunk 141,000 tonnes of shipping. The British and Americans were close to despair, for no matter what technical wizardry their scientists could produce and no matter how many ships were being built, the U-boats were winning. In the first three weeks of March, over 500,000 tonnes of shipping was sunk, and it looked as if the convoy system had at last failed.

Just at this blackest moment, three factors helped to turn the tide. First, the escorts and, above all, escort carriers taken away for Operation Torch came back to the Western Approaches. By delaying the sailing of two large convoys for Russia, the Admiralty was able to form five support groups, and the US Navy also introduced the first of its new escort carrier groups. Second, cryptanalysis using information from the ULTRA organization enabled convoys to be routed away from U-boat wolfpacks. Third, the Atlantic Convoy Conference in March led to an immediate pooling of Allied escort resources, which made for more efficient deployment of ships. Another less obvious factor was German inferiority in the technical race. Not until January 1943 did the Germans realize that the Allies were using a centimetric-waveband radar set, and a suitable search receiver could not be produced in time to affect the issue.

The losses of shipping suddenly slackened towards the end of March, and in April they dropped by half. Six U-boats had been sunk in January, 19 in February, only 15 in March and 15 in April, but in May the figure shot up to 41. The Allies were being more selective about their offensive measures now, with aircraft and ship patrols concentrated where the U-boats were most likely to be found, notably the Bay of Biscay. The U-boats saved time by crossing the bay on the surface, and if they could be forced to submerge this would cut their time on patrol in mid-Atlantic. When ULTRA revealed that U-boats were refuelling at prearranged points in mid-Atlantic from 'milch-cow' U-boats, these underwater tankers were made top priority targets for the support groups. The Allied shipbuilding and aircraft production programme was now getting into its stride, and ships and aircraft were coming forward in large numbers.

The tactics used by escorts and aircraft were improving all the time, and new weapons were introduced to exploit the ideas put forward by scientists and servicemen. The leading British anti-submarine expert, Commander F J Walker, introduced the creeping attack, using one escort to track a U-boat from a distance while directing another escort to the attacking position on

radio: the unsuspecting U-boat could not hear the slow propeller-revolutions of the attacking ship, and also believed that escorts dared not drop depth-charges while moving slowly. When Walker found that U-boats were diving deeper than ever before he asked for a 1-tonne depth-charge. In response, the Americans produced the Fido homing torpedo, designed to home onto the noise of a diving U-boat's propellers. The introduction of escort carriers meant new tactics, too, for these could be vulnerable to torpedo-attack.

A most important adjunct to radar and ASDIC was high-frequency direction-finding, or Huff-Duff, which enabled ships to pinpoint the position of a U-boat transmitting her sighting reports back to base. Although the Germans picked up information about Huff-Duff from monitored messages, their scientists were sceptical about the possibility of producing a high-precision set small enough to go into a warship, and so when unexplained losses occurred they were attributed to a new type of Allied radar. Even when a photograph of a destroyer fitted with a Huff-Duff mast was taken by agents at Algeciras, the German censor deleted the telltale mast before the photograph was circulated.

The German surface navy had virtually abandoned all hope of intervening to any effect in the Battle of the Atlantic. In February 1942, the battlecruisers *Scharnhorst* and *Gneisenau* and the heavy cruiser *Prinz Eugen* made their brilliant dash through the English Channel in broad daylight. However much this exploit might have annoyed the British, it did the Germans no good at all, for the removal of the three ships from Brest meant

Above : **The tanker** *Dixie Arrow* **sinks off the US east coast during the U-boats' second 'happy time' in early 1942.**
Right : **A US sailor watches the explosion of a depth-charge from his ship.**

that the convoys were no longer threatened. Apart from her rôle in forcing the PQ17 convoy to scatter, *Tirpitz* did nothing, and for Hitler the last straw was the Battle of the Barents Sea in December 1942. The heavy cruisers *Lützow* and *Admiral Hipper* tried to attack a convoy bound for Russia but the eight destroyers of the escort fought them off in a brilliant mixture of bluff and tactics. Hitler was so enraged by this display of ineptitude that he threatened to lay up the entire surface fleet. This provoked Grand-Admiral Erich Raeder, commander-in-chief of the navy, into resigning, and he was replaced by Dönitz. Although Dönitz did little to implement Hitler's dire threats, the change meant that the *Kriegsmarine* was now completely committed to winning the U-boat war, with no contrary opinion.

Despite brave words on 'temporary withdrawal', Dönitz and his U-boats had to concede defeat in May 1943. The U-boat remained a potent threat to the end, but after May the issue was no longer in doubt. German ingenuity produced many brilliant innovations, but as each month went by, the shortage of materials, dislocation of industry and the remorseless pressure of the Russians in the East made matters worse. When the surrender came in May 1945, new and deadlier U-boats were in existence, but only a handful. Even they had been held up while scarce resources were wasted on more exciting projects.

The Bomber Offensive
1940–42

WITH the exception of the German air bombardment of Warsaw at the climax of the Polish campaign in September 1939, the use of large-scale air bombing had at first been eschewed by both sides. Each feared that large numbers of civilian dead would spur the recipient into retaliatory action, and according to the theories of strategic air warfare prevalent in the 1930s, this would inevitably lead to the total destruction of cities, with massive civilian casualty lists. During most of 1939 and the first half of 1940, therefore, the British, French and Germans studiously avoided any possibility of attacks on major targets with civilians in the area. Only military targets were attacked, and then only with the utmost caution.

But the razing of Warsaw showed what might be achieved in the way of mass bombing, and the lesson was repeated in May 1940 with the destruction of the old quarter of Rotterdam by German bombers. There is some reason to believe that the bombing was carried out accidentally, in that the attack was meant to have been called off; but this does not alter the fact that the attack was planned in the first place.

Targets attacked during the French campaign and opening phases of the Battle of Britain were usually military, and little thought was given to retaliation. Apart from the destruction of oil installations, for example, the aircraft of Bomber Command were usually confined to raids in which propaganda leaflets were dropped, much to the disgust of the aircrews involved. But then the Germans bombed London – some aircraft had strayed off course – and Winston Churchill called for retaliation against Berlin during August. From this time, the scale of air operations of a supposedly strategic nature was gradually stepped up, principally by the British as it was the only means they had of striking at the Germans. The first raids of September and October were mere pinpricks, only about 100 tonnes of bombs being dropped on each sortie. So inaccurate was the navigation of most crews that very few of the bombs dropped landed anywhere near their targets. Daylight raids were tried, but losses were so heavy that Bomber Command decided to stick to a policy of night bombing of large targets to minimize casualties.

Although designated heavy bombers at the time of their introduction, both the British and Germans employed what were really medium bombers. All these were twin-engined machines: on the German side the celebrated Heinkel III and Dornier 17, with the Junkers 88 joining them in 1939; and the British the Handley Page Hampden, Armstrong Whitworth Whitley and Vickers Armstrong Wellington. Germany had been developing a true strategic bomber in the middle thirties, but at the death of the chief protagonist of the four-engined bomber concept, General Wever, the idea was dropped. This was to prove a grave disadvantage for the Germans during the war, for they then had to use tactical medium bombers. Subsequent efforts to design a true heavy bomber produced the Heinkel 177, an odd machine with four engines driving two propellers. The type was rushed into production too quickly and never proved really successful. It should be noted, however, that the mass use of tactical bombers at short range did give the Germans some strategic capability, as the *blitz* on London at the end of 1940 and the beginning of 1941 demonstrates. The high point of the German strategic effort against Great Britain with manned bombers, though, may be considered to be the raid on Coventry on November 14, 1940 which shocked the British considerably.

The British had given little thought in the 1930s to four-engined heavy bombers, but when they did, three types, two of which were excellent machines, emerged in the early war years. The two best of these machines were the Avro Lancaster, a four-engined development of the unsuccessful Manchester twin-engined bomber, and the Handley Page Halifax. Not very successful, but the first British four-engined bomber of World War II to enter service, was the Short Stirling. This last type pioneered many of the techniques used by the Lancaster and the Halifax, but had only a short operational career as a front-line machine before being relegated to training duties and service with the airborne forces.

Whilst these bombers were under development, Bomber Command was trying its best with night raids against targets in Germany. After the Coventry raid, the two main targets became the German oil industry and civilian centres of population. Attacks on the latter, the British hoped, would sap Germany's will to fight the war, at the same time disrupting the lives of the work force on which

Right : **Avro Lancaster heavy bombers wing their way towards Germany. The Lancaster was Britain's best four-engined bomber, and bore the brunt of RAF Bomber Command's campaign against Germany.**

the war industries depended. But if the idea was there, the weapons were not. Apart from the bombers, with their inaccurate navigation and bomb sights, the bombs themselves were all too frequently duds. An assessment of the German bombing of London showed that about 10 per cent were duds, and that 60 per cent of bombs fell in open areas, where their effect was minimal. There seems no reason to suppose that British bombs were much better.

At first, the inaccuracy of bombing was not suspected by the British, but from November 1940 photographs of raids began to reveal an alarming inaccuracy. Combined with Bomber Command's desire to strike at larger targets, this meant that from May 1941 British bombers began to attack the residential parts of German cities with incendiaries. Some high-explosive bombs were also dropped so that the civil population would keep their heads down until the fires started by the incendiaries had had a chance to get going properly.

But the problem was still inaccuracy. A partial solution was found in the pathfinder force. Drawn from the best crews in Bomber Command, the pathfinders were to use their superior navigational and piloting skills to go ahead of the main force and mark the target with special flares. Following up, the bomber force would not have to concentrate on pinpoint navigation over the target, but could instead devote its energies to dropping its bombs as close to the markers as possible. With the introduction of this method, Bomber Command's results began to improve steadily.

At the same time, Air Chief-Marshal Sir Arthur Harris was appointed to the leadership of Bomber Command, and it is with Harris that the British strategic bombing effort is most closely associated. Harris inherited a force of some 500 twin-engined bombers, and immediately set all his considerable energies to building up his force to maximum strength, hurrying the introduction of the four-engined types, and improving the combat efficiency of his crews.

The second half of 1941 may properly be considered a preparatory period, and it was only in the spring of 1942 that Harris began to secure important victories with night bombers, the most significant being the first raid by 1,000 bombers on Cologne on the night of 31 May. To launch this raid, Harris had had to take crews and aircraft from training units all over the country, but although the raid's purely military significance was small, its importance in raising the morale of the British civilian population was considerable, and put Bomber Command's efforts well and truly on the map. Harris enjoyed excellent relations with Churchill, and so was able to cut through the RAF chain of command to deal directly with the prime minister, giving Bomber Command a certain autonomy within the RAF. An example of the relationship at work was Harris's steadfast unwillingness to give Coastal Command the relatively few four-engined machines, mostly Consolidated B-24 and Boeing B-17 aircraft from the

United States, it so desperately needed. Churchill backed Harris in the latter's claims that the only thing that mattered was the bombing of Germany. Harris entirely overlooked or ignored the fact that even a few four-engined aircraft, that would hardly be missed by Bomber Command, could turn the scales in the Battle of the Atlantic and so ensure the continued supply of fuel and raw materials on which his bombers' effort was built. To Harris's credit, however, it should be pointed out that he worked very closely with the Ministry of Economic Warfare in selecting targets. Even if these were not always destroyed, at least Bomber Command was attacking the right places, which had not always been the case.

Whilst Bomber Command was gradually stepping up the quality and quantity of its raids late in 1942, the US Army's 8th Air Force was arriving in Britain to take its share of the bomber offensive. Flying B-17s and B-24s, the Americans thought that the great speed and defensive firepower of their bombers would allow them to roam at will over northern Europe, the interlocking fields of fire from great 'boxes' of bombers being sufficient to keep the German fighters at bay. With their ability to operate by day, the Americans thought the bombers' main targets should be small but vital centres of communication and war production, which could be hit from high altitude with the aid of the Norden bomb sight. Thus, whilst the British destroyed German cities by night, the Americans would knock out small but vital targets by day in a gradually increasing round-the-clock bombing offensive. The Americans made their debut over Rouen on August 17, 1942. Attacks were at first confined to targets over northern France and the low countries, and the Americans' confidence in themselves and their aircraft seemed to be

justified. With the arrival of the first Republic P-47 Thunderbolt escort fighters in Great Britain in January 1943, the bombers were allowed to start attacking targets in Germany, but the advance in this direction was slowed by difficulty in getting the P-47s fully operational. It was only in the early summer that the Americans were at last ready to attack objectives such as Bremen and Kiel. As yet they had made no daylight missions deep into occupied Europe, and this was to be their real test.

British losses had meanwhile been rising, largely as the result of the improved German night-fighter defences. Based on a line of radar stations round the north coast of Europe, these stations controlled large numbers of German Junkers 88 and Messerschmitt 110 radar-equipped fighters. Once the radar station had steered the fighter close to a bomber, the radar operator in the fighter took over and directed his pilot in to the kill, which took place once the pilot had seen the target. Radar countermeasures were at last worked out by the British, but the best solution was the insertion of British night fighters into the bomber stream. These could use their superior radar to search out and destroy the German night fighters.

Compared with what it was shortly to become, however, the combined Allied bomber offensive was still in its infancy. The weapons had been produced, but it was up to the Allied leaders to discover how they should best be used.

THE ADVANC

Like Germany, Japan entered into the war with well prepared forces and plans, and at first swept all before her. The US Pacific Fleet was crippled in Pearl Harbor, and then Japan's land and naval forces, ably backed from the air, swept into the Philippines, Malaya, the Dutch East Indies and Burma. But then in New Guinea and the Solomons Japan's land expansion was checked, while the tactical draw in the naval Battle of the Coral Sea paved the way for the decisive Allied victory in the Battle of Midway, when Japan's essential aircraft carrier force was largely crushed . . .

Pearl Harbor

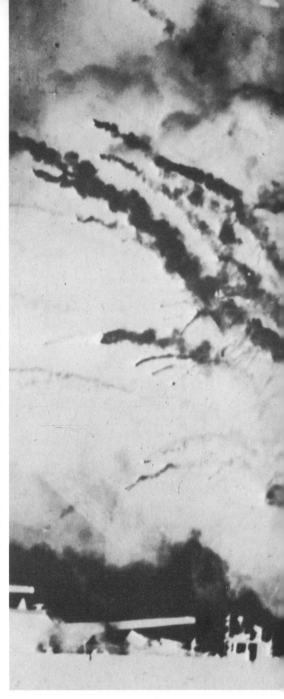

ON July 26, 1941 the government of the United States of America froze all Japanese assets in the country, a move that was shortly followed by Great Britain and the Dutch government in exile. This triple blow to Japan's position as a trading nation was taken as a result of the Nipponese Empire's continued expansion on the mainland of Asia: for ever since the beginning of the Sino-Japanese war in 1937 the USA, and in particular Britain, had been concerned about the growth of Japanese domination in eastern Asia. Various measures analogous to the freezing of Japanese assets had previously been tried, but Japan had taken little notice until this new move, inspired by the Japanese occupation of French Indo-China starting on September 22, 1941. The threat implicit in the American move of 26 July was reinforced on 17 August when President Franklin Delano Roosevelt warned Japan that any further Japanese efforts to secure a paramount position in east Asia would be met by American retaliation to safeguard her policies and financial interests. While these overt moves were setting the scene for what was to follow, it should be noted that American–Japanese negotiations on means of reducing tension between the two countries were being held in Washington, DC.

Why had the United States, in particular, taken these steps against Japan? The reason is basically a conflict of interest. Since the Spanish–American War of 1898–1899, the Americans had been well placed in the Philippines and other Pacific island groups inherited from the Spanish to play a dominant role in Chinese economic affairs. This, combined with the emergence of China from her ancient monarchism into the type of democracy acceptable to the American people, meant that in the United States China had a powerful friend. Japan, too, had only latterly emerged from her self-imposed mediaevalism. But unlike China, Japan had kept her ancient institutions, while at the same time managing to develop herself rapidly into a modern industrial nation with distinct military leanings. These military ambitions had been exercised at the expense of China in 1864–1895, Imperial Russia in 1904–1905, and Imperial Germany in 1914. Japan's major problem, however, lay in the fact that although with great energy she had turned herself into a major manufacturing nation, she had neither sufficient raw materials to feed her industries, nor markets to support them. Raw materials could be obtained from all over eastern Asia, and there was a huge market in China. Hence Japan's interest in securing a political and economic hegemony over the major economic bases in eastern Asia: Manchuria, China, South-East Asia, and the British and Dutch East Indies. Her

swift advance into these areas inevitably brought her into conflict with the western democracies, who also had considerable economic interests in the area.

By the 1930s, therefore, different political and economic interests had already set Japan and the western powers apart. These differences crystallized as Japan took over Manchuria, started a war with China, and then turned her attention south to Indo-China and the Indies. America's feelings in the matter were already plain in the supply of arms to China via the Burma Road, and Roosevelt's two moves mentioned above finally made the United States' position completely clear. But Japan could not survive without raw materials and a market, and she also needed the oil so plentiful in the Indies. Thus the western powers' freeze on Japanese assets did nothing to resolve the underlying problem: Japan's teeming population needed to live, and western interests were getting in the way.

Poor as the situation was during September 1941, it became immeasurably worse on October 17, 1941 when Lieutenant-General Hideki Tojo became Japanese Prime Minister, with the support of the nation's all-powerful military establishment. While not discounting absolutely the negotiations going on in Washington, Tojo, on 5 November, revealed to his inner circle the plans for the war he felt was increasingly certain.

By the end of November it had become clear that there could be no basis of understanding between Japan and the United States and, although negotiations continued, Japan now made the decision for war. Drawn up by staffs under the supervision of Field-Marshal Hajime Sugiyama, army chief-of-staff, and Admiral Osami Nagoya, navy chief-of-staff, the basic Japanese plan fell into three sections. It was based on Japan's inability to wage a protracted war against industrial nations. Firstly, the Imperial Japanese Navy was to neutralize the US Pacific Fleet, the western powers' major striking force in the area, while the Imperial Japanese Army and other elements of the navy seized the 'Southern Resources Area' and adjacent territories necessary to defend it. Secondly, an impregnable defence perimeter was to be set up. Thirdly, any attempts to break through this perimeter were to be repulsed so decisively that the western powers would sue for peace on the basis of a *status quo*. The whole Japanese plan was based on the two-fold premise that their forces could so maul the western powers in the first stage of the war that Japan would have the time to complete her defensive perimeter; and that the Japanese defence, based on the proven abilities of their forces, and operating on interior lines of communication, could not be breached by the westerners, operating as

they were on scanty lines of communication from main bases in the United States and Australia. Fallacies in the Japanese scheme will become apparent as the course of the Pacific war unfolds.

With the decision for war all but taken, steps to secure success in the first stage were set in hand. Here the aircraft-carriers of the Imperial Japanese Navy were to play a decisive role in crippling the US Pacific Fleet at its base, Pearl Harbor in the Hawaiian islands. Comprising six aircraft-carriers, and supported by battleships, cruisers, submarines and oilers, Vice-Admiral Chuichi Nagumo's 1st Air Fleet, otherwise known as the Striking Force, left the Kurile islands on 26 November and headed by a circuitous and little used route towards a position north of the Hawaiian islands. Strict radio silence was observed. The Americans, who had broken the Japanese Purple code, knew that Japan was finally preparing for war, but expected

that the first blow would fall on the Philippines or Malaya. Decoded radio messages indicated that Japanese forces were massing in the vicinity of both these major objectives. Several pre-war exercises had taken an attack on Pearl Harbor into consideration, but all was peaceful there early on the morning of Sunday, 7 December.

Trainee radar operators on an inefficient set north of Pearl Harbor reported that many aircraft were heading towards the islands, but the base commander dismissed the report. He thought they were some B-17 Flying Fortress bombers expected at the time, and ordered the radar crews to stand down. What the radar operators had in fact seen was Nagumo's first strike of 183 aircraft. This was soon followed by another wave of 180 machines. Surprise was complete, and the Japanese pilots found their targets neatly arranged in rows. The planes had a field day, and the score racked up by the

Above : **The Japanese air strike against Pearl Harbor decimated the battleship element of the Pacific Fleet. Here the magazines of the destroyer** *Shaw* **explode with a huge blast.** *Right :* **General Hideki Tojo brought Japan into the war.**

Japanese on that fateful 7 December was considerable : of eight battleships, three were sunk, one was capsized and the remaining four were all seriously damaged; three cruisers and three destroyers were also sunk, as was a miscellany of smaller vessels; on shore, 65 of the US Army's 231 aircraft were destroyed, as were 196 of the US Navy's and Marine Corps' 250 machines. Apart from these material losses, the Americans lost some 3,220 men dead and 1,272 wounded. Japanese losses were slight.

The blow to American strength and pride was enormous. The claim often made that Japan did not declare war before the attack

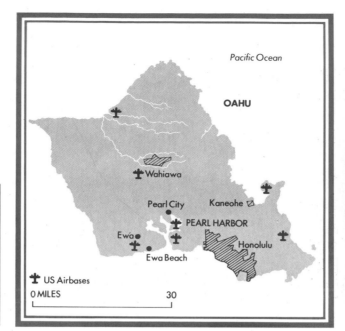

on Pearl Harbor is true, but not complete. Japan did try to declare war, but her embassy staff in Washington were so slow decoding the relevant message that the attack had started before the formal declaration was made. US intelligence, however, had decoded the message in good time, but the news was not sent out quickly enough to allow the American defences to be brought onto a war footing. Nevertheless, Japan had now entered the war, turning what had previously been a European conflict into a global one.

The only solace for the US Navy as it assessed the damage after Pearl Harbor was the fact that the Pacific Fleet's three aircraft-carriers, *Enterprise*, *Lexington* and *Saratoga*, were absent and had not, therefore, been damaged. It was these ships that were to take the war to Japan in the next few months. Despite the intense disappointment of Imperial Japanese Navy airmen that they had not been able to come to grips with their opposite numbers, the victory at Pearl Harbor was adjudged a great one, fulfilling the needs of the first stage of the Japanese war plan.

Japan's other objective in this first stage of the conflict was the securing of the Southern Resources Area. Moves to this end were being made at the time of the Pearl Harbor attack, as were mopping up operations against American bases in the Pacific. Despite the fact that they repulsed the first Japanese attack with heavy losses on 11 December, the gallant defenders of Wake island were overwhelmed in a massive second attack on 23 December; and at the foot of the Marianas islands, the tiny garrison of Guam was swept aside on 10 December.

These tiny American islands, however, were very small fry compared with the Japanese objectives on the Asian mainland and the major island groups off the coast. On 8 December (to the west of the International Date Line, this day in Asia was the same as 7 December in areas to the east of the line,

such as Hawaii) the Japanese 38th Division smashed through the mainland defences of the British colony at Hong Kong, forcing Major-General C M Maltby's forces to fall back to the island. After a call for surrender had been refused, the Japanese assaulted the island on 18 December, and by Christmas Day 1941 the small British garrison had been overrun.

Farther south, the three divisions of Lieutenant-General Tomoyuki Yamashita's 25th Army landed at Khota Bharu in northern Malaya and at Singora and Patani just over the border in Thailand on 8 December. The British command in Malaya was in turmoil, and the troops at the front poorly trained; thus after the small RAF forces in the area had been overwhelmed by superior Japanese air power, Yamashita's 100,000 men were able to move smoothly inland towards the ultimate object of any invasion of Malaya, the great island fortress of Singapore. The Japanese split into two main lines of advance, on either side of the Malayan peninsula, and moved swiftly south. The British commander, Lieutenant-General A E Percival, had some 100,000 men under his command, in three divisions, but had expected the Japanese landings to be made farther south. He now tried desperately to regroup his forces to meet the actual threat, but failed to do more than slow the Japanese marginally. Right from the beginning of the campaign, the Japanese displayed the considerable offensive tactical skill that was to make them so feared in the first two years of the war: operating on light scales of equipment, and without masses of mechanized transport, their forward elements were able to slip round through the jungle flanks of British defensive positions and establish roadblocks in their rear. Cut off, the British forces did not have the tactical skills to escape through the jungle, and so had to surrender. Thus the Japanese moved swiftly south, leapfrogging the British defensive positions to keep up the momentum of their offensive.

Above left : **Pearl Harbor was the scene for Japan's first strike of World War II.**
Above : **The blazing wreck of the battle-ship *Arizona*, completely destroyed in the Pearl Harbor attack.**
Right : **Pilots warm up the engines of their Mitsubishi A6M Zero fighters on the carrier *Akagi* before setting off for duty over Pearl Harbor.**

As 1941 ended, the British found themselves being driven steadily southwards.

Soon after the shock of the first landings, the British were further discomfited by the loss of their only two capital ships in the area. On hearing of the Japanese landings, Admiral Sir Tom Phillips had raced north from Singapore with the battleship *Prince of Wales* and the battlecruiser *Repulse* to engage the Japanese forces supporting the landings. The RAF was unable to provide air support, and on 10 December, unable to find the Japanese, Phillips turned south.

Japanese occupied

● 8.12.41

Japanese invasion Dec 8 1941 – May 6 1942

Prior Allied possessions

Japanese air strikes found him, and after a furious battle the two British capital ships succumbed to large numbers of bomb and torpedo hits.

Meanwhile the Japanese had also landed in the Philippines, when the 50,000 men of Lieutenant-General Masaharu Homma's 14th Army started coming ashore at Luzon on 10 December. The defence of this client nation of the United States rested on the 130,000 men of General Douglas MacArthur's American-Filipino forces, of which only 22,400 were fully trained. Most of the US Asiatic Fleet was withdrawn to Java, but the air forces in the Philippines, under the command of Major-General Lewis Brereton, were expected to administer a rude shock to the Japanese. Quite the contrary took place: a strike on 8 December caught the US air forces lined up neatly on their airfields. Eighteen of the 35 B-17 bombers and 56 fighters were destroyed, as well as a number of other machines. This was particularly shaming for the Americans since they had had ample warning of Japan's entry into the war. With the destruction of these aircraft, the US lost their only adequate striking force.

MacArthur's defence plans were based on the likelihood of the Japanese landing at Lingayen Gulf and driving on Manila, and so he had disposed his forces in two main group-

ings to the north and south of the capital. But between 10 and 20 December, Homma landed his forces to the north and south of Luzon, where they were able to consolidate and build airfields unmolested by the Americans. Then between 20 December and the end of the year, further landings were made to secure the islands of Mindanao and Jolo, where more airfields were built, and finally the force for the main Japanese landings on Luzon arrived in Lingayen Gulf on 22 December. The Japanese came ashore without opposition and soon moved south, the bulk of the Filipino Army being saved only by the resolution of the US forces and the Philippine Scouts. Another landing was made south of Manila in Limon Bay on 24 December and MacArthur, with his forces caught between the arms of an effective pincer, had to abandon his plan for a counterattack and withdraw towards the last-ditch defensive position in the Bataan peninsula north-west of Manila. Here he expected to hold out until reinforcements were brought in by the Pacific Fleet.

Although MacArthur was often criticized for allowing his forces to be bottled up in this way, his withdrawal was in fact the right move. The Japanese, who had allocated only 50 days for the conquest of the Philippines, expected MacArthur to defend Manila, where the better Japanese troops could have

made mincemeat of the US and Filipino forces. But MacArthur's retreat to Bataan frustrated this expectation, and delayed considerably the Japanese plans to take the Southern Resources Area.

Back in Malaya, the new year of 1942 found the British in poor shape. Pushed steadily back, their final defence line on the mainland was breached on 15 January, and by the end of the month, only the island fortress of Singapore was left. Moreover, the fortress had been designed solely against attack from the sea, whereas the Japanese were now attacking from the landward side, where there were no fixed defences or heavy artillery. On 8 February the Japanese landed on the island, and after desperate fighting captured the water reservoirs. This sealed the fate of the population and garrison, which surrendered unconditionally on 15 February, some 70,000 British troops being taken prisoner. The disaster was total, and the result mainly of poor planning and parsimony before the war. In the short term, it put the Japanese in a fine position for their planned invasion of the rich Dutch East Indies.

The new year also brought further success to the Japanese in the Philippines, albeit at great cost and delay to the overall plan. Two major assaults, in the middle and end of January, were beaten off by MacArthur's forces, but overcrowding and disease were rapidly eroding the Americans' ability to survive. Ordered to escape to Australia, MacArthur handed over command to Major-General Jonathan Wainwright on 11 March, during a period when the Japanese were waging a war of attrition. On 3 April Homma, with his forces now reinforced and rested, was able to launch the decisive offensive, and as the defence forces began to crumble the

Americans surrendered Bataan on 9 April. At about the same time, Japanese forces were mopping up on the other islands (where the defence dissolved to form nuclei of guerrilla forces); now only the fortress island of Corregidor in Manila Bay remained to deny the Japanese the use of Manila harbour. After an intense bombardment, the Japanese landed on 5 May, and after savage fighting secured this final American position in the Philippines the next day.

The skill of Japan's fighting forces is borne out by the relative losses in these campaigns: in Malaya 138,700 British against 9,820 Japanese and in the Philippines 140,000 US and Filipino against some 12,000 Japanese. Most of the Allied losses, however, were in prisoners or deserters from the Filipino Army.

Above far left : **The Japanese approached the Philippines from a number of points.** *Inset far left :* **Major-General Jonathan Wainwright (left) was one of General Douglas MacArthur's most important senior commanders in the hopeless defence of the Philippines.** *Above left :* **A Japanese machine-gun crew prepares for action during the advance on Manila.** *Top :* **The Japanese made several amphibious landings early in 1942 as they strove to clear the Bataan peninsula of its American and Filipino defence.** *Above :* **The victorious Japanese take over in captured Singapore, the 'impregnable' linchpin of Britain's Far Eastern defence.** *Right :* **Japanese round up British prisoners after the fall of Singapore, the most costly single British defeat of the entire war.**

The Japanese Tide

BY the end of 1941 the Japanese were effectively masters of the Malay peninsula and the Philippine islands, the remaining Allied forces in the areas being bottled up and incapable of taking any initiative. Yet Malaya and the Philippines were only half of the Southern Resources Area, the other two areas being the Indies, both Dutch and British, and Burma. The Indies offered rich pickings in oil and other raw materials, and Burma offered oil, tungsten and rubber. In addition, the Japanese saw that the seizure of Burma would cut the Burma Road to China, and thus sever their longest standing adversary's one remaining lifeline to the rest of the world.

Both Malaya and the Philippines offered excellent jumping-off points for the Indies campaign, and similar advantages for the Burma operation were secured by the quiet occupation of Thailand, this also providing an overland line of communication with the forces in Malaya.

British plans for the defence of Burma had been bedevilled by lack of resources, optimism that it would not be attacked, and a split command. Thus, Lieutenant-General Thomas Hutton had only two under-strength divisions, with totally inadequate reserves and logistical backing, with which to oppose the advance of the two strong divisions of Lieutenant-General Shojiro Iida's 15th Army. These heavily supported and reinforced divisions attacked from Thailand towards Moulmein and Tavoy, in the long thin 'tail' of Burma, on January 12, 1942. Hutton's forces were soon in difficulty, and had to start withdrawing behind the Salween river line by the end of January. Pressing on quickly, the 15th Army had the British outflanked by crossing the Salween upstream, forcing Hutton's tired troops to pull back once again, this time towards the Sittang river. Once again the Japanese outflanked the British by crossing the Sittang first, and part of the 17th Indian Division was lost when the only bridge over the Sittang was blown up on 23 February. Realizing that matters were becoming desperate, the British appointed Lieutenant-General Sir Harold Alexander to command, with orders to hold Rangoon. Reinforcements brought British strength back up to some two very under-strength divisions, but Alexander realized that these could not hold Rangoon. The British forces therefore prepared to retreat up the Irrawaddy and Sittang rivers, and Alexander only just escaped capture as the Japanese took Rangoon on 7 March, two days after he had assumed command. Although the situation looked hopeless, since Rangoon had been the only major means of surface communication with India, things looked up momentarily with the arrival of the first Chinese troops in the area. These had been offered by Chiang Kai-shek, the Chinese generalissimo, when he realized that his life-line to the West was in danger. The Chinese 5th and 6th Armies, each the equivalent of a strong British division, were under the command of Lieutenant-General Joseph 'Vinegar Joe' Stilwell, Chiang's American chief-of-staff.

Between 13 and 20 March a defence line was set up from Prome on the Irrawaddy and Toungoo on the Sittang, the British holding the former and the Chinese the latter. During this period, Major-General William Slim arrived to assume command of the British 'Burcorps'. By the end of the month, however, the Japanese had driven back the Chinese, forcing the British to retreat to avoid being outflanked. The same thing happened again at Yenangyaung, the location of Burma's main oilfields, between 10 and 19 April, although this time it was the British who were forced to fall back in the face of Japanese pressure.

As this battle continued, the Japanese also launched an offensive against the Chinese 6th Army in the area between the Sittang and Salween rivers in the Loikaw-Taunggyi area, and by 23 April the Chinese army had disintegrated, causing the remaining Chinese and the British to fall back, again to prevent being outflanked. But the Japanese 56th Division rushed north through the vacuum left by the Chinese 6th Army to seize Lashio on the Burma Road. The Japanese, now three divisions strong, were thus well placed to cut the Allies' line of retreat, and headed south-west towards Mandalay to do so. However, the Allies managed to fall back through this city just before the Japanese arrived on 1 May.

The Allies now split up in order to make their final escape. The British managed to fight their way north-west to Kalewa and thence over appalling mountains to the Manipur plain and India; while the remnants of Stilwell's Chinese forces continued north, some branching off towards Yunnan in China, the rest going with Stilwell north-eastwards to safety at Ledo in northern Assam.

The Japanese were masters of Burma by the end of May 1942, and China's supply route from the West was cut. Some 30,000 of the 42,000 British troops involved in the campaign had been lost, together with large numbers of the 95,000 Chinese involved, compared with Japanese casualties of only 7,000 men. As the Japanese consolidated in Burma, Stilwell set about retraining his Chinese; while the British tried setting their house in order to resist any Japanese invasion of India and to prepare the forces for a reconquest of Burma. Deprived of their land communications with China, the Americans had recourse to the expensive and difficult

Below : **Japanese troops parade through conquered Celebes.** *Right :* **The Japanese prepare to move up into an area recently evacuated and demolished by the British as they retreat north in Burma.**

Strait and the east coast of Borneo towards Java; and the Western Force moved via the South China Sea and northern Borneo towards Sumatra. Each of these forces had powerful cruiser escorts for the troopships carrying the men of the Japanese 16th Army, and support from land-based aircraft as well as Nagumo's carriers. Under the command of General Sir Archibald Wavell's American/British/Netherlands/Australian Command (ABDACOM), the mixed Allied forces could offer no real resistance, and the Japanese moved swiftly south. ABDACOM was dissolved on 25 February, the forces in the islands being left to fight on under Dutch command. With a few notable exceptions, Allied naval forces in the area came off worst in encounters with the Japanese naval task forces, and the fate of the Dutch East Indies was sealed with the decisive defeat of the Dutch Rear-Admiral Karel Doorman's force of 5 cruisers and 10 destroyers by Rear-Admiral Takeo Takagi's 4 cruisers and 13 destroyers in the Battle of the Java Sea on 27 February. The Allies lost two cruisers and five destroyers. The obsolete aircraft deployed by the Allies in the theatre had already been knocked out, and with the losses of the Java Sea battle soon augmented as the remaining Allied warships were picked off, the Japanese were in control. Between 29 February and 9 March, when the Dutch East Indies finally capitulated, they made swift progress. At the same time, other Japanese forces had secured bases along the northern coast of New Guinea and in the Bismarck archipelago. On 13 March they also landed on Bougainville, northernmost of the major islands in the Solomon chain.

American carrier forces, however, were not idle during this period. Strikes had been launched on the Gilbert and Marshall islands on 1 February, on Rabaul on 20 February, Wake island four days later, Marcus island on 4 March and on Lae and Salamaua on 10 March. Finally, on 18 April 16 USAAF North American B-25 Mitchell twin-engined bombers were flown off the carrier *Hornet* to make a nuisance raid on Tokyo. This raid had important effects on Japanese morale, and also, despite the Allied setbacks, in Australia General MacArthur was readying land forces for the counter-offensive. Equally, at Pearl Harbor the US Navy was preparing plans for an offensive across the Pacific.

In the Indian Ocean, the Japanese Navy had also been making itself felt with the arrival of Nagumo's 1st Air Fleet, five carriers supported by four battleships. In the period between 2 and 8 April, Nagumo's planes struck at Trincomalee and Colombo in Ceylon, and also sank one aircraft-carrier, two cruisers and one destroyer of the British Eastern Fleet (commanded by Admiral Sir James Somerville) before retiring back into the Pacific. Worried about the threat of further Japanese ambitions in the Indian Ocean and even Africa, the British seized the Vichy French island of Madagascar between May and November 1942.

In fact, the tide of Japanese expansion had by now reached full flood.

Above: **While their comrades hold up an extemporised footbridge over a Burmese river, Japanese infantry cross over in pursuit of the retiring Allied forces** *Left:* **The Dutch light cruiser *Java*, sistership of Admiral Doorman's flagship *De Ruyter*, was sunk in the Battle of the Java Sea.**
Right above: **The Japanese celebrate their triumph in Burma in traditional style.**
Right below: **Although poor by western standards, the Japanese tanks used in Burma met little or no effective opposition, and so proved very useful.**

means of flying supplies over the Himalayas from India as engineers set about building a new road to China from Ledo.

Meanwhile, the Japanese had been building on their successes in the southern area. Supported by the carriers of Vice-Admiral Chuichi Nagumo's 1st Air Fleet, three Japanese amphibious forces invaded the East Indies. After landings to secure bases in Borneo and Celebes in early January, the main operations gained momentum. The Eastern Force moved via Celebes, the Moluccas and Timor towards Bali and Java; the Centre Force advanced via the Macassar

Coral Sea & Midway

MANY disasters followed in the train of Pearl Harbor, the fall of Malaya, the East Indies and the destruction of Allied naval strength in the Battle of the Java Sea. The rickety command structure which had been set up in December 1941 was in ruins; the first requirement for the Allies was to find new, secure bases from which to plan the destruction of the Japanese.

The war theatre was vast, stretching from New Zealand to the Aleutian islands, but by April 1942 General Douglas MacArthur had taken over as Supreme Allied Commander, South-West Pacific, and his naval opposite number, Admiral Chester Nimitz, was Commander-in-Chief, Pacific. The Japanese, of course, were not going to wait for the Allied forces to recover their balance, and on 20 April a Japanese invasion force left Truk in the Carolines, heading for the Solomon islands and New Guinea. From bases to be captured there they could easily attack Australia, the cornerstone of Allied power in the south-west Pacific.

Nimitz was alerted to the Japanese intentions by the same team of cryptanalysts whose warning of the Pearl Harbor attack had been ignored. He wasted no time in sending two aircraft-carriers, *Yorktown* and *Lexington*, under Rear-Admiral Frank Jack Fletcher, to the new extemporized base at Espiritu Santo. Against these the Japanese had mustered two fleet carriers, *Shokaku* and *Zuikaku*, the smaller carrier *Shoho* and the seaplane carrier *Kamikawa Maru*.

Battle was joined on 3 May when the Japanese landed on Tulagi in the Solomons. The Americans soon launched strikes against the invasion force, and these inflicted considerable damage. Both carrier task forces manoeuvred for two days without making contact, but at first light on 7 May reconnaissance aircraft sent back their sighting reports and air strikes were launched by both sides. The first American strike against *Shoho* did no damage, but *Yorktown*'s aircraft inflicted heavy damage shortly afterwards. Within ten minutes of the first torpedo-hit,

Shoho was sinking.

The Japanese had no such success, for their aircraft erroneously sank a fleet oiler and a destroyer under the impression that they were a carrier and a light cruiser. A later strike which sought *Yorktown* was mauled by her combat air patrol and lost nine aircraft. When a group of Japanese aircraft mistook *Yorktown* for a friendly ship gunfire accounted for a further 11 planes, making a loss of 17 per cent of the Japanese carriers' strength without a proper attack having been launched against either *Lexington* or *Yorktown*.

Next day, the American carrier planes attacked again, and managed to damage *Shokaku* with two bomb hits, but further attacks were not successful. This time the Japanese pilots were able to strike back, catching *Lexington* and *Yorktown* together about an hour before noon. The nimble *Yorktown* was hit by only one bomb and managed to contain the fire which broke out, but the older *Lexington* was hit by two torpedoes and two bombs. Her fire was much more serious and about an hour later she suffered a severe internal fuel explosion. She continued to blaze and was finally abandoned four hours later, sinking three hours after that.

The US Navy was bitterly disappointed by the outcome of the Coral Sea battle, but the tactical reverse was small consolation for the Japanese. They were forced to cancel the amphibious landing at Port Moresby, in favour of an overwhelmingly difficult overland advance. As important in the long run was the damage to *Shokaku* and the depletion of the two surviving carriers' air groups, which meant that both were unable to fight at Midway. The Battle of the Coral Sea robbed the Japanese of an objective for the first time, and ultimately made an Allied victory in the south-west Pacific certain.

The Japanese were troubled by their failure to secure New Guinea, but this did not stop them from pursuing their other objectives in the north and central Pacific. The grand strategic aim had always been to force the Americans into a main fleet action, and although Pearl Harbor had eliminated virtually all the US Pacific Fleet battleships, its aircraft-carriers were still at large. Realizing that Nimitz was far too wily to fritter away his strength in attacking the Japanese homeland, the commander-in-chief of the 1st Fleet, Admiral Isoroku Yamamoto, decided to lay a more subtle trap. If he occupied Midway island at the western end of the Hawaiian chain of islands, Yamamoto knew that the Americans would have to fight him. The island, known as the Sentry of Hawaii, was far too valuable as an outpost of the American defensive perimeter to fall into Japanese hands.

The plan called for an ambitious assault on Midway backed up by a powerful surface fleet and four fleet carriers. Another force would simultaneously occupy the Aleutian islands, 2,400 km (1,500 miles) to the north. On paper, this was more than enough to crush the Americans, and the plan deserved to succeed. But there was one big advantage on the American side: cryptanalysis had in good time revealed the broad outlines of the enemy deployment and Nimitz was able to plan his counter-stroke in advance. Nevertheless, the Americans had so few ships that the margin between defeat and victory remained very narrow. Only two carriers were available, and they had to be brought from the south-west Pacific. *Yorktown* had been damaged in the Coral Sea battle, but repairs were effected in an unbelievably short time – three days – at Pearl Harbor. Although *Yorktown* had lost many of her air group, she made up her strength with survivors from *Lexington*, and as a result boasted the most battle-hardened aircrews of all the US carriers.

The Coral Sea actions had shown that more fighters were needed, and so 50 per cent more Grumman F4F-4 Wildcats were embarked. The Douglas TBD Devastator torpedo-bomber had already proved most unsatisfactory, being too slow and carrying an ineffective torpedo, but there was no time to replace it with the new Grumman TBF-1 Avenger. The Japanese made no changes to their aircraft (Mitsubishi A6M5 Zero fighters, Aichi D3A Val dive-bombers and Nakajima B5N Kate torpedo-bombers), apart from embarking a pair of fast Yokosuka D4Y1 Judy reconnaissance aircraft in the carrier *Soryu* to improve their chances of sighting the US fleet. Against the American *Enterprise*, *Hornet* and *Yorktown* the Japanese could muster *Akagi*, *Kaga*, *Hiryu*, *Soryu* and *Hosho* and two seaplane carriers. In addition they had 9 battleships, including the giant *Yamato* (64,000 tons and nine 18-inch guns) and 11 cruisers.

Forewarned about the true Japanese objectives, Fletcher, commanding at sea under Nimitz's overall supervision, could ignore the thrust towards the Aleutians. On 2 June

Far left: **Out-thought and outfought, Vice-Admiral Chuichi Nagumo commanded the Japanese fleet crushed in the Battle of Midway.** *Left*: **Admiral Chester Nimitz commanded the Pacific Ocean Areas with very great distinction right through the war.** *Right*: **Douglas SBD Dauntless dive-bombers fly over the key island of Midway. The main strike component of the three US carriers, they played a decisive part in the Japanese defeat at Midway, which cost the imperial navy four irreplaceable carriers, their aircraft and highly skilled aircrews.**

Task Forces 16 and 17 (*Enterprise, Hornet* plus six cruisers, and *Yorktown* plus two cruisers) were in position some 560 km (350 miles) north of Midway. The invasion force was sighted next day, but Fletcher let shore-based aircraft from Midway attack it as he had still no idea of where to find Vice-Admiral Chuichi Nagumo's main carrier force. By nightfall on 3 June both carrier groups were approaching Midway, 740 km (460 miles) apart and completely ignorant of each other's whereabouts. All this time, Midway was under attack from Japanese bombers but held its own, leaving Fletcher and Rear-Admiral Raymond Spruance (*Enterprise* and *Hornet*) to concentrate on their main objective, the location and destruction of the Japanese carriers.

By next morning, Nagumo's carriers were only 320 km (200 miles) north-west of Midway; the dawn patrol from the island spotted them. Five minutes later Task Force 16 received orders to launch a strike, and soon 97 torpedo- and dive-bombers were airborne. Meanwhile some 50 shore-based bombers had made an attack on Nagumo's carriers without success, with a loss of 17 aircraft. Stung by this attack, Nagumo decided to reinforce the assault on Midway by throwing in the 93 aircraft which he had retained in case of a strike by the American carriers. The aircraft were sent down to the hangars for rearming with bombs, just 14 minutes before Fletcher's task force was sighted. But the report omitted any mention of a carrier, and so Nagumo's calculations still seemed to make sense.

The Japanese admiral was caught off balance, even if he did not fully realize the fact. A series of unsuccessful attacks on his carriers by shore-based aircraft prevented Nagumo from recovering those aircraft which had been bombing Midway, with the result that many ran out of fuel. Nearly a third of the aircraft which had taken off were lost, but two hours after the first sighting report, Nagumo's carriers were finally ready to face Task Forces 16 and 17.

The first strike by *Hornet* and *Enterprise* was not coordinated with the one launched by *Yorktown*, and sustained heavy losses. But there were still 50 aircraft left from the *Enterprise* and *Yorktown* air groups; these finally succeeded in crippling the *Akagi*, Nagumo's flagship, then destroyed *Kaga* and *Soryu*. All three Japanese carriers succumbed quickly to devastating fires which swept through their hangars. The fourth carrier, *Hiryu*, immediately launched a counter-strike and her aircraft flew straight to the *Yorktown* and hit her with three bombs. The American carrier proved better able to cope with the fire which inevitably followed, but the ship was badly damaged and could not recover her own fighters. Yet by heroic

Left: **These combat and supply vessels of Task Force 16 are seen from the flight deck of the carrier** *Enterprise* **in the Coral Sea.** *Right:* **The carrier** *Yorktown* **begins to list before sinking in the decisive Battle of Midway, which turned the tide of the war.**

exertions she was able to get under way again and even to launch eight fighters to cope with a second strike from *Hiryu*. However, this time she was unable to dodge two torpedoes.

The last fight of *Yorktown* had a decisive effect on the outcome of the battle. The Japanese had assumed that they were opposed by only two carriers, not knowing that the Pearl Harbor dockyard workers would achieve the impossible by repairing *Yorktown*'s Coral Sea damage in only three days. Having hit one carrier badly earlier that day, they could not believe that the same carrier would be operational again in less than three days. Therefore the carrier which had just been sunk must be the second carrier, and it could now be safely assumed that both American carriers were knocked out. In fact there were still two undamaged ships.

Enterprise and *Hornet* had very few aircraft left, and only 40 bombers took off for a last desperate strike against *Hiryu*. Their target was carrying about half the aircraft with which she had started, and although the Zeros were able to punish the attackers they could not prevent the second wave from scoring four bomb hits on the flight deck. She began to burn, and the fires slowly got out of control. Incredibly, the other three carriers were still ablaze: *Kaga* and *Soryu* did not sink until the evening and *Akagi* lasted until dawn. *Hiryu* finally sank at 0900 next morning.

Yamamoto and his Main Body had been too far away to help, but he did realize that the plan had gone badly wrong. By ordering the three smaller carriers *Zuiho, Ryujo* and

Junyo south from the Aleutians he hoped to concentrate a fresh force to trap the Americans in a night action; but Spruance, in command after the disabling of Fletcher's *Yorktown*, wisely took Task Force 16 well clear to the east as soon as he had recovered the last aircraft. In theory, Yamamoto's four small carriers mustered enough aircraft to defeat Spruance, but in practice the vast distances made it impossible to bring the ships together soon enough to score decisive hits. Yamamoto decided to bow to the inevitable and ordered his invasion force to withdraw early on the morning of 5 June.

This was the decisive moment of the Battle of Midway. It went on for another two days, during which other ships were sunk and a submarine put two more torpedoes into *Yorktown* to seal her fate. But these events were only a postscript. Midway marked the high tide of Japanese expansion in the Pacific, and although it did not appear obvious at the time, Japan was never to recover the initiative. The losses of Japanese aircrew were much heavier than the Americans'. Much worse, the Japanese found it almost impossible to replace their pilots. Nor could the shipyards turn out more carriers to replace the four sunk, whereas US shipyards were already turning out fleet carriers in large numbers. But the most important result of Midway was that the Japanese failed in their attempt to dislodge the Americans from their defensive perimeter. For Nimitz it was only a matter of waiting until the new ships were ready before launching his drive across the central Pacific towards Japan.

New Guinea & Guadalcanal

Left : **US Marines patrol in hot, humid conditions typical of the thick jungle to be found on most of the islands of the Solomons 'ladder' towards New Britain.**

IN May and June 1942, the Japanese decided to expand the defensive perimeter they were establishing around their newly won possessions. This expansion was to take place primarily in the south-east, where Papua, the Bismarck and the Solomon Islands were all to be taken by the forces of Lieutenant-General Hitoshi Imamura's 8th Area Army. The keys to the territory, the Japanese decided, were Port Moresby on the southern coast of Papua, and the island of Guadalcanal in the Solomons.

Major airfields in these two spots would allow the Japanese to detect and destroy any Allied force attempting to break through the perimeter. Despite a first rebuff in the Battle of the Coral Sea, Imamura remained determined to press on with his plans, but now decided that the only way to take Port Moresby was by means of an overland advance from the north coast across the formidable Owen Stanley range, and from the east after a landing at Milne Bay. His first steps were therefore to land troops at Gona on the northern coast of Papua (July 11, 1942) with another landing at nearby Buna shortly afterwards, and on Guadalcanal on 6 July. The troops on Guadalcanal immediately set about building an airfield, whilst those in Papua started to prepare for the advance towards Port Moresby.

The Americans were also trying to decide what they should do next. General Douglas MacArthur, commanding the South-West Pacific Area, favoured a direct thrust by the army on Rabaul, the town on New Britain where the Japanese presence in the area had its centre; and Admiral Ernest King, head of the US Navy, favoured naval operations in the Bismarcks and New Guinea area to disrupt the Japanese action against the supply line across the Pacific to Australia, combined with an island-hopping campaign towards Rabaul. The joint chiefs-of-staff mediated between the commander of the South-West Pacific Area and the head of the US Navy, and plumped for a three-phase operation: the seizure of the southern Solomons by the forces of Vice-Admiral Robert Ghormley's South Pacific Area; the seizure of the rest of the Solomons by MacArthur's forces, and finally the seizure of the north coast of New Guinea, New Britain and New Ireland, also by MacArthur's forces supported by the navy. Ghormley's forces were able to move quickly to their task, but MacArthur's first move was forestalled by the Japanese advance towards Port Moresby.

On 21 July the men of Major-General Tomitoro Horii's 18th Army set off south-west from their beach-head between Gona and Buna. Local Australian forces could not halt the advancing Japanese, and pulled back before them into the Owen Stanley mountains, fighting desperate rearguard actions but failing to stop the skilful and determined Japanese advance up the Kokoda Trail. By 12 August the Japanese were over the crest of the mountains, and the exhausted Australians, starving and short of all essential supplies, were still falling back. As they approached the Port Moresby area, the Japanese too began to suffer from the effects of their nightmare crossing of the mountains, and were gradually slowed by strengthening Australian and American resistance, ably led by the Australian Lieutenant-General Edmund Herring. By 26 September the Japanese had been halted at Ioribaiwa, only 50 km (30 miles) from Port Moresby. Three days earlier, the 7th Australian Division had started a counter-offensive, soon joined by the US 32nd Division. Ordered by Imamura to fall back, Horii started his retreat at the end of the month, harried unmercifully by the Americans and Australians. This time it was the Japanese who suffered the most terrible privations, especially shortages of food. Many men died after trying to eat grass and earth. By 19 November the Japanese were back where they had started in Buna and Gona.

Meanwhile, the other prong of the Japanese assault on Port Moresby had been defeated. On 25 August a regiment had landed at Milne Bay, but after serious fighting with the local forces this was wiped out. Port Moresby was now safe from overland assault.

Despite their losses and hardships, the Japanese were determined to hold Buna and Gona to the end. Long awed by the speed and aggressiveness of Japanese offensive tactics, the Allies were now to be taught a desperate lesson in the Japanese skill and determination in defence, especially from prepared positions. The Allied assault started on 20 November, but at first made no progress whatsoever. Disease had decimated the Allied formations, and morale was low. Matters were improved by the takeover of a new commander, Lieutenant-General Robert Eichelberger on 1 December, but it was not until 7 December that the Australians were able to batter their way into Gona against the

shattered opposition. Buna still held out, the Australians and Americans failing to take it against fanatical resistance on January 22, 1943. The Japanese had lost over 7,000 dead and 350 prisoners, all wounded very badly. The Allies had lost 5,700 Australian and 2,783 American dead, with a further large number incapacitated by disease.

The campaign is a fascinating one. For the first time, the Japanese had been beaten, but had showed how costly it was to be for the Allies to win back all that they had lost. The Australians and Americans, on the other hand, had learned the hard way about survival in the jungle, and how to play the Japanese at their own game. The experience of the campaign was digested by the various planning staffs, and the lessons passed on to the other formations which would be taking on the Japanese all over the southern Pacific.

Realizing that the Japanese had landed on Guadalcanal, in July and August, the Americans accelerated their plans to retake the island. Commanded by Rear-Admiral Frank Jack Fletcher, whose three aircraft carriers were to provide tactical air support and long-range protection, an expedition was prepared. The commander of the landing forces was Rear-Admiral Richmond Turner, and the formation to be landed was Major-General Alexander Vandegrift's reinforced 1st Marine

Division, 19,000 strong.

Moving forward from Noumea in New Caledonia, the 1st Marine Division landed on 7 August, the main force coming ashore on Guadalcanal and subsidiary forces on Tulagi and Gavutu, just off Florida island. On these two latter islands, some 1,500 Japanese put up a spirited defence before being overwhelmed. On Guadalcanal, however, where the marines landed on the north coast on each side of Lunga Point, opposite Florida island, the 2,200 Japanese quickly dispersed into the jungle and the Americans occupied the airfield area, renamed Henderson Field. As the Japanese pondered their riposte and gathered their forces in, the Americans set about expanding and strengthening their defensive perimeter around Henderson Field.

Meanwhile the invasion fleet, lying in the roadstead between Guadalcanal and Florida islands, was coming under intense Japanese air attack from bases in New Britain. Then the Japanese sprang a major surprise on the Allies in the naval Battle of Savo island, just off Cape Esperance, up the coast from Lunga Point. Vice-Admiral Shigeyoshi Inouye, commanding the 4th Fleet from Rabaul, sent Vice-Admiral Junichi Mikawa with seven cruisers and a destroyer to attack the Allied naval forces covering the landings. Arriving

off Savo island on the night of 9 August, Mikawa encountered a force of one Australian and four American heavy cruisers commanded by the British Rear-Admiral V A C Crutchley. In a confused night action lasting only 32 minutes, Mikawa's cruisers sank all but one of the Allied cruisers, the last being crippled, without loss to themselves. Mikawa then retired, although he should have gone on to destroy the Allied transport fleet. He did not know, however, that Fletcher had pulled his carriers out of the area. One Japanese cruiser, *Kako*, was sunk by an American submarine on its way back to New Britain. Shocked by his losses, Turner pulled out with all his naval forces, leaving the marines without naval support.

Left much to themselves apart from air raids, for the next week the marines continued to consolidate and prepare for the inevitable Japanese attack. On 18 August, however, a regiment commanded by Colonel Kiyonao Ichiki landed east of the marine base. Moving overland, Ichiki's force attacked Henderson Field on 21 August. The day before, the marines had received their first aircraft, and these played an important part in repulsing this and later attacks. For two days, Ichiki launched a series of determined assaults, all of which were beaten off by the marines. Surprised in the rear by the

Left : **Colonel Carlson and some of his Marine Raider battalion pose with some of the trophies taken during the clearing of Guadalcanal in February 1943.** *Above :* **This Japanese painting skates over the mental and physical horrors of the terrible fighting for Guadalcanal, which finally halted Japan's expansive drive.**

1st Marine Division's reserve regiment on 22 August, Ichiki's force was driven into the sea and annihilated.

On the next day, the US Navy salvaged some of its pride in the Battle of the Eastern Solomons. A force under Rear-Admiral Raizo Tanaka was trying to run some 1,500 reinforcements through to the Japanese defenders of the island, covered by three aircraft carriers under Vice-Admiral Chuichi Nagumo. The carrier *Ryujo* was sunk, but the Americans suffered damage to *Enterprise*, and Tanaka's transport group got through to deliver its troops and bombard the Henderson Field area on the return journey.

On the night of 7 and 8 September a marine raiding party attacked the Japanese base at Taivu and captured the plans for the next Japanese attack on Henderson Field. This materialized on 12 September in the form of a series of punches by Major-General Kiyotaki Kawaguchi's 35th Brigade. The fighting raged for two days before the marines finally repulsed the 35th Brigade, which suffered some 1,200 dead. The action is now remembered as the Battle of Bloody Ridge.

Both sides were now reinforced. Vandegrift received the 7th Marine and 164th Infantry Regiments, bringing his strength to 23,000, and the Japanese landed the head-quarters of the 17th Army and two divisions, some 20,000 men under Lieutenant-General Harukichi Hyakutake. This reinforcement period lasted until 22 October, and was marked on Guadalcanal by intensive skirmishing and patrol activity.

It also led to a naval battle off Cape Esperance between 11 and 13 October, when a cruiser squadron commanded by Rear-Admiral Norman Scott, escorting American transports, caught Rear-Admiral Aritomo Goto's cruiser force, also escorting troop transports. Scott's forces sank a cruiser and a destroyer and crippled the other two cruisers, but the Japanese landed their troops, although losing two destroyers to land-based bomber attacks afterwards. Between 13 and 15 October two Japanese battleships bombarded Henderson Field, a clear indication that naval superiority was back in the hands of the Japanese.

Between 23 and 26 October, and under the personal command of Lieutenant-General Masao Maruyama, the Japanese launched a series of furious assaults on Henderson Field, losing some 2,000 men in the process. None of the attacks came near to succeeding. As the Japanese licked their wounds, Vandegrift expanded his perimeter considerably. Had the 1st Marine Division been capable of taking the offensive, there is little doubt that the Japanese would have lost heavily, but the marines were exhausted, and a land stalemate ensued as elements of the 2nd Marine Division began to arrive in the period up to 8 December.

Activity at sea continued, however, with the Battle of Santa Cruz on 26 and 27 October. Vice-Admiral William Halsey had replaced Ghormley, and Rear-Admiral Thomas Kinkaid replaced Fletcher. Kinkaid now met a Japanese carrier force in an action that damaged two Japanese and an American carrier, and also led to the loss of the US carrier *Hornet*. Although the Japanese had won, it was by a great sacrifice in experienced aircrew, a fact that was later to be of great importance.

On Guadalcanal, the exhausted Vandegrift and 1st Marine Division had at last been withdrawn on 9 December, their places being taken by XIV Corps and Major-General Alexander Patch. Whilst Japanese strength hovered around the 20,000 mark, by January 9, 1943, the Americans had 58,000 men of the 2nd Marine, 25th and American Divisions.

During the three-phase Battle of Guadalcanal, the Americans once again regained command of the sea. In a series of confused battles, the Japanese lost the battleships *Hiei* and *Kirishima*, and the Americans the cruisers *Juneau* and *Northampton*. Starting on 12 November, the battle finished only on 15 November.

Finally, all was ready for the elimination of the Japanese from Guadalcanal. Patch's offensive started on January 10, 1943, and in the next two weeks drove the Japanese back from their positions in the jungle west of Henderson Field. By the end of the month, the Japanese 17th Army was penned up in Cape Esperance. From here the destroyers of Tanaka's Tokyo Express, as usual brilliantly handled, evacuated some 11,000 survivors between 1 and 7 February, leaving the Americans in sole command of Guadalcanal.

The battle had been costly, but the psychological boost to the Allies following this major victory over the Japanese was very considerable.

US 495

PA13-13

N EUROPE

By 1943 the strategic initiative on the Eastern Front had passed completely to Russia after the great tank battle at Kursk, and by the end of the year the Germans were reeling back from Russia. In the Mediterranean, too, the Allies had invaded Italy, and when in June 1944 the great cross-Channel onslaught was launched against Normandy, the Germans were reduced to defence on three major fronts. The Germans fought on tenaciously and at times brilliantly, but there was nothing that could stop the armed strength and massive industrial power of the Allied powers as they moved in concentrically to crush the final embers of resistance in Germany itself.

Kursk

IF the destruction of the 6th Army in Stalingrad had at last proved that the Germans were not invincible, and that the Russians had an effective army, the Battle of Kursk five months later showed that Germany could not hope to win her war with Stalin's Russia. This great armoured clash, the greatest tank battle to date, was the last time that Germany was able to take the initiative on the Eastern Front. Fighting on ground of their own choosing, and at a time they considered best for their tactics, the German armies were first halted and then thrown back by the size and skill of the ever improving Russian forces.

With the spring thaw in March, operations

Above : **Russian troops manhandle an anti-tank gun forward. Such guns exacted a heavy toll of Germany's armoured strength.** *Left :* **A German PzKpfw III medium tank, obsolete by the time of Kursk, beats a hasty way through burning grassland.**

on the Eastern Front came to a temporary halt, and the Germans at last had the time to plan their next moves. But what was to be done? As the Russians licked their wounds and tried to ready themselves for whatever might come next, the planning staffs in Germany were trying to make up their minds. The *Oberkommando der Wehrmacht* (OKW), or Armed Forces High Command, which ran the German war effort in every theatre but Russia, was of the opinion that the German armies there should go over to the strategic defensive. This would free forces for the western theatres, in which the great Allied invasion was expected shortly. The *Oberkommando des Heeres* (OKH), or Army

High Command, which ran the war against Russia under Hitler's overall supervision, agreed with OKW to a certain extent, but thought it essential that Germany launch a limited offensive in Russia during the summer to spoil Russian intentions for their own offensive. Hitler agreed with OKH, principally because he felt that a striking victory was needed to bolster the flagging spirits of his European allies.

Once they had decided that a limited offensive was needed, the OKH planners decided that the best place for such a blow was the great salient that jutted into the German lines west of Kursk. The trouble was that the salient was such an obvious choice for an offensive. Thus speed in planning was vital if tactical surprise were to be achieved. The German plan was in essence simple, and based on the familiar pincer theory. Field-Marshal Walther Model's 9th Army of Army Group Centre (Field-Marshal Günther von Kluge) was to advance on Kursk

from the northern half of the salient, whilst Colonel-General Hermann Hoth's 4th *Panzerarmee* and General Wilhelm Kempf's Army Detachment Kempf, both supplied by Field-Marshal Erich von Manstein's Army Group South were to advance on Kursk from the south. The Central and Voronezh Fronts would be trapped in the salient and then destroyed, after which German forces would be freed for service in the west.

OKH wished the offensive, codenamed *Zitadelle* (Citadel), to take place as early in April as possible after the spring mud had dried out enough to allow armoured vehicles to move. But no sooner had the basic plan been formulated than reasons for delay began to pour in: troops could not be moved up in time, and Model decided that his forces were not sufficient for the task in hand. The April date passed, as did one in May, and at this stage several senior commanders began to have second thoughts about the whole operation: of these the two most important

were General Alfred Jodl, chief of the Armed Forces Operational Staff, and Colonel-General Heinz Guderian, recently recalled to service as Inspector-General of Armoured Forces following his dismissal after the battle for Moscow. Both these men thought that the offensive was very dangerous in concept and should be abandoned. Guderian also felt that the new Panther tanks and Elephant tank-destroyers coming from Germany's armament factories would be wasted since the divisions which were to use them had not yet been able to train properly. Hitler himself began to have doubts, as did von Manstein, but Field-Marshal Wilhelm Keitel, head of OKW, and Colonel-General Kurt Zeitzler, the OKH chief-of-staff, managed to overcome the *Führer*'s doubts. The offensive was finally scheduled for July, by which time ample supplies of ammunition, troops and new tanks would be available. Utmost secrecy was to be observed as the preparations for the attack were made.

Despite the Germans' precautions in the matter of secrecy, the Russians were kept fully informed of all that was happening. Based in Switzerland, and run by the apparently innocuous Rudolf Rössler, was the Lucy spy ring. This was one of Russia's most

important weapons of World War II, and details of Lucy activities have never since been revealed. The base in Switzerland was only a clearing house for information before it was passed on to the Russians. But somewhere in the German high command there was a superb Soviet spy, probably in the communications or coding department. This man clearly had access to Germany's major military decisions, which he passed on to Lucy in Switzerland.

By such means, the Russian high command or *Stavka* was able to keep a close watch on the progress of German preparations and make its own plans accordingly. Just about the only thing that the Russians did not know was the time appointed for the actual attack, but they were to be told of this too by a deserter just before the offensive started. Although they did not know it, the German armies were to attack without any element of strategic surprise, and in only a few places did the first attacking formations achieve any measure of tactical surprise.

With the exception of the immediate German start lines, the Kursk salient is excellent terrain for armoured warfare, with low rolling hills of firm sandy soil and relatively few towns, the whole dotted with sunflower fields

Left : **Soviet troops prepare to beat off a German armoured attack during the climactic Battle of Kursk.** *Below left :* **A German crewman bales out of his blazing tank.** *Above :* **A column of T-34 medium tanks, complete with 'tank-rider' infantry, moves up towards the great armoured clash in the Kursk salient.**

and orchards. Accordingly, the Germans massed most of their mobile forces to the north and south of the salient for the offensive. Model's 9th Army totalled some 1 *Panzergrenadier*, 6 *Panzer* and 14 infantry divisions, although only 8 of the infantry divisions were to be used for *Zitadelle*. Supported by some 730 aircraft of the 6th Air Fleet's 1st *Fliegerdivision*, the 9th Army could field about 900 tanks, although most of these were obsolescent PzKpfw II, III and early mark IV types.

In the south, von Manstein had more numerous and better-equipped forces : 2 *Panzergrenadier*, 9 *Panzer* and 11 infantry divisions, although only 7 of the infantry divisions were to be used in the planned offensive. More significantly, von Manstein's forces had some 1,000 tanks and 150 assault guns, these armoured fighting vehicles including about 200 of the new Panther and 94 of the new and even more powerful Tiger I tanks. Air support was provided by the 1,100 aircraft of the 4th Air Fleet's VIII *Fliegerkorps*. Artillery support comprised some 6,000 guns and mortars in the north, and 4,000 similar weapons in the south.

All in all, this was a formidable offensive force, but it did have limitations. The most important of these were the fact that many formations had only recently been reorganized after the *débâcle* at Stalingrad and Germany's subsequent defeat in the south. They had not achieved their true potential as fighting units as yet, trained reserves and replacements were in short supply and although Hitler and the staff generals had high expectations of the new armoured vehicles, Guderian and the front-line commanders were all too aware that these had been rushed into

premature action, and were still very prone to teething troubles. The Panther, Tiger and Elephant were all somewhat unreliable mechanically, and the Elephant suffered from the distinct tactical disadvantage of not having a defensive machine-gun with which to ward off enemy infantry with demolition charges.

Forewarned is forearmed, so the proverb says. But the Russians were leaving nothing to chance, and massed truly enormous forces in the Kursk salient for the forthcoming battle. The overall plan devised by Georgi Zhukov, who had been promoted to Marshal of the Soviet Union in January 1943, was not content with just stopping the Germans' attempt to eliminate the Kursk salient. Once German forces were firmly embedded in the Russian defences of the salient proper, massive offensives were to be launched into the German salients north and south of Kursk in the regions of Orel and Kharkov. The whole Russian front was then to grind forward remorselessly.

In the Kursk salient proper, the Russians had had four months in which to prepare their defences, based on a series of very strong field fortifications. The first line consisted of five lines of trenches some 5 km (3 miles) deep, reinforced with numerous anti-tank strongpoints. In this area, anti-tank and anti-personnel mines were laid at a density of 2,400 and 2,700 mines per mile of front. Eleven kilometres (7 miles) behind the first line lay a similar second line, with a strong third line 32 km (20 miles) behind the second. Behind this third line were the front reserves, dug into formidable defences of their own. Finally there were the theatre reserves, the Reserve or Steppe Front commanded by the redoubtable Colonel-General I S Konev, holding the neck of the salient. Here could be formed a final line of defence should the Germans break through that far; at the same time, the salient could not be cut off and it was capable of reinforcing either of the two first-line fronts.

In the salient were General K K Rokossovsky's Central Front, facing Model, and

General N F Vatutin's Voronezh Front, facing von Manstein. It was Rokossovsky who had suggested the astute location of the Steppe Front at the neck of the salient. Even allowing for differences in designation (a Russian army being equivalent to a strengthened western corps, and a Russian corps to a reinforced western division), it is clear that the three fronts were very strong: the Central Front had one tank and five infantry armies, as well as two tank corps; the Voronezh Front had one tank and five infantry armies, together with one infantry and two tank corps; and the Steppe Front had one tank and four infantry armies, with the support of a further one tank, one mechanized and three cavalry corps.

Russian numbers were therefore considerable. So too were the resources available: 13,000 guns, 6,000 anti-tank guns and 1,000 rocket-launchers for the two forward fronts, some 2,500 aircraft deployed by the 2nd and 16th Air Armies, and at least 3,600 armoured fighting vehicles, although some Russian sources put the figure as high as 5,000. The Battle of Kursk was therefore to see the deployment of at least 5,600 armoured fighting vehicles, and perhaps even 7,000 such machines.

The Russians knew what the Germans were planning. The Germans, however, had no comparable source within the Soviet high command, and their reconnaissance aircraft had failed to reveal the extent and thoroughness of the Russian preparations. Having carried all before them in the air for the first two years of the Russian war the aircraft of the *Luftwaffe* had at last been matched by Soviet planes. Superior Russian numbers and a modicum of skill were to prevail in the long run. The Russians demonstrated at Kursk that heavy tactical air support of ground forces with masses of aircraft such as the excellent Ilyushin Il-2 *Shturmovik* would be decisive.

All was finally ready on 5 July, after a delay occasioned by Russian artillery bombardment of the German forming up areas. There was an intense two-hour bombardment of the Russian positions, and then the 9th Army swept into the attack. The bombardment failed to crush the Russian defences, and the one infantry and three *Panzer* corps immediately encountered stiff resistance. By 11 July Model had fed all available forces into the fray, but the maximum penetration along the 50-km (30-mile) offensive front was a mere 25 km (15 miles), in the region of Ponyri and Olkhovatka. Near these two villages the Russian 2nd Tank Army put up a sterling defence, and furious armoured battles raged at very close quarters. Although the latest German tanks had good armour and armament, making them formidable opponents at long range, the Russians used the superior mobility and speed of their tanks to keep at close range, where their inferior armament was just as good as the Germans' long-barrelled 7.5- and 8.8-cm guns. In one small area were engaged some 2,000 tanks and self-propelled guns; losses on both sides were extremely heavy. The 9th Army was now

exhausted; the German advance slowed and finally stopped just short of the ridge after which it was downhill all the way to Kursk. Rokossovsky's forces had broken the northern arm of the pincer intended to eliminate the Kursk salient, causing Model to lose 25,000 dead, over 200 of his tanks, and more than 200 aircraft from the 6th Air Fleet.

In the south, von Manstein attacked earlier, and at first enjoyed better results. For these his tactics were to a certain extent responsible: Model, with a high proportion of infantry to armour, had decided to use conventional tactics, with infantry, engineers and artillery opening the way for the tanks to move up; von Manstein, on the other hand, did not have the infantry for such tactics, and decided instead to use his armour to open the way for the supporting forces. The tactic evolved to meet von Manstein's need was the *Panzerkeil* (armour wedge): a Panther or Tiger at the head of the wedge, with PzKpfw IIIs and IVs fanning out behind it along the sides of the wedge. During the battle, von Manstein realized that this formation was wrong since the Russian tanks were closing in to a range where the new tanks' superior guns could not be used to full advantage. He changed the composition of the wedge so that the older tanks led to flush the Russian tanks and anti-tank guns, whilst the Panther or Tiger followed behind to engage the flushed target at long range.

The 4th *Panzerarmee*, which was to strike for Kursk by way of Oboyan, made good progress through the Russian 6th Guards Army, but then ran into the 1st Tank Army and had to slow down. At the same time, Army Detachment Kempf was striking north-east from just south of Belgorod to protect the 4th *Panzerarmee*'s right flank from Russian reinforcements coming in from the east. By 6 July both the 4th *Panzerarmee* and Army Detachment Kempf had driven deep into the Russian defences, but Soviet reserves were beginning to arrive in some considerable numbers. The most important of these arriving forces was the 5th Guards Tank Army, an élite and powerful armoured force. Determined resistance was gradually overcome, and by 11 July, Hoth's left wing, with XLVIII *Panzer* Corps as its main striking element, had pushed forward some 25 km (15 miles) against the 40th, 6th Guards and 1st Tank Armies. On Hoth's right wing, II SS *Panzer* Corps, under the command of General Paul Hausser, was making even better progress, and had pushed forward as far as Prokhorovka after an advance of 50 km (30 miles). Army Detachment Kempf was also moving forward well and had reached Rzhavets on the upper Donets, with a line of Russian forces keeping it separated from II SS *Panzer* Corps. On 12 July the head of the 5th Guards Tank Army reached Prokhorovka and engaged the tanks of the SS *Panzer* corps. The biggest tank battle in history was about to start.

Hausser's tanks and their crews were by now in fairly poor shape, but the Russians were able to stop their advance only on first engagement. With more Russian tanks on the

way, Hausser's position was just becoming precarious when III *Panzer* Corps, Army Detachment Kempf's spearhead, arrived from the upper Donets and took the 5th Guards Tank Army in flank. The battle was confused and desperate, but late on 13 July the Germans definitely seemed to be in the ascendant.

On this day, however, von Manstein and von Kluge had been summoned to a meeting with Hitler, who told them that *Zitadelle* was to be called off. The Allies had landed in Sicily three days before, and troops were needed for the West. A day earlier, moreover, the Central, West and Bryansk Fronts had launched a great offensive against von Kluge's Army Group Centre. Model's small gains were wiped out almost immediately, and by 18 August the German salient round Orel was destroyed. So von Kluge was only too pleased to hear of the cancellation of *Zitadelle*. But von Manstein was not happy with the decision. Although he had been against the operation from the start, he felt that he was in a position now to destroy a major portion of Russia's armoured strength in the battle around Prokhorovka. Hitler reluctantly agreed with von Manstein, who then urged Hausser to complete the destruction of the 5th Guards Tank Army as swiftly as possible. Just as victory was in sight, however, on 17 July Hitler ordered the attack to be broken off, and the SS *Panzer* corps to be sent to Italy. The Battle of Kursk was over. It had failed in its major objective, and had in the end also failed in the *ad hoc* objective of destroying the Russian armour just as the distinct possibility of victory came in sight. On 3 August the Voronezh, Steppe and South-West Fronts went over to the general offensive, and by 23 August the Kharkov salient had fallen once again to the Russians.

A general offensive had now started right along the Russian line from west of Moscow down to the Black Sea, and in a series of co-ordinated strikes that ended only on 23 December, the Russians drove the German Army Groups Centre, South and A to the line of the Dniepr river. The 17th Army was cut off in the Crimea, and the Russians also secured huge bridgeheads across the Dniepr from north of Gomel to south of Kiev (these fell on 6 November) and between Kremenchug and Zaporozhye.

The most significant event of the year had been the German failure to eliminate the Kursk salient. This was the last time the Germans held the initiative in Russia, and from now on all they could do was to try to maintain their hold. Hitler steadfastly refused to sanction retreat, but the weight and size of the Russian forces gradually drove the Germans back, despite the latter's great skill and determination in defensive fighting. Stalingrad had signalled the high point of the German advance; Kursk signalled the beginning of the decline.

Right : **A German tank moves up towards the line past a knocked-out anti-tank gun.**

The Invasion of Italy

A S the last battles were being fought in Tunisia, the Allied staffs were already planning the invasion of Italy. Although a heavy toll had been taken of the Axis forces on land and in the air they could still offer strong resistance and it was believed, especially by Montgomery, that the Italians would fight hard in defence of their own soil. Allied air forces were waging a war of attrition to wear down the *Luftwaffe* and the *Regia Aeronautica*, but Axis planes could still be a menace to the ships of an amphibious operation, so it was necessary to advance step by step within range of land-based fighter cover.

The intention was to capture first Sicily with its airfields and then, as opportunity offered, to cross over to the toe and heel of the mainland. However, the next main thrust would again be made by sea to a point south of Naples still within range of effective air cover. The ultimate Allied objective was to drive Italy out of the war, but how it was to be done no one clearly knew for at least a year after the invasion of Sicily.

The expedition was to be a joint American-British campaign under a supreme commander based in Africa (at first General Dwight D Eisenhower, later the British

General, Sir Maitland Wilson). General Sir Harold Alexander was to command two field armies, Lieutenant-General George S Patton's 7th and General Sir Bernard Montgomery's 8th. The assault on Sicily was the biggest amphibious operation in terms of numbers so far attempted – more divisions were landed in fact than on D-day in Normandy.

On the right, the 8th Army, preceded by a brigade of glider-borne troops, was to land on the east coast with four divisions, turn right and advance north making for the straits of Messina so as to cut off all the Axis troops on the island. On the left, the US 7th Army was to land three divisions, with an armoured division close behind, over an 80-km (50-mile) front on the south coast. It was preceded by four battalions of parachute troops whose task was to seize airfields and other vital points inland. Patton's rôle was to protect the flank and rear of the 8th Army from interference by the six Axis divisions in the island, two of them German *Panzer* or *Panzergrenadier* of the highest quality.

This was a perfectly good plan, but it was plain to the Americans that Alexander had selected the British 8th Army for the decisive rôle: a choice they resented. Some American

Above left : **Scenes of apparent (and often real) confusion were common at all the main Allied amphibious landings, especially when large landing craft were being unloaded.** *Above :* **A British 3-inch mortar crew brings its weapon into action for close support of the infantry advancing inland.**

divisions had in fact not shown up well in their first actions in Tunisia, but they were now blooded, anxious to show their form, and so resented the slur. No one, however, resented it more than Patton, a brilliant, highly temperamental and intensely patriotic officer who, to make matters worse, had taken a strong dislike to the able, but arrogant and tactless Montgomery.

From 1943, the tremendous power of the Allies, especially in the air, made the chance of failure remote, but they were still inex-

perienced. Amphibious operations are always hazardous and the opening phase of this one was almost a disaster. On D-day, 10 July, Montgomery's troops disembarked efficiently, consolidated and moved off to capture their first objective, the naval base of Syracuse. But the entire airborne operation was a fiasco. The US Troop Carrier Command was really a logistic force: its pilots were unaccustomed to flying in the combat zone and incapable of the pin-point navigation at night required for airborne operations. Confused by bad weather and enemy fire, the pilots landed 12 gliders on target and no less than 47 of the 144 in the sea. On the American front, 3,400 of the paratroops reached the mainland, but some as much as 40 km (25 miles) off target and mostly in scattered parties.

The weather was rough, and although Patton's infantry got ashore successfully, there was delay in landing tanks and artillery. At that moment, with one foot in the sea and the other on land, they were violently counterattacked at Gela, in the centre of the intended beach-head. Here the Americans, especially their regular 1st Division (The Big Red One) and parties of paratroops literally 'marching to the sound of the guns', showed a tremendous fighting spirit, stopping the Hermann Göring Division with its 100-odd tanks just short of the beach, aided by some astonishingly accurate fire from the guns of the US Navy cruisers covering the landings. This dispelled any notion that the Americans could not fight or were not a match for German armoured forces.

The 8th Army, having got off to a good start, then met with stiff resistance. Sicily, with its narrow roads, terraces and sharp ridges was ideal for defence and gave a fore-taste of what the Allies were to face for the next two years: Montgomery was slowed down and almost halted.

Patton viewed this delay with intense impatience, and eventually persuaded Alexander to let his army go over to a full offensive. Once off the leash, he turned away to his left, made a remarkable dash for Palermo, captured it, and started to race Montgomery for Messina along the northern coast. He won by a short head, but the Germans in a masterly withdrawal behind a series of defence lines got clean away across the straits, without their equipment, but with most of their principal asset, the men.

The 8th Army then hopped unopposed over the straits (after a huge and unnecessary bombardment), and its 5th Division began to work up the coast from Calabria to Salerno, where the next act was to be performed. Salerno proved a desperate affair. It had been preceded by the dramatic fall of Mussolini and the surrender of Italy, and the Allies vainly hoped that the Italian army might even change sides; after all, the United States was a second home to many Italians. The Germans, however, had foreseen the danger and brutally disarmed their late ally to prevent the occurrence. (When the Italian general commanding the coastal defences of Salerno demurred, he was shot on the spot by the German major issuing the order.) What many simple soldiers thought would be a walk-over turned, therefore, into a bloody battle. Lieutenant-General Mark Clark's US 5th Army with two British and one US division leading, landed smoothly enough on 9 September, but the Germans were ready for them. Salerno is ringed by mountains affording splendid observation, and between artillery fire and counterattack the invaders were pinned near the beaches; indeed, the British and Americans could not join up, and for a time no further landings could be made in the British sector. The British 56th (London) Division was driven back, and when the *Panzers* broke through the front of the US 36th Division they were stopped only just short of the beaches by American divisional artillery fire at close range. The whole of the shallow beach-head and the beaches themselves were under observed artillery fire, as was the fleet lying in Salerno bay under air attack with the new glide-bombs – prototype guided weapons. There was talk of re-embarkation, but this was sternly squashed by Alexander, who was at the beach-head. Reinforcements were landed, two British 15-inch gun battleships arrived to give added fire support, US heavy bombers were called in and the British 5th Division (whose efforts have always been underrated) pressed up north from the toe of Italy, distracting the defence.

German opposition began to wilt under the terrific fire-power which met each of their attacks. The British and Americans began to take the offensive, pushing out the perimeter and making room for the British 7th Armoured Division (the Desert Rats) to start punching along the road which led to Naples.

Field-Marshal Albert Kesselring saw that he had to choose between being destroyed where he stood, or breaking clear to fight a rearguard action protected by an immense belt of demolitions prepared by his engineers. Not a bridge was left standing and every road was mined. He abandoned Naples and fell back slowly to his main defensive position, the Gustav Line. This ran from coast to coast from the mouth of the Garigliano river in the west to Ortona in the east. Towards this the Allied armies, the 5th on the left and the 8th on the right, began to advance, driving in the German rearguards and outposts. This preliminary was in itself a major task. The Germans proved masters of defensive fighting in Italy, and it was not until the 5th Army had fought one battle to cross the Volturno river and another to capture Monte Camino, that its patrols could even

Above: **A prime-mover tows a gun off the beach after the Salerno landings.** *Right:* **General Eisenhower (in jeep) has a word with British troops in a Bren gun carrier near the front line.** *Far right:* **The Allied invasion of Sicily, featuring Patton's dash to Messina.**

examine the formidable Gustav defences of which, so to speak, the Garigliano and Rapido rivers formed the moat, the mountains the bastions, and Monte Cassino the guardtower of the gateway through which the road led to Rome.

Fighting went on until Christmas, during which period the 8th Army took Bari and Foggia, fought a three-day battle for Termoli and crossed the Trigno and Sangro rivers against strong resistance and in vile weather. They took Orsogna after three attempts and Ortona after 12 days which were notable for some savage street fighting between Canadian infantry and German paratroops.

All this hard fighting on the Adriatic coast wore the Germans down but was strategically useless. Behind each ridge and river was another just as doggedly held. The solution, the Allies felt, was to use their sea-power for yet another landing to outflank the Gustav Line positions and open the road to Rome. The site chosen was Anzio. If the 5th Army could break through the western end of the Gustav Line and the force landed at Anzio could cut inland, the right wing of the German 10th Army might well be trapped and destroyed. The problem was how to pierce the Gustav Line. An attempt in early January 1944 to cross the Garigliano and Rapido rivers failed dismally. It was then decided that the correct strategy was to force a passage through the Cassino gap along Route 6 to Rome, but that this would not be possible until Monte Cassino itself was captured. Accordingly, on 22 January Major-General John Lucas, commanding the US VI Corps, landed a British and an American division on the beaches at Anzio, and on 24 January Major-General Geoffrey Keyes launched his US II Corps at the Cassino defences.

Lucas has been blamed for not immediately advancing after his successful landing and so creating confusion in the rear of the Gustav Line, but military historians now agree that

this would have been folly. German reaction was famous for its speed and aggression, and had Kesselring been able to cut in behind to sever communications, Lucas would have been helpless for lack of supplies. He wisely paused to secure his beach-head and base, but in doing so was to be besieged for four months.

Kesselring had been fully prepared for such a landing. His first move was to send batteries of 88-mm *Flak* guns from the air defences of Rome to form a screen of anti-tank guns round Anzio, and the simultaneous issue of a single codeword (Richard) sent pre-designated units from his reserves racing down Italy to form a perimeter defence. These were followed by a division from France and another from Yugoslavia, three regiments from Germany itself and two heavy tank battalions. Hitler sent frenzied messages: 'Anzio abscess must be lanced' and 'the *Führer* expects the bitterest struggle for every yard of ground' in the Gustav Line. The result was that by the time the Royal

Allied troops landing by sea

22.7.43

Allied advance and dates of capture

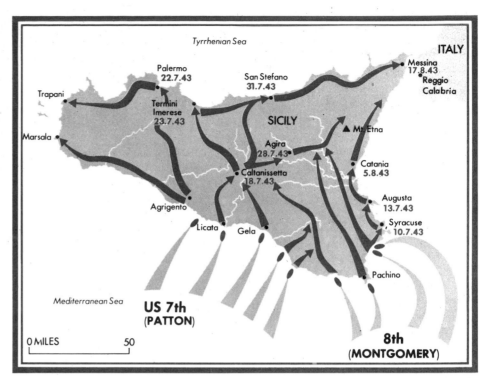

Tyrrhenian Sea

ITALY

Palermo
22.7.43

San Stefano
31.7.43

Messina
17.8.43

Reggio
Calabria

Trapani

Termini
Imerese
23.7.43

SICILY

Mt. Etna

Marsala

Agira
28.7.43

Catania
5.8.43

Agrigento

Caltanissetta
18.7.43

Augusta
13.7.43

Licata

Gela

Syracuse
10.7.43

US 7th
(PATTON)

Pachino

Mediterranean Sea

0 MILES   50

8th
(MONTGOMERY)

Navy and the US Navy had with exemplary speed unloaded Lucas's formations and he was ready to attack with four divisions, Kesselring had assembled eight divisions to block him. The result was that far from being able to break out and help the 5th Army Lucas was subjected to powerful counter-offensives which threatened to liquidate his position altogether. With his 14th Army containing the beach-head, and the 10th comfortably holding off both the 8th and the 5th, Kesselring was well placed to carry out the *Führer*'s orders. Lucas's VI Corps, however, stood firm, and never looked like being beaten. Lucas himself was vindicated by events, and very unfairly dismissed when the crisis was over. In the meantime, Alexander felt it essential to help Lucas by a full-scale attack, and on 24 January the US II Corps began the first of the four battles for Cassino.

Monte Cassino is the name of a spur crowned by the ancient monastery overlooking Italy's Route 6; its intricate defensive system, garrisoned by three battalions of paratroops, embraced a whole group of peaks. Any attacking force had first to fight its way over the Rapido river, past the town and then climb 450 metres (1,500 feet) under fire first to locate and then to assault the cunningly sited German positions in the crags and gullies behind the crest, from which came streams of interlocking machine-gun fire. It was not possible for the Americans to deploy their massive fire support or their tanks in this situation; the issue had to be decided by close fighting with sub-machine gun, grenade and later the Gurkha *kukri*. The US 34th Division and the Moroccans and Algerians of the French Expeditionary Corps reached the crest-line and battled there for 18 days, arriving within a kilometre of the monastery, but a kilometre is a very long way in mountain warfare. Eventually they gave up when the US battalions had lost three-quarters of their fighting strength.

These were replaced by the 2nd New Zealand and 4th Indian Divisions. After much discussion, it was decided to attack the monastery direct and the highly controversial decision was taken to use heavy bombers. Major-General F I S Tuker, a highly experienced Indian Army officer, had urged a widely circling attack in the higher ground in which his skilled mountain troops would bypass the monastery defences, but this was disregarded. Bombing had no effect, for the buildings themselves were not occupied, and after two days the New Zealand Lieutenant-General Sir Bernard Freyberg, who was in command, stopped the attacks. On 15 March he started them again, this time asking for Cassino town to be bombed, but this also had little effect, except to create a miniature Stalingrad where *Panzer-grenadiers* and Maoris fought at close quarters in the ruins. No attempt was made to co-ordinate bombardments with attack, and the defenders repeated their fathers' tactics of the Western Front, going to ground in the impregnable rock and concrete shelters, to pop out and man their weapons when the bombing stopped and the assaulting troops appeared. Every scrap of food, can of water and box of ammunition for the attackers had to be carried up by hand, and when not fighting the attackers defended their gains under continuous artillery fire which caused a drain of casualties.

As Tuker had foreseen, it was useless to attack the Germans at their strongest point. The Indian engineers brought off the extraordinary feat of building a secret track up the mountain. It was fit for tanks, and a squadron drove up it, but to no avail.

Freyberg persisted for three weeks, by which time he had lost 4,000 men: that fine regiment, the 1st Royal Sussex of the 4th Indian Division, alone lost all but three of its officers and 162 out of 313 men in 48 hours. Finally, on 23 March, the offensive was halted, the forward troops pulled back and the ground won consolidated. Both sides now paused to rest and recover. Every soldier was mentally and physically exhausted by the cold, the wet, the ceaseless bombardments and the strain of months of bitter fighting. Alexander, advised by his able chief-of-staff, Lieutenant-General Harding, decided to rest and regroup his troops. The spring, with fine weather and dry ground would allow him to use his two assets, planes and tanks. He would launch a properly coordinated offensive, using all his resources at the same time, to break through the Gustav Line with one concentrated punch and advance at the same time with maximum possible force from the beach-head at Anzio. This, he felt sure, would break the deadlock. Better, if he could destroy the bulk of the 10th Army where they stood facing him in southern Italy, it would open up the whole peninsula to a rapid Allied advance to the north. This great operation, since it was to set the crown on a year of hard fighting, was to be called Diadem.

All Russia Liberated

THE rapid pace and wide geographical extent of their military activities, in 1943, had been achieved at great cost to the Russians. Many hundreds of thousands of men had been lost, and tanks, guns, aircraft and other war *matériel* had been used up at a prodigious rate. Yet, thanks to the efforts of her growing armaments industry in the area beyond the Urals, Russia was able not only to resupply her armies, but to equip on a relatively lavish scale the new formations that were also coming forward in great numbers. Hitler had gambled on a quick war, so that Russia's resources in industry and manpower could

not be used to their full extent, and he had lost. No matter how great the casualties inflicted on the Russian forces, Germany was unable to destroy enough to force them out of the war. The Russians fought in a relatively unsophisticated fashion, with ample supplies of the right types of weapon, such as the excellent T-34 tank, and they were prepared to spend the lives of large numbers of men. Germany, on the other hand, could not do this: her armies fought an advanced type of warfare using the latest weapons, but she could not keep up with the losses inflicted by the Russians, and although in 1943 and 1944 her armies were still superior in

quality to those of the Russians, this was more than counterbalanced by the enormously superior quantity of the Soviet forces. Supplied by the Americans and British with considerable war *matériel*, including large numbers of trucks, the Russians were gradually developing a type of hard-hitting, fast mobile warfare, admirably suited to their armies and the terrain of western Russia. With supply outstripping demand, the Russians were able to keep up an almost nonstop offensive, with fresh troops always ready to take over from exhausted formations.

In 1941, Hitler had ordered Field-Marshal Wilhelm von Leeb's Army Group North

Above : **Supported by armour, Russian infantry clear a village of its German defenders.** *Right :* **Well equipped against the bitter winter, Russian infantry move up against the Germans on the northern sector of the long Eastern Front, near Leningrad.**

not to take Leningrad by direct assault, but rather to invest the city and destroy it by starvation and bombardment. The investment had been completed when Leeb's forces reached the southern shore of Lake Ladoga, completing the ring of Axis forces round the birthplace of Soviet Russia; the Finns holding the region to the north. Leningrad's trials in the following months were appalling, with thousands dying of starvation every day, and disease and cold taking their toll. It is estimated that at the end of 1943, the people of Leningrad were dying at the rate of 20,000 every day. Nevertheless the city held out and continued to hold off the Germans.

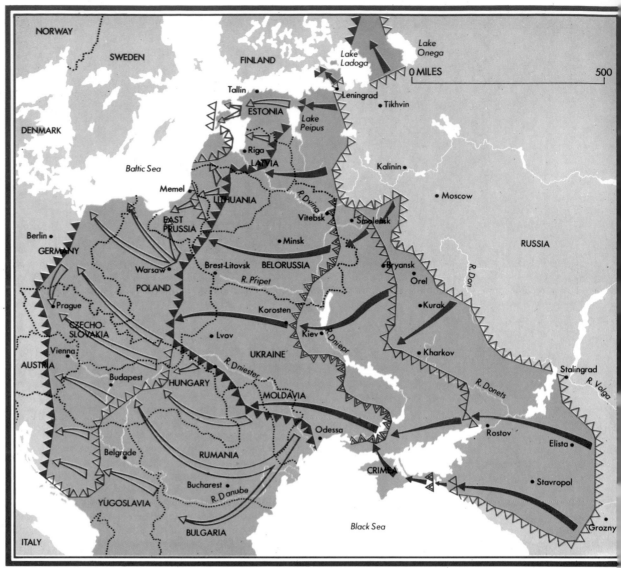

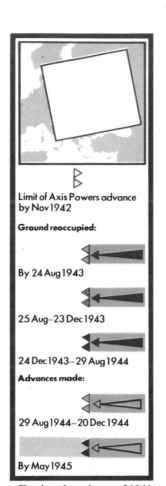

Limit of Axis Powers advance
by Nov 1942

Ground reoccupied:

By 24 Aug 1943

25 Aug–23 Dec 1943

24 Dec 1943–29 Aug 1944

Advances made:

29 Aug 1944–20 Dec 1944

By May 1945

During the winter of 1941 and 1942, supplies were brought in over the frozen surface of Lake Ladoga, but of course this ended with the thaw in March 1942, and conditions deteriorated rapidly.

In August 1942, the Leningrad and Volkhov Fronts launched a joint offensive, with the aim of cutting the corridor from Tosno north to Lake Ladoga held by the German 18th Army, but this failed and Leningrad remained under siege. An attempt to link up with the forces locked up at Oranienbaum, further to the west along the Gulf of Finland, failed at the same time. In January 1943, however, hope of eventual relief appeared when the Leningrad and Volkhov Fronts finally managed to cut their way through just south of Lake Ladoga and link up near Sinyavino. Although this 'Corridor of Death' was under the constant threat of German artillery, a trickle of supplies reached Leningrad, and German efforts to cut the Russian land bridge failed. The limits of this supply route precluded the total relief of the city, which lost perhaps 1,000,000 people during the siege, but it did stop conditions worsening.

Almost exactly a year after the link to Leningrad had been opened, the Russians at last managed to free the city from the constant

threat of German conquest. At the same time, they drove the forces of Army Group North, commanded by Field-Marshal Georg von Küchler, back to Lake Peipus in Estonia. On January 15, 1944 the forces of the Leningrad and Volkhov Fronts, commanded by Generals L A Govorov and K A Meretskov, swept forward and caught the Germans completely off their guard. The Leningrad Front crossed the frozen Gulf of Finland and fell on the left of the German 18th Army (General Georg Lindemann) whilst the Volkhov Front crossed the frozen lakes and marshes further to the south to attack the 18th Army's right. By the end of the year, the Russians had advanced to the line of the Luga river and taken the historic capital of the area, Novgorod. Lindemann pulled his army back smartly, but only just escaped encirclement. The 2nd Baltic Front, under General M M Popov, had made limited attacks further yet to the south, but in February burst into major offensive action to push the Russians' front forward to the line running along the Velikaya river south from Pskov, at the southern end of Lake Peipus. When the thaw started at the beginning of March, bringing hostilities to a temporary halt, Field-Marshal Walther Model, who had replaced Küchler on 29 January, had only just managed to begin

to check the Russians. The threat to Leningrad had at last been removed after the greatest siege of modern times.

Meanwhile, in the south, the Russians had been continuing their offensive against the Germans in the Ukraine. Supported on its right by Colonel-General P A Kurochkin's 2nd Belorussian Front, on December 24, 1943 the 1st Ukrainian Front under General N F Vatutin struck west in a savage offensive from its great bridgehead around Kiev. General I S Konev's 2nd Ukrainian Front also swept over to the offensive further to the south, between Kanev and Kirovograd, on January 5, 1944 with General R Ya Malinovsky's 3rd Ukrainian Front and General F I Tolbukhin's 4th Ukrainian Front, on each side of Zaporozhye at the head of the Dniepr bend, joining in on 10 and 11 January respectively. There was nothing that the Germans could do except try to extricate themselves as best they could. Field-Marshal Erich von Manstein's Army Group South and Field-Marshal Ewald von Kleist's Army Group A tried to stem the Russian winter advance, but their forces were unable to halt the vast Soviet fronts or army groups. On 29 January, two corps were trapped at Korsun-Shevchenkovsky, and although von Manstein immediately set

138

about putting together a relief force, a large part of the two corps was lost, together with all their heavy equipment, by the time the relief force and the cut off garrison linked up on 17 February. Von Manstein's efforts had been greatly hampered by terrible winter conditions and the overall exhaustion of his men.

The Russians continued to grind forward right into April, despite the brilliance of many counterattacks mounted by the indefatigable von Manstein, who yet again demonstrated his remarkable tactical genius. In the confusion of such operations, it was hardly surprising that another German army was now cut off. This was the 1st *Panzerarmee*, commanded by General Hans Hube. Isolated to the east of Kamenets Podolsky on 10 March, Hube did not allow his forces to become pinned down by the superior Russian armies opposing him. Keeping constantly on the move, and supplied from the air, the 1st *Panzerarmee* fought a brilliant campaign against the Russian lines of communication, as ordered by von Manstein, who kept a close personal supervision over the whole operation by radio. Unable to pin down this highly mobile force, the Russians were at a loss what to do, and slowed down the pace of their general advance in the area. Finally Hube turned west, and in conjunction with an attack south from Tarnopol by the 4th *Panzerarmee*, now commanded by Colonel-General E Raus, broke out through the Russian front line with his forces almost intact.

Yet the Russians were still moving steadily forwards. Commanded by more than competent generals, and supervised from Moscow by Marshal Georgi Zhukov and Stalin, who kept a personal link open to all senior commanders, the Russians seemed invincible. Regardless of the tactical genius of their commanders, the German soldiers were outnumbered and beaten back for all their skills and determination. History shows that von Kleist conducted an exemplary retreat, and von Manstein a brilliant one; Hitler's reward to these excellent commanders was to fire them on 30 March. Colonel-General Ferdinand Schörner, a hard-line Nazi but adequate general, took over von Kleist's Army Group South Ukraine, latterly Army Group A, whilst the ubiquitous Field-Marshal Walther Model, the '*Führer's* fireman' as he was dubbed, took over von Manstein's Army Group North Ukraine, latterly Army Group South.

Vatutin, killed in March, was replaced on 1 April by Zhukov, and the Russians pressed forward. The Germans' 6th and 8th Armies in the south were badly mauled, and the great Black Sea port of Odessa fell on 10 April. By the middle of the month, the Russians had cleared the Axis forces out of all Russia to the south of the Pripet marshes. The Bug, Dniestr and Prut rivers had all been crossed,

and the Ukrainian fronts were now deep into southern Poland and northern Romania. Trapped in the Crimea, the German 17th Army was faced with the impossible problem of holding off the 2nd Guards and 51st Armies of Tolbukhin's 4th Ukrainian Front, which attacked south along the Perekop isthmus on 8 April, and General A I Eremenko's Independent Coastal Army, which crossed from the Taman peninsula into the Kerch peninsula on 11 April. The 17th Army was driven back towards Sevastopol, from which only a few men could be evacuated. Hitler had insisted that the Crimea be held as a jumping off point for the reconquest of southern Russia, and his dementia now cost Germany the fine 17th Army when the last parts of Sevastopol fell on 12 May.

The winter and spring campaigns had cleared southern Russia, and Stalin now planned to use the summer offensive to clear central Russia, Belorussia, just to the north of the Pripet marshes. The offensive was entrusted, from south to north, to Marshal K K Rokossovsky's 1st Belorussian, Colonel-General M V Zakharov's 2nd Belorussian, Colonel-General I D Chernyakovsky's 3rd Belorussian and Colonel-General I Kh Bagramyan's 1st Baltic Fronts, with the destruction of Field-Marshal Ernst Busch's Army Group Centre as their main objective. The offensive was to be launched from the area just to the west of Smolensk and Gomel, the axis being west towards East Prussia. As usual, immediate overall command of the whole operation was entrusted to Marshal Georgi Zhukov, by now deputy supreme commander of the Russian armed forces under Stalin. Massing some 250 guns per kilometre of front (400 per mile), the four Russian fronts started their offensive against the hapless Army Group Centre after a devastating barrage on 23 June. Disorganized at the front by the Russian artillery, and in its rear areas by the ever increasing activities of Russian partisans, now a formidable force, Army Group Centre could not even retreat before the armoured offensive. The Russians

smashed a 400-km (250-mile) gap through the Germans' front, through which poured the armour and infantry. The Red Air Force had total command of the air, and the armour pushed on forwards as swiftly as possible, leaving the infantry to mop up and follow on as best it could. Hitler, as usual, forbade any thought of retreat, and ordered cut off formations to stand and fight until relieved. However, Hitler did not consider where the relieving forces were to come from. Vitebsk fell on 25 June, Bobruysk on 27 June and Minsk on 3 July. For the first time in the war, an entire German army group was destroyed: 25 of Busch's 33 divisions were cut off and destroyed, and the Russians claimed to have killed 400,000 Germans, with another 158,000 taken prisoner, and to have captured or destroyed 2,000 armoured vehicles, 10,000 guns and 57,000 vehicles. The loss of Belorussia and the destruction of Army Group Centre, by 4 July, was a catastrophe of immense proportions for the Germans, yet the size of the forces deployed by the Russians cannot detract from Zhukov's genius in planning and controlling such a successful and speedy campaign. The Russians had come a long way from being the military 'illiterates' defeated so soundly by the Germans a mere three years earlier. Zhukov's Belorussian campaign bears very favourable comparison with the best German staff work of the beginning of the war. Busch was inevitably sacked by Hitler, who entrusted command of the shattered Army Group Centre to Model, who also kept command of Army Group North Ukraine.

This was only the first stage of Russia's summer offensive. The Belorussian fronts continued westwards, taking Vilnyus on 13 July, Brest Litovsk on 28 July and reaching the outskirts of Warsaw by the end of August. Colonel-General Georg-Hans Reinhardt, previously commander of the 3rd *Panzerarmee* badly mauled near Vitebsk, took over from Model as head of Army Group Centre on 16 August when Model left for France; where the situation was worsening after the

Above left : **In a series of titanic offensives, the Germans were driven out of Russia.** *Right :* **The Russians were great believers in heavy artillery fire.**

Allied break-out from the Normandy beachhead. Model's other hat, as commander of Army Group North Ukraine, was assumed by Colonel-General J Harpe, although he was only confirmed in this post after the army group had become Army Group A in September.

No amount of reshuffling could halt the Russians, however. On 13 July Konev's 1st Ukrainian Front, just to the south of the 1st Belorussian Front, had gone over to the offensive, and was joined still further to the south on 5 August by General I E Petrov's 4th Ukrainian Front, only recently formed. By the end of August, the Ukrainian and Belorussian fronts had reached a north and south line running from Jaslo in southern Poland, past the east of Warsaw, round East Prussia and thence into Lithuania. The advance since the end of July had been small, for the Russians had advanced some 725 km (450 miles) and their lines of communications could no longer sustain further advance. Yet just as the Russians began to slow down at the beginning of August, there occurred one of the most remarkable and heroic actions of the war. In Warsaw the Polish Home Army had, secretly, long planned a rising against the German garrison, once the Russians were within reach of the city. Despite their anti-communist feelings, the men of the Home Army, under the command of General Tadeusz Bor-Komorowski, rose against the Germans on 1 August. Unfortunately, the 1st Belorussian Front halted just over the river from Warsaw, and after a hopeless but heroic defence, the Home Army was crushed in bitter fighting by SS troops by the end of September. The fact that Rokossovsky halted just too soon to help the Home Army has been a controversial point ever since the war, and will in all probability remain so. The most likely reason is that the Russians wished to see this pro-western force in Poland destroyed, so facilitating the establishment of a puppet government loyal to the Soviet Union. What was left of Warsaw after the German campaign of 1939, and the reduction of the Jewish ghetto afterwards, was almost totally destroyed in the vicious two-month campaign by the SS.

On 4 July, General A I Eremenko's 2nd Baltic Front, General I I Maslennikov's 3rd Baltic Front and General L A Govorov's Leningrad Front extended the Russian general offensive to the north. Together with the 1st Baltic and 3rd Belorussian Fronts they swept into the Baltic states occupied by Russia in 1940 and lost to the Germans in 1941. Army Group North, commanded by Colonel-General Georg Lindemann, could not stem the Russian advance and fell back towards the Baltic. Although this army group was threatened by the distinct possibility of being cut off by the Belorussian fronts' advance towards East Prussia, Hitler again would not even consider the possibility of retreat from the Baltic states. Forced back from the line of the Narva and Velikaya rivers, Army Group North eventually found itself in western Latvia, where it was cut off in the peninsula north of a line between Tukums on the Bay of Riga and Liepaja on the Baltic Sea, when the forces of the 1st Baltic Front reached the sea on 10 October. Narva had fallen on 26 July, Daugavpils (Dvinsk) on 27 July, Kaunas on 1 August and the bastion of Riga was to fall on 15 October. Colonel-General Heinz Guderian, who had replaced Colonel-General Kurt Zeitzler as OKH chief-of-staff, was appalled by Hitler's decision to allow this important and powerful force to be locked up by the Russians where it was paralysed to further Germany's war aims. The men of Army Group North remained immobilized and useless in the Kurland peninsula right up to the end of the war, although some units were evacuated by ships of the German navy.

With the German threat to Leningrad removed, the Russians could turn their attention in the area to Finland. In the middle of June, five Russian armies attacked up the Karelian isthmus and round each end of Lake Onega, and after skilful Finnish defence had at first halted them, began to make ground. The Mannerheim Line was finally breached, and on 20 June Viipuri fell to the Russians. Realizing that their position was hopeless, the Finns sued for and were given an armistice on 4 September. Under the terms of this armistice, the Finns had to clear their former co-belligerents, the Germans, out of the country, and there was some sharp fighting before this was accomplished. In the far north, on the shores of the Arctic, the German 20th Army was driven back out of Russia by Meretskov's Karelian Front in October, and the Russians eventually pushed on into Norway, although the little ports of Petsamo and Kirkenes held out.

The Russian advances in the northern Ukraine and Belorussia had by now placed Army Group South Ukraine, now commanded by Colonel-General Johannes Friessner, in a difficult position. Any Russian advance into southern Poland and Hungary would put it in danger of being cut off, together with Army Groups E and F in Greece and Yugoslavia respectively, particularly if Hitler, as usual, refused permission to pull back. The Russians realized this as clearly as the Germans, and launched an attack into Romania on 20 August with the 2nd and 3rd Ukrainian Fronts. The German 6th and Romanian 3rd Armies were quickly trapped, and the Russians pressed on to the Danube river by 29 August. Romania, long disaffected with the Axis cause by lack of success, capitulated on 23 August and declared war on Germany two days later. The Romanian 3rd and 4th Armies quickly joined forces with the Russians to press the campaign against their former allies. Reaching the Romanian capital on 31 August, the Russians wheeled west and then again northwest to drive into southern Hungary. The entire country of Romania was overrun by 24 September.

The 37th and 57th Armies of the 3rd Ukrainian Front continued south-west, however, and plunged into Bulgaria, which surrendered on 4 September and joined Russia four days later. Beset by partisans and

Above: **In April 1944 the Germans defence in the Crimea ended.** *Below right:* **The Russians roll into another 'liberated' city as the Germans retreat.**

the Bulgarian 1st Army, Army Group E succeeded in pulling back from Greece to link up with Army Group F in Yugoslavia.

Greatly weakened by the loss of much of the 6th and 8th Armies, Army Group South Ukraine tried to hold southern Hungary, with Army Groups E and F to its right in Yugoslavia. It was an impossible task, and the Russians moved with ease into Hungary and eastern Yugoslavia where, with the aid of Tito's partisans, they took Belgrade on 19 October. By the end of 1944, the Russians were firmly ensconced in the Balkans, and ready to drive forward into Austria and Czechoslovakia.

Russia had been cleared of the invaders. Finland, Romania and Bulgaria had dropped out of the war. The Russian armies were poised to sweep into the territories bordering Germany and thence into Germany proper. Stalin had every reason to be pleased with the performance of his forces. All Germany could do, in the absence of a leader who could see the paramount reasons for trying to secure peace, even at the price of unconditional surrender, was fight on desperately in the hope of slowing down the Russian war machine. The Russians were still to have a hard time of it in 1945.

The Gothic Line

IT is ironical that the attitudes of the United States and Britain in Italy and South-East Asia were completely opposed. Over Burma and China the Americans were all for an offensive strategy and felt that the British were dragging their feet, while the British saw no merit in becoming entangled in the mountains and jungles of upper Burma to help China – a doubtful and inert ally – when they were free to strike further south and east by sea. By contrast, in Italy the British felt they already had a foothold in Europe and wished to exploit it without putting all their money on the hazardous Channel crossing. Winston Churchill, always a great exponent of the 'indirect approach', envisaged a wide movement into Austria and central Europe and thence into southern Germany. The Americans would have none of this. 'Overlord' and the direct approach was their chosen strategy, followed up by another landing, 'Dragoon', in the south of France. In addition, General Sir Harold Alexander in Italy was to hand over seven divisions immediately for Overlord, and six more later in 1944 for Dragoon. His rôle was limited to keeping as many German divisions occupied in Italy as possible.

Alexander himself was a devoted supporter of Churchill's strategy, but he was commanding a multi-national army; his second in command was a US officer; one of his armies was American; and one corps was French – and the French wanted desperately to fight to liberate France herself, not any other country.

Alexander had to be extremely diplomatic, both in command and in his recommendations: he was not a purely British general. He was not a man to sulk, or intrigue, or bend his orders; he was a very determined and clear-headed man. He decided, therefore, that the most effective way to carry out his mission was to fix his eyes on the Po valley, the Julian Alps and the Ljubljana gap in Yugoslavia leading to central Europe, and drive there as hard as he could with all his force. Even short of divisions as he was, he had command of the air, overwhelming resources in weapons and engineers to build bridges. A remorseless drive to the north would keep his opponent as busy as any other more cautious and limited offensives. Such was the background of the Italian campaign in 1944, employing more troops – some 40 divisions on two sides – than any other theatre of war, apart from the Russian Front.

Alexander had decided that his next task was to reorganize and tidy up his armies, and then put plan Diadem, to liquidate the Cassino–Anzio stalemate, into action. The plan was to let operations die down on the Adriatic coast and shift the 8th Army to the centre. Some military experts believe that the secret of mountain warfare is to avoid it, as it offers endless opportunities for delaying

Above: **A British Bren gunner waits for his target in the dire battles in front of the Cassino massif.** *Above right:* **Heavily armed Americans move up towards the front in Italy.** *Right:* **An infantry support version of the Sherman tank moves up at speed in typical Italian summer conditions.**

action. The new effort was to be made along the valley floor below Cassino to burst through the Liri valley. The British XIII Corps under Lieutenant-General Sidney Kirkman, the man who had devised the fireplan at El Alamein and, in Montgomery's opinion, the best artilleryman in the British Army, with three infantry divisions and one armoured division and 1,000 guns, to be followed by I Canadian Corps of one armoured and one infantry division, was to bridge the Rapido river and break into the valley defences under cover of a dense continuous smoke screen. This lasted from 12 May to 18 May and used 813 tonnes of smoke munitions and 135,000 artillery smoke shells alone. Altogether something approaching 1,000,000 shells of all kinds were fired. Hostile batteries received a barrage of seven tonnes of heavy shells in a few minutes, and when the Canadians attacked the rear edge of the Gustav Line, known as the Hitler

Line, their preliminary bombardment was at the rate of 1,000 shells an hour.

This vast mass of artillery was to switch to the Cassino heights as necessary to support two Polish divisions, who were to clear the heights once and for all. On the left of the Liri valley the French Expeditionary Corps with two colonial divisions, one Algerian and one Moroccan, all experienced mountaineers, was to clear the heights on the left with startling success. The US II Corps was to attack near the coast. Then, at the appropriate moment, one US armoured, three US infantry and two British divisions were to mount an offensive from the Anzio beach-head and make for Valmonte. Their task was, as before, to cut Route 6 and trap the German divisions as they were driven back from the Gustav Line.

The RAF and the USAAF were to concentrate on attacking the German reserves as they were moved up, and also on giving close air support to the advancing troops, using new and highly developed methods of communication from ground to air.

Altogether 41 divisions were involved in this great battle: 8 German divisions encircling Anzio; 10 in the crucial area of the Gustav Line; 6 Allied divisions in Anzio; and 17 between Cassino and the sea. It will be seen, therefore, that Operation Diadem can be ranked as one of the great battles of military history, and one which could have been one of the decisive battles of the war. Although it was a resounding success (pushed out of the news and public notice by the launching of Overlord on 6 June, just after the Gustav Line defences had collapsed) it fell short of complete victory. This was partly due to the extraordinary bravery and resilience of the Germans, who never admitted defeat. They extricated their mauled battle-groups, formed rearguards and in spite of the unceasing attacks of the Allied air forces retreated in order up through Italy to their next main position in the Apennines: the Gothic Line.

The other cause was a decision by Clark of the 5th Army to vary his orders. Whether it was national pride, personal vanity or because he genuinely thought it was politically and strategically important, has long been the subject of controversy: the fact remains that he decided to capture Rome. Leaving only one division to follow the thrust line laid down by Alexander, he swung four US divisions away to the left. He was held up along an intermediate line, called Caesar, and it can be argued that had this been allowed to solidify there would have been a long hold up, had not Clark broken through it; but there can be no doubt he had departed from his orders, and the delicacy of Alexander's position was that Clark was allowed to get away with it. As a result the 10th Army escaped.

One of the surprises of the battle was the success of General Alphonse Juin's French-African troops. These were sent into the rugged, roadless, mountain sector between the Americans and the British XIII Corps, more or less to keep the Germans in that sector occupied. Using troops better suited to the Imphal battle in far-away Burma than to the massed fire-power and technology of war in Europe, Juin first infiltrated his infantry and captured a vital peak which controlled the Liri valley on the south side, as Cassino did on the north. Then, using his *goumiers* or irregular Moroccan mounted infantry, Juin cut through the Hitler Line, came out behind it and caused the defences of the German left flank to collapse, while the British and Canadian armoured divisions, choked with their abundant transport, were still stuck in traffic jams in the Liri valley. Had this been foreseen, or exploited when it happened, the battle might have turned out very differently.

On the other side of the valley, it cost the Poles 4,000 casualties to capture the Cassino heights. Thus the defence of the position by Major-General Heidrich and his paratroops, cost the Allies altogether some 12,000 casualties and the battle remains one of the epics of defensive warfare. It was fitting that the Germans were overcome by their deadliest enemies: on 18 May the 12th Podolski Lancers, fighting as infantry, raised the Polish flag over the ruins of the monastery. The bodies of six nationalities were scattered among the Cassino defences, and in this connection it is worth noting that Alexander had at one time or another 25 nationalities or language groups under his command: Americans; French; Brazilians; Algerians; Moroccans; Canadians (who could count as two); British (who could count as four); South Africans, who included Basutos; Indians, who included Sikhs, Mahrattas, Madrasis, Jats, Rajputs, Punjabis, Pathans, Baluchis and Gurkhas, who strictly speaking come from Nepal; Poles; Jews from Palestine; Nisei (US native-born) Japanese; Greeks; and Italians.

If Alexander had achieved nothing else he had fulfilled his mission of drawing in reserves. By 6 June, D-day for Overlord, four divisions had been sent to Kesselring to prevent a total collapse of the German position in Italy and later he was to be given three more. (It remains clear that whatever the Americans might have thought about Churchill's central European strategy, Hitler was under no illusions about the dangers of any army appearing to threaten Germany from the south while he tried to hold off the Russians from the east.) The result was that when the battle to pierce the Gothic Line began, Alexander's numerical superiority had changed to an adverse balance of 20 to 22. However, in air-power, weapons and supplies he had still a great advantage. He began his campaign against Kesselring's rearguards as soon as the confusion of the breakthrough and 5th Army's change of course could be cleared up.

'Push', not 'pursuit', is the word. The experience of Sicily was endlessly repeated. The advancing Allies found that every bridge was down, every verge and detour mined and everything attractive was fiendishly booby-trapped. To pick up a trophy, such as a Luger pistol, to pluck a delicious peach in an orchard or even luxuriously to use a flush lavatory in an abandoned house was to risk

being blown up. For the troops who had fought through the Gothic Line there was none of the excitement of a triumphant advance. All through the hot, dusty Italian summer the long columns of tanks and lorries rumbled forward, hit the enemy, stopped, patrolled, positioned the artillery and attacked uphill through the terraced fields and orchards, losing a platoon here and a tank or two there, only to find the Germans gone. They then had to form up again, advance to the next ridge and start all over again. What kept the Allied soldiers going was one thing only: they were always advancing. Eventually in August, they began to close up on to the Gothic Line.

North of Florence the Apennines lie diagonally across Italy and offer a natural line of defence from Spezia to Pesaro, which had been enormously strengthened by the German engineers. The route through the centre was via two mountain passes. Going round the Adriatic flank meant crossing 7 river valleys with 12 more rivers barring the way in the wide valley of the Po. It was a battle demanding vast resources as well as good tactics.

Good military plans are usually very simple. All they require is good staff work, brave troops, good weather and reserves. The first two were assured, although some of the best divisions were already very tired and sapped by casualties, which always fall hardest on the leaders of companies and platoons; but the third was not going to last for more than a few weeks and the last was non-existent. Kesselring's veterans were equally tired and depleted but they had been reinforced with fresh troops and their defences were ready. As things stood there was no question of a quick Allied breakthrough and little chance of exploitation should one be achieved, but Alexander and his army commanders decided to try.

The plan suggested by Lieutenant-General Sir Oliver Leese, who had taken Montgomery's place, was for the 8th Army to be moved back to the Adriatic for a concentrated

Allied troops landing by sea

Allied troops landing by air

3.9.43

Allied advance and dates
of capture

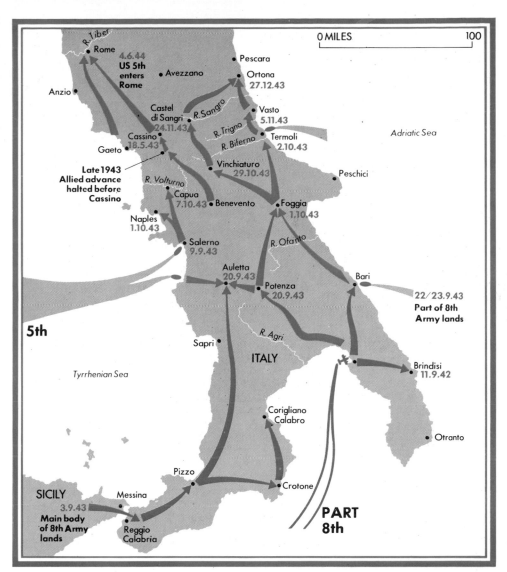

Above left : **Italian partisans, such as
this band near Milan, greatly helped
the Allies by harassing the German
rear areas. Right: The Allies' advance
went well as far as the Cassino line.**

punch effort up the coast with the Polish and
Canadian corps. The main thrust would come
from the British V Corps with four divisions
some ten miles inland through the foothills,
with the aim of letting his tanks loose in the
Po valley behind Kesselring's eastern flank.
This was to commence on 25 August. Hoping
that after two weeks most of Kesselring's
reserves would have been attracted to the
east, the 5th Army was to attack the Futa and
Il Giogo passes north of Florence, early in
September. A great deal of care was taken to
conceal the 8th Army's *Schwerpunkt* (point of
main effort) by the elaborate pretence of a
build-up in the centre. The first attacks by a
master of infantry tactics, Major-General Sir
John Hawkesworth, commanding the 46th
Division, made in silence without any preliminary air bombardment or covering fire,
were a rapid success. The *Intention* heading
Hawkesworth's operation order was 'The
46th Division will BUST the Gothic Line.'
It nearly did.

As a preliminary, his division, with the
famous 4th Indian Division on its left,
crossed the Metauro river and attacked outposts manned by the German 71st Division,
who were driven back in panic. By the end
of August the whole 8th Army was hard up
against the main position, its patrols looking
at hillsides converted to bare slopes, houses
knocked down, trees and vines cleared to
provide fields of fire, fields of anti-personnel
and anti-tank mines and the villages converted to machine-gun strongpoints. What
looked to be impregnable was pierced, not
simply by weight of fire but by infantry fighting. Like the battle in Imphal earlier that
year, the issue was finally decided by the outcome of combats between platoons in which
sometimes the courage of a single man won
the day.

Lieutenant Norton, a South African serv-

ing with the Hampshires who led the way up
Monte Gridolfo, took two positions single-
handed and then, wounded, went on with his
platoon to take the whole position. He won
the Victoria Cross.

A company of the 2/7th Gurkha Rifles took
a fortified village by night using only *kukris*
and grenades after four hours of fighting.
Only 30 could stand at daylight but all the
defenders were dead or taken prisoner.

Another Gurkha, Rifleman Sherbahadur
Thapa, a Bren-gunner of the 9th Gurkha
Rifles, held up a counterattack for two hours,
quite alone, charging out to shoot up the
enemy as he formed up. He was awarded a
posthumous VC.

Similar stories could be told of the
United States infantry. On 10 September it
was the turn of the 5th Army to attack the
fortified passes through the Apennines.
Monte Altuzzo, commanding the Giglio pass
and stiff with concrete machine-gun posts,
was taken by a platoon of the 1st Battalion,
338th Infantry. (The platoon leader radioed
his CO, Lieutenant-Colonel Willis O Jackson: 'I've got your birthday present. We've
captured Altuzzo.') Jackson's battalion had
lost 250 out of 400 men. The successful
struggle to hold the castle at Battiglia for three
days by the 2/350th against repeated counterattacks remains an epic of American arms.

All this heroism in the end went for
nothing. Alexander ran out of infantry reserves. The hope of a tank breakthrough on
the east flank was a vain one. The British 1st
Armoured Division was thrown repeatedly
into action against their old, deadly enemy,
the German batteries of 88-mm anti-tank
guns. At Ceriano the Bays of the 2nd
Armoured Brigade were shot to pieces in a
few minutes, and eventually the division had
to be disbanded. The 8th Army lost 14,000
men killed, wounded and missing. It had
advanced 48 km (30 miles), losing 200 tanks
on the way and now it was stuck. Moreover,
it had begun to rain.

At one moment it looked as if the 5th Army,
having cleared the passes, might almost crack
the position open in the centre: there was
only another 24 km (15 miles) to go and from
the forward positions Bologna could just be
seen in the plain far below. At that desperate
moment even Kesselring himself thought he
had lost but rain, mud, bad flying weather
and a dour defence stopped the 5th Army
infantry in the mountains as it had stopped
the 8th Army tanks in the plain.

145

D-Day

OPERATION Overlord, the cross-channel invasion of France, was the most critical and the most dangerous operation of the whole war. It was critical because it opened the only route by which the military strength of the United States could be brought to bear on Germany and the war ended quickly. It was dangerous, because in an amphibious operation failure is complete. Overlord was the core of Allied strategy and all resources had been devoted to it; even the Japanese had been given second place. So far three assault landings had been attempted (in Sicily, at Salerno and at Anzio, against relatively weak opposition and an unfortified coast) and each had been a near thing. By contrast, in France one complete army group awaited the invaders, commanded by no less than Field-Marshal Erwin Rommel, with 32 divisions ready to intervene, 3 more in Holland, and another army group with 13 divisions stationed in southern France. The vulnerable parts of the French coast were defended by the Atlantic Wall, a formidable belt of obstacles and minefields covered by batteries of guns in concrete emplacements. The disastrous Dieppe raid of 1942 had shown just how different breaching the Atlantic Wall would be from landing on an Italian beach or a Pacific atoll.

For logistic reasons the largest force the Allied planners could put ashore in the first wave was five divisions, with six more to follow when there was room for them to deploy. All possible scientific and military ingenuity, therefore, had to be devoted to solving three very difficult problems. The first was to put the assault troops safely ashore in the face of intense fire. The second was to get tanks and artillery over the ditches and tank-traps barring the way inland. The third was to supply the two armies which would pour into the beach-head, and bring in over the beaches the thousands of tonnes of petrol, ammunition and food needed. New methods and new weapons had to be invented for the battle of the beach-head.

It was planned to saturate the whole defence system by bombing and naval bombardment, but all experience showed that however heavy a bombardment, enough men and weapons survived to decimate the attackers, so close support for the actual run-in to the beach had to be provided. This was achieved by putting armoured self-propelled artillery and also multiple-rocket launchers in the landing craft. The guns then rolled ashore to give normal support until the rest of the ordinary artillery was landed. Large numbers of battle tanks were fitted with 'DD'

Left : **Part of the Allied armada for the invasion of Normandy prepares itself for the great day while lying in the security of a southern British port.**

flotation gear, a British invention which enabled them to swim ashore to fight with the first wave. No less important was the part played by the tanks adapted for special jobs in the physical breaching of the defences and operated by assault engineers. These carried super-heavy mortars for blowing up concrete bunkers, flail equipment to explode minefields and rolls of matting, fascines, ramps and bridges to make roads inland from the beaches.

The battle would be very hard, and there would be no hope of the rapid capture of a port, or ports in working order: the defenders would be certain to render them unusable. Instead, it was decided to build two harbours off the invasion beaches. A fleet of old ships was steamed across and sunk in groups to provide breakwaters, and two artificial harbours – 'Mulberries' – made up of floating concrete cylinders were towed across the Channel. Oil was brought ashore by pipe-line, into which tankers discharged directly, and 'Pluto' (Pipe-Line Under The Ocean) was later laid direct from England to France.

All this was essential, not in order to win the Battle of Normandy – that itself was another huge problem looming ahead – but to make certain that Field-Marshals Gerd von Rundstedt and Rommel did not win the 'Battle of the Beach-head'. For both battles the Allies had three great assets. Air Chief-Marshal Sir Arthur Tedder and General Carl Spaatz, USAAF, had won complete command of the air without which, of course, Overlord could not have been launched at all. The air forces were to help blast the armies forward, block the movement of reserves and massacre the defeated German columns in retreat.

Unseen, but as effective as another army, were the forces of the French resistance, which attacked the German lines of communication and the German reserve divisions marching up actually had to fight their way through them.

The third asset was the *Führer*, Adolf Hitler himself. As a supreme commander he was a disaster, for the simple reason that he regarded war as a giant game of chess, which he played on a map sitting in his bunker in East Prussia, giving futile orders no one dared to disobey. A single one of these was to lose the war in France.

To these three could be added the American habit of 'thinking big': something the British simply could not afford to do, because they had a small population, resources were scarce and British generals were not allowed to throw away lives on the scale of a Hodges or a Patton. (Montgomery was always being criticized for his slowness and over-preparation.) Roosevelt, advised by his own chiefs-of-staff, thought that 'the best way to kill the most Germans' was 'to mount one great big invasion and then slam them with everything we've got . . . it's the quickest way to win the war.' Both, of course, were right in their way (Desk strategists should compare the battered brigades Montgomery had available for the pursuit after El Alamein with what Patton was free to use in the ensuing weeks: a force bigger than the whole 8th Army of 1942.) Only by quoting numbers can the scale of Overlord be realized.

The assault was led by 3 airborne divisions, followed by 5 assault divisions with tanks landing on the beaches, followed by 6 more divisions, with 21 more waiting in England. They were carried by 4,262 aircraft and 4,266 ships of all kinds and supported by 2,300 combat aircraft, which flew 14,600 sorties on D-day alone. In the weeks before D-day the heavy coast artillery batteries which were the main threat to the landings were bombed out of existence and all the railways and rolling stock, which might move von Rundstedt's strategic reserve to the threatened point, were wrecked. Some 80,000 tonnes of bombs were dropped. At sea two fleets guarded the flanks of the assault force and stood by to give covering fire to the landings, while 29 flotillas of mine-sweepers cleared the Channel coast.

The bombing pattern was carefully arranged to avoid giving away the landing site and an elaborate deception plan was mounted to make the Germans believe that the invasion would be launched in the Pas de Calais. In fact, after a very thorough study the Allied planners had chosen the Normandy coast in the Seine Bay a long way to the west as the landing place. The reasoning behind the choice was long and complex, but the most obvious and important consideration was room to put ashore in the first wave a force strong enough to resist any initial counter-attack: on this General Sir Bernard Montgomery, the land force commander for the invasion, had been insistent.

His detailed plan – an enlargement on the original – was as follows: the British 6th Airborne Division was dropped or glidered in to seize vital bridges over the Orne river to protect the left flank of the proposed beach-head while the US 82nd and 101st Airborne Divisions fulfilled a similar function on the extreme right. Then the seaborne forces landed between the mouths of the Orne and Vire from left to right as follows: the British 3rd, Canadian 3rd and British 50th Divisions leading the assault of the British 2nd Army, and the US 1st and 4th Divisions of Lieutenant-General Omar Bradley's US 1st Army. One of the most crucial rôles in the whole enterprise was that of the special parties who had to land just ahead of the assault waves at exactly the right point of the tide to blow up the underwater obstacles on the beaches.

This question of timing was critical, for only certain infrequent days gave the optimum conditions of moon, tide and sunrise. The tidal flow arrives at different times on different beaches so there had to be different zero hours along the front and this, com-

bined with varying distances to be travelled, demanded a complicated timetable which had to be followed exactly and could not be easily altered. As the perfect combinations only occurred at intervals and a postponement was fraught with terrible difficulties the decision faced by General Eisenhower on 3 June and 4 June was appalling: the weather forecast was gales and rough seas, with a faint improvement possible. Faced with the alternatives of postponement and the assault divisions being cut off by storm and surf when most vulnerable, he took a historic and courageous decision. D-day was to be 6 June. The storms had not altogether abated and the bad weather hampered the landings, but it also caused the defenders to relax their vigilance. Early that morning the airborne troops landed, and at half tide and precisely 40 minutes after 'nautical twilight' the assault divisions landed under cover of a barrage along the beaches; the fleet standing in to give a final battering to the coast artillery casemates and radars; and 2,000 aircraft attacking the defences in depth. The Allies were ashore and from then on never looked like being driven off.

The only hitch occurred on the front of the US V Corps, where all the DD tanks but two foundered in the rough sea and the infantry, checked by heavy fire, lay down on the beach, their morale entirely lost, until late afternoon. Then leadership began to assert itself. Colonel Taylor of the US 1st Division rallied the paralyzed GIs with the repeated call that those who remained on the beach were all going to die: 'Now let's get the hell out of here,' he said and walked off inland, followed by a few brave men. Then by some magic impulsion more and more little groups and then platoons and companies began to follow. By nightfall all the 'Big Red One' was inland and digging in.

By 12 June Montgomery had 326,000 men ashore and the series of battles necessary to put the second half of the plan into action had fairly begun. There was much misunderstanding of this plan, which was Montgomery's own, at the time, and some ill-informed criticism of alleged failure on the part of his troops. In fact, both Montgomery's army group of British, Poles and Canadians and Bradley's Americans fought with great tenacity against the best professional soldiers of modern times, and broke them.

In brief, the questioned strategy was for Montgomery's group to attack on the left, round Caen, where a break-out would spell the greatest danger to the Germans and where they would be expected to mass their reserves. This would ease Bradley's task in the west

Above left : **Men and supplies stream ashore from their landing craft at Gold Beach.** *Above right :* **The invasion of Normandy.** *Right :* **Grim expectancy marks the faces of these American infantry as they wait to come ashore from their landing craft onto the beach.** *Far right above :* **Eisenhower gives some last minute advice to US paratroops.** *Far right below :* **British paratroops synchronise their watches.**

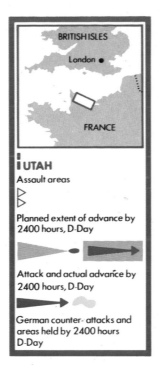

BRITISH ISLES

London

FRANCE

UTAH

Assault areas

Planned extent of advance by 2400 hours, D-Day

Attack and actual advance by 2400 hours, D-Day

German counter- attacks and areas held by 2400 hours D-Day

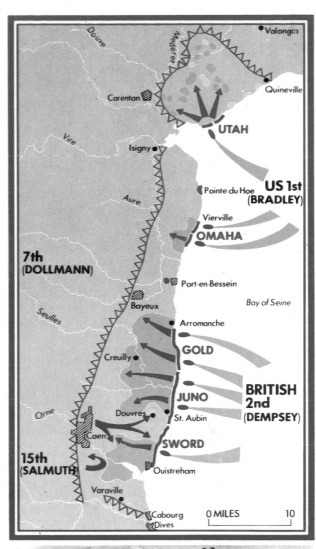

Douve

Médere

Valognes

Carentan

Quineville

UTAH

Vire

Isigny

US 1st
(BRADLEY)

Aure

Pointe du Hoe

Vierville

OMAHA

7th
(DOLLMANN)

Port-en-Bessein

Seulles

Bayeux

Bay of Seine

Arromanche

GOLD

Creully

BRITISH
2nd
(DEMPSEY)

JUNO

Orne

Douvres

St. Aubin

SWORD

Caen

Ouistreham

15th
(SALMUTH)

Varaville

Cabourg

0 MILES   10

Dives

149

where he was battering away at the defence perimeter hemming him in, in order to make a gap for his armoured divisions under Patton to burst out into the open country and the enemy rear. In fact, this is what happened and Montgomery reached the Seine 11 days earlier than he had predicted in his plan.

There were three phases in the series of battles that followed: all on the largest scale. In Africa and Asia the battles involved half a dozen divisions at most; in Italy nine or ten on each side. In France in 1944, the Allies deployed a Canadian, a British, a French and three American armies.

Once the first phase of seizing and expanding the foothold in Normandy was over Montgomery, with overall operational control, commanded his own 21st Army Group (Canadian 1st and British 2nd Armies) and Bradley's 12th Army Group (US 1st and 3rd Armies). The last of these, under the redoubtable George Patton, had been formed in the field during the fighting. Bradley was promoted to 12th Army Group commander from the 1st Army, taken over by Lieutenant-General Courtney Hodges.

On 7 July Montgomery reduced Caen to rubble with heavy bombers (which only served to block the line of advance of his own tanks) and then, on 18 July, tried to drive three armoured divisions down an avenue 3,650 metres (4,000 yards) wide blasted open by more than 5,000 tonnes of bombs dropped by the RAF – Operation Goodwood. Most of this tonnage hit nothing but the soil of France, for conforming to their usual tactics, the Germans' main defence line was several miles in the rear and this mighty hammer blow fell only on their battle outposts. The three armoured divisions found themselves facing an unshaken defence. They lost rather more than half their tanks, mainly to the guns, but the 1st *Panzer* Division claimed 80 destroyed in counterattacks using their new Panther tanks. This was rough going, but the British and Canadians had by 29 June attracted four *Panzer* divisions to their sector.

After a pause imposed by storms which turned the whole Normandy battlefield into mud, Montgomery kept up the pressure on the left by repeated sledgehammer blows against the yielding, but still unbroken, fence of guns and tanks facing the 21st Army Group.

Then, on 25 July, Bradley struck the decisive blow of the second phase, from St Lô to the west, to capture Coutances. It was on the same pattern as Goodwood with massive air support, but larger and on a wider front. The air bombardment included 1,500 heavy and 400 medium bombers, but the main effort was made by infantry supported by tanks, with hundreds of fighter-bombers acting as close support flying artillery. These were linked to the forward battalions by radio, using the new techniques for air–ground co-operation, and as soon as the tanks or infantry ran into opposition the aircraft were in action within a few minutes.

On 1 August Patton's 3rd Army was able to break through south of Coutances to begin the third phase, of open warfare. He cleared

enough of Brittany to remove any threat from the remaining German garrisons there, and then, on Bradley's orders on 4 August, swung his axis from south-west to due east: for Paris. This was, perhaps, a strategic error. The correct objective was to trap the German 7th Army, now about to be encircled from the left, while its right was still gripped by yet another Montgomery power-drive which was to take the British to Villers-Bocage. (The American commanders had made the same mistake, of being seduced by the prestige of liberating a great capital, which had led to Clark's dash for Rome, allowing the German 10th Army to escape Alexander's trap two months before.) Fortunately for the Allies, at this point Hitler took charge.

On 29 July, when von Rundstedt advised the *Führer* that the Battle of the Beach-head was lost and the moment had arrived to retreat and establish a new defence line, running north and south along the Seine, he was sacked. Rommel had been wounded, and the new commander was Field-Marshal Günther-Hans von Kluge, a good professional like all the German generals, but lacking the nerve necessary to stand up to Hitler.

That great strategist saw a peculiar picture on his battle-map. From the eastern end of the semi-circular bulge marking the Allied perimeter a long narrow tentacle began to appear curling first south and then east and growing daily. This was not of course a soft limb, but a phalanx of 3rd Army tanks. 'Some goddamned fool once said that flanks must be secured,' said the flamboyant Patton to his commanders, 'and ever since sons of bitches all over the world have gone crazy over their flanks. We don't want any of that in the Third Army: flanks are something for the enemy to worry about, not us.' Patton was a braggart, but one who made his brags good, as von Kluge was to discover. Hitler's orders to him were to advance into the loop and cut the tentacle off at its root at Avranches. Von Kluge dutifully assembled six divisions, including 250 tanks, all clearly visible to Allied air reconnaissance, and launched them, fatally, so that the head of the force was jammed between the expanding bridgehead and Patton's army. At this moment Montgomery ordered the Canadians to attack southward to Falaise and Patton to swing one of his corps north to meet it, so the German counter-offensive was now threatened in its rear. Von Kluge asked permission to withdraw, but was refused and ordered to press on to Avranches. The German 7th Army was now crammed into a narrow corridor 64.5 km (40 miles) long, tanks and vehicles blocking the roads three abreast: a perfect target for the air forces who proceeded to massacre them. Meanwhile, the Canadians and Poles fought their way towards Falaise and Patton's XV Corps captured Argentan 15 miles away. Fighting as German soldiers always did, the 2nd *Panzer* Division, against heavy odds and bombarded from the air, threw back the Canadians and held the gap open just long enough to enable some thousands of men to escape the trap,

Top: **American paratroops, destined for a hard time in Normandy, prepare to move by Douglas C-47.** *Above:* **Part of the myth of Germany's impregnable anti-invasion defences was fostered by propaganda photographs of large-calibre coastal guns in vast concrete emplacements. In fact there were relatively few of these.** *Right:* **After a number of precarious days in the beach-head area, the Allies moved steadily inland.** *Above right:* **USAAF C-47 transports line an airfield during the preparations for launching the airborne side of the D-day landings.**

but the bulk of 15 divisions and 2,000 tanks and vehicles were destroyed in the greatest *débâcle* of modern military history. The Battle of Normandy was over and the pursuit began. Montgomery and Bradley turned left and westward to trap the remaining German divisions against the Seine, while Patton raced for Paris, and beyond.

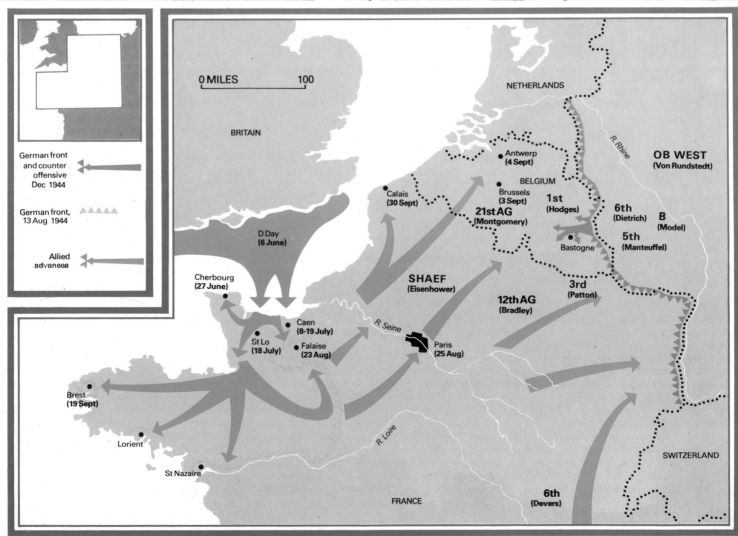

German front
and counter
offensive
Dec 1944

German front,
13 Aug 1944

Allied
advance

0 MILES   100

BRITAIN

NETHERLANDS

Antwerp
(4 Sept)

Calais
(30 Sept)

BELGIUM

Brussels
(3 Sept)

21st AG
(Montgomery)

1st
(Hodges)

6th
(Dietrich)

5th
(Manteuffel)

B
(Model)

OB WEST
(Von Rundstedt)

R. Rhine

Bastogne

D Day
(6 June)

Cherbourg
(27 June)

SHAEF
(Eisenhower)

3rd
(Patton)

12th AG
(Bradley)

Caen
(8-19 July)

R. Seine

St Lo
(18 July)

Falaise
(23 Aug)

Paris
(25 Aug)

Brest
(19 Sept)

R. Loire

Lorient

St Nazaire

SWITZERLAND

FRANCE

6th
(Devers)

151

Dragoon

IT has been mentioned in the chapters on the campaign in Italy that the Allies, not without heated and prolonged argument, had decided not to exploit Field-Marshal Sir Harold Alexander's victories in Italy; but rather to withdraw as many divisions from that theatre as possible, including all the French troops there and in North Africa, and open a new front in southern France. This was to be called Operation Dragoon.

On the purely political side the Americans were adamant that neither their forces nor those, like the French, built up with American resources, were to become involved in any far-flung adventures into central Europe. As far as the French were concerned their hearts were fully committed to the liberation of their own soil, and no other. On the

Far left: **An American armoured unit, equipped with Sherman tanks, moves up to its embarkation point for Operation Dragoon.** *Above:* **American infantry stream ashore during the landings in the south of France.** *Left:* **As in the Normandy landings, the assault in the south was preceded by an airborne operation, though this one was successful and carried out in full daylight. As the Allies approached their main objectives German resistance stiffened.**

strategic side, General Dwight D Eisenhower's plan made sense. Firstly, by mid-August (the earliest Dragoon could be mounted) the German last-ditch garrisons still held the Atlantic ports in western France and the two northern Allied army groups were still being maintained across the Normandy beaches. If Toulon and Marseilles could be seized intact then the situation would be eased and divisions still standing idle in the United States could be ferried over to join in the fight. Secondly, the quickest way to end the war was to destroy the German armies defending their western frontier, and this is where the maximum force was to be concentrated.

Ideally, Dragoon should have coincided with Overlord, but there were not enough landing and other craft. It was not until 15 August that three divisions of Lieutenant-General Alexander M Patch's US 7th Army assaulted the stretch of coast extending from the east of Toulon to St Raphael. The following day the leading divisions of the French 1st Army, commanded by General Jean Marie Gabriel de Lattre de Tassigny, landed near St Tropez with the mission of capturing and clearing the two ports.

De Lattre's initial status was a corps commander under Patch, but, once his mission was achieved, he would separate to lead his army as its full complement came ashore and his French 1st and the US 7th Armies would form the 6th Army Group under Lieutenant-General Jacob L Devers. Devers's axis of advance was to be northwards towards Grenoble and Belfort and then swinging to the east it would form a front with General Omar Bradley's 12th Army Group.

The opposition faced by Dragoon was numerically formidable, consisting as it did of Colonel-General Johannes von Blaskowitz's Army Group G with 11 divisions. However, these divisions were all of poor quality, and largely occupied in ferreting out the 'resistance' – officially the 'French Forces of the Interior' (FFI) – and could maintain only a thin defence of possible invasion beaches. Twenty-four battalions were of Soviet prisoners of war, mostly Ukrainians and Georgians who, for various reasons, had turned their coats. Von Blaskowitz could not stand up to the blow aimed at him by Patch, and the German Supreme High Command (OKW), for once, wisely chose to cut its losses and run. Von Blaskowitz was ordered to leave strong garrisons in Marseilles and Toulon, in order to deny them to the Allies for as long as possible, and to withdraw his main body northwards thus concentrating the remaining German forces on the defence of the *Reich*.

Dragoon was a text book success; an amphibious operation exercise embodying every lesson learned to date and launched with every refinement of tactics and equipment. Four hundred aircraft dropped a combined American/British airborne division, to control the road network by which any counter-attack forces might reach the beach-head. This was to be established by the US 3rd, 45th and 1st Divisions, supported by the 36th Division and Combat Command No 1 of the French 1st Armoured Division, all covered by a powerful air force and preceded by a tremendous naval bombardment. Among the spectators of the landings was Winston Churchill, who had fought so long and hard to prevent Dragoon taking place at all. He sent a congratulatory telegram to Eisenhower, who had had to bear the burden of standing up to him and who was now deeply gratified.

Patch wasted no time. He sent his VI Corps off post-haste on two axes to hurry the German rearguards along: the left through Avignon and up the Rhône valley, and the right along the *Route Napoléon* through Digne and Grenoble. The FFI had been called out, and it was important that they should not be exposed too long to counter-attack, having engaged the withdrawing German columns with only light weapons. As it was, the resistance leader Cammaerts with two companions, was captured, and only escaped the firing squad through the inspired protests of 'Pauline', the celebrated Christine Granville, who kept their captors dithering with threats and arguments until the timely arrival of the Americans.

De Lattre's original orders were to await the concentration of his forces, which were

likely to be complete by about D-day plus 10, and then embark on the serious business of breaking into Toulon. This looked like being a costly affair. The port was held by some 25,000 troops ensconced in a ring of 30 forts of old vintage but proof against all but the heaviest weapons, and more modern defences based on earthworks and pill-boxes. A deliberate assault with maximum force was required, but to give a German commander ten whole days to improve his defences further seemed unwise to de Lattre if it could be avoided. It happened that the initial landing had gone so smoothly and the turn-round of the ships had been so rapid that the build-up was much faster than expected. De Lattre was an exceptionally able commander, and, like all his troops, burning to get to grips with the enemy who had so humiliated them four years before. (He was also a cavalryman, full of the cavalry spirit, and not inappropriately an old 12 Dragoon.) He decided not to wait, and exerting his full powers of persuasion, which were considerable, obtained the permission of Patch and Devers to begin his operation on 20 August, five days ahead of schedule.

De Lattre had under his command and, as yet, incomplete, the 1st Free French Division (de Brosset), the 3rd Algerian Division (de Goislard de Monsabert), the 9th Colonial Division (Magnan) and the 1st Armoured Division (du Vigier). All these commanders had plenty of dash, but exercised with considerable tactical skill. The French colonial infantry were adept at operating in broken country, and intimate knowledge of the topography of their own country told them that the range of hills inland running parallel to the coast, north of Hyères all the way to Marseilles, offered the most difficult, the most unlikely and therefore the most promising approach; just as General Juin had perceived that the rugged route through the Gothic Line had been the most promising.

Accordingly de Lattre sent Monsabert, a Gascon, reinforced by a *tabor* (squadron) of *goumiers*, in a wide sweeping movement round the north and west of Toulon. The *goumiers* were the lethal, semi-regular Moroccan infantry enlisted by the French and who were allowed to wear their own dress and fight in their own way, specializing in reconnaissance and infiltration. For guile, stratagem and ferocity they had no equals, except possibly the Pathan mountaineers of the Indian North-West Frontier.

Du Vigier, still lacking one combat command, was sent off on an even wider encircling movement outside Monsabert to protect his right flank (no one knew at this moment of the total extent of the German withdrawal) and to hook in south and west of Marseilles. Patch had agreed to release his other combat command as soon as it could be disengaged, and this was to intervene in the main battles in the centre.

De Brosset, reinforced by French Commando troops, moved directly on the axis Hyères–Toulon. The 9th Division would be attached between the 3rd and the Free French as it disembarked, its units marching

without a pause into action.

The speed with which de Lattre developed his manoeuvre was astonishing. The German units may have been of doubtful quality, but the Free French had to do some hard fighting for Hyères. Three strong forts on commanding heights outside Toulon were taken only at the cost of severe casualties, by the divisional reconnaissance regiment – which was not its proper job – and the Commandos, on 22 August. In one of the forts, 250 German dead were counted. The reconnaissance regiment then slipped through the ring of pill-boxes and strongpoints into the city centre. De Magnan went forward to see where to introduce his leading troops and came back to spur them on with the succinct and

Left : **The French acquired a considerable reputation for street fighting during the operations in southern France and also during the advance up the Rhone and over to the Rhine.**
Above : **Allied operations in the Mediterranean included the liberation of the island of Corsica. A Corsican soldier examines a piece of artillery abandoned by the Germans as they pulled out.**

typically French order: 'Come along! I have kissed at least 200 girls already!' An intensely confused situation then began to develop inside the city, with the badly shaken Germans holding on while de Magnan's men surrounded them; their precise positions being pointed out by delirious bands of French civilians and the FFI, while bullets and kisses flew about in equal numbers. De Magnan was given the task of mopping up the port and, on 26 August, the last strongholds surrendered and Toulon was free.

Encouraged by this success and divining that the two things he must avoid were to check the *élan* of his troops or to give his opponents time, de Lattre without waiting to consolidate decided to attack Marseilles

immediately. He disengaged de Brosset and sent him together with the 1st Armoured Division's Combat Command No 1 (Sudre) to join Monsabert, reinforcing him with more *goumiers* as they arrived. He then ordered the commanders to close in on a given line surrounding the city and not commit themselves, except for reconnaissance, until he could assess the situation. This was achieved by 23 August.

Marseilles was defended by German marines, the 244th Infantry Division and a jumble of units who had been scattered from the beach-head area by the shock of the US VI Corps landing, and 200 assorted guns. In the old days to evict such a German garrison from a city in house-to-house fighting might have taken weeks, but with the whole population of the city against them and every street or suburban road on the perimeter offering a route for infiltration, and with scores of FFI squads harassing them, the German position was untenable. Nevertheless, de Lattre was right to pause momentarily to regroup. He had, apart from his task of reducing Marseilles, to cover the left flank of the US VI Corps and as an army commander he had to be thinking even further ahead and poising his troops for the pursuit northward; for which he had to assemble his 1st Armoured Division, less the tanks for the attack on Marseilles.

All this was very well planned and the French staff work appears to have been both prompt and accurate. As it turned out, but happily enough, the forward troops did not take the slightest notice. Supported by the FFI, one combat team of Sudre's tanks and motor infantry, plus a battalion of Monsabert's Algerians, penetrated into the heart of the city and started to wreak havoc. In a short time they were up against the inner defences of the dock area, the ultimate objective of the whole operation. On the outside, the remainder of the 3rd Division with two more *tabors* of *goumiers* were steadily reducing the concrete defences outside the city. Fortunately the fortresses were stronger than the defenders, although the Algerians and the *goumiers*, without the benefit of prolonged or heavy bombardment, suffered severe casualties in clearing them. De Lattre, with his memories of World War I, compared the fighting in severity with the assaults on the forts at Verdun.

Monsabert's own behaviour was hardly to be approved of by any staff college, but was typical of the Gascon character. At the earliest possible moment, he himself entered the city and established his HQ right inside it where, de Lattre complained, he had to crawl part of the way under fire if he wished to visit his divisional commander. From this point Monsabert was able to establish contact with the German garrison commander, and after the French had carried the main defences covering the docks persuaded him to surrender on 27 August. Marseilles thus fell one whole month ahead of schedule.

The subsequent exploits of the French 1st Army were equally distinguished, but form part of the story of the final defeat of the armies of the Third *Reich* by the Allied forces under Eisenhower.

Pursuit to the Siegfried Line

BY 1 September the whole German defence system in the West had been blown to fragments. The troops who had survived the catastrophe at Falaise had been scattered, and had lost most of their remaining equipment in a vain attempt to hold the line of the Seine river, which the Allied armies had crossed with great dash. Hitler had sacked the luckless von Kluge, who had shot himself, and his replacement, the tough, competent, Nazi-orientated Field-Marshal Walther Model,

had no option but to rally what troops he had and try to organize the defence of the frontiers of the *Reich*. The *Westwall*, the so-called 'Siegfried Line', was unmanned and many of its guns had been removed for use in the East. The western frontier of Germany, in fact, was wide open and professional German opinion is quite firm that had the Allies mounted a rapid armoured thrust of some 15 divisions without delay, they could have been through the *Westwall* and over the Rhine in the autumn of 1944; and the war might have

been over that year, with the saving of thousands of lives. There is no doubt that this is what the Germans themselves would have done.

Why Eisenhower did not attempt it has since been the subject of debate. Whatever the verdict, the facts are all well known. The first, mental, obstacle was that astonishingly the Allied planners had given no thought to what should be done after breaking out of the Normandy bridgehead: there was no 'master plan' agreed in advance. Their unexpected

Above : **A British infantryman takes advantage of the natural cover provided by a knocked-out German tank during the push towards the Siegfried Line. The feet of a dead German sniper can be seen in the foreground.**
Far right : **Men of the US 7th Army outside one of the Maginot Line forts adapted for use by the Germans against attack from the west. The forts were of little more use than they had been to the French.**

early success had taken all the Allied generals by surprise. As if it were by common agreement, all the armies swung east or north-east and advanced as best they could. On 1 September the Canadian 1st Army was driving up the Channel coast (and affording great relief to the south coast towns in England by overrunning the V-2 launching sites); the British 2nd Army was racing for Brussels; the US 1st Army was some 130 km (80 miles) beyond Paris; and Patton with his pearl-handled six-shooters and triumphant 3rd Army was as far forward as Verdun, his eyes on the *Westwall* and the Rhine beyond. The US 7th Army and the newly formed French 1st Army had advanced some 320 km (200 miles) north from their landing sites in the French Riviera. This was a satisfactory picture in the eyes of General Dwight D Eisenhower, who had at this point assumed full control of all operations and had relegated General Sir Bernard Montgomery to the limited command of his own army group. Eisenhower favoured a broad advance, so

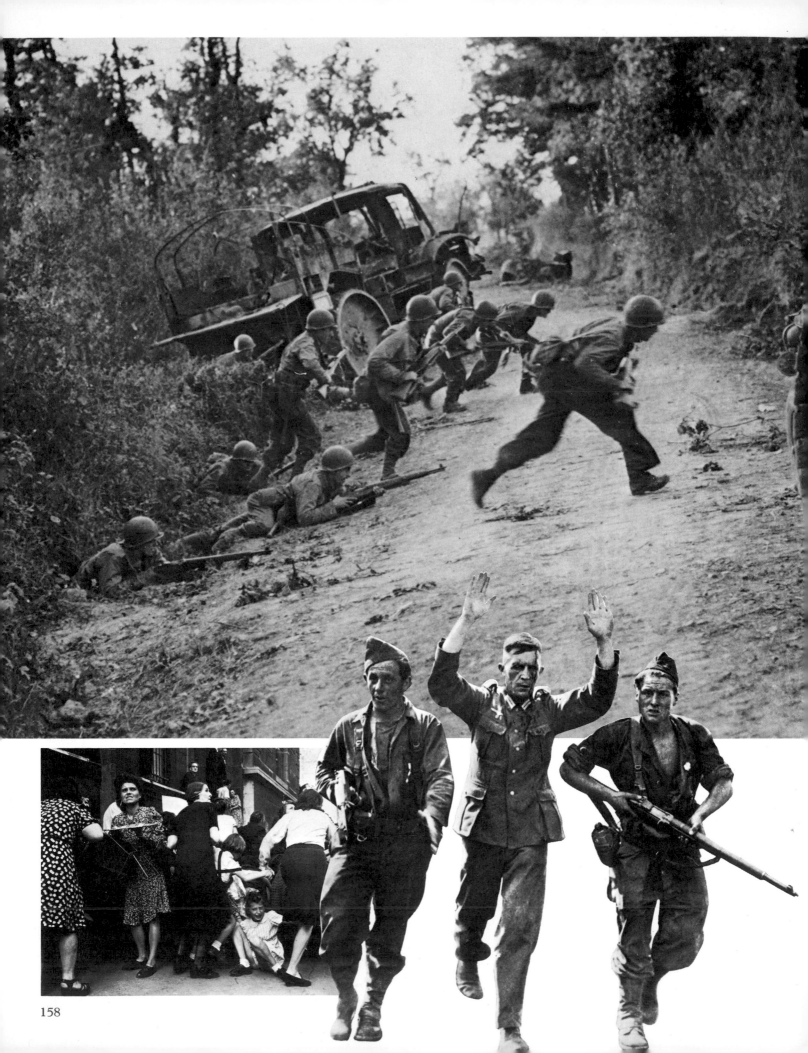

Above: **Mindful of the possibility of German snipers, American infantry double across a road past the wreckage of a knocked-out German Panther tank. The Germans proved to be masters of defensive fighting, but the speed of the Allied advance took them completely by surprise.** *Far left:* **French civilians dive for cover from German snipers after the arrival of General de Gaulle.** *Left:* **A German is captured during the street battle for Paris.**

that all his divisions might exert their full force; their flanks secure as they spread across France like a flooding tide. The immediate difficulty he faced was that, partly as a result of winning the battle of Normandy 11 days ahead of schedule, the necessary ports had not yet been captured and cleared.

Therefore the supply for his vast armies had still to come via the 'Mulberry' harbours, over the beaches and then up the lines of communication by lorry, for the Allied *blitz* which had totally wrecked the French railway system also, of course, effectively denied it to the Allies. To give some idea of the logistic task, Eisenhower had 2,250,000 mouths to feed (about two-thirds the present population of Israel or New Zealand) and find petrol for nearly 450,000 vehicles, of which some 5,000 were front-line battle tanks. An ordinary division at 'contact rates', that is, fighting the enemy with maximum effort, required 406 tonnes of supplies, petrol and munitions a day, and an armoured division 900.

As the communications lengthened, the supply lorries themselves began to eat up supplies on an increasing scale: it was a complicated calculation. Inevitably, therefore, either units not needed for the pursuit had to be grounded and the available supplies trucked forward to small, spearhead formations, or the whole advance slowed down. If the advance slowed down the German general staff, always reacting fast in an emergency, would have time to consolidate the defence of the German frontier before the pursuing forces could arrive. The answer was simple; to carry it out fraught with difficulties.

Montgomery argued vehemently that the northern route was strategically the most important (which was correct) and that the best course was to concentrate all resources on it for a swift major advance. However, this meant stopping the US 1st and 3rd Armies, an action which was politically impossible. The fact is that it is remarkable that the Anglo-American alliance worked as smoothly as it did, for grass-roots public opinion in the United States remained stubbornly anti-British throughout the war. The verdict on Eisenhower is that he was both an excellent supreme commander and a selfless one, but however good the strategic arguments (with which, in fact, he did not wholly agree), he could not afford to halt his American armies and give a British general the honour of carrying the ball to the goal-line.

Moreover, the chickens of Sicily had come home to roost. Bradley's and Patton's violent dislike and contempt for Montgomery had increased. They saw his plan simply as a trick to grab all the limelight. Patton was determined to press on, and gave Eisenhower the choice of either halting or even recalling him, or of keeping him supplied. Even a supreme commander could not override two such powerful subordinates, and the best he could do was to give the northern front priority.

This situation was aggravated by an ongoing and abrasive argument between Montgomery and Eisenhower over the command control system. Montgomery bluntly indicated that Eisenhower could not control the battles from his headquarters at Granville hundreds of kilometres behind the fighting: he should appoint a land forces commander operating from a command post well forward, and it was clear that Montgomery

wanted this post for himself.

While the armies were advancing and the high command was distracted with these dissensions and the acute problem of supply, it was guilty of another astonishing omission. The key to solving the supply problem of the northern sector was to capture the port of Antwerp and all the routes to it as soon as possible, but this was entirely overlooked. Montgomery himself was intent on another expedient to accelerate his advance, which was to use the airborne armies lying idle in England to clear the network of river obstacles ahead of him, as far as the bridge at Arnhem; the operation to take place in mid-September.

In the meantime the German defences began to take shape and resistance to stiffen. German morale had somehow managed to survive the worst shocks of the war, but by July 1944, the generals at least had seen that the game was up. Von Rundstedt, always outspoken, was asked at the crisis of the Normandy battle by one of Hitler's entourage what should be done? 'Make peace, you idiots,' was his reply. Unfortunately any hope that the winter battles could be avoided by a collapse of the German will to resist was destroyed by the publication of the Morgenthau plan, which condemned Germany to death as a nation: large portions of German territory were to be surrendered on the east and west; Germany was to be partitioned; her heavy industries and mines were to be destroyed physically; German slave labour was to be used to make good the ravages of war in the occupied countries; and what was left was to be converted to dependence on agriculture. The call for unconditional surrender was a double-edged weapon: now the Germans knew exactly what it meant. It was one of the great miscalculations of the war. Evil as the Nazis and the Nazi system were, the ordinary German soldiers were patriotic and considered military courage and refusal to admit defeat a supreme virtue, and they all determined to fight on until the bitter end. The results were soon apparent.

The Allied armies had some enjoyable weeks of motoring through France with an occasional skirmish, amid kisses from the girls and cheers and drinks from the men, and a rain of flowers in place of armour-piercing shot. They were then brought abruptly to a halt.

The *Westwall* was not a 'line' like the Maginot Line (or the Bar-Lev Line along the Suez Canal). The Germans were great artists in defence in depth, to use the technical term: each position was covered by more behind, and backing these up were more parties of troops ready to counterattack and drive successful intruders out. Into this the Americans had to batter a way, bit by bit, with heavy artillery. In Holland the 21st Army Group was held up by the maze of defended waterways. The last shot in the locker was to be Market Garden, the great airborne operation, but it was to be too late. The Allies had lost the race to the frontiers and the 'watch on the Rhine' was established. A whole series of costly battles lay ahead.

Arnhem

FIELD-MARSHAL Sir Bernard Montgomery's perhaps extravagant hopes of being given the troops and logistic support for a huge drive in the north had been dashed by General Dwight D Eisenhower's decision to advance across the whole Allied front, but he was not a man who gave up easily. His goal was the Ruhr, the heart of the German war industry, and there were two routes to it. One ran due east, which would mean a bloody battle of attrition to breach the *Westwall* or 'Siegfried Line'. The other ran north-north-east, in the direction of Arnhem. The Siegfried Line defences ended near Cleve, and if Arnhem with its great road bridge over the Rhine could be secured the wall could be outflanked.

The northern route would not be any easier. Holland was the worst possible terrain for armoured mechanized fighting: flat, low-lying, wet and cut up by a network of dykes and drainage ditches. To reach the lower Rhine at Arnhem it was first necessary to cross three wide navigation canals and the Maas and Waal rivers. One option was as unattractive as the other for ground operations, but there was lying idle in England the whole Allied 1st Airborne Army, fretting at its lack of activity since D-day. No fewer than 17 plans to employ bits of it had been made and cancelled, because the objectives had been overrun by the ground forces, or later on, like the one code-named 'Comet', because the weather had deteriorated and German resistance had stiffened. Comet's objective had been Nijmegen and Arnhem, but proposed to use only a reinforced division.

Montgomery now revived this plan on a grand scale, renamed 'Market Garden'. His forward troops were up to the line of the Meuse–Escaut Canal, 110 km (70 miles) from Arnhem. The new plan was to drop a whole airborne corps. The US 101st Airborne Division would seize and hold the bridges over the Wilhelmina Canal at Son and the Willemswart at Veghel, the US 82nd the bridges over the Maas at Graye and the Waal at Nijmegen, and the British 1st the bridge at Arnhem. This was Operation Market. At the same time the British XXX Corps would drive up the road through Eindhoven which connected all these points, the Guards Armoured Division leading, and join up with the lightly armed airborne troops as rapidly as possible: Operation Garden. This armoured advance was absolutely essential for success, as the strength of airborne forces lay in the surprise of their sudden descent, and their weakness in lack of heavy weapons, especially for prolonged defence against tanks. This applied with most force to the British at the last bridge of all; 'a bridge

Above : **A 3-inch mortar of the 6th Airborne Division fires on the Germans in the outskirts of Arnhem.**
Above right : **Part of an Airspeed Horsa glider's load of 28 airborne soldiers troop aboard its aircraft.** *Right :* **British paratroops sway down towards a landing zone already littered with the discarded aircraft of the initial glider landings, unopposed by the Germans.**
Far right : **As swift to react as usual, German armour and infantry, mostly of SS origins, moved into Arnhem to contain the British airborne troops.**

too far' as the British Lieutenant-General F A M Browning, commanding I Airborne Corps and no pessimist or defeatist, prophetically called it. There were indeed those who argued that the whole operation was too risky, but it was agreed by all responsible that it must go on. Planning had gone too far, the morale of the troops would be in danger if they were not used, and in any case the conduct of war is nothing but a choice between dangers. Great strategic rewards demand great tactical risks.

The tactical risks at Arnhem were clear enough. Airborne troops, most experts believed, should be dropped in the dark, to obtain surprise, and as close to their objectives as possible, if not on top of them. For various reasons, the most cogent being that the RAF firmly believed that the Arnhem area was strongly defended by AA artillery, the assault was made by day, and the dropping zones for the paratroops and the landing zone for the gliders chosen was 13 km (8 miles) from the vital bridge: the pace of a heavily loaded infantryman on his feet, be it noted, is at best 4 kph (2.5 mph). Three hours is too much time to give gratuitously to an enemy famous for rapid and aggressive reaction, from generals to corporals. All the same, had Major-General R E Urquhart, commanding the 1st Airborne Division, been able to implement his plan all might yet have been well. He proposed to put one whole brigade in close defence of the bridge and three more round it in a solid defence perimeter, and with some 10,000 *élite* infantry supported by light artillery and anti-tank guns (the adequate British 57-mm 6-pdr) dug in and ensconced in houses he would have taken a deal of shifting even by the best troops. Unfortunately, the lack of aircraft imposed a three-day build-up on 17, 18 and 19 September, by which time the hornet's nest was fully stirred up and only one battalion of the whole force had been able to reach its objective.

Even these self-imposed handicaps might have been overcome but for the date. The third week in September was too late, and it was not only a question of the weather. All the battlefield intelligence showed that the efforts of Field-Marshal Walther Model of Army Group B to reinvigorate the shattered German troops and man the *Westwall* were succeeding. Everywhere resistance was stiffening. The most serious problem was that the II SS *Panzer* Corps – 9th and 10th SS *Panzer* Divisions, commanded by the able General Willi Bittrich – were actually in the Arnhem area resting and re-equipping. (This fact was known to at least some Allied intelligence agencies, but how or why it came to be disregarded is too long and complex a question to discuss here.)

On the German side there had been much discussion about the next possible move by the Allies, but no firm plans had been made. It proved enough to have, in the area, Model in overall command, Colonel-General Kurt Student, himself a paratrooper, in command of the sector, and Bittrich, with their HQs in the vicinity of the drops. All acted imme-

diately, and their speed was matched by that of the ordinary German soldiers, who were schooled, whether *Panzergrenadiers* or office clerks, to seize their weapons and throw themselves into action at once, without panic or even doubt, under the first leader who rallied them. (Twenty riflemen, a tank and a gun crew became an instant combat team by some magic; it was the great secret of German success in battle.) German officers were expected to behave as the situation demanded without asking permission or waiting for orders. II SS *Panzer* Corps was therefore immediately appropriated; Student called up some parachute *Kampfgruppen* (*ad hoc* battle-groups, being built up into regular divisions) from the Cologne area, and kidnapped an infantry division that happened to be passing by train through his sector to another command. In a very short time the German defences were being mobilized and local counterattacks being mounted. A series of misfortunes were about to fall upon the luckless 1st Airborne Division which no amount of heroism could overcome.

The first of these was to find a stop-line made up from the youths of an SS *Panzergrenadier* training battalion in their way. Behind this was another battle-group from the 9th *Panzer* Division's infantry with some light armoured vehicles, while another was forming up and a third moving post haste to the road bridge. The airborne troops were therefore involved in precisely the kind of operation for which they were not fitted: a deliberate infantry attack on a strong all-arms force, without benefit of tank co-operation and the massive artillery support the best of troops require in modern warfare. All the same, the redoubtable Lieutenant-Colonel J D Frost managed to fight his way with most of his 2nd Parachute Battalion to the Arnhem road bridge, and held on there.

The second misfortune was that far away to the south the Germans found, on the corpse of an American officer killed in a crashed glider, an operation order outlining the entire plan. Thus in hours Student and Bittrich knew every move to make and the fog of war, then very dense, became clear. The landing zones near Arnhem thus revealed were soon ringed with AA artillery.

The third was a complete breakdown (possibly technical, due to lack of maintenance and training: the issue is again too complex to discuss here) of the 1st Airborne's radio sets, with the solitary exception of the light regiment of the Royal Artillery. (The Germans, too, had few working radios but they managed exceptionally well with runners, cyclists and the Dutch civil telephone system.) Everyone from Urquhart's HQ down to battalions was out of touch with each other and the air force. Urquhart himself went forward with one brigadier, very correctly, but was unable even to talk back from his own jeep to his own HQ – some 3.5 km (2 miles) – and he himself was caught up in the fighting and could not get back, while the brigadier was wounded. The command system thus disintegrated at this crucial stage of the battle, and the battle itself into a series

of furious, uncoordinated little combats. Only Frost's battalion, less a company, and some divisional troops who had rallied to him, hung on grimly to the area commanding the north end of the unblown Arnhem road bridge. (The rail bridge had gone, blown up in the face of Frost's C Company, who were ordered to take it.)

Meanwhile things had been going successfully, if behind schedule, on the road from the south. The Americans had had a much easier landing; their troubles were to start later when Student's counterattacks began to make themselves felt. By Monday 18 September the 101st Division (the future defenders of Bastogne) had a firm grip on their objectives and had joined hands with the tank battalion of the Irish Guards. Eindhoven was clear. Major-General James Gavin, commanding the 82nd Airborne Division, had the bridge over the Maas at Grave and was fighting hard in Nijmegen for access to the Waal bridge. The Guards' tanks, supported by the guns of XXX Corps and air-strikes, were rolling, but were soon to roll to a stop. It was hardly tank country, as it was impossible to deploy off the roads without bogging, and to make matters worse, the roads ran along high embankments, along which the tanks slid like beads in a shooting gallery to be picked off by the 88-mm anti-tank guns sited to left and right. To make matters more difficult the weather worsened, so that both the re-supply of the Arnhem troops by air and the direct air support to the troops fighting up the road were interrupted. (Given fine weather, of course, the tremendous air superiority of the Allies, combined with the

Above: **A British 17-pounder anti-tank gun guards the approaches to Nijmegen bridge.** *Right:* **Operation Market-Garden was boldly conceived.**

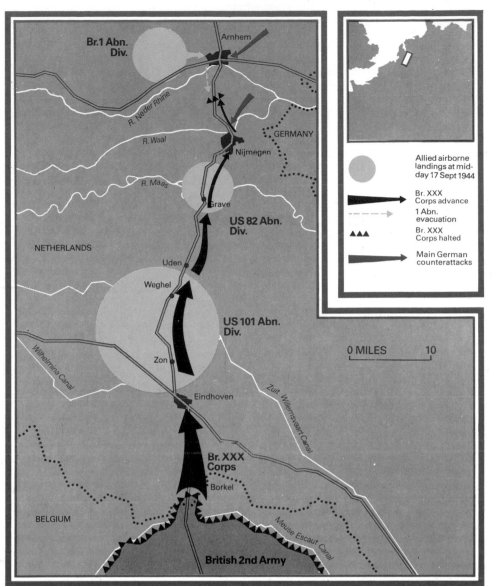

lack of cover in Holland, could have punished the German forces south of the Rhine so severely that a breakthrough to the Arnhem bridge while Frost was still holding on might have been possible; but this must remain conjecture.) It was not until 22 September that after a great combined effort elements of the British 43rd and US 82nd Divisions crossed the Waal and secured the Nijmegen bridge, but on the same day the Guards had to send a brigade back to assist the 101st at Veghel, where it was being attacked from east and west simultaneously. Although the fighting along the corridor was severe, it was overshadowed by the tragedy in Arnhem: the 82nd lost 1,400 men and the 101st over 2,000, and they were to lose another 3,600 between them before the ground taken was finally secured.

In Arnhem close-quarter fighting of an intensity seen nowhere else in the West and probably only equalled in Kohima or at Stalingrad continued unabated although, it must be added, not untempered by chivalry. Urquhart must be the only general officer in the war who killed an opponent with his pistol, and both his paratroop brigadiers were severely wounded. By 19 September it was clear to him that he could not fight his way through to reinforce Frost or take up his planned positions, and he decided to form a close defensive perimeter in the small town of Osterbeek, 6.5 km (4 miles) on the Rhine downstream of Arnhem, with its south face

on the river. If he, and Frost at the northern end of the Arnhem bridge, could hold out in house-to-house fighting there was still a chance that XXX Corps might break through in time, but this hope soon dwindled. Nevertheless, the division fought on. The gallant Poles, after tragic delays, were dropped opposite Osterbeek south of the river, but their mission was hopeless. They suffered heavy casualties on landing, and they could neither cross the river to reinforce Urquhart nor turn south to help open the road, for Bittrich had sent a battalion of *Panzergrenadiers* with a company of Panther tanks to block them.

The situation at the end of a week was that the 9th *Panzer* Division was systematically reducing the Arnhem positions, while the 10th was still blocking the last few miles between XXX Corps and the Arnhem bridge, and both the US airborne divisions were under counterattack from east and west. It soon became clear that the only course was to use the infantry of the 43rd (Wessex) Division to close up to the river bank at Osterbeek and evacuate what was left of Urquhart's men before they were annihilated: they for their part had determined to

fight to the bitter end, but the end was very near.

The division carried out this plan with courage and skill, actually making an assault crossing to the north bank, while the massed guns of XXX Corps put a box barrage round Osterbeek, and the engineers in boats brought out most of the unwounded men of the garrison under intense fire. So intense was the whole level of the fighting and so numerous the acts of gallantry that this fine feat was not seen as very remarkable. Some idea of the nature of the fighting is given by the casualty figures: 1st Airborne lost 6,400 men, of whom 1,200 were killed, while the 9th *Panzer* Division and its reinforcing units lost 3,500. Five Victoria Crosses were awarded to men of the 1st Airborne Division for the week's fighting, four of them posthumously.

Much has been written since that date and there has been much argument about the chances of success and the wisdom of attempting such an operation, but one stark fact remains clear. Market Garden, where the *élite* of four armies met in battle, was unsurpassed for courage and self-sacrifice in any part of World War II.

The Battle of the Ardennes

BACK in 1870 in the war between Prussia and France a cavalry leader called von Bredow led a sacrificial charge that had become one of the cherished traditions of the German Army. Perhaps it was in Hitler's subconscious mind when he planned personally and in great detail his final offensive in the West, codenamed 'Autumn Mist', officially the Battle of the Ardennes and better known as the 'Battle of the Bulge'. On 15 December three German armies crashed into a weakly held sector of the Allied front in a hopeless counter-offensive. By January 28, 1945 they were back on their start line, leaving behind 19,000 dead and having suffered 111,000 wounded, missing or prisoner, and lost hundreds of tanks and assault guns that could never be replaced. It was an astonishing episode, not least because not a single German general involved believed in it, but all executed it with great loyalty and also the military efficiency for which the German general staff were famous.

With regard to timing, Hitler's intuition, always better than his strategy, was perfect. By the end of the year the Allies were mentally balanced between the over-confidence born of their great victories and the unpleasant shock, particularly to the Americans, of what was involved in trying to break into the Siegfried Line. The series of costly battles were reminiscent of the static holocausts of World War I. But breaking in was only a matter of time and resources: the long term assessment was that the German war machine was running down, and that lack of fuel for its *Panzers* alone would prevent anything but a dogged defence for what remained of the war. Some intelligence agencies had noticed some significant troop moves and correctly, as it turned out, predicted an offensive but

not its locality. No notice was taken, and everyone was relaxed with the exception of the unfortunate GIs battering at the Siegfried Line positions. Field-Marshal Montgomery, it is related, was playing golf when the battle started.

Hitler's plan was to repeat the success of the happy year of 1940 and mount a *blitzkrieg* on the least likely and most weakly held part of the Allied front: the Ardennes, a tangle of forests, hills, steep ridges and deep ravines. Three armies under the command of Field-Marshal Model's Army Group B were to take part. The 6th *Panzer* Army (Colonel-General 'Sepp' Dietrich), newly raised, was to make for Liège and Antwerp, the 5th *Panzer* Army (General Hasso von Manteuffel) for a vital communication centre at Bastogne and then to Namur and Brussels, and thence Antwerp, while the 7th (infantry) Army, having broken through, was to swing left to protect von Manteuffel's left from a counterattack from the south. The assembly of tanks, withdrawal of troops from other sectors, stockpiling of ammunition and rail moves were to be made with the utmost secrecy, and so well was this done that the size, scale, direction and axis of the attack were a complete surprise to the Allied commanders. It took them a week to discover what Hitler was up to; at first they thought it only a spoiling attack to hinder Patton's advance towards the Saar. Fortunately Hitler no longer had the resources for war on this scale, nor did he have the men, tanks, aircraft or even fuel. The bulk of the new infantry (grandiosely called *Volksgrenadiers*: 'people's grenadiers') were made up of under-age boys and sick old men. They fought well, but they had not the battlecraft of the vanished generation of 1940 and 1941. Even the once *élite* paratroops were of a low standard. Only the tank crews in their good PzKpfw V Panthers and PzKpfw VI Tigers were up to the old standard, and many of the junior officers and sergeants, bred in the old German tradition, were full of the attacking spirit.

The strangest element of the German plan was a raid, led by one Otto Skorzeny who had rescued Mussolini back in 1943. Groups of German troops, preferably English-speaking and dressed in British or American uniforms, in captured jeeps and with Allied weapons, were to intrude into the rear areas to commit mayhem and generally spread alarm and con-

fusion. The raid proved a farce and had no real effect apart from the annoyance caused by American identification procedures. (One zealous sergeant asked Lieutenant-General Omar Bradley who Betty Grable's husband was.) What was to upset the Allied high command was the sudden onslaught by 12 infantry and 9 *Panzer* divisions, totalling some 700 tanks and supported by 2,000 field guns. This blow was to fall on a thin screen of some nine infantry regiments (27 battalions, say 20,000 men) backed by a single armoured division spread out over 100 miles of front, a front, moreover, very easy to infiltrate. It was not in military terms a proper defensive position at all, but a line of outposts which would normally be used to screen a 'main line of resistance'.

The troops themselves were either resting, like the 4th Infantry Division, terribly mauled in the recent fighting along the Siegfried Line, and becoming acclimatized, or grass-green and half-trained, like the 106th Infantry Division fresh from the USA. The weather was bitterly cold and the day's work was mostly spent in learning how to live comfortably in the field; the night's in unenthusiastic patrolling. Sickness rates were high. Much of the equipment, especially the vital radio sets, were out of order and under repair. Altogether the two corps of the US 1st Army in the sector were unready, morally and physically, for a full scale battle.

Early in the morning of 16 December the American forward posts came under a violent bombardment in the dark and prevailing fog, followed by a major assault. As might be expected in any army in such a posture and against such an opponent, there was panic, the front was broken in many places, some troops leapt into their vehicles and bolted to the rear, guns were abandoned and many men surrendered; but the majority, some seasoned troops, some in their first action, fought so hard and so well that it was they who actually won the battle. Americans do not like dwelling on apparent failure, and regarding the opening moves as somewhat disgraceful, they naturally are prouder of the all-American victory which ended the affair. However, the way their 1st Army, told to stay put and fight, stopped Army Group B in its tracks for vital hours and days was one of the finest feats in US military history.

It is the reaction to a set-back, with communications cut and confusion and disaster everywhere, that is the real test of any army, and this the Americans passed with honours. Typical of the many small combats that go to make up the fabric of a great battle was the

Left: Obersturmbannführer **Jochen Peiper of the** *Waffen-***SS spearheaded the German thrust in the Ardennes.** *Right:* **Bastogne, defended by the 101st Airborne Division, after the battle.**

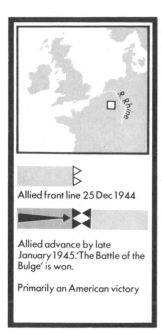

Allied front line 25 Dec 1944

Allied advance by late
January 1945. The Battle of the
Bulge' is won.

Primarily an American victory

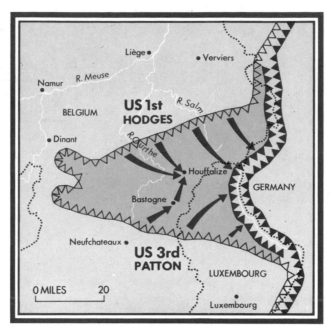

defence of Holtzhum where the *Volks-grenadiers* were repulsed by one American AA half-track, whose crew commander had the nerve to beckon them up as if he were part of their reconnaissance and then shot them to pieces with a quadruple .5-inch machine-gun; or the 25 men of a local HQ who sallied out to make a successful counter-attack; or the single platoon at another post at Walhausen who ended by calling their artillery fire down on their own position as they were overrun and of whom only one man survived. At Berdorf another platoon held out for four days. At Buchholz railway station the men of a company of 1/394th Infantry, in reserve well behind the lines, were in the 'chow-line' queuing for their breakfast when, to their astonishment, a company of *Volks-grenadiers* appeared out of the fog marching in column down the railway line. The Americans were alert, and dropping their mess-tins and grasping their rifles they killed 75 of the Germans. Forty men of the 99th Infantry Division, another 'green' formation, restored their position with a bayonet charge, a very rare thing in modern warfare. On the same front, the assaulting infantry broke through even after being terribly mangled by riflemen and anti-tank guns only to be re-pelled point blank by the artillery. The romantically named 38th Cavalry, a recon-naissance unit not equipped for static defence, inflicted hundreds of casualties and stood its ground.

In bits and pieces, counterattacking where they could and hanging on grimly where they could not, the Americans held points vital in terrain offering little opportunity for cross-country tank manoeuvre: the cross-roads, bridges and communication centres. St Vith and Houffalize held out for long enough and Bastogne, where six roads meet, never fell. Its siege is a famous page in history, and Brigadier-General McAuliffe's barrack-room phrase used to refuse a formal invitation to surrender is now a legend.

The result of all this was that the whole time-tale of Autumn Mist was delayed,

and every hour and day that passed allowed the massive resources of Bradley's army group to be redirected and positioned for a massive counter-stroke.

All the same, the picture as seen from command posts of the Allied armies was enough to cause great dismay. There was a great shortage of information and no one knew how well the fragments of the 1st Army were still fighting. What seemed ominous was that the Ardennes front had been blown wide open, and both ominous and mortifying was the fact that US soldiers were being actually outfought and, worse, surrendering in droves. The 28th Infantry Division was a write-off and the luckless 106th lost its two forward regiments in what the Germans called a 'kettle' (*Kessel*), the Americans a 'sack'. They were encircled and tamely rounded up inside a thin cordon of the enemy. All the back areas with their rich stocks of food, munitions and petrol seemed wide open to capture (but one brave Belgian cap-tain guarding a dump used the petrol to fuel a barrier of flame as a successful roadblock). The winter weather in the mountains – snow, sleet, low cloud and fog – from the first day of the battle onward had grounded the Allies' most potent weapon: their fighter-bombers. Command decisions were difficult to take, because the wedge driven into the Ardennes cut off Lieutenant-General Courtney Hodges and most of his 1st Army from Bradley's 12th Army Group HQ and Patton's 3rd Army in the south.

Eisenhower at once saw the correct solu-tion and insisted on it, unpalatable as it was, to the fractious team of Bradley and Patton. He put the US armies north of the bulge, the 1st and 9th, under Montgomery, with instructions to hold the line of the Meuse, to shorten the defence line, withdrawing here and there if necessary, to create a reserve and then to attack from the north. The 3rd Army was to stop its battle of attrition along the Saar, and swing its bulk for a massive blow against the German southern flank. Nothing was more to Patton's taste, and the feat by

his staff of picking up the bulk of his army, turning it through a right angle to start it marching north across the cluttered lines of communication will long be studied.

The only snag arose from bad British–American relations and their difference in outlook. Bradley in particular was incensed that any American troops should be placed under British command, especially when that commander was Montgomery. Furthermore, the US Army did not believe in withdrawal, even for the best tactical reasons, partly be-cause it was thought cissy, partly because of the glare of publicity in which US generals had to command and the difficulty of explain-ing the reason, and partly for the good reason

that the US Army was taught only to hold ground, or attack. Bradley privately ordered Hodges to ignore orders to withdraw and go over to the attack as soon as possible. This disagreement combined with a violent row over the self-congratulatory interview given to the press by Montgomery has marred the memory of this great battle, but had little effect on the way it was fought.

Montgomery's highly professional moves secured the line of the Meuse with his own troops, thus freeing Hodges and Lieutenant-General William Simpson to organize the northern counter-offensive; the long, poking finger of the *Panzer-Lehr* and 2nd *Panzer* Divisions stubbed up against the US 2nd

Above left: **The German salient was eliminated by the Americans.** *Above:* **Captured Germans march off to the rear.** *Right:* **Earlier, the Germans looked more happy.**

Armored Division and the British 3rd Royal Tank Regiment (the only British unit to be seriously engaged) near Dinant, while Patton's three corps attacked north-east astride the Bastogne axis and into the base of the salient due north of Luxembourg. Patton's tactics (a headlong rush without preparation) were extremely costly against unbroken *Panzers* ('*Our* blood, and *his* guts,' as one GI cynically observed, referring to Patton's melodramatic nickname) but if the cost could

be afforded they worked. What in fact turned the whole battle was the change in the weather. Mud and slush turned to ground frozen hard, and the skies became sparkling and clear with the frost, allowing the US 9th Air Force to fly 10,305 sorties between 23 and 31 December. Once it was flying weather Army Group B was doomed.

So ended Hitler's own offensive, planned, executed and commanded by himself, and all his hopes. The sacrifice of his best troops only opened the way into the Third *Reich*.

The Bomber Offensive

1943-45

IN January 1943, after Morocco had been occupied in the 'Torch' operations, Churchill and Roosevelt met at Casablanca to decide on the general strategy of the war after Africa had been cleared. High on their list of matters to be discussed was the problem of what was to be done with the new and potent offensive weapon they had in Bomber Command and the 8th Air Force, both stationed in Great Britain and launching an increasing number of raids into Europe. Bomber production was still increasing, so in the months to come the force should continue to grow into a more devastating weapon yet. Now it was up to Roosevelt and Churchill, together with their military advisers, to choose the main types of target to be assaulted. From the Casablanca Conference there emerged the 'Pointblank' directive, setting forth the order of priority of targets to be attacked by the bombers. The list's order was subsequently changed quite often, but as it emerged from the Casablanca meeting, its priorities were as follows: U-boat construction yards; the aircraft industry; transportation systems; oil plants; and finally other targets vital to the German armaments industry. The British were allowed to continue their night area raids on centres of civilian population.

Whilst this directive was assimilated and target lists drawn up by the relevant planning staffs, raids continued as before. However, by the middle of the year a new sense of purpose was discernible in the activities of Bomber Command and the 8th Air Force, joined from October 1943 onwards by the US 9th Air Force operating from bases in the Foggia area of southern Italy. Between 20 and 24 June Bomber Command undertook its first 'shuttle' mission, when aircraft set off from Great Britain, bombed Wilhelmshaven and then flew on to North Africa. On the return trip the Italian naval base of La Spezia was attacked. Nine days earlier the

8th Air Force had attacked the U-boat yards at Wilhelmshaven, but damage caused was slight. The problem bedevilling the 8th Air Force at this time was the lack of escort fighters with an adequate range, and it was not until the end of the year that the North American P-51 Mustang arrived, allowing the bombers to make deep penetration raids with proper escort all the way. The Americans devoted July to attacks on the German aircraft industry, principally the part producing fighters. Although the short-term results were good, the concentrated raids had finally persuaded the Germans of the wisdom of dispersing their production facilities, and this was now set in hand as a matter of urgency. At the end of July the British struck the first major blow against a German city, when four massive raids ruined virtually the whole of Hamburg. Firestorms caused by the incendiaries did most of the damage. Apart from the dead, the Germans also had about 750,000 homeless with which to cope after the raids. And on the night of 17 and 18 August Bomber Command struck at the German secret weapon research centre at Peenemunde on Germany's Baltic coast. Although not absolutely certain of the importance of the target, Bomber Command sent off a heavy raid, and this caused a great deal of damage, slowing the development of the V-2 considerably.

The Americans now learned a hard lesson in the need for escort fighters on deep penetration missions. On 1 August 178 bombers set off from North Africa to bomb the oilfields at Ploesti in Romania. Picked up by German radar in Greece, the bomber force was harried mercilessly by German and Romanian fighters, losing 54 of their number. Damage was caused to the refinery, but this did not halt production for long. As if this had not been enough, the Americans next lost 60 out of 376 B-17s sent off to bomb the

Below : **Powered by a Rolls-Royce Merlin, the P-51 Mustang was the war's best escort fighter.** *Inset above :* **B-17s blast the ball-bearing works at Schweinfurt.** *Right :* **US 8th Air Force B-17F bombers.**

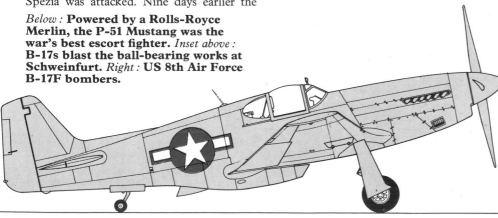

ball-bearing factories at Schweinfurt. A similar raid on 14 October was even more costly: 60 B-17s lost out of 291. The machine-guns of the Flying Fortresses were not enough to defeat the cannon-armed fighters, flown by the Germans with great determination and courage. After the Schweinfurt *débâcle*, the Americans suspended deep penetration daylight missions pending the arrival of P-51 escort fighters. The first of these arrived on 3 December, and the Americans then resumed the daylight offensive.

The culmination of the British bombers' year was the beginning of the Battle of Berlin in November. Up to March 1944, some 16 major raids were sent against the German capital, causing great damage and giving the Germans a very hard time of it. By this time the British bomber force had been joined by large numbers of the latest bomber, the comparatively small de Havilland Mosquito. Of wooden construction and powered by only two engines, the Mosquito could carry a very useful bomb load, and was in fact a far more cost effective aircraft than most heavy bombers. It could deliver its load with great accuracy at all altitudes, although its optimum was low to medium altitude, and its speed made it more than a match for any German fighters. So versatile was the basic design that all sorts of variants of the aircraft were produced; night fighter, strike fighter, fighter-bomber, passenger plane, photographic reconnaissance machine and meteorological workhorse. The German night fighters were also improving, and the electronic battle became very intense late in 1943 and early in 1944. By this time also, the British were using a number of electronic navigation aids, with good results.

During the first half of 1944, relentless pressure was maintained against Germany. The Americans had now grouped together as the Strategic Air Forces, under Lieutenant-General Carl Spaatz, the 8th Air Force in England and the 15th Air Force in Italy, enabling a single command organization to direct very large numbers of bombers onto the chosen targets with great ease. Spaatz also worked closely with Air Chief-Marshal Sir Arthur Harris in coordinating the American and British efforts: a target might well be visited by Bomber Command in the night and by the 8th and 15th Air Forces the following day, or *vice versa*.

Most important for the Americans, however, was 'Big Week' during the period between 20 and 26 February. The object of the week was to grind down German fighter strength. Although Bomber Command raided the same targets at night, the week was really an American effort. Whilst the bombers attacked fighter production factories to destroy the Germans' source of supply, the escort fighters had a field day with the German fighters that came in to attack the bombers. Here the true worth of the superb Mustang was shown to its full extent. Although Spaatz lost 244 bombers and 33 fighters during 'Big Week', the Germans lost 692 fighters in the air, plus many more on the ground and in the factories. The

Left: **A formation of B-17s releases its bombs over the marker bomb indicating the target area in Berlin.** *Above:* **The Martin B-26 Marauder was a fast and hard-hitting medium bomber used in most theatres of the war.**

factories themselves were also severely damaged. The same basic task of grinding down the *Luftwaffe* was continued through to May, causing the Germans to lose 2,442 fighters in action and 1,500 more from other causes.

There was now a change in emphasis. The strategic bombers were taken off conventional targets and set to 'isolating the battlefield' in northern France. The object of this campaign, in May and June 1944, was to prepare for the Allied landings in Normandy. Both the strategic and tactical air forces joined to destroy all the Germans' means of communication in northern France, the low countries and western Germany. Tunnels were caved in, bridges dropped, railway lines cut, marshalling yards destroyed, canals breached and roads bombed. The idea behind the campaign was that Normandy and Britanny be isolated, so that when the Allies landed in June, the Germans would not be able to rush up reinforcements with their usual speed. Great care had to be taken, however, that no pattern emerged from the bombing, lest the Germans work out where the landings were to take place. At the same time as this campaign against communications were being waged, the Allied air forces attacked and ruined nearly every airfield in the area. By the time of the Normandy landings, there were scarcely any German aircraft in northern France, those that had survived the Allied onslaught having been withdrawn.

Once the Allied landings had secured a good beach-head, the strategic bombers went back to their proper task of ruining Germany's ability and will to wage war. From July to December the heavy bomber campaign reached its peak. Virtually without a break, British and American bombers launched concentrated attacks on Germany's transport system, oil industry and other sources of power: electricity-generating stations were demolished, coal mines attacked, and all Germany's land and water transport

systems totally wrecked. By the end of 1944, Germany's ability to fight a war had at last been seriously affected. There was little fuel left for vehicles and aircraft, and even though the production of *matériel* was still rising, the Germans had no way of delivering such guns, tanks and aircraft to the fighting troops. And even if the troops had received them, they could not run them. To all intents and purposes, by the end of 1944 Germany was paralyzed by her lack of fuel and the absence of a transport system.

The campaign continued into 1945, with German resistance slowly dying away. Even though the Germans had the best jet fighter of the war, the Messerschmitt 262, which could have posed a very real threat to Allied air superiority in 1944, the type had not been placed in full-scale production early enough, and the few examples in operations could not stem the tide. With no fuel for training, the German pilots had also deteriorated in quality from the great days of 1940 to 1943.

The area bombing concept reached its conclusion on the night of 13 and 14 February, when the baroque city of Dresden was utterly destroyed. Although the city had little military significance and was full of refugees fleeing from the Russians, a great Bomber Command raid was launched. The incendiaries took an immediate hold in the old city, and uncontrollable firestorms of horrific intensity swept all before them. Winds of over 650 kph (400 mph) have been estimated in the centre of the storm, and the temperatures were high enough to melt steel. Many thousands of people taking cover in deep shelters were found dead because the fires had used up all the oxygen in the air, and those in shallower shelters were killed and burned though they were underground. All that was found was the dry dust of their bodies. The 8th Air Force completed Bomber Command's work with a great raid on the day after.

The last remnants of the *Luftwaffe* were eliminated in the period between 21 and 24 March, when the Allies' air forces flew more than 40,000 missions to seek out these last survivors of the German air force. Thereafter the strategic bomber force was used in direct support of the ground forces for the rest of the war.

The End for Germany

DURING 1944 the Russians had launched three major offensives, and each one of them had succeeded well. The first offensive, in the spring, had pushed the Germans back out of the Ukraine and away from Leningrad. The second, in the summer, had concentrated in the central sector of the front, and driven the Axis forces out of Belorussia, back into Poland and the Baltic states, and had halted with its spearheads just outside Warsaw. The third, in the autumn, had once again been a two-part drive: in the south, the Ukrainian fronts had pushed the Axis forces back into the Balkans and then forced them to retreat into Hungary and Czechoslovakia after the defections of Bulgaria and Romania; and, in the north, the Baltic fronts had moved forward once again, driving through to the Baltic and trapping Army Group North in the Kurland peninsula.

It was a magnificent feat, made possible by the ruthless determination of the Russian soldiers and the first-class staff work of their commanders. The Germans had fought back with great courage and skill; and taking into account the fact that they were greatly outnumbered, had also fought a campaign of considerable tactical skill.

The Russians were now poised near the borders of Germany, ready for the final act. The curtain rose on January 12, 1945 when the armies of Marshal K K Rokossovsky's 2nd Belorussian Front swept over the Narew river just north of Warsaw and fell on the German 2nd Army. At the same time, the Russian 47th Army set about taking Warsaw, which fell on 17 January. Rokossovsky's troops pushed all before them, and drove north-west up the right bank of the Vistula river towards the Baltic. When the Russians reached the sea between Elbing and Danzig, Colonel-General Georg-Hans Reinhardt's Army Group Centre was cut off.

Whilst their right was threatened by Rokossovsky's front, the troops of Army Group Centre also found that their left was in no better position: General I D Chernyakovsky's 3rd Belorussian Front had also driven swiftly forward, in conjunction with General I Kh Bagramyan's 1st Baltic Front, to reach the sea north of Memel. Reinhardt had begged to be allowed to disperse his forces

in order to meet this threat, but Hitler had refused, and now the whole army group was cut off and in desperate straits. By 8 February the Germans, despite a grim defence, were pinned against the coast in a few isolated pockets, in all some 500,000 men. Hitler at last saw that he had been wrong and gave permission for the survivors to be taken off. This the German Navy did, in an extraordinary evacuation quite the equal of Dunkirk, leaving the last German beachheads to hold out as best they could for the rest of the war – the last ones surrendered only on 9 May. Some of the troops in Kurland were pulled out at the same time, as were some 1,500,000 German civilians. But the cost was appalling, as the Germans had no air cover to fight off the Russian attack planes: by the end of the evacuation the German Navy consisted of only one heavy and one light cruiser.

East Prussia, having fallen, was the first part of the Third *Reich* to be taken by Russia in World War II. It was in this very area during 1914 that the Russian invaders had suffered the terrible double defeat of Tannenburg and the Masurian Lakes, but now they were avenged. The refugees, however, brought back wild tales of the rapacity of the

Right: **Acute shortages of manpower made Germany recruit even boys into the fighting services.** *Far right:* **Germany's capital, Berlin, fell to the Russians, whose armour is here seen close to the Brandenburg Gate.**

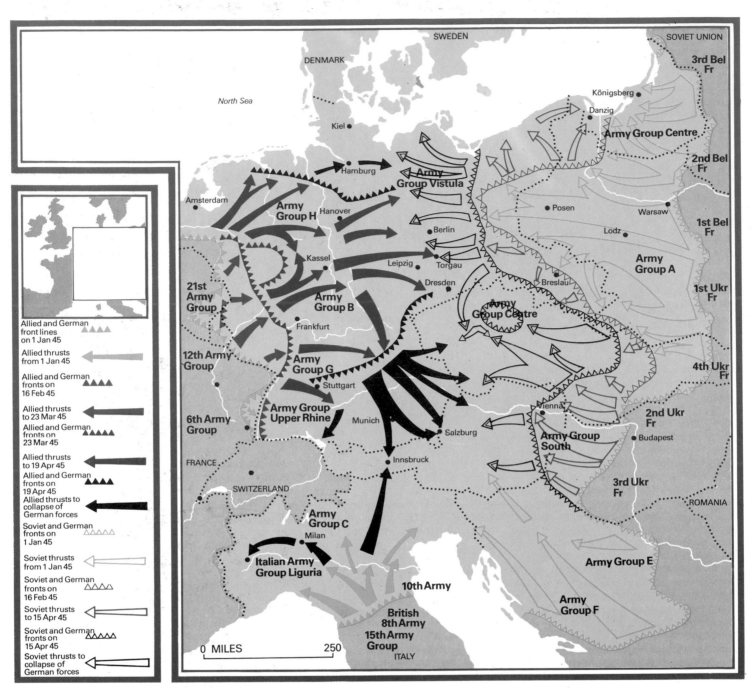

average Russian soldiers. The rest of Germany was shortly to learn of this characteristic at first hand.

Whilst these northern forces were conquering in East Prussia, the armies of Marshal Georgi Zhukov (1st Belorussian Front) and Marshal I S Konev (1st Ukrainian Front) had surged forwards under devastating artillery support across the Vistula river south of Warsaw. Only the 9th, 4th *Panzer* and 17th Armies of Colonel-General Johannes Harpe's Army Group A were there to make the vain effort to stop the Russians. The Germans' task was an impossible one, and by 17 January the Russians had advanced almost to the German/Polish border near Katowice and Czestochowa. Confident of their vastly superior manpower and *matériel* strength, Zhukov and Konev pressed on as far and as fast as their hard working logistics organizations could support them.

The supply echelons had a difficult task:

over 1,500,000 Russians were pressing steadily forwards, supported by 28,000 guns, nearly 3,500 tanks and self-propelled guns and some 10,000 aircraft. The Germans, on the other hand, could not find even a fraction of the supplies needed by their 600,000 men, 8,250 guns, 700 tanks and 1,300 aircraft, despite the fact that they were working on interior lines of communication.

Zhukov, in particular, appeared to move forward irresistibly, and by 31 January the 1st Belorussian Front had reached the Oder river, only some 65 km (40 miles) to the east of Berlin. In Zhukov's rear, however, as in everyone else's rear, there were large numbers of German pockets, bypassed and contained in the furious advance, but now ready to be mopped up. Most of the smaller pockets were eliminated in short order, but some held out for long periods in dogged displays of defensive fighting. It is a point to note that the troops in these pockets were not

all young, fanatical, well trained and well equipped. Quite to the contrary, they were a mixture of whatever formations fell into the pocket in their disorganized retreat. Hitler, as ever insistent on the need to hold ground, had demanded that the key cities such as Deutsche Krone, Poznan, Glogau, Breslau and Oppeln be held, and held they were for some time: right up to the end of the war in some cases.

Zhukov's great central drive had also had the effect of splitting Army Groups A and Vistula, the latter surprisingly commanded by *Reichsführer*-SS Heinrich Himmler who had apparently decided that he could command an army group, without any military training, as well as the next man. Admittedly his force was a motley of troops from the bottom of the barrel, but this was all the more reason to have an experienced commander. After a short time Himmler retired from his command in favour of Colonel-

Left : **The Allies closed in concentric-ally on what was left of the German** *Reich. Above :* **Russian armour rolls into the outskirts of Berlin, which suffered terrible losses of life in the battle.**

General G Heinrici, who was able to pull the command together to a certain extent.

In the middle of February both Russian fronts attacked again, Zhukov's in Pomerania and Konev's in Silesia, to straighten their lines. Konev's advance took him to the line of the Neisse river, and so by the end of the month the two fronts were lined up only 65 km (40 miles) from Berlin along 160 km (100 miles) of the Oder and Neisse rivers. By the end of March, the 1st Belorussian Front had reached the sea at Kolberg and was opposite the great port of Stettin on the left bank of the Oder. In the south, meanwhile, the 1st and 4th Ukrainian Fronts had again pushed forward well into Czechoslovakia, defended by Field-Marshal Ferdinand Schörner's Army Group Centre.

Further south, in Hungary, Budapest had fallen to Marshal R Ya Malinovsky's 2nd Ukrainian Front on 14 February, and the 2nd and 3rd Ukrainian Fronts had then pushed on to the general line Nagyatad–Lake Balaton–Lake Velencei–Esztergom–Banska Stiavnica by 6 March. From here it was an easy push into the rest of Hungary and thence into Austria, in the direction of Vienna.

But then Hitler's desperate preoccupation with oil once more came into play: SS *Oberst-gruppenführer* (Colonel-General) 'Sepp' Dietrich's 6th SS *Panzerarmee*, resting in the area after its mauling in the 'Battle of the Bulge', was to strike south-east between Lakes Balaton and Velencei to retake the Balaton oilfields. Other formations were to join in to the south to expand the offensive and administer a sharp check to the Russians' general drive.

Dietrich's attack went in on 6 March, and at first good progress was made; but the weather was very bad, the ground thick with mud, and the Russian defence steadfast. As Dietrich's *Panzers* were gradually slowed by the terrain and lack of fuel, the Russians counterattacked and drove the Germans back pell-mell. General Otto Wöhler's Army Group South could find no reply, and soon the 2nd and 3rd Ukrainian Fronts were over the border into Austria. Vienna fell on 14 April, and a day later the Russians were well past the Austrian capital.

Between December 1944 and April 1945, therefore, the several Russian fronts had pressed on from the line Kaunas–Bialystok–Warsaw–eastern Czechoslovakia–Budapest–Belgrade to a line from Stettin in the north to Vienna in the south, with a large German salient in eastern Czechoslovakia. Only in two places could the Germans make a defence: what was left of Germany between the Western army groups advancing from France and the Russians advancing from Poland, and Czechoslovakia. By prior political agreement, the Western Allies were to halt on the Elbe river, to the west of Berlin, leaving the rest of Germany to the Russians, with Berlin as the chief prize.

Under the overall supervision of Zhukov, the plans for the Berlin campaign were laid carefully. Whilst the 2nd Belorussian Front drove across northern Germany from the Oder to the Elbe, the 1st Belorussian and 1st Ukrainian Fronts would close in on Berlin from the north and south, cut it off and then fight their way in to final victory. Zhukov and Konev had no illusions about how bloody this fight for Germany's capital would be: with their backs to the wall, the Germans would fight as never before. The figures of men and *matériel* are available for this climactic battle of the war against Germany. In Berlin itself, for example, were 2,000,000 civilians and a garrison of 30,000. But holding the outer defences were about 1,000,000 German troops. To take on this formidable array,

Zhukov and Konev could between them muster some 2,500,000 men. Although the German troops were on the whole a mediocre lot, with little in the way of munitions, the Russians knew that they would put up an excellent defence. The defences themselves were mainly to the south of the city, for here there was no natural defence line like the Havel river to the north. Of course these were last-ditch defences, and nothing like as strong as the Germans' positions 65 km (40 miles) away on the west bank of the Oder and Neisse rivers, which is where the sober military men knew was their only possible chance of beating back the Russians.

The Russian offensive started on 16 April, preceded by one of the most intense artillery bombardments ever seen: along Zhukov's and Konev's fronts there was one gun every 4 metres (13 feet). After enormously thorough artillery preparation the Russians stormed across the rivers, only to be met by heavy and well-organized German fire. By 18 April the two Russian fronts had each secured only two small bridgeheads, some 5 to 11 km (3 to 7 miles) deep. Two days later, however, the Germans had been crushed in scenes of terrible carnage. Zhukov and Konev pressed on as quickly as they could, and linked up west of Berlin on 25 April. The only part of the German river defence force to remain reasonably intact was the 9th Army, soon joined by part of the 4th *Panzerarmee*, in a pocket near Markisch Buchholz, some 50 km (30 miles) south-east of Berlin.

The 2nd Belorussian Front attacked on 20 April and soon drove through the defences of Colonel-General Kurt Student's Army Group Vistula. Army Group Centre, well to the south of Berlin, had been split from the rest of the German defences by Konev's wedge-shaped advance. On 25 April US and Russian forces met on the Elbe at Torgau. The shattered remnants of the river defence forces were desperately trying to break through to the west before the Russians' rear areas were consolidated – it was the Germans' only chance of surrendering to the Western Allies.

Finally, it was Berlin against the 1st Belorussian and 1st Ukrainian Fronts, as the Russian attack was launched on 26 April. By 28 April Zhukov's 2nd Guards Tank Army had reached the Spree river in the northern outskirts, but to the south Konev's 8th Guards and 1st Guards Tank Armies had nearly reached the Tiergarten in the centre of the city. If the two Russian forces could link up, Berlin would be cut into western and eastern halves.

Hitler, by now totally demented, spent all the time he had left calling on the 9th Army to break through and relieve the capital. The 9th Army could barely hold its own any more. Although the two Russian fronts were only 1.5 km (1 mile) apart on 28 April, it was to take them another four days of murderous close fighting to link up across the *Reichstag* and Chancellery, where Hitler's bunker was situated. On 30 April, however, Hitler committed suicide after appointing Grand-Admiral Karl Dönitz as his successor.

Although still titular head of the 1st Belorussian Front, Zhukov's task of co-ordinating the joint 1st Belorussian and 1st Ukrainian Front offensives meant that he had to appoint a deputy to run the front in every-day respects. The man designated to this position was General V D Sokolovsky.

The fall of Berlin, one of the bloodiest battles fought this century, left only one other major pocket of German resistance: Schörner's last-ditch defences in Czecho-slovakia. Schörner, a die-hard Nazi had been given this command by Hitler because of his political loyalty. Although the war was lost, Schörner was determined to fulfil his orders to hold this important industrial area north-east of Prague, and his methods of securing the cooperation of his men were simple: anyone refusing an order or showing any signs of dilatoriness was shot. To the north was the 1st Ukrainian Front; to the east was the 4th Ukrainian Front; to the south-east and south was the 2nd Ukrainian Front; to the south-west was the US 3rd Army; and to the west was the US 1st Army. Only to the south was there any hope of escape, and here the 3rd Army and 3rd Ukrainian Front were hourly closing the gap.

Schörner had some 1,000,000 men, but without fuel and ammunition they were un-

Above: **A tank is ferried across the Rhine on a Bailey raft as engineers of the US 9th Army build another raft on the bank.** *Right:* **German civilians wander about in the ruins of Pirmasens, deva-stated in the US 7th Army's advance.**

able to halt the Allies. By 6 April the 2nd and 4th Ukrainian Fronts had overrun Slovakia in the east. Two months later they were well into the prosperous region of Moravia, and at this moment the Czech par-tisans rose in the Germans' rear, severely affecting their communications. Two days later, on 8 May, the Russians to the north, east and south launched a massive onslaught. Prague was taken on 9 May, and Schörner finally surrendered with his last German forces still fighting on 11 May.

The Russians have estimated that German losses in the last three months of the war on the Eastern Front were 1,000,000 dead plus 800,000 men, 12,000 armoured vehicles, 23,000 guns and 6,000 aircraft captured.

While the Russians were overcoming German resistance in the east, the western Allies were advancing.

After the fighting in the Ardennes had died down, it would have been clear to anyone except Hitler that the only hope for Germany was an end to the war. This was not to be,

176

and as long as the German Army held together and could use the remnants of the *Westwall*, the floods in the Low Countries and the barrier of the Rhine as a defensive system, it was plain that the task of defeating it would be long and bitter.

It was for this reason that General Dwight D Eisenhower insisted on the maximum concentration of force in France. The supreme commander has been compared by some to the chairman of a board of directors, steering a middle course and sometimes weakly giving in to first one pressure group and then to another. This is a mistaken view. Eisenhower was a general of outstanding ability and strong personality. He was politic and mild in manner, but impossible to deflect from what he believed to be the best course, resisting pressure from Churchill, Field-Marshal Sir Bernard Montgomery, Field-Marshal Sir Alan Brooke, the British CIGS, and the powerful combination of General Omar Bradley and the obstreperous Lieutenant-General George Patton alike. The British were once more pressing for a main effort in the north, Patton clamouring for more action with as many divisions as he could take command of in the 3rd Army sector, while General Jean de Lattre de Tassigny was demanding a greater share of the action for his army and for France.

Eisenhower only considered these demands insofar as they suited what his insubordinate subordinate, Montgomery, would have called his 'master plan'. Broadly, this was to uncover the Rhine from end to end by driving in the German bastions remaining on the west side. Then he intended to follow the classical strategy for forcing a river line by attacking on as many points as possible, 'bouncing' a crossing where he could and making a formal assault with maximum artillery and air support where the defences were strong; then advancing from these bridgeheads into the heart of Germany. The next move was to encircle the Ruhr industrial area on which the German economy depended – already wrecked by the bomber offensive – and mop it up, while the Allied armies drove forward to the Elbe to meet the Russians.

The first move was by Devers' army group in the south. A local counter-offensive aimed at the recapture of Strasbourg was beaten off in January and then the French 1st Army, its colonial troops much reduced in numbers after sacrificial fighting and suffering with cold and frostbite, were initially checked in an attempt to liquidate the 'Colmar pocket', which was badly dented but still holding. Devers then reinforced the French with the US XXI Corps – a great mark of trust in de Lattre – and the attack was resumed. De Lattre deployed Major-General J-P Leclerc's 2nd Armoured Division (which had emerged from West Africa to join the 8th Army in 1943, reformed in England and had so far operated with the US Army), the Free French and his US corps on the north of the salient; covered the nose which protruded into the Vosges with the French 10th Division; while his I Corps – the 2nd and 4th Moroccan Divisions and the 9th Colonial

Division – attacked from the south. The US 109th Infantry Regiment drove the Germans from Colmar on 1 February, chivalrously allowing the French troops to enter the city first. By 5 February the attacks from north and south had joined up, and by the 9th the last Germans not killed or captured were over the Rhine.

On 8 February, away in the north, Montgomery launched the Canadian 1st Army under Lieutenant-General Sir Henry Crerar in Operation Veritable, whose aim was to advance from the Nijmegen salient, break through the *Westwall* and clear the Germans out of the Reichswald forest, Cleve, Goch and Xanten. The extreme care with which the British attacks were planned and their reliance on their powerful and highly skilled artillery were, oddly enough, adversely criticized in some American circles; but it must be remembered that both British and Canadian man-power were wasting assets ('Shells save lives' was the motto of those days) and there was no room for manoeuvre: as the commander of the leading British XXX Corps said: '. . . I had to blast my way through three defensive lines, the centre of which was the Siegfried Line.' A fire-plan of great complexity was prepared, first to suppress hostile artillery fire and then to soften up the enemy positions, with special attention to precision fire on concrete bunkers. Once the attack had started a barrage was to be put down on the forward enemy localities, to stand there for 70 minutes until the assaulting divisions had closed up to the German positions, before beginning to roll forward at the rate of 274 m (300 yards) every 12 minutes, with six regiments on each divisional front providing four belts of fire altogether 457 m (500 yards) deep. The total number of guns and howitzers employed was 1,050, supplemented by light anti-aircraft guns, anti-tank guns, the guns of tanks, machine-guns, heavy mortars and a regiment of 12 32-barrelled rocket projectors. Some idea of the intensity of the fire is given by the ammunition statistics: 500,000 rounds, of all kinds, weighing 11,000 tonnes were dumped, of which 5,953 were used in the preliminary bombardments and in the barrage 160,338 25-pdr and 5.5-inch shells. The Reichswald was cleared by 13 February, Goch by the 21st and Xanten on the 26th. This was the most severe fighting on the left bank of the Rhine, the 21st Army Group casualties numbering 16,000 and the defenders losing 23,000 prisoners and an unknown number of killed and wounded.

On 23 February Lieutenant-General William H Simpson's US 9th Army, under command 21st Army Group, crossed the flooded valley of the Roer in assault boats (Operation Grenade) and made sufficient progress to deploy armour by 1 March. Simpson cleaned up his objectives with a loss of 7,300 men, but captured another 30,000 prisoners. These two battles went a long way to crack the still unbroken will of the German Army.

In the meantime, the US 1st Army (Lieutenant-General Courtney Hodges) was

grinding its way forward in the sector from Cologne to Koblenz when the battles of attrition were enlivened by a flashing *coup de main*. The defenders were withdrawing in some confusion and without a continuous front when some American tanks and armoured infantry drove between them to capture Remagen, to find the Ludendorff Bridge across the Rhine unblown and lightly guarded. It was being kept open to allow the units still west of the Rhine to cross. This was reported and the local commander, Brigadier-General William M Hoge, ordered it to be seized. There was a blunder on the German side; the demolition charges were ready laid but when they were triggered only one exploded, causing a crater at the west end. The Americans rushed the bridge on foot under small arms fire, cutting the wires to the explosive charges as they went. Soon they had fought their way across and dug in on the far side. Curiously enough, Hoge's initiative was not followed up, the superior officers in the command chain – in marked contrast with German action in similar circumstances – referring ever upwards in succession until Bradley at 12th Army Group HQ was reached. Bradley, naturally, ordered Hodges to push across every formation he had in hand and by 12 March a bridgehead 23 km (14 miles) wide was securely held by three divisions supported by tanks. In this way, the formidable obstacle was cheaply crossed and

the way to the heart of Germany lay open. Counterattacks were beaten off as were, for a time, suicidal *Luftwaffe* missions by a huge concentration of anti-aircraft artillery. But between the air attacks and a continual bombardment by heavy artillery the bridge collapsed; too late, for by that time the US engineers had thrown sufficient bridges across the river to ensure that the forward troops could be maintained.

Patton was not to be outdone. He had a stiff task which had to be undertaken methodically by stages: a task not suited to his temperament, but nevertheless carried out with precision. He first broke through the *Westwall* in the Saar and then crossed the Mosel, which meant an advance through broken and hilly country until he could uncover the Rhine from Koblenz to Mainz. He had his eyes fixed on the river, for he was determined to cross before Montgomery's projected date, 24 March, and the day before managed to put six battalions across at Oppenheim at the cost of 28 casualties.

On 31 March de Lattre, anxious lest the Americans should cross the Rhine first, secured a bridgehead at Speyer.

On 24 March Montgomery launched his grand spectacular: Operations Plunder (the Rhine crossing), followed by Varsity, an airborne descent on the far side. Again this has been represented as an example of over-caution and adversely compared with the un-

planned 'bouncing' of the upper Rhine, but the same considerations applied as to Veritable. In addition the German high command, which was apprehensive about the northern thrust, had made a fair appreciation of its scope and direction and one of the last of their good formations, the 1st Parachute Army, was barring Montgomery's way. The river at his intended crossing point, between Emmerich and Homberg, was 900 m (1,000 yards) wide, flowing at $3\frac{1}{2}$ knots, and it was Montgomery's intention not to have a fight for the bridgehead but to drive through to a great depth in order that the subsequent advance could continue without a check.

The planning for Plunder was based on the technique for landing on a coast rather than on a simple river crossing and, like Dragoon, embodied every possible refinement to ensure that the crossing was successful and with minimum casualties. The main assault was to be carried out by the 1st Commando Brigade directed on Wesel, the 15th (Scottish) Division in the centre of the British sector, and the US 30th and 79th Divisions of Simpson's 9th Army south of the Lippe canal. H-hour was 0200 on 24 March. At 1000 two airborne divisions, the British 6th and the US 17th, were to parachute in or be landed close enough to the river to be within supporting range of the artillery on the left bank.

On the British sector the difficulty of putting enough artillery across in the early stages made it necessary to deploy it in full view of the Germans on the right bank, and therefore a permanent smoke screen was generated to cover the whole front, while to aid manoeuvre at night banks of searchlights sited near the river provided 'artificial moonlight'. The artillery fireplan was once more large and elaborate, with a preliminary bombardment by 25 batteries of 5.5-inch, 7.2-inch and 240-mm guns, followed by covering fire in a complex schedule from 706 25-pdr and 5.5-inch guns for the 15th (Scottish) Division's crossing. Two hundred heavy bombers blasted a path for the commandos as they approached Wesel. Over 660 tanks were poised to follow up. Some of the Scots companies were in tracked amphibians (LVTs or Buffaloes) with orders not to disembark on the further bank but motor on, providing their own covering fire to objectives deep in the proposed bridgehead. The Scottish troops met with resistance near the east bank described as 'fanatical', but eventually cleaned it up; even the German paratroops were beginning to feel that they had had enough.

Eisenhower himself, having looked at his 9th Army, went to view the fly-in by daylight of 400 aircraft carrying paratroops, followed by 1,300 more towing gliders, a total of 14,000 troops of the British 6th and US 17th Airborne Divisions arriving in an endless procession which filled the sky. This required the most careful coordination with the field artillery fire, as shell trajectories were high enough to intersect the aircraft flight paths, and meant that at times fire on the German AA artillery and other fire-support had to be denied. All went well, however, and by the end of the first day's fighting the British and Americans had joined up and were 10 km (6 miles) over the river.

On the second day Montgomery and Simpson took two distinguished visitors across the river, Churchill and the British CIGS, Brooke. Brooke afterwards confessed that Eisenhower had been correct in his broad-front plans for the Rhine crossing, as proved by events. To the south Eisenhower's other two Army Groups were advancing from their bridgeheads, with no substantial resistance. It was estimated that only some 6,000 disorganized troops were opposing Devers.

The orders for the December and January counter-offensives, followed by Hitler's desperate command to hold ground without yielding had in fact placed the surviving German formations on the execution block. Some divisions were by now just an HQ and a few scratch troops like the *Volksturm*, some only combat teams (*Kampfgruppen*). Altogether facing west there was only the equiva-

lent of some 26 full strength divisions, representing the last scrapings of the manpower of the *Reich* collected for sacrifice – old men, sick men and boys. (Some of the latter proved as fanatical as their elders.) Nevertheless there was much sharp fighting ahead, first on all fronts and then in pockets as small groups of SS troops or paratroops determined to hold out to the bitter end.

The scheme of manoeuvre for the Ruhr battle was for the 9th Army to encircle it from the north and the 1st Army from the south, linking up at Lippstadt and trapping the German forces who had intended to use its cities to fight a long delaying battle. This was complete by 6 April. Three corps were given the task of entering the sack so formed, carving it up and reducing it sector by sector. Within was Army Group B HQ, under Field-Marshal Walther Model, who refused a futile order from OKW to break out, but at the same time felt unable to surrender formally. He told his troops to fight on or just go home as they chose, and committed suicide. Some 317,000 prisoners, including two dozen generals, representing some 19 divisions and various army and corps HQs, plus 100,000 air defence troops, were captured.

While this last great battle of the war in the West was going on, the remaining American armies surged forward to the Elbe with ever-increasing momentum, while further north the Canadians and British advanced against more dogged resistance from formed bodies of troops. Eisenhower then made a much discussed alteration to his final plan. He had originally intended to make Berlin his final objective, but a number of considerations supervened. Allied intelligence quite mistakenly concluded that the Germans might take to guerrilla warfare and that there was a plan to establish a 'national redoubt' in the mountains of Bavaria, and he ordered the 3rd and 7th Armies to swing to the south. To go on to Berlin, Eisenhower estimated, might be too costly to be worth while so late in the war. With the main German armies facing him destroyed, Berlin had ceased to be a purely military objective, apart from which the Russians were closer to it than he was. He feared that a head-on contact between the Russians and Allied troops might lead to awkward confrontations and sought some clear natural feature on which they could

meet in orderly fashion; for this the Elbe was ideal. He also felt that there was little point in capturing territory only to hand it back to the Russians according to political agreements already entered into by the Allies. He therefore resisted the British demands to be allowed to go on to Berlin and also Simpson's similar request when he had secured a bridgehead over the Elbe. On 24 April officers of the US V Corps met Russian representatives at Torgau on the Elbe and forward movement ceased.

The national redoubt proved a myth. The military disintegration of Germany accelerated, until on some occasions when commanders of units attempted to hold out they were actually overpowered by citizens who saw no point in further destruction of their homes. With Hitler's death on 30 April, what central authority there was disappeared and the *Reich* began to surrender piecemeal. The representatives of the Germans in the north surrendered to Montgomery, with effect from 0800 on 5 May. At the same time, large German forces east of the Elbe surrendered to Simpson, many civilians attempting to cross to the west bank to escape the Russians. For a formal surrender the Allies insisted on complete capitulation on both fronts, and this was agreed at Allied supreme headquarters in Rheims at 0200 on 7 May by Colonel-General Alfred Jodl in the presence of Eisenhower's chief-of-staff, Lieutenant-General Walter Bedell Smith, and high staff officers from the British, Russian, French and United States armed forces.

At this point it is as well to remember that the United States sent 3,000,000 men to Europe, committed 61 divisions and lost 120,834 killed and 344,649 wounded. The British troops numbered 907,000 with 13 divisions and their casualties were 141,291 killed and wounded. Canada sent 188,000 men and her five divisions (excluding action in Italy) suffered 43,249 casualties. The French eventually raised four colonial and eight French divisions and joining in the battle on August 20, 1944, suffered a total loss of 115,600, of which 24,000 were killed. Nor must 6,000 Polish and 1,000 Dutch, Belgian and Czech casualties, in units fighting with the 21st Army group, be forgotten. Such was the cost of breaking into Hitler's 'Fortress Europe' and destroying his armies and his régime.

Left : **German industry was destroyed by the Allied heavy bombers.** *Right :* **General Jodl, with Admiral von Freideburg on his left, signs the surrender documents at General Eisenhower's headquarters in Rheims on the morning of 7 May 1945 ending the war in Europe.**

The End in Italy

IN the spring of 1945 the same dogged, battle-worn opponents faced each other in Italy: the Allied 5th and 8th Armies *versus* the German 10th and 14th Armies. Only some of the principal actors had changed rôles. Kesselring and Alexander had been promoted to theatre commanders. Army Group C was now led by a sound Prussian general, Colonel-General Heinrich von Vietinghoff, and the ambitious Lieutenant-General Clark had succeeded Alexander in command of the 15th Army Group. Major-General Lucian Truscott, who had commanded the corps at Anzio after Lucas, now had the 5th Army, and the jovial Leese had gone to Burma to be succeeded by Lieutenant-General Sir Richard McCreery, a specialist in armoured tactics.

Alexander's orders from the chiefs-of-staff for 1945 were to continue to lean on Army Group C hard enough to prevent any German divisions from being withdrawn from Italy, and if von Vietinghoff withdrew to a new defence line in the foothills of the Alps, to follow him. This was an invitation to limit operations to a few cautious, small-scale attacks. Two more good divisions of Canadians had been taken away, and although Clark had received a Brazilian division and an excellent specialist US mountain division fresh from the US, and McCreery two Polish brigades and a Jewish Palestinian brigade, the numerical odds against 15th Army Group

were still 17 to 23 against in terms of divisions. The war was nearly over. Eisenhower's armies had crossed the Rhine in three places in March, the Russian vanguards were at the frontier of Austria, Army Group C was well-equipped and up to strength and in an extremely strong position, and there was no point in incurring a lot more casualties. Moreover, a German emissary was secretly in touch with Alexander's HQ sounding out the prospects of a negotiated surrender in Italy. Another costly offensive, it could be argued, made little sense.

Alexander and his commanders were of a different opinion. What they lacked in numbers they possessed in terms of fire and air power, and they argued, as before, that the only way to carry out their mission effectively was to mount a full-scale offensive. They felt that they had fought too hard and for too long to relax now without the victory they believed

Above: **DUKW amphibious trucks proved their worth time and time again in the river-obstructed advance northwards through Italy.** *Above right:* **Surprisingly, after the success of previous landings, the Allies attempted no major landings in northern Italy during the closing stages of the campaign.** *Right:* **Engineers of the 5th Army's US 10th Mountain Division shelter in the lee of a tank destroyer while awaiting the rout of German snipers ahead of them.**

to be theirs by right. Strangely enough the soldiers felt the same. Much deserved praise has been given to the astounding morale of the Germans in defeat, but they believed that they were fighting for personal and national survival. An Allied soldier would not have been blamed if he decided to go canny and stay alive for the rest of the war. In fact, the American, British, Polish and Indian veterans, tired as they were, fought a tremendous battle and broke the Germans inside a month.

The front was divided by geography into two distinct sectors, both ideally suited for defence. Opposite the 5th Army the road north was barred by ten miles of crags and precipices, fortified and garrisoned by the best of the German infantry: *Jägers*, mountain troops and paratroops. The 8th Army's front line was along the flood banks of the Senio river and four more defended river lines lay beyond. On the right the way was barred by the waters of Lake Comacchio and floods created by the breaching of the dykes along the rivers. Across the whole 80 km (50 miles) of front there was only one dry gap, where the road north to Argenta ran between the lake and the floods, and offered a way round the whole river network. McCreery fixed his sights on this.

Clark's plan was for the 8th Army to attack early in April using all the air power available, and when McCreery had attracted the German reserves to his side, the 5th Army would in its turn take it over for a thrust in the centre.

The 8th Army's last offensive was a triumphant combination of tactics and technology. A large number of DD tanks had arrived in Italy (battle-tanks fitted with flotation gear as used on D-day in Normandy) and of tracked amphibious infantry carriers, and these converted the expanse of water facing the 8th Army's right from a barrier to an avenue reaching the heart of the 10th Army's defences. As a first move British commandos and Royal Marines secured a safe start line on the south and east of Lake Comacchio, and then two brigades of the 56th (London) Division in assault boats attacked the eastern shore and secured the wedge of dry land leading to Argenta. This was the doorway through which McCreery

intended to pass his armour. If the bridge over the Reno river at Bastia could be secured he would have the side door to the whole 10th Army defence system, for then, after crossing the Senio, his right-hand divisions could join up with the Londoners and fan out towards the Po.

On 9 April the 10th Army artillery areas were struck with thousands of tonnes of fragmentation bombs from heavy bombers, then by medium bombers, followed by fighter-bombers in close support of the attacking infantry. A series of barrages were fired by 1,000 guns (25-pdrs and 5.5-inch) supplied with 2,000,000 tonnes of ammunition. The far bank was doused with burning fuel from flame-throwing tanks, and the assault began. The infantry crossed, followed by tanks and the welter of specialist armoured vehicles. By 16 April the 10th Army was still fighting doggedly, but the 6th Armoured, the 78th and the 56th Divisions, all veterans of Africa and Italy, had fanned out north of Argenta in the Po valley and were inching forward. Von Vietinghoff's line was very near the breaking point.

Truscott began his attack in clear skies on 14 April. It was a sign of the times, perhaps, when a German division in defence actually disintegrated and ran. The 10th Mountain Division was enthusiastic and fresh, and it had been specifically trained in mountain warfare, unlike the normal US troops. It had already shown its form when it surprised the defence in a preliminary operation by roping a whole battalion up an apparently unscaleable precipice. Now, in the same manner as the Moroccan *goumiers* had sneaked through the Gustav Line, the American mountain troops led the way through the remaining northern foothills of the Apennines. The remnants of the 14th Army had to come down from the peaks or be cut off. Truscott's main thrust was directed east of Bologna, because one of the peculiarities of von Vietinghoff's position was that its final stop-line was the Reno river, which curled all round his centre and left, but could be outflanked in the west by Truscott where it rose in the Apennines, or at the Argenta gap. The Americans and British were now travelling with tremendous impetus, while throughout the back areas of Army Group C the RAF and the

USAAF were ready to pounce on any movement of German troops.

Clark's intention was to catch the whole German force south of the Po, and destroy it there with the river at its back: this he achieved. Any remote possibility that it could not have been destroyed was scotched by Hitler himself. Before the Allied offensive had started von Vietinghoff had asked the *Führer*'s permission to fight a mobile battle of withdrawal and so keep his army intact, and was accused of 'wavering' or holding 'defeatist attitudes' as his reward: 'The *Führer* expects the utmost steadfastness in fulfilment of your present mission, to defend every metre of the northern Italian areas entrusted to your command.' When von Vietinghoff at last nerved himself to give the order to retreat his front had already collapsed. As he had foreseen, the only hope would have been to duck the hammer blows of Allied air power and artillery and slip back across the wide and flooded Po.

On 22 April the 6th South African Division, leading the 5th Army's advance, and the British 6th Armoured Division, travelling west, met each other behind the retreating Germans at a village appropriately called Finale. The Germans were trapped, and in complete disorder, except on the Mediter-

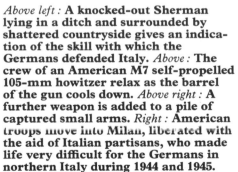

Above left : **A knocked-out Sherman lying in a ditch and surrounded by shattered countryside gives an indication of the skill with which the Germans defended Italy.** *Above :* **The crew of an American M7 self-propelled 105-mm howitzer relax as the barrel of the gun cools down.** *Above right :* **A further weapon is added to a pile of captured small arms.** *Right :* **American troops move into Milan, liberated with the aid of Italian partisans, who made life very difficult for the Germans in northern Italy during 1944 and 1945.**

ranean coast where a mountain corps fell back in good order to the end. Even the paratroops began to surrender. Their Major-General Heidrich, the gallant defender of Cassino, was not the surrendering kind, and swam to freedom across the Po. Most of the German heavy equipment was left on the south bank, the units which got away were harried by the Italian partisans, while the Allied divisions, hardly able to realize that their battle was won, crossed the Po and raced for the Alpine passes. The cease-fire was ordered for 1800 hours on 2 May, 21 months and 13 days after the touchdown on the Sicily beaches, and the long, bitter and forgotten war was over.

THE DEFEA

Like Germany, Japan continued to fight on with fanatical courage against ever-lengthening odds after the Battle of Midway. Though US priorities lay in the European theatre, the strength of the US Navy was sufficient to harry the Japanese mercilessly, isolating her island garrisons and crippling her supplies of raw materials. Then land forces crushed the garrisons in campaigns of appalling bloodshed, while the air forces devastated Japan's industries and cities. But Japan refused to consider surrender until the undreamt of power of the atom bomb eliminated Hiroshima and Nagasaki in two swift moments.

The Philadelphia Inquirer
An Independent Newspaper for All the People
PUBLIC LEDGER

CIRCULATION: July Average: Daily 569,159; Sunday 1,102,515

TUESDAY MORNING, AUGUST 7, 1945

FINAL CITY EDITION

THREE CENTS

Atomic Bomb, World's Most Deadly, Blasts Japan; New Era in Warfare Is Opened by U.S. Secret Weapon

Bong Killed Testing New Jet Plane

Leading Air Ace Burns to Death In Crash on Coast

Terrific Missile Unleashes Basic Force of

The Solomons' 'Ladder'

THEIR defeats in Papua and in Guadalcanal naturally worried the Japanese high command. In this area, the generals and admirals in Tokyo felt, was the greatest danger of an Allied breakthrough into the Southern Resources Area so vital for Japan's continued ability to wage the war and prosper economically after it. It was therefore decided to reinforce the area heavily. The nodal point of the region's defences was Rabaul on New Britain, and hence great numbers of reinforcements were sent, as well as vast quantities of *matériel* to replace that lost in the Papua and Guadalcanal battles. From Rabaul

these additional resources were allocated as the local commanders saw fit, mostly to the garrisons in the Huon Gulf in north-east New Guinea and in the Solomons as far south as New Georgia. It should be remembered that the Japanese had no joint command structure, and it depended on the good sense of commanders whether or not the army and navy acted in cooperation. In this area the cooperation was good: overall command was exercised by Vice-Admiral Jinichi Kosaka, who had under him the 8th Area Army of Lieutenant-General Hitoshi Imamura. The 8th Area Army controlled two formations, Lieutenant-General Hotaze

Adachi's 18th Army in New Guinea, and Lieutenant-General Iwao Matsuda's 17th Army in the Solomons. In view of the fact that this threatened area was the key to the naval-controlled defence perimeter on which Japan's fate hung, Admiral Isoroku Yamamoto, commander-in-chief of the Combined Fleet, kept a watchful eye on the situation from his headquarters in Truk, far to the north in the Caroline islands.

The general Allied strategy for the area had been fixed in July 1942, and following the defeat of the Japanese attempts on Port Moresby and Guadalcanal, General Douglas MacArthur's South-West Pacific Area forces

Chester Nimitz's Pacific Ocean Areas for men and *matériel*. MacArthur and Halsey worked very smoothly as a team, however, and this overcame many of the problems that might have defeated two less tolerant commanders, especially on the Japanese side.

The advance through New Guinea was finally made possible by the capture of Buna on January 22, 1943. Some preparatory movements had already been carried out, the most important of these being the airlift to Wau, some 50 km (30 miles) south-west and inland of the major Japanese coastal garrison of Salamaua, by an Australian brigade from Lieutenant-General Edmund Herring's New Guinea Force. The brigade established a forward base and threatened the Japanese, whilst MacArthur put the finishing touches to the main assault plans and made ready his forces.

To make the Japanese think that his drive would be a straightforward one along the coast, on 30 June a battalion of the US 32nd Division was landed at Nassau Bay, just to the south of Salamaua, and this battalion, together with the 17th Australian Brigade from Wau, now threatened Salamaua from the west and south. At the same time the US 158th Infantry Regiment took Trobriand island, and the US 112th Cavalry Regiment, Woodlark island, both of these lying north-east of the south-eastern tip of Papua. This completed the clearance of Japanese garrisons in Papua between Buna and Milne Bay undertaken in October and November, 1942.

The Japanese were considerably shaken on September 4, 1943 when the 9th Australian Division of the New Guinea Force, now commanded by General Sir Thomas Blamey, landed east of the main base of Lae in the Huon Gulf. A day later the US 503rd Parachute Regiment dropped at Nazdab, inland from Lae, thus completing the isolation of the garrison. The paratroops were

quickly reinforced by the 7th Australian Division, airlifted from Port Moresby. The Allies' forces at Salamaua and Lae now attacked simultaneously, Salamaua falling on 12 September and Lae on 16 September. While the 9th Australian Division advanced round the coast, the 20th Australian Brigade was shipped round to Katika, where it landed on 22 September and cut off the garrison of Finschhafen, which fell on 2 October.

The 7th Australian Division had not rested on its laurels. After the capture of Lae it moved off up the Markham river valley, inland of the Saruwaged and Finisterre ranges of mountains, and then crossed into the Ramu river valley *en route* towards Madang, which fell to the 11th Australian Division on April 24, 1944. Overland advances and landings from the sea completed the isolation and destruction of other Japanese garrisons on the Huon peninsula during the same period. Of the 10,000 Japanese troops in the area, half had been killed, and the other half dispersed into the terrible jungle of the region.

While the Australians were mopping up on the Huon peninsula, the men of Krueger's 6th Army had secured a toehold on the western end of New Britain. The 112th Cavalry Regiment made a diversionary landing at Arawe on the south coast of New Britain on December 15, 1943, and 11 days later the 1st Marine Division came ashore on Cape Gloucester at the western tip of the island. The division quickly secured a beachhead with two airfields, after 1,000 Japanese had been killed in a hard-fought four-day battle.

Halsey's forces had also been active during this period, moving up the 'ladder' of the Solomons. After a brief pause to rest and reorganize after the defeat of the Japanese on Guadalcanal, the Americans started to climb the ladder. The Russell islands, just to the

Above: **Men of the 1st Marine Division watch for signs of Japanese activity in the Cape Gloucester region of New Britain.** *Right:* **Men of the 163rd Infantry Regiment, part of the US Army's 41st Division, storm ashore on Wake island during the landing of May 18, 1944.**

were ready to start the drive on Rabaul. The South Pacific Area was dissolved, Vice-Admiral William Halsey's naval forces in the area becoming the 3rd Fleet, allocated to MacArthur's overall command.

The drive on Rabaul was to be a two-pronged affair. Supported by the aircraft of Lieutenant-General George Kenney's 5th Air Force, Lieutenant-General Walter Krueger's 6th Army was to advance up the coast of New Guinea and then invade the western end of New Britain before making the final assault on Rabaul. At the same time Halsey's forces were to 'island-hop' through the Solomons in the direction of Rabaul. The one major problem that had to be overcome was a command and allied logistical one: although under MacArthur's strategic command, Halsey was still dependent on Admiral

north-west of Guadalcanal, were taken by the 43rd Division in February, but this was only a preliminary move. The basic US plan was now to bypass the main Japanese garrisons, concentrating instead on a series of outflanking movements to secure key air bases and so isolate the Japanese garrisons. This would avoid heavy losses and, it was hoped, neutralize the enemy bases.

First step up the ladder was New Georgia, where Japan's main airbases in the Solomons were located. As an initial move, the island of Rendova, just off New Georgia, was taken as an artillery base on 30 June. The main landings went in near Munda on 2 July, the assault forces being the 37th and 43rd Divisions with marine support. Overall control of the ground force was exercised by Major-General John Hester, later replaced by Major-General Oscar Griswold. The Japanese were commanded by Lieutenant-General Noboru Sasaki, who led his men ably. Fighting was extremely bitter, and at first the raw American troops came off the worse in desperate struggles in the jungle. The 25th Division had to be committed on 25 July, and after regrouping and resting his forces, Griswold finally took Munda airfield on 5 August. The back of the Japanese resistance had been broken, and all organized opposition ended on 25 August. Heavy casualties had been suffered by both sides.

On 15 August, meanwhile, an American regimental combat team (about the equivalent to a British brigade) had leapfrogged past Kolombangara, which had an important airfield, to land on Vella Lavella. After building an airfield the Americans were withdrawn. Their replacement was the 3rd New Zealand Division, which crushed the last Japanese resistance by the middle of September. The Japanese on Kolombangara, realizing their impossible situation, evacuated the island, and the central rung of the Solomons was in Allied hands by 7 October.

The last major rung before New Britain was the large island of Bougainville, which had several airfields. To distract the Japanese, the 3rd Marine Parachute Battalion landed on nearby Choiseul on 27 October. Having distracted the Japanese, the battalion was evacuated a week later. Also on 27 October, the 8th New Zealand Brigade Group landed on Treasury island. This was quickly secured as an advanced base for the Bougainville operation. Moving forward from here, the 3rd Marine Division poured ashore at Empress Augusta Bay on Bougainville, on 1 November. At first Japanese resistance was light, and a naval base and airfields were soon operational within the beach-head, measuring some 16 km (10 miles) wide by 8 km (5 miles) deep. Thereafter Japanese opposition grew, and by the end of the year the perimeter had hardly been advanced. The only real chance the Japanese had had of evicting the Americans from Bougainville had been in the Battle of Empress Augusta Bay on 2 November, but the radar-equipped US task force proved too powerful for the Japanese force, which lost a cruiser and a destroyer, and had most of its other vessels damaged. To complete the move up the Solomons ladder, on February 15, 1944 the 3rd New Zealand Division took Green island, wanted as a forward airfield site for attacks on Rabaul.

Realizing that the actual conquest of New Ireland and eastern New Britain would be extremely costly, the Americans had decided merely to cut them off and leave them to 'wither on the vine' in their isolation. So it was necessary, finally, to take the islands north of New Britain and New Ireland to complete the encirclement. Accordingly, MacArthur's forces moved on the Admiralty islands and Halsey's on the St Matthias islands. A reconnaissance of Los Negros in the Admiralties on 29 February met little opposition and the 1st Cavalry Division was quickly moved in to secure the island by 23 March. A landing was also made on Manus on 15 March. Halsey's 4th Marine Division landed unopposed on Emirau in the St Matthias group, and quickly moved on to Mussau. New Britain and New Ireland, with their great bases at Rabaul and Kavieng, were cut off. On New Britain, the 1st Marine and 40th Divisions had been moving steadily eastwards, and on 6 March the 1st Marine Division had made a forward landing at Talasea on the Willaumez peninsula. It was now decided to halt the American forces

Above left: **US Marines in the wake of a tank on Bougainville in 1943.** *Above:* **US infantry mop up a party of Japanese infiltrators on Bougainville.** *Left:* **A B-25 bomber makes a low-level pass over a Japanese merchant ship.**

where they were and to contain the Japanese. Gradually Australian forces took over the task of keeping a watch on the Japanese for the rest of the war, freeing MacArthur's American divisions for further operations. The successful neutralization of Japanese strength in the area also allowed the 3rd Fleet to be returned to Nimitz in June.

The Japanese perimeter had been horribly dented, but the authorities in Tokyo decided that the western end of New Guinea could still be held by Lieutenant-General Jo Imura's 2nd Area Army, based in Hollandia, just over the border in Dutch New Guinea. Here a great complex of airfields and supply dumps was built, but there were few troops in the area. Most of the 18th Army's surviving men, some 65,000 strong, were based in the areas of Wewak and Madang.

In an action of some genius and great risk, MacArthur decided to bypass the 18th Army and go for Hollandia itself, even though this was beyond the range of Kenney's aircraft. Although Nimitz had lent him Vice-Admiral Marc Mitscher's Fast Carrier Task Force to

provide air cover, MacArthur decided to land forces at Aitape, at the same time as the Hollandia landings, to secure the airfields there. The Aitape landing could be covered from Saidor-based aircraft, and once Aitape's airfields were in US hands, the Hollandia landings could be covered by Kenney's aircraft, freeing Mitscher for other tasks.

Whilst the Australians were pressing into Madang, far to the rear, MacArthur's two landings went in on 22 April. The 24th and 41st Divisions landed on each side of Hollandia, which fell on 27 April; and in two days a pair of reinforced regiments secured Aitape. In both places the fighting was very heavy, and although the Americans lost only 550 killed, Japanese dead totalled more than 14,000, other forces in the area being dispersed into the jungle.

MacArthur's forces now advanced in bounds along the coast, taking Sansapor island at the western end of New Guinea on 30 July and bringing the New Guinea campaign to an end. Blamey's Australian forces, meanwhile, had been fighting to a halt a last-breath offensive by the 18th Army in the area of Wewak and Aitape. This was finally crushed on 5 August.

Japan's defensive perimeter had been breached, and MacArthur now turned his attention to the Philippines.

Island Hopping in the Pacific

ALTHOUGH Halsey's forces in the advance up the Solomons ladder had tried a certain amount of 'island-hopping', the technique could not be used to full effect there. In the Central Pacific, however, there was ample scope for such tactics. In the vast open spaces of the ocean, with Japanese bases scattered on a multitude of little islands and atolls across hundreds of thousands of square miles of sea, the steadily growing strength of the US Navy could be used to transport and support US Army and Marine units to overwhelm the lesser Japanese garrisons with local superiority of forces. Having fewer ships, the Japanese could not match the Americans' strategic mobility, and this should make it possible to edge gradually closer to Japan without having to deal with the major bases until the end of the campaign.

Whilst General Douglas MacArthur and his South-West Pacific Area were firmly in favour of a methodical approach to Japan via

Left : **US Marines advance cautiously into thick jungle, wary of Japanese snipers, booby-traps and concealed bunkers.** *Below :* **A pair of Marines return Japanese fire from a beach position on the islet of Roi in the Kwajalein atoll area of the Marshall islands, invaded in January 1944.**

New Guinea and the Philippines, the US Navy (in the persons of Admiral Ernest King, commander-in-chief, and Admiral Chester Nimitz, commanding the Pacific Ocean Areas) favoured a more indirect approach across the Central Pacific to take Formosa or part of the Japanese-held mainland of China. The Japanese empire would then be cut in two, separating Japan's industry and population from the raw materials and food they obtained from the south. This, the US Navy thought, would greatly weaken Japan and so facilitate the final assault should it prove necessary. The grand strategic question of which plan was better. did not have to be answered until 1944, and until then there was room for both the US Army and the US Navy to advance in their own areas, MacArthur in the South-West Pacific and Nimitz across the Central Pacific. The US armaments factories were turning out *matériel* so prolifically that there was ample for MacArthur and Nimitz, even though the Pacific in general enjoyed a lower priority than the theatres in which the Germans could be engaged.

To a great extent Nimitz was helped by MacArthur's efforts: feeling that the South-West Pacific was in the greatest danger, the Japanese had responded by sending the best of their air units, from both the army and navy, with the result that the Central Pacific

garrisons were left with handfuls of aircraft and indifferent pilots. The good aircrews, moreover, were cut down in droves, and their replacements were nothing like as capable. The Japanese suffered yet another blow with the death of Admiral Isoroku Yamamoto on April 18, 1943, when his plane was shot down by Lockheed P-38 Lightnings operating from Henderson Field on Guadalcanal. The Japanese naval code had been broken and the Americans sent the P-38s to intercept Yamamoto over Bougainville. Admiral Mineichi Koga replaced Yamamoto as commander of the Combined Fleet, but he did not possess the strategic genius or popularity of his predecessor.

Throughout the first nine months of 1943, Nimitz carefully built up his forces and planned his first westward moves. With the return of Vice-Admiral William Halsey's 3rd Fleet from the Solomons in June, Nimitz had the foundation of the greatest naval force ever assembled, and this was growing all the time. The main striking force was built round new, fast battleships and aircraft carriers emerging from the American yards at a remarkable pace, supported by heavy and light cruisers and by powerful destroyers. When commanded by Halsey, this force was known as the 3rd Fleet, whilst under Vice-Admiral Raymond Spruance it became the 5th Fleet. The main offensive element of this force was the Fast Carrier Task Force led by Vice-Admiral Marc Mitscher. Other air support came from the US Army's 7th Air Force, under Major-General Willis Hale, operating from the Ellice islands. For landing operations, Nimitz had some 100,000 men, plus all their transports and the necessary supply facilities for far-flung operations.

The first objective for the Central Pacific drive was the Gilbert and Marshall groups of islands, where airfields could be built for the next step forward. The Gilberts and Marshalls, two large groups of tiny atolls, were to be taken in two phases: in November 1943, the southern part (Makin, Tarawa and Apamama in the Gilberts), and in late January and early February 1944, the northern part (Eniwetok, Kwajalein and

Majuro in the Marshalls). With no previous experience to refer to, the landing forces had little idea what they were up against: each major component of each atoll lagoon had been heavily fortified, and was defended by first-class troops.

Makin and Tarawa were to be assaulted on 20 November, and for a week before this they were saturated with bombs and naval shells. It made hardly any impression at all. Deep in their coral, concrete and coconut-log bunkers the Japanese were safe from anything but a direct hit, and waited for the inevitable assault. Makin fell to the 165th Regiment of the 27th Division on 23 December, but its 600 defenders had held up the Americans for far too long to suit Major-General Holland 'Howling Mad' Smith, commander of V Amphibious Corps. All of the 250 combat troops were killed and only 100 prisoners were taken; all of them Korean labourers.

However, compared with Tarawa, Makin was a walk-over. Rear-Admiral Keiji Shibasaki had some 4,700 seasoned troops, and formidable defences including 8-inch guns and 400 pillboxes. Reconnaissance had not revealed the presence of an inner reef, on which most of the landing craft got stuck, forcing the men of the 2nd Marine Division to wade hundreds of yards through a curtain of fire. Their losses were appalling. The marines were then trapped on the beaches, and by nightfall 1,500 of the 5,000 men landed had become casualties. Reinforcements in the next two days suffered comparable losses, but gradually the marines forced the defenders back. The last pocket of Japanese resistance was overwhelmed on 23 November, by which time the Americans had lost 985 dead and 2,193 wounded. The Japanese lost all but about 100 taken prisoner, of whom only 17 were combat soldiers. Well covered by war photographers, Tarawa came as a terrible shock to the American people, just as photographs of the fighting for Buna and Gona had been. In the long run, however, the Central Pacific forces benefited from the experience on Tarawa, learning the tactics necessary and seeing the need for landing craft that could crawl over reefs and onto the

Below left: **US troops line up for 'chow' on a Pacific island.** *Above:* **Marines on the alert for Japanese snipers hidden in dense cover.** *Far right above:* **A 75-mm pack howitzer shells Japanese positions.** *Far right below:* **Advance in the Marianas.**

shore. These emerged as Landing Vehicles Tracked, in reality armoured and tracked amphibious personnel carriers and tanks. Apamama fell quickly on 21 November.

Koga's Combined Fleet, bereft of aircraft, could no nothing but lie impotently at Truk.

Kwajalein was defended by some 8,000 men under Rear-Admiral M Akiyama. The 7th Division landed and overran the island quickly between 1 and 7 February. The 4th Marine Division took other islands in the group. The lessons of Tarawa had been well learned, and the Americans suffered only 372 dead and about 1,000 wounded out of some 41,000 men landed. All but 230 of the Japanese defenders were killed. Majuro had been occupied on 30 January, but the islets of the Eniwetok atoll were to prove another tough nut to crack.

On 17 February two battalions of the 22nd Marine Regiment came ashore on Engebi, at the north of the atoll, and met little resistance; but on 19 February two battalions of the 106th Regiment met very determined and fierce resistance when they landed on Eniwe-

tok atoll itself. Only after two days of heavy fighting was this little area of coral declared secure. Two battalions of the 22nd Marine Regiment encountered similar opposition on Parry when they landed on 22 February, and it took a day's hard fighting to crush the Japanese. This sterling defence had been put up by Major-General Nishida's 1st Amphibious Brigade, an experienced unit some 2,200 strong. The Americans suffered some 339 dead, but all the Japanese were killed. The flamethrowers of the Americans proved particularly effective in assaulting bunkers, which could absorb the explosions of all but heavy shells and bombs.

Mitscher's carriers had meanwhile struck at Truk on 17 and 18 February. Although Koga managed to escape with the Combined Fleet, the carrier aircraft sank 200,000 tonnes of merchant shipping and destroyed 275 aircraft on the ground. Koga retired from Truk as a permanent base in favour of anchorages in the Philippines. On 1 April Koga was killed in an accident, and his place as commander of the Combined Fleet was taken by Admiral Soemu Toyoda, a far more energetic individual – so energetic, in fact, that he sent his forces into the disastrous Battle of the Philippine Sea in June.

Late in May 1942, the Japanese had, as part of their deception plan for the Midway operation, sent a force north against the Aleutian islands off the coast of Alaska. The task of Vice-Admiral Boshiro Hosogaya's Northern Area Force of 2 light aircraft carriers, 7 cruisers and 12 destroyers was to attack the Aleutians at just the right moment to allow the Americans to divert forces north from the Midway region. Hosogaya was then to establish bases in the Aleutians, in the islands towards the western end of the chain.

Having broken the Japanese naval code, the Americans were able to plan accordingly, and Nimitz detached about one third of his forces to protect the Aleutians. Hosogaya managed to outmanoeuvre Rear-Admiral Robert Theobald's force, however, and twice shelled Dutch Harbour, much to the embarrassment of the Americans, before retiring westwards to establish his bases on Kiska and Attu on 6 and 7 June respectively. These attacks had achieved nothing worthwhile, as a result of the Americans breaking the code and thus having prior knowledge of Japanese intentions. Air support for the garrisons of Kiska and Attu was provided by land-based aircraft operating from Paramushiro, the most northern of the Japanese-owned Kurile islands, and just to the south of the tip of Kamchatka.

There was no real military need for Nimitz to eject the Japanese from his Northern Pacific Area other than injured American pride about the Japanese occupation of part of their possessions. Nevertheless, the decision to do this was taken in 1943.

On 26 March Hosogaya was convoying reinforcements to the islands with two heavy and two light cruisers, as well as four destroyers, when he fell in with Rear-Admiral Charles McMorris's one heavy and one light cruiser, as well as four destroyers. In a long-range gun duel, the Battle of the Komandorski Islands, *Salt Lake City* was crippled and *Nachi* very seriously damaged. As the Japanese closed in for the kill, however, three of the US destroyers also closed in for a torpedo attack and forced Hosogaya to turn away for home.

Rear-Admiral Thomas Kinkaid, commanding in the North Pacific, ordered Rear-Admiral Francis Rockwell to land the 7th Division on Attu to clear out the Japanese. This landing went in on 11 May, and after 18 days of fighting in appalling terrain and bitter weather Attu was declared secure. Only 29 of the 2,500 Japanese defenders were captured, and the Americans lost 561 dead and 1,136 wounded. On 15 August a joint Canadian and American force landed to fulfil a similar function on Kiska, but found that the Japanese had gone. The 4,500 defenders had in fact been lifted off a fortnight earlier, when the Japanese high command realized that their loss would serve no purpose whatsoever.

Burma

IN 1943 the will of the Allies to strike back at the Japanese was strong, but they lacked the means. The Japanese position, on paper at any rate, was weak. The new Japanese empire, or 'Greater East Asia Co-Prosperity Sphere', had expanded suddenly like a balloon, ready to be pricked. It stretched from the Indian frontier to the faraway Pacific, and the Japanese armed forces were fully committed to a war in China and another in the Pacific against the greatest military power in the world. In Burma a small fraction of their army faced the British-Indian army to the west, a threat from Lieutenant-General Joseph Stilwell's Chinese Army in India (CAI) in the north

Left above: **A mixed Japanese column wends its way towards the front in northern Burma, where the Allies were slowly preparing for the fight back to the south.** *Left below:* **Most of the major bridges were blown by the British as they pulled back.** *Above:* **In the absence of major roads and railways, the Allies made very extensive use of air transport in the Burma campaign.**

and the many Chinese armies to the east.

Unfortunately for the Allies, the best of the Indian divisions had been sent to the Middle East, and the remainder were dispirited and badly in need of training for jungle warfare. While the Chinese mainland armies, under a corrupt administration and feeble leadership, were useless. Only the CAI under the formidable old 'Vinegar Joe' Stilwell were in a position to fight. Only Stilwell was determined to get to grips with the Japanese as soon as possible, come what may. The British generals, who were later to inflict a crushing defeat on the Japanese, were equally determined not to strike until they had educated their soldiers in the art of fighting the Japanese. The disastrous outcome of the offensive in the Arakan, in 1943, strengthened this resolve.

In January 1943 three brigades of the 14th Indian Division were with great difficulty advancing down the coast with the port of Akyab as their goal. Japanese resistance was light; indeed their outposts were distributed in single companies of infantry. The real obstacles were mountains, roadless jungles, mangrove swamps, tidal creeks, disease and the difficulty, or impossibility, of moving supplies and heavy infantry weapons. (One battalion lost half its strength before it sighted a Japanese.)

There was also the peculiarity of fighting the Japanese, who could attack with dash and great tactical skill, but often preferred to dig themselves into 'bunkers' impervious to all but the heaviest artillery shell on a piece of ground demanding attack, and hold it until the very last individual Japanese had been killed. No other soldiers in the whole war did this and fighting them was a unique experience. At Donbaik, for instance, four separate attacks were made on one of these positions using the 1st Royal Inniskilling Fusiliers, 1st Punjabis, 7th Dogras, 1st Lincolnshires and 1st Royal Welsh Fusiliers, resulting in severe losses. The Welshmen alone left 150 dead in the area of one of these miniature forts. Even reverting to the methods of a previous century and digging in a 3.7-inch howitzer at close range, and blasting away over open sights, failed. (This was the germ of the 'bunker-busting' techniques using both tanks and guns, which was perfected later.)

For six weeks the 14th Indian Division, reinforced with brigade after brigade, tried to break through without success. Then, when they were exhausted, the Japanese counterattacked, the Allied resistance broke and the whole force, badly shaken, returned to India.

Another threat to the Japanese appeared 1,000 km (600 miles) away in the extreme north of Burma. The CAI was created by Stilwell from the remnants of the Chinese divisions he had led on foot out of Burma, in 1942, together with some raw material flown in from China. They had been collected at Ramgarh, in Bihar, and trained on American lines under Stilwell's direction. Only he, with his deep understanding of the Chinese and fluent command of their language, could have persuaded the Chinese to accept such foreign ideas as hygiene in the field and punctuality, and their officers to submit to basic retraining with their men without feeling they had lost face. Training was on a 'conveyor belt' system; squads of hundreds of men, learning to aim and fire their weapons, on a strict schedule with a minimum of frills; squads which were then grouped in companies and battalions for training under their own Chinese officers. It was not a 'colonial army', but all Chinese from top to bottom. Stilwell retained control by introducing 'advisers' and liaison officers at regimental and divisional headquarters. His greatest handicap was a system of dual command by Generalissimo Chiang Kai-shek, who interfered constantly by signal and always on the side of urging caution and obstructing Stilwell's orders for offensive action. For all that, it was an effective force and proved a match for the Japanese.

Stilwell's task was to drive the Japanese south and clear the way for a new highway through northern Burma along which munitions and supplies could be taken to the Chinese, now cut off by land and sea and being expensively supplied by air. With the newly organized 38th Division leading, the CAI started south: 'At 1706 hours on 28 February, 1943, the leading bulldozer of the US Engineers crossed into Burma proper at milestone 43.2 from Ledo.'

The Japanese posture in Burma was entirely defensive, but this did not mean that it was passive. Lieutenant-General Sinichi Tanaka's 18th Division, in northern Burma, was strung out in a series of outposts from south of Ledo to Fort Herz, 160 km (100 miles) away, but Tanaka was still able to make local attacks and administered some sharp jolts to the intruders. Such was the prestige of the Japanese and their aggression that the British-Indian outpost garrisons were soon retreating north and the Chinese 38th Division was halted. Stilwell, who was primarily adviser and chief-of-staff to Chiang Kai-shek, felt he had to take command of the CAI in the field, and after a great deal of persuasion he managed to get it crawling forward in December: crawling, because even in comparison with the rest of Burma the Patkai hills and the Hukawng valley were an appallingly difficult environment in which to live, let alone stage an offensive.

What deterred Tanaka from exploiting his easy successes in the north, was the unexpected and alarming intrusion of a brigade of British and Gurkha troops into northern Burma. These had somehow infiltrated, largely undetected, across the Chindwin river which was then the line of contact between the British in Assam and the Japanese. This was no ordinary raid. Brigadier Orde Wingate had been ordered to study the possibilities of warfare behind the enemy lines by Field-Marshal Sir Archibald Wavell. Wingate had evolved from guerrilla methods he had already tested in Ethiopia, a strategy called 'long-range penetration', using scattered company-strong 'columns' controlled by radio and supplied from the air; which would move through the jungle and use it as a covered approach for attacking vulnerable Japanese rear areas.

Operation Longcloth had been intended as part of a combined British and Chinese offensive, but when this was cancelled Wingate persuaded Wavell to let him go ahead alone, in order that his new strategy and novel methods of training troops on guerrilla lines could be fairly tested in battle.

By no purely military criterion could this first Chindit experiment be judged a success, for all the courage and self-sacrifice shown by the troops, who accepted that no sick or wounded could hope to be evacuated. All went fairly well at first; some successful skirmishes were fought against the Japanese

and the railway to the north was cut. Wingate, whose intentions were never clear in his own mind, then rashly moved into an area where he was in grave danger of being trapped. He extricated part of his force by the expedient of jettisoning all his heavy weapons and animals and breaking up into small parties. However, part of his force did not receive the orders to withdraw and failed to return: the survivors suffered terrible hardships from fatigue, starvation and disease. Of 3,000 men, some 800 failed to return and of the survivors only 600 were fit for further active operations. Nevertheless, when the public learned that for three months a commando-type force had been at large and on the rampage behind the lines of the apparently invincible Japanese, there was an enormous uplift in morale; not least in India, where it had been depressed by the news of constant defeats and setbacks and a Japanese invasion seemed likely.

Above: **Wingate's men from the first Chindit expedition, looking remarkably fit after their time behind the Japanese lines are evacuated.** *Right top:* **Lieutenant-General 'Vinegar Joe' Stilwell, commander of the China-Burma-India theatre, was an enigmatic character.** *Right centre:* **Chiang Kai-shek (leading) had been fighting the Japanese longer than any western leader.** *Right:* **'Merrill's Marauders' were well supported by loyal Burmese levies.** *Superimposed:* **Another eccentric figure was Brigadier Orde Wingate.**

Wingate's message was simple and its effects were far-reaching. For the British it was that the Japanese could be defeated; for the Japanese, that the jungle could be penetrated and therefore the Chindwin front was vulnerable. They now thought less about the defence of Burma and more about attack and began the planning that was to lead them to Imphal and Kohima.

Success in the Central Pacific

WITH the Gilberts and Marshalls safely in his hands, and the Aleutian problem in the process of being cleared up, in spring 1943 Admiral Chester Nimitz, commander of the Pacific Ocean Areas and of the Pacific Fleet, could turn his attention to his next objectives in the Central Pacific, the Marianas. Another large group of islands, these were rocky rather than coral, and offered a different set of problems for the assaulting land forces. The three main islands to be taken were Saipan, Guam and Tinian, to be attacked in that order. The three islands were needed for the long-range bombing of Japan by the new Boeing B-29 Super-fortresses. Judging from prewar maps and aerial reconnaissance photographs, US Army Air Force engineers calculated that they could build an enormous complex of airfields on the islands, sufficient to allow the war to be taken to Japan with a vengeance. Industrial targets would be destroyed, ruining Japan's ability to wage a modern war, and civilian targets would be attacked, if necessary, to destroy morale and disrupt the industrial plants' work forces.

The targets in the Marianas were softened up on 11 and 12 June by a visit from Vice-Admiral Marc Mitscher's Fast Carrier Task Force. Some 200 Japanese aircraft and many merchant ships were caught and destroyed. Vice-Admiral Richmond Turner's V Amphibious Force of 530 ships, and the 127,000 men of III and V Amphibious Corps (commanded by Major-General Holland Smith and Major-General Roy Geiger respectively) arrived off the islands on 15 June after steaming up from the new rendezvous point of Eniwetok.

Commanding in the Marianas was Vice-Admiral Chuichi Nagumo, well remembered by the Americans as the leader of the Japanese forces in the attack on Pearl Harbor that had brought the United States into the war. Now, however, Nagumo's command, the Central Pacific Area Fleet, was a paper force. Nominally in command of the land forces, the 31st Army, was Lieutenant-General Hideyoshi Obata. At the time of the American invasions Obata was away in the Palau islands, and so command of the ground forces devolved on the senior commanders on each island.

After a feint attack on Mutcho Point, on the centre of Saipan's western coast, by V Amphibious Corps' reserves, the real attack went in on each side of Afetna Point, farther to the south. To the north of the point Major-General Thomas Watson's 2nd Marine Divi-

sion landed, whilst to the south of the point Major-General Harry Schmidt's 4th Marine Division made the landing. Both were hotly contested by the troops commanded by Lieutenant-General Yoshitsugo Saito. Although American intelligence had estimated that there were 20,000 Japanese on Saipan, Saito had 25,469 army troops and 6,160 naval personnel. By 18 June the Americans had reached the eastern coast of the island, and turned north and south to crush the two halves of the Japanese defence into the ends of the island. The 27th Division, commanded by Major-General Ralph Smith, had been committed on 17 June, but this did little to speed up the pace of the Americans' advance.

The southern pocket of Japanese at Nafutan Point was soon contained by a single battalion of the 27th Division (the pocket was wiped out on 28 June), and the rest of the division was ordered to line up between the two marine divisions for the northward advance, scheduled for 23 June. Fighting to a different set of tactical precepts, the army division was soon lagging behind the adventurous marine divisions, and Holland Smith precipitated an argument, yet to be resolved satisfactorily, by sacking Ralph Smith in favour of Major-General Sanderford Jarman. The problem was not Ralph Smith's but rather that of the differences in tactical doctrine between the US Army and US Marine Corps.

After heavy fighting, the three divisions had reached a line running roughly across the island from Garapan on the west coast by the end of the month. The 2nd Marine Division was pulled out of the line as the advance continued to move into a narrower part of the island. By 7 July the Japanese position was desperate, and Saito issued orders for a last suicidal counterattack from Makunsha. Beaten back with great loss by the 27th Division, this marked the end of the road for the Japanese. Although American progress had been slowed by the absence of tactical air support, as a result of Mitscher's departure for the Battle of the Philippine Sea with his Task Force 58, the Japanese were finally crushed by 9 July. Rather than surrender, hundreds of civilians killed themselves by jumping off the cliffs at Marpi Point. The Japanese troops suffered some 27,000 dead, but 2,000 were taken prisoner. The Ameri-

Right : **US Marines move cautiously and steadily into the ruined outskirts of Garapan, on the island of Saipan in the Marianas group, on June 23, 1944. Soon bomber bases were operating on the island.**

cans suffered some 3,126 dead, and 13,160 wounded, most of them marines. This is perhaps an apt commentary on the different tactics that had incensed Holland Smith: the army troops advanced methodically and slowly, incurring few casualties; the marines advanced with greater 'dash' and speed, but suffered correspondingly heavier losses. Both Saito and Nagumo committed ritual *seppuku* to avoid capture.

Guam was next on the list of targets, and was to be taken by the 3rd Marine and 77th Divisions and 1st Provisional Marine Brigade of Geiger's III Amphibious Corps, lately I Marine Amphibious Corps, the formation that had taken Bougainville. Command of the Japanese forces on this largest of the Marianas had been entrusted to Lieutenant-General Takeshi Takeshina, the commander of the 29th Division, although only one regiment of the division was present on the island. In all, Takeshina had some 13,000 soldiers, and some 5,500 naval personnel were commanded by Captain Yutaka Sugimoto. (Obata had hurried back from the Palaus on hearing of the American landings on Saipan, but had been unable to get further than Guam. He left the command arrangements as they were, but when Takeshina was killed by machine-gun fire from a marine tank on 28 July, Obata assumed command of what was left of the defence.)

The two marine formations landed on each side of the Orote peninsula on 21 July, with the 77th Division following the 1st Provisional Marine Brigade later in the day. Fighting was again severe, but not as hard as it had been on Tinian. The two halves of the corps linked up in a good beach-head on 22 July and then turned north to the capital of Agana and on to the tip of the island at Ritidian and Pati Points. As on Saipan, the Japanese defended with great courage, launching counterattacks when they were able, but were slowly driven back. The end of the organized resistance came on 10 August on Mount Machanao, at the north-western tip of the island. US casualties totalled 1,919 dead and 7,122 wounded, but as usual the Japanese total was far higher at 17,300 dead and 485 prisoner. Some of the Japanese escaped and went into hiding, one surrendering finally as late as 1972.

This left only Tinian to be secured, and the invasion of this was scheduled for 24 July. The assault was undertaken by the 2nd and 4th Marine Divisions of V Amphibious Corps, now commanded by Major-General Harry Schmidt since the elevation of Holland Smith to the post of Commanding General, Fleet Marine Force, Pacific. The 27th Division was in reserve after its hard time on Saipan.

Although the senior commander on the island was Vice-Admiral Kakuji Lakuda, commander of the 1st Air Fleet, practical

Above left : **Marines take cover on Guam after hitting the beach, and prepare to move off inland.** *Above :* **Marines on the invasion beach at Saipan wait for the arrival of amphibious tanks before attacking inland.** *Left :* **The Americans met fanatical opposition taking coral atolls such as Kwajalein.**

command was exercised by Colonel Kaishi Ogata of the 50th Infantry Regiment. Ogata had some 4,700 army personnel, and Captain Goichi Oya led 4,110 naval personnel of the 56th Naval Guard Force.

Whilst the 2nd Marine Division launched a feint towards Tinian town on the south-west of the island, the 4th Marine Division landed on two tiny beaches on the north-west tip of Tinian early on 24 July, meeting only relatively light resistance. The 2nd Division then arrived from its feint and landed across the same beaches. The two divisions fought off an ineffectual night counterattack, and the next day set off south, the 2nd Division on the left and the 4th on the right. Progress was steady, and by 28 July the two divisions had taken half the island. The Japanese were gradually penned up in the south-east of the island, and the final assault went in on 31 July, all organized resistance ending on 1 August.

As usual, Japanese losses had been very heavy: 6,050 dead and 235 prisoners, compared with the marines' loss of 290 dead and 1,515 wounded.

With the three islands secured, the engineers could begin to move in with their equipment to start work on the great airfield complexes needed for the air side of the three-pronged strategic offensive against Japan: air attacks on industry from bases in China and the Marianas; submarine attacks on shipping, especially tankers to starve Japan of raw materials and oil; and the combined land and sea offensive to retake Japan's conquests and invade the home islands if necessary. B-29 operations from the Marianas started on 28 October with a raid on Truk, but soon great numbers of these strategic heavy bombers were winging their way to Japan from the Marianas.

Nimitz's Central Pacific offensive was now complete, and he could turn his attention once more to the debate on the best route by which to approach the Japanese home islands. Both he and MacArthur, the main protagonists of the two different schools of thought, attended the presidential conference in Hawaii during July at which President Roosevelt made his decision.

The fall of the Marianas and the defeat in the Battle of the Philippine Sea had the result, in Japan, of bringing about the fall of Lieutenant-General Hideki Tojo's government on 18 July, to be replaced by a slightly more realistic one under General Kuniaki Koiso.

Battle of the Philippine Sea

I N March 1944 the Americans set in motion an operation to capture the Mariana islands, a Pacific chain about 1,125 km (700 miles) long. Only the four southernmost (Guam, Rota, Saipan and Tinian) were important, for the rest were too volcanic to allow the construction of airfields needed for the Boeing B-29s which were to bomb the Japanese homeland, but the Marianas were also a useful staging post for Japanese ships and aircraft in transit between the home islands and the south-west Pacific.

The Japanese naval forces were commanded by Admiral Soemu Toyoda, with the 1st Mobile Fleet under Vice-Admiral Jisaburo Ozawa, comprising 5 battleships, 9 carriers and 13 cruisers. Toyoda was certain that the next American thrust would be to the south, so he and Ozawa planned to use a decoy force to lure the Americans from the Marshalls towards Ulithi or the Palau islands. From there they could be attacked in strength by carrier-aircraft, but somehow the Japanese ships had to be kept out of reach of the much-feared American carrier planes. The Americans had a fast carrier force of seven large and eight smaller carriers, carrying the staggering total of 700 fighters and nearly 200 bombers. In addition, the American invasion forces would be covered by escort carrier groups carrying more than 300 fighters and bombers. The Japanese could muster over 600 aircraft in the Marianas and western Carolines and, furthermore, were able to reinforce them by flying in fresh aircraft from the home islands via Iwo Jima.

To preserve their carriers the Japanese decided to launch strikes from them at extreme range and then land the aircraft on shore airfields. There was one flaw in this plan: all Japanese experience to date showed that a carrier strike against a base, from their own attack on Pearl Harbor onwards, was most likely to catch the defenders on the

wrong foot. Also the Japanese were now desperately short of skilled pilots, whereas the American air groups were composed of experienced and confident aircrews, with hundreds of replacements on the way.

On June 6, 1944 Vice-Admiral Marc Mitscher's Task Force 58 left Majuro lagoon and five days later the first sweeps were made over Guam, Saipan and Tinian. The Americans reported enormous successes, but their intelligence had underestimated the numbers of shore-based aircraft, and they mistakenly believed that they had wiped out the Japanese defenders. A heavy bombardment of Saipan started on 13 June, followed by the landing of 20,000 men two days later. As soon as the Japanese were certain that the attack was not a diversion Ozawa was given the order to sail, and on 13 June he left Tawitawi in the Sulu archipelago, with the giant battleships *Yamato* and *Musashi* amongst other ships. Unfortunately for him, a lurking US submarine reported the departure of this fleet, and another spotted it emerging from the San Bernadino Strait into the Philippine Sea on the evening of 15 June.

Admiral Raymond Spruance, commanding the US 5th Fleet, was kept informed of the expected attack, and wisely postponed the landing on Guam to allow the transports to be kept well clear of the battle area. Leaving only a force strong enough to cover the Saipan invasion, the American admiral concentrated his ships about 290 km (180 miles) west of Tinian, for he was determined not to be lured away until he knew the whereabouts of the main Japanese fleet. Ozawa, for his part, was confident that his plan was going well, for he had kept out of range of the American carrier aircraft, and his own aircraft had reported the position of the enemy forces. On the night of 18 to 19 June he divided his force into an advance guard under Vice-Admiral Takeo Kurita, with four battleships and three

Left : **The escort carrier** *White Plains* **steams through bomb bursts, photographed from another small carrier,** *Kitkun Bay.* *Below :* **The Mitsubishi A6M Zero fighter was obsolete in the Philippine Sea battle.**

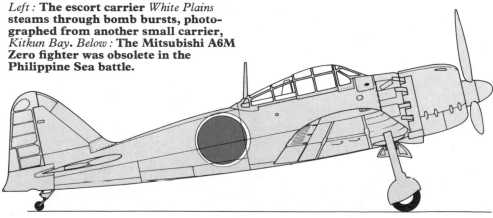

medium-sized carriers, while keeping the main force of six carriers under his own command. He hoped that Kurita's force some 160 km (100 miles) ahead of him would draw the fire, and so leave his five carriers intact for a decisive blow against Spruance.

Thereafter things began to go wrong. During the evening of 18 June Ozawa imprudently broadcast an appeal to the shore-based air forces for a maximum effort next day: American high-frequency direction-finding stations picked it up and passed a fairly accurate estimate of Ozawa's position to the 5th Fleet the same evening. Spruance reacted with his customary caution and refused to close at once, but he did order Mitscher's Task Force 58 to strike against the Guam air forces to make certain that Ozawa would get no support from that quarter.

On the following morning Ozawa's carriers started to fly off the first strikes against the 5th Fleet, but just after the Japanese flagship *Taiho* had flown off aircraft for the second wave she was torpedoed by the submarine *Albacore*. The brand-new 30,000-ton carrier was in no danger of sinking from a single hit but the blast had ruptured her aviation fuel lines, and the ventilation system allowed lethal fumes to permeate the entire ship. All that was needed was a spark and, according to survivors, this resulted when the electric starter of a pump was pressed. A series of explosions ripped through the ship, and to make matters worse an improperly refined grade of oil was being carried as furnace fuel; this also produced inflammable vapour, and when it exploded it blew the bottom out of the engine room. Most of the 1,700 men aboard *Taiho* died with her in the holocaust.

Ozawa suffered another disaster about three hours later when the submarine *Cavalla* put three torpedoes into another of his carriers, *Shokaku*. She sank quickly, leaving Ozawa only four carriers. Meanwhile, the air strikes against the 5th Fleet were not going as well as hoped. Most of the bombers and torpedo-bombers were detected on radar and intercepted before they got within range of their targets. But the later strikes gave the Americans a close shave. The battleship *South Dakota* was hit by a 250-kg (551-lb) bomb and a damaged torpedo-bomber crashed into the side of her sister *Alabama*; two carriers were damaged by bombs and several more escaped damage by good luck and frantic manoeuvring. Over 50 Japanese aircraft had got through the screen, a penetration rate of more than 14 per cent, which would have produced impressive results for experienced pilots. Had the aircrews of Pearl Harbor, the Coral Sea and Midway been alive, there is no doubt that the Americans would have suffered heavy losses.

The Mobile Fleet had launched four strikes, totalling nearly 400 aircraft with the reconnaissance 'shadowers'. The losses ran to 243 aircraft, and a further 30 or more returned with serious damage. By next morning the surviving seven Japanese carriers had only 68 fighters and 32 bombers still operational. The aircraft based on Guam had been wiped out, with 52 destroyed on the ground, 58 shot down and many more seriously damaged. In contrast, the Americans had lost only 30 aircraft, 6 of them by accident and not in action. But the most grievous loss of all was in aircrew. Over 400 Japanese aircrew died, whereas the Americans were able to save 17 out of the 44 aircrew shot down.

The most worrying aspect of the day's battle had been the extremely good performance of the Nakajima B6N *Tenzan* single-engined torpedo-bomber. Codenamed 'Jill' by the Americans, this aircraft had remarkable speed and manoeuvrability, and was capable of over 467 kph (290 mph). It could out-dive and out-turn the Grumman F6F Hellcat fighter, and therefore very few were stopped by the Combat Air Patrol or the ships' anti-aircraft guns throughout the battle. The combination of this bomber with the right aircrew would have been hard to beat. The Americans found that the scale of attacks had tended to swamp their fighter-direction organization (FDO) and it became hard to distinguish between friendly and hostile radar contacts. Under the stress of protracted combat the American pilots tended to forget the need for radio discipline, and the controllers had difficulty in getting through top-priority messages about enemy attacks.

Early in the afternoon of 19 June Ozawa turned north-west to refuel his task force, but Spruance contented himself with recovering his aircraft and continued on a westerly course. As a result, Spruance was subsequently criticized; although his reasoning was that he had no accurate idea of Ozawa's movements, he did not order a night search, which might have produced some news. Next morning at first light a reconnaissance revealed nothing, and a special long-range search was sent too far north of Ozawa's position to achieve anything. Nothing was known until mid-afternoon, by which time the Mobile Fleet was 480 km (300 miles) away. This meant that any strike launched would have to reland in darkness, and few of the American fighter pilots had been trained in this difficult technique. But Mitscher did not hesitate to order a strike, and by 1630 85 Hellcat fighters, 77 Curtiss SB2C Helldiver dive-bombers and 54 Grumman TBF Avenger torpedo-bombers were airborne.

The American aircraft caught up with the Mobile Fleet in fading light and between 1840 and 1900 they launched into a series of coordinated attacks. The defending fighters, about 40 Zeros, fought with skill and determination. They managed to hold off the Hellcats and broke into the large American formations. In spite of being outnumbered the Zeros succeeded in shooting down 6 fighters and 14 bombers, but they were so heavily outnumbered that they lost 25 of their number. The carrier *Hiyo* was hit by aircraft from the USS *Belleau Wood* and sank. Ozawa's flagship, the veteran *Zuikaku*, was set on fire by several bomb hits, and *Junyo* was hit by a single bomb from one of *Lexington*'s aircraft. The smaller carriers

Chiyoda and *Ryuho* were also damaged as were the battleship *Haruna* and the heavy cruiser *Maya*, but Ozawa was able to extricate his force and returned to Okinawa without further loss.

The Americans paid a heavy price for making their attack at such a distance. The desperately weary pilots and observers, many of whom had been in combat throughout the day, had to fly back as night fell. As the needles on their fuel gauges flickered towards 'Empty', pilots looked for a friendly warship near which they could 'ditch'. For those who managed to land on their carriers there were still the hazards of a night-landing to cope with, and many crashes resulted. The story is told of how Mitscher ignored the risk of giving his position away to any lurking Japanese submarine by switching on the deck landing lights, in order to give his aircrew a chance of survival. Eighty aircraft were lost through lack of fuel or landing accidents, but fortunately the escorting destroyers were able to rescue 160 out of the 200 aircrew who were forced to 'ditch' in the sea.

The 5th Fleet was angry and frustrated by its failure to destroy Ozawa's entire Mobile Fleet, and many felt that Spruance's caution had robbed them of a decisive victory. The disaster of the *Taiho* went unnoticed, and if the US Navy had known that three fleet carriers had been sunk rather than two, feelings might not have run so high. On the

Right : **As her aircraft prepare to take off,** *Kitkun Bay* **is shrouded by smoke from an exploding Japanese bomb.**
Above : **Grumman TBF Avenger torpedo-bombers warm their engines.**

Japanese side there was no such doubt about the decisiveness of the victory, and Ozawa offered his resignation to the Emperor. Another large part of Japanese air power had been wiped out with virtually nothing to show for the sacrifice. The Philippine Sea and the Marianas were now under American control, a prerequisite for the invasion of the Philippines, and the Japanese defensive perimeter was badly breached. The performance of the US Navy's submarines had been remarkable, not only in the combat rôle, sinking two carriers, but in the less glamorous job of reporting the passage of the Mobile Fleet at two vital moments.

In retrospect the only doubt about the Battle of the Philippine Sea can be over Spruance's failure to locate Ozawa on the night of 19 June. Had that happened it would have been possible to strike earlier the next day. Other criticisms about his retention of Mitscher's task force do not hold good, for the heavy attacks on the 5th Fleet were only defeated by the overwhelming strength of the fighter defence. Had Spruance been closer to Ozawa, as his critics advised, his fighters might well have been away escorting the bombers. Once again Spruance's caution had saved the Americans from disaster.

The Battle of Leyte Gulf

AS with the landings in the Marianas, the Japanese planned a bold counter-stroke against the American invasion of Leyte in the Philippine islands in October 1944. But this time there was a difference. Japan's leaders at last began to admit the possibility of defeat, and a final gambler's throw of the dice was planned in a desperate attempt to retrieve their fortunes. The result was to be decisive, and so it was, but not in the way planned.

The plan had been carefully worked out by the staff of Admiral Soemu Toyoda, commander-in-chief of the Combined Fleet. Known as the *Sho-1* Plan (*Sho* means victory), it involved the use of virtually the whole of the surface fleet as well as the surviving carriers, with a decoy force to lure the Americans away and three surface forces to smash their way through to the invasion beaches. The surface forces were to be used as a sledgehammer to make up for the desperate shortage of aircraft and aircrew.

The Japanese forces were divided into four parts, and for convenience they are described as follows:

1. The Main Body or 'Northern Force' under Vice-Admiral Jisaburo Ozawa, comprising the fleet carrier *Zuikaku*, three small carriers *Chitose*, *Chiyoda* and *Zuiho*, two battleships partially converted to carriers (but without aircraft), three cruisers and eight destroyers;
2. Vice-Admiral Takeo Kurita's Force A, otherwise the Centre Force, comprising the battleships *Yamato*, *Musashi*, *Hagato*, *Kongo* and *Haruna*, 12 cruisers and 15 destroyers; and
3. Force C, otherwise known as the 'Southern Force', which was divided into a Van squadron under Vice-Admiral Shoji Nishimura and a Rear squadron under Vice-Admiral Kiyohide Shima. These forces comprised only two old battleships, four cruisers and eight destroyers. Although the Southern Force had the same objectives, its two admirals were responsible to different superiors, a division of command which was to prove disastrous.

Ozawa's Northern Force had the unenviable task of steaming southwards from Japan towards the Philippines with the sole object of luring Admiral William Halsey's Fast Carrier Task Force away from the invasion area in Leyte Gulf. Ozawa's rôle was to accept casualties in order to make certain that the other three groups could have a free hand in sinking the invasion fleet. Kurita's Centre Force was to steam from Borneo through the San Bernardino Strait to Leyte Gulf, where

it would unite with the two halves of the Southern Force which had fought their way through the Surigao Strait between Leyte and Mindanao. This massive concentration of ships would then fall on the huge fleet of transports lying helpless off the invasion beaches.

For once the American submarines were not efficient in detecting Japanese movements, and Ozawa's departure from the Inland Sea on 20 October went unnoticed, with the result that he was not yet functioning properly as a decoy. But submarines did spot Kurita's force passing Palawan three days later, and *Darter* succeeded in sinking his flagship, the heavy cruiser *Atago*, and damaging her sister *Takao*. *Dace* sank a third heavy cruiser, *Maya*, giving the *Sho* plan a bad start. Part of Shima's force was also sighted and that night Kurita was seen in the Mindanao Strait. However, the watching submarines still failed to report the whereabouts of Ozawa's decoy force.

The Americans acted on the assumption that such major Japanese forces must be on their way to Leyte Gulf through the Surigao Strait, and Halsey disposed his forces accordingly. Vice-Admiral Marc Mitscher's Task Force 38 was divided into four task groups, and three of these were stationed to the east of the Philippines at a distance of 200 km (125 miles) from each other. Task Group 38.3 under Rear-Admiral Forrest Sherman was the northernmost, off central Luzon with four carriers, two battleships and four light cruisers. Task Group 38.2, under Rear-Admiral G F Bogan, had three carriers, two battleships and three light cruisers, and was off the San Bernardino Strait. To the south, off Samar island, was Task Group 38.4 under Rear-Admiral R E Davison. Halsey's flagship, the battleship *New Jersey*, was with Bogan's Task Group 38.3 to the north. This was the most powerful fleet assembled during the entire war, but it could still be caught off balance if the intentions of the Japanese were misunderstood.

At dawn on 24 October Halsey ordered air searches from Lingayen on the west side of Luzon down to the north of Mindanao, but not to the north or north-east. The result was that the Central and Southern Forces were sighted by noon making for the San Bernardino and Surigao Straits, but the Northern Force still went undetected. Halsey prudently ordered his three task groups to concentrate and took the precaution of ordering the fourth group, Task Group 38.1 under Vice-Admiral J S McCain, back from its refuelling position 800 km (500 miles) to the

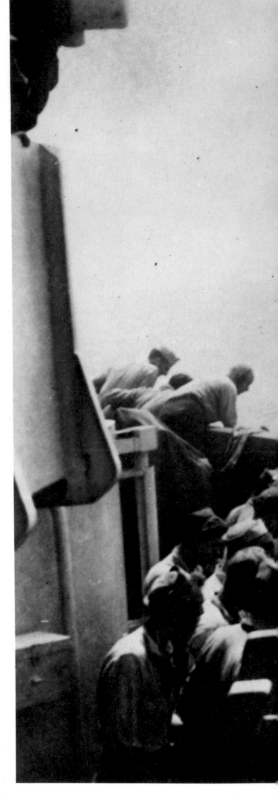

east. But, in the meantime, Task Group 38.3 was attacked by shore-based aircraft, which succeeded in damaging the light carrier *Princeton*. While other ships were trying to help the blazing carrier, Ozawa launched his aircraft against them, but the raw pilots had great difficulty in finding their targets.

Although Ozawa had only about 30 aircraft left after his fruitless attack on Task Group 38.3, this hardly affected the plan, his purpose being to attract attention to himself. At last Halsey ordered a search to the north, the

direction from which the attack had come, but of course Sherman's task group was under heavy air attack and could not comply until about 1400. It was 1640 before the American reconnaissance aircraft found the Northern Force, by which time it was 305 km (190 miles) away to the north-north-east, too far for an attack.

Kurita's Centre Force was all the while under heavy attack from American carrier aircraft. After incessant attacks the 64,000-ton *Musashi* was hit by some 20 torpedoes and

Left : **The American light aircraft-carrier** *Princeton* **burns after being hit by a single Japanese bomb during the Battle of Leyte Gulf. The ship was abandoned after the internal fires got out of control. The cruiser** *Birmingham* **suffered over 600 casualties when** *Princeton* **finally blew up with** *Birmingham* **still lying alongside her.** *Right :* **Admiral Soemu Toyoda was commander in chief of the Imperial Japanese Navy at the time of the disastrous Leyte Gulf battles.**

slowly became unmanageable. The heavy cruiser *Myoko* was also badly damaged, but otherwise Kurita's force had not been hit. Nevertheless, he decided to reverse course for a while to escape further attacks and to wait until he received confirmation that the Americans had swallowed the bait. Halsey obliged by concluding that the Centre Force had been so severely mauled that it could no longer be considered a threat to the 7th Fleet, which was covering the invasion in Leyte Gulf. Acting on that assumption he declared that Ozawa's force was the main Japanese force, and ordered all his battleships and carriers in pursuit. The trap had been sprung.

The American staff organization now compounded the error. At 1512 on 24 October Halsey sent a message to his forces indicating his intentions of forming a new task force of battleships and carriers to stop Kurita's

Centre Force off the San Bernardino Strait. This was only an intention, but it was read by Vice-Admiral Thomas Kinkaid of the 7th Fleet and others to mean that the force had already been formed, and so they assumed that the exit was guarded. In fact no ships at all were guarding the strait, and there was nothing to stand between Kurita and the invasion fleet.

Far to the south Nishimura's fleet was ploughing steadily towards the Surigao Strait, where the 7th Fleet had been alerted to the danger. The old battleships under Rear-Admiral Jesse B Oldendorf which had been detailed for shore bombardment were warned at midday to prepare for a night engagement. Unfortunately the battleships had only a small proportion of armour-piercing ammunition aboard, and had already expended half their outfit of high-explosive

Left above: **The battleship** *Pennsylvania* **takes part in the pre-invasion bombardment of Leyte island.** *Left below*: **Vice-Admiral Marc Mitscher commanded Task Force 38 in the Battle of Cape Engano.** *Top*: **The giant battleship** *Musashi* **pours out smoke as she makes for shore to beach herself in the Battle of the Sibuyan Sea.** *Above*: *Musashi's* **sistership** *Yamato* **survived Leyte, only to be wasted later.**

shell against the beach defences; the destroyers and cruisers were also low on ammunition. But Oldendorf's battleships were still confident that they could hold their own in a night action, thanks to their efficient radar and fire-control.

Just after 2236 on 24 October the Van of the Southern Force was picked up by a motor torpedo boat (PT-boat) patrol off Mindanao, followed by the Rear Squadron about 30 miles astern. As both forces steamed up the strait the PT-boats attacked, firing a total of 34 torpedoes, but only one hit was scored on a light cruiser. By 0200 the next morning Shima and Nishimura were still going well, but they were attacked by destroyers an hour later. The battleship *Fuso* was damaged by one torpedo and the *Yamashiro* by another. Neither ship suffered serious damage, but three out of the four Japanese destroyers were sunk or badly damaged. A second wave

of destroyers was sent in, hitting *Yamashiro* a second time and sinking a destroyer. At 0349 the battleship *Fuso* blew up from a succession of torpedo-hits; she broke in two and drifted southwards. The flagship *Yamashiro* seemed indestructible for she took another two torpedoes at about 0411 without stopping.

The attacks by the destroyers stand out as a classic of destroyer tactics. They completely shattered the Japanese formation, and finally only *Yamashiro*, the cruiser *Mogami* and a single destroyer were left to face Oldendorf's six battleships. In fact the destroyer attacks were still in progress as the head of the line came into gun-range. The waiting battleships and cruisers poured fire into *Yamashiro* and soon she was ablaze from end to end. *Mogami* escaped by a miracle, but Nishimura's flagship capsized at 0419 taking him and most of the crew with her. Shima, seeing the destruction which overtook the other ships, turned about in an attempt to avoid the same fate. He lost only one destroyer in the process, but when daylight came his ships were subjected to heavy air attacks, which at last accounted for the gallant *Mogami*.

While Nishimura was being annihilated in the Surigao Strait battle, Kurita seemed to be in sight of victory. Not until 0412 on 25

October did anyone check whether or not the San Bernardino Strait was guarded, and even then an answer from Halsey was not available until 0645. When the escort carriers learned the news they were practically within gun-range; at 0655 *Yamato* opened fire on them with her 18-inch guns at a range of 27.4 km (17 miles). Despite the fact that these small carriers were almost defenceless, with their aircraft carrying only light bombs, they fought an heroic action against Kurita's ships. The screening destroyers sacrificed themselves to save the carriers, and only the *Gambier Bay* was sunk, at a cost of three US destroyers. Baffled, the Japanese withdrew northwards, just as it seemed to the Americans that they were going to brush aside the puny opposition to get to the invasion fleet.

We will never know what caused Kurita's change of plan, but it was probably the strain of incessant attack coupled with his lack of adequate intelligence. He was aware that Nishimura's forces had been wiped out, and he was also worried about his fuel-supply. But whatever the cause, it was a golden opportunity thrown away, the finest chance since Pearl Harbor to inflict a major defeat on the Americans. After more aimless manoeuvres he withdrew at midday.

Kurita was harried by US carrier aircraft but it was Ozawa who suffered Halsey's full wrath. The American carriers took a terrible revenge, sinking the carriers *Zuikaku*, *Zuiho* and *Chiyoda*. This was later called the Battle of Cape Engano, and it marks the end of the series of titanic battles which, collectively, are known as the Battle of Leyte Gulf. In terms of tonnage and numbers of ships involved it was the greatest sea battle in history, and it achieved the virtual extinction of the Imperial Japanese Navy. Leyte is also noteworthy as the last action in which classic ship-types fulfilled their designed rôle: battleships engaged battleships, destroyers attacked battleships with torpedoes etc. The Japanese came close to victory, but more thanks to American mistakes than their own skill. Had the Americans used the intelligence at their disposal the Centre Force would have been stopped sooner and the Northern Force would have been dealt with as well.

The Invasion of Leyte

IN July 1944, the Americans were faced with the difficult and thorny problem of what to do next in the Pacific. General Douglas MacArthur favoured an assault on the Philippines and thence Japan: he had given his word in 1942 that he would free the islands from the Japanese as soon as he could, and felt that the Americans should honour his pledge; there were also, of course, convincing military reasons why MacArthur thought this the best course. Admiral Chester Nimitz, on the other hand, thought that the American forces should now move to an invasion of Formosa or of a Japanese-held part of China before the final assault on the Japanese home islands. President Franklin D Roosevelt was thus faced with the task of deciding to take the opinion either of the general commanding the South-West Pacific Area or the admiral commanding the Pacific Ocean Areas. The protagonists argued their cases at a conference held at Pearl Harbor in July, but Roosevelt finally came down on the side of MacArthur, and Nimitz, with great magnanimity, threw his planning staffs wholeheartedly into the job of coordinating army and navy plans for the Philippines operation: MacArthur's forces would take Mindanao, the southernmost large island of the Philippines group, whilst Nimitz's forces took Yap

Above: **US Navy gunners duck for cover as a Japanese kamikaze attacks.**
Right: **Japanese pilots are briefed for air operations against the US invasion fleet. Their attacks, however, proved abortive.**

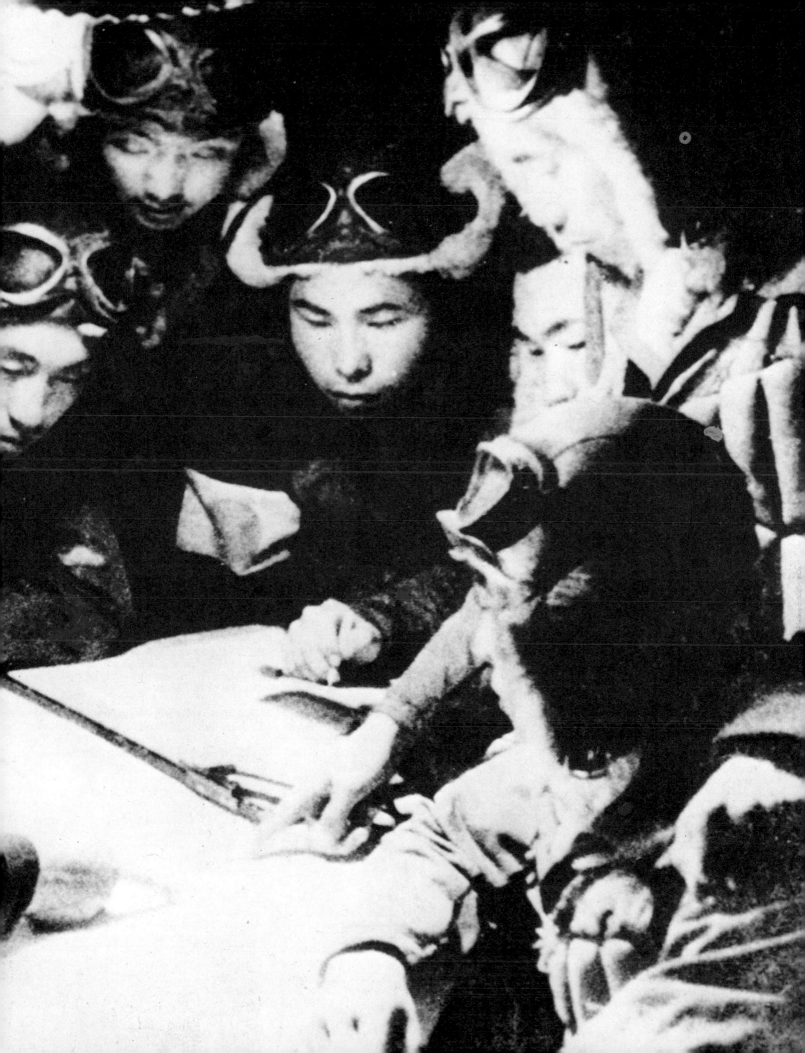

as an advanced base; the two forces would then link up for the assault on Leyte; and finally as MacArthur went on to take Luzon, the main island of the Philippines, Nimitz would take Iwo Jima and Okinawa as bases for the final landings on Japan itself.

First of all the two commanders set about securing themselves adequate forward bases. On 15 September army troops landed on Morotai, just north of Halmahera island in the Moluccas, secured the island against little Japanese opposition and set about building an airfield. On the same day US Marines of Major-General Roy Geiger's III Amphibious Corps landed on Peleliu, towards the southern end of the Palau islands. Here they were met by the usual fanatical Japanese opposition, however, ably directed by General Sadal Inone. Peleliu was only secured on 13 October after both the marines and Japanese had suffered the usual very heavy losses. The fighting finally ended on 25 November, by which time the army's 85th Division had been brought in to reinforce Major-General W H Rupertus's 1st Marine Division. Meanwhile, army troops of Geiger's immediate superior, Vice-Admiral Theodore Wilkinson of III Amphibious Corps, had taken the southernmost island of the Palaus, Angaur, between 17 and 20 September and the vast atoll of Ulithi, some 160 km (100 miles) west of Yap. The last was

taken without opposition, and soon became the US 3rd Fleet's main base.

To support the Morotai and Peleliu operations by diverting the attention of the Japanese, the aircraft carriers of Admiral William Halsey's 3rd Fleet had launched strikes against targets in the Palaus, Ulithi and Yap on 6 September, but met with little opposition. Halsey then moved north to try his pilots' luck against targets in the Philippines between 9 and 13 September. Yet again there was minimal opposition, and so Halsey informed Nimitz that he thought the landings planned for Yap and Mindanao unnecessary, and that the target date for Leyte should be brought forward. The American chiefs-of-staff agreed, and with Nimitz's offer of the loan of III Amphibious and XXIV Corps, MacArthur was able to bring forward the Leyte operation from 20 December to 20 October. The whole history of the planning for the Philippines operation is remarkable for its flexibility and far-sightedness, and nowhere is it more clear than in this last-minute change of plan on 15 September.

The actual landings on Leyte were preceded by the usual naval operations to suppress Japanese air power. Between 7 and 16 October Halsey's planes struck at Okinawa's airfields before turning to do the same at Formosa. Here, however, two of his cruisers were damaged, and Halsey took the con-

Above: **General Douglas MacArthur (in the lead and wearing dark glasses) wades ashore from a landing craft onto the beach at Leyte, thereby fulfilling his promise that 'I shall return'.**
Right: **The invasion of Leyte was only the first step in the US reconquest of the Philippines, parts of which were still held by the Japanese right up to the end of the war.**

siderable gamble of using these as a decoy for the Japanese air forces, which rose beautifully to the bait and were decimated by Halsey's air power. These fast carrier sweeps had cost Japan some 650 aircraft and their irreplaceable aircrew. Just as significantly, most of the planes lost had been the replacements for those lost in the Battle of the Philippine Sea, sent to Formosa from Japan by Admiral Soemu Toyoda, commander-in-chief of the Combined Fleet. Japan's carriers were now almost naked of aircraft. Halsey's success off Formosa was added to by the success of three US Army Air Force formations, the 5th Air Force from New Guinea, the 7th Air Force from the Marianas and the XX Bomber Command from China, all of which launched major raids at Japanese targets within their ranges.

All was now ready for the landings on Leyte by General Walter Krueger's 6th Army. Between 14 and 19 October, the 700 ships of

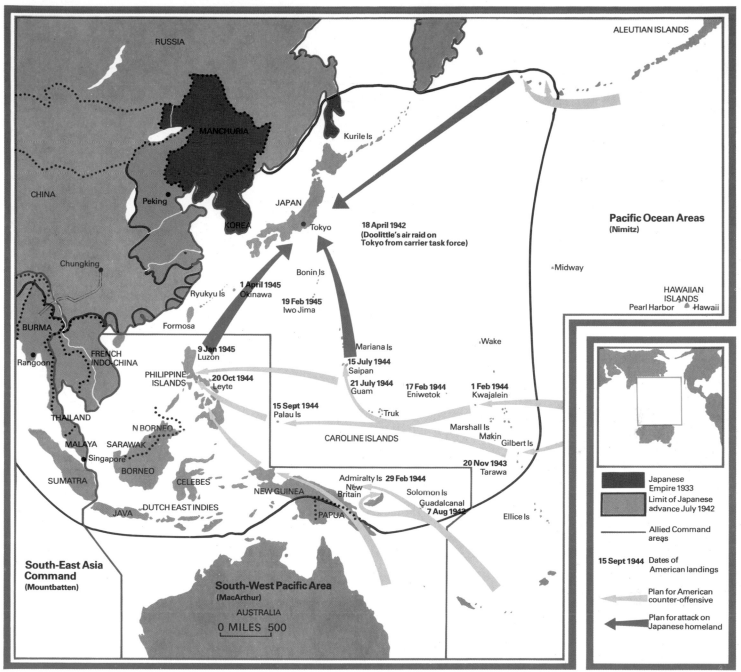

RUSSIA

ALEUTIAN ISLANDS

MANCHURIA

Kurile Is

CHINA

JAPAN

Peking

KOREA

Pacific Ocean Areas
(Nimitz)

Tokyo

18 April 1942
(Doolittle's air raid on
Tokyo from carrier task force)

Chungking

Midway

Bonin Is

Ryukyu Is

1 April 1945
Okinawa

HAWAIIAN
ISLANDS
Pearl Harbor   Hawaii

19 Feb 1945
Iwo Jima

Formosa

BURMA

Mariana Is

Wake

FRENCH
INDO-CHINA

9 Jan 1945
Luzon

15 July 1944
Saipan

Rangoon

PHILIPPINE
ISLANDS

20 Oct 1944
Leyte

21 July 1944
Guam

17 Feb 1944
Eniwetok

1 Feb 1944
Kwajalein

THAILAND

15 Sept 1944
Palau Is

Truk

N BORNEO

Marshall Is

MALAYA   SARAWAK

Makin   Gilbert Is

Singapore

CAROLINE ISLANDS

SUMATRA   BORNEO

20 Nov 1943
Tarawa

CELEBES

Admiralty Is **29 Feb 1944**
New
Britain

Solomon Is

NEW GUINEA

JAVA   DUTCH EAST INDIES

Guadalcanal
7 Aug 1942

Ellice Is

PAPUA

**South-East Asia
Command**
(Mountbatten)

South-West Pacific Area
(MacArthur)

AUSTRALIA

0 MILES 500

Japanese
Empire 1933

Limit of Japanese
advance July 1942

Allied Command
areas

15 Sept 1944 Dates of
American landings

Plan for American
counter-offensive

Plan for attack on
Japanese homeland

Vice-Admiral Thomas Kinkaid's 7th Fleet moved Krueger's 200,000 men from their advanced bases towards Leyte. The two attack forces, VII Amphibious Force under Rear-Admiral Daniel Barbey and III Amphibious Force under Wilkinson, were supported by the six battleships of Rear-Admiral Jesse Oldendorf, which could lay down a formidable volume of heavy gunfire to aid the land forces, and by the aircraft operating from the 16 escort carriers of Rear-Admiral Thomas Sprague's Task Group 77.4. Providing long-range support and protection were the eight fleet carriers, eight light carriers and six battleships of Halsey's 3rd Fleet. As usual, all these naval forces were provided with ample cruiser and destroyer support. The one blemish in the otherwise excellent organization for the Leyte operation was a measure of divided command, MacArthur controlling the 6th Army and 7th Fleet, and Halsey the 3rd Fleet. Still smarting from their failure to

sink all the Japanese carriers involved in the Battle of the Philippine Sea, the men of the 3rd Fleet had the primary function of seeking out and destroying the Japanese Fleet should the occasion arise, and the secondary function of covering the Leyte operation. This was nearly to have disastrous consequences in the Battle of Leyte Gulf, as revealed in the preceding chapter.

To defend the Philippines General Tomoyuki Yamashita, the 'Tiger of Malaya', had the 14th Area Army of 350,000 men. But to cover the possible landing areas and to keep the active Philippine guerrilla movement in check meant that these troops had to be spread over a wide area. On Leyte there was only the 16th Division, commanded by Lieutenant-General Shiro Makino, totalling only 16,000 men. This was part of Lieutenant-General Sosaku Suzuki's 35th Army, entrusted with the defence of the southern Philippines.

The landings went in as planned on 20 October against minimal opposition. The 1st Cavalry and 24th Divisions of Major-General Franklin Sibert's X Corps landed in the area just to the south of Tacloban on the eastern side of the island, and the 96th and 7th Divisions of Lieutenant-General John Hodge's XXIV Corps slightly further south, in the area of Dulag. By midnight on the 20th, the Americans had landed 132,500 men and nearly 200,000 tons of supplies. The Americans pressed on inland quickly before the Japanese could strengthen their defences. Part of the 16th Division had established a beach-head on each side of the Juanico Strait between Samar and Leyte by the 24th. By the 30th, the Americans had occupied most of the north-eastern corner of the island, as far west as Carigara on the north coast, and in the west as far as the lower slopes of the central mountain chain as far south as Burauen, although the front line was only

lightly held. MacArthur and President Sergio Osmena of the Philippines came ashore on the 22nd, MacArthur at this time making his celebrated 'I have returned' speech.

By 30 November the Americans had pushed further forwards, but Suzuki had moved into Leyte. As the 16th Division fought stubbornly to delay the Americans, Suzuki shipped in another 45,000 men and 10,000 tons of supplies before 11 December, when all Japanese ship movements to Leyte were halted. Progress into the mountains was virtually halted, and extraordinarily heavy rainfall made other movement very difficult. X Corps edged slowly towards Limon and Pinamopoan on the north coast, by means of land and amphibious advances, by 7 November. XXIV Corps tried unsuccessfully to take the mountains overlooking the main Japanese base of Ormoc on the west coast against superb defence by the 16th and 26th Divisions. The Japanese defence was finally outflanked on 7 December when the US 77th Division was landed just south of Ormoc. Limon and Ormoc both fell on 10 December, and forces from north and south linked up at Libungao on 20 December. The Japanese were now cut off from their one remaining port, Palompon, to which a few sailing vessels were still operating. Organized resistance

Above : **The light carrier** *Belleau Wood* **burns furiously after being hit by a** *kamikaze* **aircraft.** *Above right :* **The fleet carrier** *Essex* **is hit by a** *kamikaze* **in the area just forward of the island during the Leyte operations.** *Right :* **A comrade ties the** *hachimachi,* **round the head of a kamikaze pilot.** *Far right :* **The Japanese heavy cruiser** *Kumano* **blazes after being hit by dive-bombers.**

ended on 25 December, but mopping up operations against the starving Japanese continued for some time yet. A beach-head on Samar had already been secured, and on 15 December an American brigade landed on the island of Mindoro, to start building an airfield for the forthcoming Luzon operations. By the beginning of 1945 the Americans had secured Leyte, the southern tip of Samar and enclaves on the south and west coasts of Mindoro. Japanese losses so far were in excess of 70,000, and those of the Americans 15,584. Small as these figures may seem in comparison with other casualty figures, Leyte features prominently in any history of World War II because the Japanese decision to fight it out here cost the Nipponese Empire the war: Japan was bound to lose in the long run, but the naval defeat at Leyte Gulf set the seal on it.

Imphal

'THE Army has now reached the stage of invincibility and the day when the Rising Sun proclaims our definite victory in India is not far off . . . Despite all the obstacles of river, mountain and labyrinthine jungle we must sweep aside the paltry opposition and add lustre to Army tradition by achieving a victory of annihilation . . .'

With these stirring words from Lieutenant-General Renya Mutaguchi the Japanese 15th Army, 'aided by the Gods and inspired by the Emperor', crossed the Chindwin river, early in March 1944, with every man laden with enough ammunition and food for three weeks, a supply train of 3,000 horses and 5,000 oxen, and 17 mountain guns carried on 10 elephants. Their objective was not Delhi (although it might have been, had the despised British-Indians collapsed once again under the *banzai* attacks of the Japanese) but Imphal, the great base the British were building up for the liberation of Burma. With enemies on three sides building up their strength helped by the United States, the Japanese generals believed that a passive, defence war was too dangerous. The best course and one suited to the Japanese temperament was to knock out the nearest opponents. It was an awesome gamble, because there were no roads or bridges between Burma and Assam and the victory had to be won while the supplies lasted. The Japanese, however, had spotted the weakness in the widely dispersed British positions. Although Mutaguchi had only three divisions, he could choose the points to strike. In February a limited offensive in the Arakan had drawn Lieutenant-General William Slim's reserves to that area. Mutaguchi believed it would be a month at least before the 14th Army could be reinforced in Assam. He was to be proved wrong. The British flew in reinforcements and supplies in days, but Mutaguchi's utter defeat was due not only to the Allies' superior air power, tanks and artillery, but also because the British, Indian and Gurkha infantry for four bloody months consistently beat the Japanese in their own speciality: close combat.

'Imphal', of course, is simply a label for a whole series of battles fought from 15 March to 22 June. Some of them have only been heard of by military specialists – Sangshak, Nungshigum and Shenam, where whole battles lasting for days were fought for little hills, with nicknames like 'Scraggy' or 'Nippon Hill'. Somehow eight divisions manoeuvred through the jungle and along the forest tracks, but most of these 'battles' were desperate encounters between companies and even platoons. The key position in Kohima, which was the key of the whole Imphal battle, was held by companies of the Royal West Kents and the 1st Punjab Regiment who fought with grenades for their own key position – in peacetime a tennis court! Six Victoria Crosses were won in the Imphal battles.

John Harman, a lance-corporal in the Royal West Kents, when the Japanese with their great tactical skill moved a single machine-gun to a point where it threatened the whole battalion defence, told his section to give him covering fire and attacked it single-handed. He bayoneted the crew without firing a shot and finally held up the machine-gun so his section could see it and threw it away. He was killed on his way back.

Sergeant Victor Turner, commanding a platoon of 20 men of the 1st West Yorkshires, repelled the Japanese by making five one-man counterattacks with showers of grenades. He returned for more grenades and was killed during his sixth foray.

Jemadar (Lieutenant) Abdul Hafiz of the 9th Jats won another posthumous Victoria Cross leading an attack on a Japanese who, for the first time, fairly ran away, an unheard-of event, and the hill on which this happened came to be known as 'Run-Away Hill'. After being mortally wounded he seized a Bren gun from a wounded sepoy and gave covering fire until he died.

Netra Bahadur Thapa, a *subhadar* (captain) in the 5th Gurkha Rifles, told to hold a position to 'the last round and the last man' did so, and was found dead with his *kukri* wedged in

Left : **The Japanese were always able to convince themselves that things were going better than in fact they were.**
Right : **Japanese pioneers set about improving the way forward for the combat formations.**

the skull of a Japanese.

Ganju Lama, of the 7th Gurkha Rifles, with a broken left wrist, a bullet wound in his right hand and another in his leg, crawled to within 28 metres (30 yards) of two Japanese tanks with a PIAT (Projector, Infantry, Anti-Tank, a hand-held weapon throwing a hollow-charge armour-piercing bomb) knocked them out and killed the crews when they bailed out.

Naik (corporal) Agansing Rai, of the 5th Gurkha Rifles, led his section after an attack had 'faltered' (it took a good deal of fire to make a Gurkha attack falter). In three successive attacks, weapon in hand, his section reduced to three men, he killed a machine-gun crew, captured an anti-tank gun and finally, sub-machine gun in one hand and a grenade in the other, took a Japanese bunker holding up the advance, killing its occupants.

The important point to make here is that in Hong Kong, Sarawak, Malaya, Burma and during 1943 in Arakan, the Japanese had appeared invincible, as Mutaguchi had boasted in his order of the day announcing the great offensive called 'U-Go' to smash the 14th Army, and the retraining of the British and Indian troops had not merely improved tactics and weapon skills but had released courage and devotion fully equal to coping with the suicidal Japanese. Also the medical services had greatly reduced losses from tropical diseases.

When the battle began the British had drawn back from 32 to 80 km (20 to 50 miles) from the Chindwin river, which they watched with army patrols and an observation corps of tribesmen (called V Force) organized by British officers (the Nagas west of Imphal were directed by an Englishwoman, Miss Ursula Graham Bower). The nearest point of the railway from India to Jorhat in the far north-east was Dimapur. From it the only supply route was the road through Kohima, a pleasant little town on a ridge which provided a natural defensive position, to Imphal, a valley about 24 km (15 miles) wide overlooked by mountains rising up to 2,100 metres (6,900 feet). Four roads joined there: from Kohima, Sangshak, Tamu and Tiddim, and a subsidiary road from Bishenpur, soon to be the scene of a gruelling battle, to Silchar which also gave access to Imphal. 'Roads' is a purely descriptive term: they were un-metalled and only just motorable until the military engineers improved them. Troops who moved by road could be blocked or ambushed: movement through the jungle up and down the dense forest on the mountain slopes was painfully slow.

Imphal was therefore a strategic centre of communications. Three airfields had been made there (two all-weather), in it were dumps of supplies and ammunition of all kinds, the headquarters of IV Corps, commanded by the outstanding Lieutenant-General G A P Scoones, and garrisoned by the 23rd Indian Division. Another division, the 17th Indian, was based on Tiddim and the 20th Indian on Tamu. (Indian divisions were two-thirds Indian and one-third British, usually two Indian battalions and one British in each brigade. The 2nd Division, which reinforced Kohima, was all-British. 'Indians' means Rajputs, Punjabis, Jats, Mahrattas, Dogras, Pathans, Madrasi Tamils and Gurkhas. British and Indian battalions in the Indian divisions respected each other and got on well together. The all-British 2nd Division fresh from England looked down on Indian troops and in return was heartily disliked.)

The three divisions, because of the width of the front and the nature of the country, were each spread out over some 65 to 80 km (40 to 50 miles). Imphal is 209 km (130 miles) from Dimapur and 145 km (90 miles) from Kohima, and the 17th Division was 257 km (160 miles) south and the 20th 129 km (80 miles) to the south-east. There was nothing except V Force and a battalion of the Assam Rifles between Homalin, where the right flank division of the Japanese was to cross the Chindwin, and Kohima, where Colonel Richards, lately turned out of the Chindits by Wingate because he was over age (at 40!) had been sent to organize its defence with such details as could be scraped up from reinforcement camps and logistic units. The initial dispositions of IV Corps were in any case for an advance, not defence. They were very vulnerable to an aggressive enemy like the Japanese who had the initiative and could strike wherever they chose. When the excellent British intelligence system began in February and March to receive evidence that the Japanese were about to launch a full-scale offensive, plans had to be made to form a solid defensive ring round Imphal. This meant pulling in the outlying units, but not too fast: they had to delay the Japanese in order to allow the mass of civil labour working on the roads and in

Above left : **Careful siting was an important consideration in ensuring accurate reports from forward observation posts such as this one for an Indian mountain battery, a type of artillery that proved very useful in the battles for Kohima and Imphal.**
Above : **While the British and Indians were involved in the desperate battles for the Manipur plain, the Chinese, equipped with American weapons and vehicles, were fighting their way south.**

the depots to be removed to safety, but they were not to tangle with the Japanese too closely and become pinned down.

The real danger was in the north, or British left. The great weakness of IV Corps' position was that its supply lines did not come from rear to front but along the front from left to right. If the Japanese could take or bypass Kohima and cut the railway at Dimapur, not only IV Corps, but Stilwell's Chinese divisions, could be starved to death. British intelligence thought that the biggest force that could come by this roadless northern route was a regiment. In fact a nasty shock was in store: the whole of the Japanese 31st Division arrived at Kohima and cut the road between that place and Dimapur.

The Japanese tactics which so far had proved successful against the British were simple and effective. They would encircle them and set up road blocks of bunkers behind them – they were able to do this at great speed for Japanese soldiers could dig like moles – and the brigades thus trapped were either caught between two fires or, panic-stricken, would leave the road and escape

through the jungle, leaving all their guns and heavy weapons and vehicles behind. However, the Japanese were to discover this was no longer the pattern of events. The 14th Army had a new spirit. If cut off they stood to fight until they had beaten the enemy, or were relieved, and if they could not be supplied by road they were supplied from the air. All the logistics units were taught to do the same. This the Japanese had yet to find out, although they could have taken warning from the beating they had taken in Arakan in February. Accordingly the Japanese spread their effort out: their 33rd Division against the 17th, the 15th against the 23rd, two separate columns from the 33rd and 15th reaching clawlike for the 20th, and the 31st against Kohima.

At first the situation as seen by Slim looked very dangerous. Parts of all three of his divisions were cut off and had to fight their way out with some loss, and an enemy force appeared in the heart of the Imphal base and seized the commanding height of Nunshigum. Colonel Richards in Kohima was cut off and the Japanese then blocked the road behind the relieving brigade. To the spectators it looked as if once more the Japanese would succeed in routing their opponents. Stilwell, who had a very low opinion of 'Limeys' and their fighting ability, became very alarmed. He halted his operations and offered Slim a Chinese division to protect Dimapur and the railway on which he and his large engineer force building the road entirely depended. Slim, however, and his chiefs, General Sir Henry Giffard and

Admiral Lord Louis Mountbatten, were men of strong nerves. Stilwell's offer was politely refused and he was told to get on with his own operations. To the surprise of the Japanese the 5th Indian Division, which had been drawn into the Arakan fighting as they had planned and should have been a month's journey away, was flown in complete with its artillery to Imphal. The 5th Division won the battle of Nunshigum. The 50th Indian Parachute Brigade, sent hastily to Sangshak, was cut off but stood and fought until ordered to break out, thus giving Scoones invaluable days to rearrange his defences. The British 2nd Division was sent to break through to Kohima and open the road to Imphal. The Japanese here made the fatal mistake of fighting tooth and nail for the Kohima ridge: had they bypassed it and made a dash for Dimapur things might have turned out badly for the British, for a long delay might have starved out the Imphal garrison.

As it was, in the eyes of spectators who had no notion of jungle marching and jungle fighting things went at snail speed while Scoones tightened his defences and fought battle after battle, slowly going over to the offensive. Mutaguchi, who had told Lieutenant-General Kotoku Sato of the 31st Division at Kohima: 'A resolute will makes the Gods give way', wrote on 4 June: 'withholding my tears . . . I shall . . . withdraw from Kohima.' Shortly afterwards his 15th Army collapsed and only fragments of its fine regiments, ill and starving, staggered back across the Chindwin, leaving behind 30,000 dead.

Clearing the Philippines

THE reduction of the last Japanese resistance on Leyte by the end of 1944 opened the way for the assault on the main Philippine island, Luzon, where General Tomoyuki Yamashita and the majority of the men of his 14th Area Army were located. Yamashita had some 260,000 troops under his command, and these he divided into three main groupings to defend the key areas of the island. Yamashita himself and 152,000 men formed the Shobo Group in the north of the island; Lieutenant-General Rikichi Tsukada and 30,000 men formed the Kembu Group in the Bataan peninsula area; and Lieutenant-General Shizuo Yokoyama with the 80,000 men of the Shimbu Group held the rest of the island, including the capital, Manila. Yamashita knew that once the Americans had landed he could expect no reinforcements and therefore

decided on a slow defensive campaign, with the intention of tying down as many American troops as possible for as long as possible. With only 150 operational aircraft he could not hope to contest mastery of the air even at the outset of the campaign, and so *kamikazes* were to be launched as the American invasion fleet approached the landing areas, thus giving the pilots as many targets as possible. Once the Americans had landed, unopposed, as Yamashita thought it unwise to risk his forces in the presence of overwhelming US air and naval gunfire support, Yamashita would pull back slowly to the inaccessible mountains, where strong defensive positions had been prepared, and sell the lives of his men as expensively as he could. The Japanese commander had no intention of being drawn into a costly street battle for Manila, and on the whole his plans were sound.

The American plan was also simple. General Walter Krueger's 6th Army, veterans of the Leyte campaign, was again at a strength of some 200,000 men. It was to be lifted from Leyte and convoyed to Lingayen Gulf, 160 km (100 miles) north of Manila, on the west coast, by the 850 vessels of Vice-Admiral Thomas Kinkaid's 7th Fleet. As at Leyte, Vice-Admiral Jesse Oldendorf's battleship force was to provide heavy gunfire support, while long-range cover and air support would come from the aircraft carriers of Admiral William Halsey's 3rd Fleet and from the airfields on Leyte, now occupied by the aircraft of General George Kenney's Far East Air Forces. After landing, the 6th Army would advance south across the central plain of Luzon to Manila and its magnificent harbour. Other forces would spread out to engage the Japanese wherever found.

Above: **Vehicles roll off landing craft in Lingayen Gulf during the invasion of Luzon. Japanese opposition to the landings took the form only of** *kamikaze* **attacks on the vast amphibious invasion fleet.** *Above right:* **Two American officers pause to examine a well camouflaged Japanese 77-mm tractor-mounted gun knocked out by American artillery during the Luzon operations. At first Japanese land opposition was minimal.**

The invasion fleet set sail from Leyte Gulf on January 2, 1945, and made for Lingayen Gulf, where the landings were to take place on 9 January and where the Japanese had also made their main landings earlier in the war. Although the *kamikaze* aircraft did not achieve the results they had hoped for, many warships were severely damaged and the escort carrier *Ommaney Bay* was so badly damaged that she had to be abandoned. On 7 January, however, the Americans launched a series of major raids against Japanese airfields on Luzon, and the planes that escaped this were flown out to Formosa. It was a sad tactical mistake, on the part of the Japanese, that the main damage done by the *kamikazes* was to warships rather than the more vulnerable and important troop transports.

On 9 January, the 6th Army started to pour ashore at Lingayen: on the left was Major-General Innis Swift's I Corps of the 6th and 43rd Divisions, and on the right was Major-General Oscar Griswold's XIV Corps of the 37th and 40th Divisions. By nightfall, the two divisions were well placed in a beachhead of 68,000 men some 27 km (17 miles) wide and 6.5 km (4 miles) deep. There was no sign of the Japanese. XIV Corps' task was to drive through to Manila, whilst I Corps on the left flank dealt with any Japanese interference from Yamashita's Shobo Group. Swift's corps found the Japanese prepared positions very tough opposition, and Griswold was unwilling to advance very far until I Corps had cleared his left flank. But by 23 January, XIV Corps was in the Clark Field area, where it was involved in a week of heavy fighting before it could move on yet again.

Lieutenant-General Robert Eichelberger's 8th Army had assumed responsibility for the southern islands of the Philippine archipelago when the 6th Army sailed north for the Luzon campaign, but it was now decided to use this to help along Krueger's forces. So, on 30 January, Major-General Charles Hall's XI Corps landed in the Subic Bay area and seized Olongapo before moving off east to Danilupihan, which fell on 5 February, completing the isolation of the Kembu Group in the Bataan peninsula. Yamashita had seen this as a possibility, however, and refused to have major forces locked up in the peninsula as had been the case with the Americans in 1942. So before the pincers of XIV and XI Corps closed at Danilupihan most of the Kembu Group had reached temporary safety to the north-east. Nevertheless, XI Corps had two weeks of serious and costly fighting before it had cleared the remnants of the Japanese group from Bataan on 21 February.

The other 8th Army formation used on Luzon was the 11th Airborne Division, commanded by Major-General Joseph Swing. On 31 January, two regiments of the division were landed south of Manila, at Nasugbu and moved quickly inland. The third regiment was dropped on Tagaytay Ridge further inland, on 3 February, encountering only small-scale resistance before linking up with the rest of the division, which then moved north towards Manila, which was reached on the following day.

But here the Americans were in for a nasty shock. Although ordered by Yamashita not to defend the city, Rear-Admiral Mitsuji Iwafuchi and 18,000 fanatical naval troops decided to make a last stand here. The 37th Division drove down from the north into the city, whilst the 1st Cavalry Division moved round the east of Manila to link up with the 11th Airborne Division. Casualties on both sides were appalling, and by the 22nd of the month the Japanese had been driven back into the old walled town, where they made their last stand. Manila was almost totally destroyed in the fighting, the Japanese firing great sections of streets as defensive measures. By the end of the battle, on 4 March, some 100,000 Filipino civilians, at least 16,665 Japanese and 1,000 Americans had been killed, with another 5,500 Americans wounded. An 11th Airborne Division company commander is quoted as saying: 'Tell Halsey to stop looking for the Jap Fleet; it's dying on Nichols Field.' The battle for Manila was the only urban fighting of the Pacific War, and rivalled that of Stalingrad in intensity.

Manila was only half the prize, though, for the harbour in Manila Bay could not be used until the Japanese garrisons on Corregidor and Fort Drum had been eliminated. An amphibious assault and airborne landing on Corregidor, on 16 February, were followed by severe hand to hand fighting before the island was declared secure on 27 February. Some 4,417 Japanese dead were found, and only 19 prisoners were taken. US losses were

209 killed and 725 wounded. Fort Drum fell quickly on 13 April – fuel oil and petrol were poured into the ventilators of the fort and set on fire, incinerating the entire Japanese garrison. Caballo island was landed upon during the same day, but did not fall for two weeks, whereas Carabao island fell without a fight.

By the middle of May the southern half of Luzon had been cleared, but Yamashita was still fighting an excellent campaign in the mountains of the north. For the rest of the war the Americans tried in every way they could to flush the Japanese out, but in the end were content to keep them bottled up in the Cordillera Central and Sierra Madre. At the end of the war, when Yamashita surrendered, he still had 50,000 disciplined men under arms. Yet the Luzon campaign had cost the Japanese 192,000 dead and just under 10,000 captured in combat, compared with just under 8,000 American dead and 33,000 wounded. Both Yamashita and MacArthur, the latter ably supported by Krueger, had fought exemplary campaigns. The only criticism that can be made of Yamashita's is that had he not divided his forces, and then lost contact with them, he might have done better still.

Whilst Krueger's 6th Army was reducing Luzon, Eichelberger's 8th Army was involved in clearing the southern Philippines, defended by the remaining 100,000 men of Lieutenant-General Sosaku Suzuki's 35th Army. Between February and August the 8th Army was involved in some 50 amphibious landings. Normally the pattern was similar: as the Americans landed, the Japanese would pull back into the interior of the islands, to be mopped up by local Filipino forces once the Americans had secured their main objectives and pulled out for the next landing. The exception to this rule was Mindanao, where Suzuki had two good divisions. A series of American landings on the north, south and west coasts, with all forces pushing on into the centre of the island, led to the 35th Army being cut off; it held out in two major groups in the east of the island for the rest of the war. The 8th Army's campaign had cost 2,556 American dead and 9,412 wounded, but as usual Japanese losses were much higher: some 50,000 in all. MacArthur could now turn his attention to his next objective, the Japanese home islands. Once the main Japanese forces in the Philippines had been defeated or bottled up, MacArthur and his staff concentrated on this great undertaking, eventually ruled out by the A-bombs on Hiroshima and Nagasaki.

Above right : **An American flamethrowing tank pours forth a gout of fire on a Japanese strongpoint on Luzon, watched with interest by a pair of GIs.** *Above far right :* **Despite the deployment of considerable US strength in the islands, the Japanese in some areas held out for the rest of the war.** *Right :* **Infantrymen pinned down by Japanese machine-gun fire wait for support.** *Far right :* **A patrol moves through devastated Intramuros in Manila.**

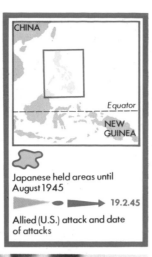

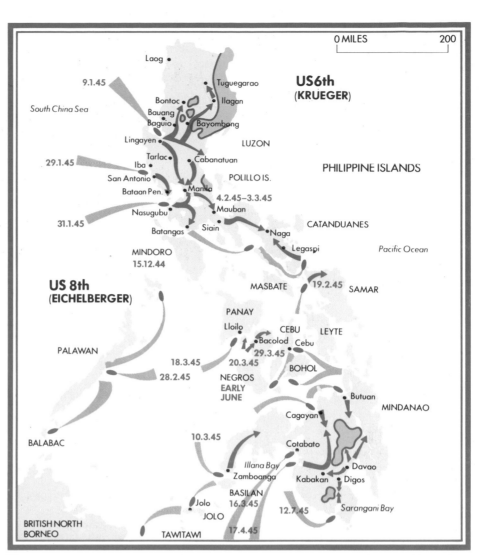

0 MILES 200

Laog

9.1.45

South China Sea

Tuguegarao

Bontoc
Bauang
Baguio

Ilagan

Bayombong

US6th
(KRUEGER)

Lingayen

LUZON

29.1.45

Tarlac
Iba
San Antonio
Bataan Pen.

Cabanatuan

PHILIPPINE ISLANDS

POLILLO IS.

Manila

Nasugubu

4.2.45–3.3.45

31.1.45

Batangas

Mauban

Siain

Naga

CATANDUANES

Legaspi

Pacific Ocean

MINDORO
15.12.44

MASBATE

19.2.45 SAMAR

US 8th
(EICHELBERGER)

PANAY
Lloilo

CEBU

LEYTE

PALAWAN

Bacolod

Cebu

29.3.45

18.3.45
20.3.45

BOHOL

28.2.45

NEGROS
EARLY
JUNE

Butuan

MINDANAO

Cagayan

BALABAC

10.3.45

Cotabato

Illana Bay
Zamboanga

Davao

Kabakan

Digos

BASILAN
16.3.45

Jolo

12.7.45

Sarangani Bay

BRITISH NORTH
BORNEO

JOLO

17.4.45

TAWITAWI

223

Iwo Jima & Okinawa

THE fall of the Philippines had sealed the fate of Japan, principally because Japanese shipping could no longer move between the home islands and the rich 'Southern Resources Area' with its vital raw materials and precious oil. However, the Americans were still to face serious problems in their final approach to the Japanese archipelago, principally from fanatical Japanese defence on the islands of Iwo Jima and Okinawa. The capture of these two islands was to be one of the three final preparatory phases to the invasion of Japan proper; the other two being the destruction of what was left of Japan's merchant fleet by the US submarine force, and the destruction of Japan's industrial potential by Boeing B-29 Superfortress heavy bombers, operating from China and the Marianas.

Iwo Jima is a small volcanic island 7.5 km ($4\frac{2}{3}$ miles) long by 4 km ($2\frac{1}{2}$ miles) wide, but despite its small size it was of considerable tactical importance. Lying at the foot of the Bonin chain south of the main Japanese island of Honshu, Iwo Jima was a great asset to the side which controlled it: in Japanese hands, aircraft could operate from its two airfields to attack B-29s *en route* between the Marianas and Japan; in American hands, the island's airfields could be used as emergency landing fields for crippled bombers, and also as bases for long-range escort fighters to protect the bombers over Japan itself. (A third airfield was under construction.)

Fully conscious of the island's strategic importance, the Japanese were determined to prevent it from falling into American hands. Lieutenant-General Tadamichi Kuribayashi had under his command some 22,000 men from army and navy combat units. For months these men had been honeycombing the northern plateau with strong-points, gun emplacements and other bomb and gunfire-proof positions. Kuribayashi realized that this type of defence would limit him to static operations, but saw that there could be no other type possible in the face of overwhelming American *matériel* superiority.

The US assault was preceded by the most intense 'softening-up' seen in the Pacific war: more than two months of incessant bombing, followed just before the landings by a continuous three-day barrage by six battleships and their supporting forces. Under the overall command of Admiral Chester Nimitz in Hawaii, the assault force was under the local command of Admiral Raymond Spruance's 5th Fleet. (The 3rd and 5th Fleets were in fact the same ships, the former designation being used when Admiral William Halsey was in command, the latter when Spruance led.) The land force commander was Lieutenant-General Holland M. Smith, known not too affectionately as 'Howling Mad'

Below : **An aerial photograph of Okinawa, two days after the invasion, reveals the size of the invasion fleet off the beaches and the ideal situation of Yontan airfield.** *Right :* **Tracer rounds in US anti-aircraft fire form a pattern in the sky above Yontan airfield during a Japanese raid.**

Smith, and the assault force itself was Major-General Harry Schmidt's V Amphibious Corps of three US Marine divisions.

The landings went in on February 19, 1945, and met with determined and accurate Japanese fire: the vast pre-landing bombardment had failed to crush the Japanese defences. The landing area was a black volcanic sand beach on the south-east side of the island, and two marine divisions landed in the first wave: Major-General Keller Rockey's 5th on the left and Major-General Clifton Cates's 4th on the right, with Major-General Graves Erskine's 3rd Marine Division remaining at sea as a floating reserve. Despite some 2,420 casualties, the marines made good progress and cut the island in two by the end of the first day. Part of the 5th Marine Division turned south the next day to assault the dominating heights on Mount Suribachi at the southern tip of the island. As usual, Japanese defence was unflinching, and it was not until the morning of 23 February that the American flag was hoisted on the summit of the volcano, recorded for posterity in a rerun, with a larger flag, later in the day.

The 4th Marine Division was meanwhile making slow progress towards the north, fighting every inch of the way through the elaborate and well-concealed Japanese defences. Elements of the 3rd Division came ashore to aid the 4th on 21 February, with the rest of the division landing two days later. Thereafter, all three divisions of V Amphibious Corps crept forward a few hundred yards every day, the 5th Division on the left, the 3rd in the centre and the 4th on the right, supported the whole way by the guns and aircraft of the 5th Fleet. Vastly superior American strength had its effect, however, and the Japanese were driven steadily north before the marines. By 11 March Kuribayashi's last survivors were penned up in an area round Kitano Point, Iwo Jima's northernmost extremity. But it was only on 16 March that the island was declared secure, and on 26 March that the last Japanese

resistance ceased.

Marine losses had been 6,891 dead and 18,070 wounded; those of the Japanese, almost the entire garrison—only 212 prisoners were taken. Yet the value of the island was proved when 16 crippled B-29s landed safely on the island. By the end of the war, it has been estimated, the lives of 24,761 aircrew had been saved, 2,251 B-29s having landed on the island in emergencies. Yet the planners had to ask themselves what the lessons of the conquest were, for if so small an island could be taken only with casualties such as these, what would the conquest of Japan proper cost in lives?

The final stage of the advance towards Japan was to be the conquest of the Ryukyus, a tail of islands stretching south from Japan itself. Okinawa is the largest island in the chain, some 95 km (60 miles) long and between 3 km (2 miles) and 30 km (18½ miles) wide, with a considerable variety of terrain. Virtually unknown outside Japan before the war, Okinawa was a difficult problem for the American planners, and reconnaissance aircraft had not been able to secure good information about the island. It was estimated that the garrison numbered about 65,000 men, with the main defensive area likely to be in the southern third of the island, where the island's four airfields were located. In fact, Okinawa was garrisoned by the 130,000 men of Lieutenant-General Mitsuru Ushijima's 32nd Army. There were also 450,000 civilians on the island. Ushijima, as was normal for the Japanese, had been ordered to hold the island at all costs: it was expected by the Japanese high command that *kamikaze* attacks on the American fleet during the landing would be decisive, and the losses in ships sufficient to force the Americans to withdraw, enabling the 32nd Army to mop up any forces that had landed. Ushijima elected to fight the same sort of campaign as Yamashita in Luzon: he would attempt to hold the strategically important southern end of the island from a great complex of fortifications built into the hills, thus forcing the

Above left : **Men of the 1st Marine Division blast forward to Naha.** *Above :* **Cautious Marines cover a Japanese on Okinawa, the first island in which large-scale surrenders took place.** *Left :* **Taking no chances, two Americans flame a Japanese strongpoint guarding the approaches to Mount Suribachi.**

Americans to mount a costly series of frontal assaults in order to break through his defences. Despite the hopes of the high command, Ushijima had no illusions about being able to hold the Americans on the beaches should the *kamikaze* attacks fail.

The American assault force was a powerful and well integrated team. As at Iwo Jima, the responsibility of getting the troops to Okinawa and protecting them once they had landed was given to Spruance's 5th Fleet, with the Joint Expeditionary Force being led by Vice-Admiral Richmond Turner. The land operations were to be the job of Lieutenant-General Simon Bolivar Buckner's 10th Army of 180,000 men, with ample reserves being held in New Caledonia and other islands further north. The beach area selected for the landings was just to the north of Hagushi Bay, on the western side of the

island. Two corps were to land in the first wave: the 6th and 1st Marine divisions of Major-General Roy Geiger's III Amphibious Corps on the left, and the 7th and 96th Divisions of Major-General John Hodge's XIV Corps on the right. As the island was beyond the range of any American tactical support aircraft, the 10th Army and the invasion fleet were dependent for air support and protection on the carriers of Vice-Admiral Marc Mitscher's fast carrier force, Task Force 58, and the four British carriers of Vice-Admiral Sir Bernard Rawling's Task Force. Unfortunately for the Americans, Okinawa was within range of Japanese aircraft from Formosa and Japan. Scheduled for 1 April, the main landings would be preceded by the usual intense bombardment and the capture of a number of subsidiary targets in the area as forward bases.

On 26 March, the 77th Division was landed in the Kerama group, some 32 km (20 miles) south-west of the main beaches on Okinawa, to secure them as a fleet anchorage. Little resistance was met, and the capture of a large number of suicide boats eased the minds of the naval command. On 31 March, the 77th Division moved forward to capture the Keise group, only 16 km (10 miles) from

the main assault area, as a heavy artillery base for the support of III and XIV Corps. During the same period, the carrier forces ranged over the area to try to neutralize the Japanese *kamikaze* aircraft. Some 193 *kamikaze* missions were dispatched, the Americans and British destroying 169 of them. Those that got through, however, inflicted heavy losses on the American carriers, which lacked the armoured flight decks of the British vessels. Nonetheless, the carrier activities had destroyed part of Japan's *kamikaze* potential that might otherwise have been used against the more vulnerable invasion fleet.

The great armada of ships carrying the invasion force, some 300 warships and 1,139 other vessels, had meanwhile been approaching Okinawa, and the four assault divisions went ashore without opposition on 1 April, securing a good beach-head for the 60,000 men who landed on the first day. A feint attack by the 2nd Marine Division against the south-east coast helped to distract the 32nd Army's attention as the main force landed. The next day the two corps set about their allotted tasks. III Amphibious Corps turned left, and encountered little resistance in securing the northern two-thirds of the island by 13 April. This was a reversal of

Buckner's earlier decision to leave the clearance of the north until after the main Japanese positions in the south had been overrun. The last organized resistance in the north was finally overcome on 20 April, although many Japanese escaped into the hills to wage a guerrilla campaign against the Americans. Whilst the 6th Marine Division undertook this task, Buckner had also changed his mind about another earlier decision, and now ordered the 77th Division (Major-General Andrew Bruce) to take the island of Ie Shima, where there were 2,000 Japanese troops and a labour force for building airstrips. Buckner had somewhat belatedly realized the importance of these. The division landed on 16 April and secured the western half by the end of the day. But it was to be a bloody eight days before the rest of the island was overrun. The divisional commander said: 'The last three days of this fighting were the bitterest I ever witnessed.'

Back in the south, XIV Corps had been having a far tougher time of it. After pushing through to the east coast across from the landing areas on the west coast by 3 April, they had turned right as III Amphibious Corps turned left. As yet little opposition had been met, but the few prisoners taken revealed the reason: the 32nd Army was waiting in the

south, and the real battle had yet to start. On 4 April, XIV Corps ran into the Machinato Line. The Americans pressed on slowly against strengthening resistance, and by 12 April had been brought to a halt. Ushijima's plans were going just as he had planned, but he then deviated with costly results. The Japanese 24th and 62nd Divisions launched a two-day counter-offensive that the Americans were able to repel with heavy losses. A temporary lull settled over the southern battlefield on 14 April as both sides rested and reappraised their plans. His frontal assaults having failed, Buckner now determined to launch a surprise attack by the 27th Division, previously the army's floating reserve. The attack went in on 19 April and was a failure, as was that of the following day. A bitter comment to come out of this stage of the fighting was: 'You can't bypass a Jap because a Jap does not know when he is bypassed.' The Machinato Line was finally pierced on 24 April, but the Americans were again brought to a halt on 28 April, this time in front of the Japanese main defence line, the Shuri Line. Buckner paused again to reconsider his attack and rest his weary divisions.

Meanwhile, there had been high drama at sea. The first *kamikaze* attacks by aircraft had

Left : **A reconnaissance patrol of the 1st Marine Division surveys Yontan airfield on Okinawa on April 1, 1945.**
Above : **A wounded Marine is evacuated from the beach-head area on Iwo Jima.**
Right : **Colonel R P Ross raises the stars and stripes on Okinawa.**

been launched on 7 April against the ships lying off the island, and although 383 of the 355 *kamikaze* and 340 conventional attack aircraft had been shot down, damage had been caused to many ships, and quite a few smaller vessels had been sunk. At the same time, the biggest *kamikaze* of them all was approaching the island. This was the super-battleship *Yamato*, escorted by one light cruiser and eight destroyers. Bunkered with just enough fuel to get to Okinawa and loaded with as much ammunition as she could carry, *Yamato* was to sink as many American ships as possible before being sunk herself. Encountered by Mitscher's carrier planes on the afternoon of 7 April, *Yamato* took four hours of attack before sinking, together with the cruiser and four destroyers. Aerial *kamikazes* were resumed, with more than 3,000 missions being launched on 12 and 13 April. American losses were heavy: 21 ships sunk, 43 very seriously damaged and 23 badly damaged.

Ushijima launched an offensive by the 24th Division on 3 May, but this was bloodily repulsed by the next day. Buckner was meanwhile reorganizing his forces for the final offensive. III Corps moved into the right of the line, with XIV corps on the left, for Buckner's attack of 11 May, which pierced the Japanese defences at both ends of the line. Ushijima began to pull back from the Shuri Line on 21 May, and by the end of the month the Americans had broken through towards the south coast. However, there was still plenty of fight left in the 32nd Army, and the hills of the southern tip of Okinawa suited their tactics admirably. Buckner pressed home his offensive against gallant resistance, and the last organized defence ended on 22 June. Ushijima committed suicide just before the end, and Buckner had been killed by artillery fire four days earlier. Fighting continued sporadically for another few days, and Okinawa was declared secure on 2 July.

The cost to both sides had been appalling: the Americans lost 7,373 killed and 32,056 wounded on land, and 5,000 killed and 4,600 wounded at sea; the Japanese losses were 107,500 dead and 7,400 prisoner, with possibly another 20,000 dead in their bunkers as a result of the US tactics of using flame-throwers and burning petrol, and then sealing the bunkers with demolition charges. In *matériel*, the Americans had lost 36 ships sunk and 368 damaged, as well as 763 aircraft; the Japanese had lost 16 ships sunk, and the staggering total of at least 4,000 aircraft.

229

Bombers Against Japan

BOTH the Americans and the British placed great reliance on strategic bombing in World War II, partly because in this way costly land operations might be avoided or made less costly by the reduction of the enemy's ability to fight, and also because (in the early stages of the war at least) there was little other way of striking back at Germany and Japan. Once the campaigns had got under way they generated their own momentum and thus became almost impossible to stop, even should Allied leaders have wished to flout public and military opinions.

In the war against Germany, the bombing campaign had been waged by Great Britain and the United States, the former concentrating on area bombing by night and the latter on pinpoint bombing by day. In the war against Japan, the bombing campaign was exclusively an American pursuit, with the Boeing B-29 Superfortress heavy bombers making both day and night, pinpoint and area attacks on Japan's vulnerable civilian, industrial, communications and fuel centres.

The campaign got under way in a very small but significant way on April 18, 1942. Launched from the deck of the aircraft carrier *Hornet* some 1,300 km (800 miles) from Tokyo, 25 North American B-25 Mitchell twin-engined medium bombers struck at Tokyo and then flew on to land in China. The raid lacked any military importance, but it was a profound shock to the Japanese people, and came as an important boost to Allied morale at a very black time.

No further raids were made in 1942, and 1943 was devoted mostly to the building up of Major-General Claire Chennault's 14th Air Force in China. This had started life as the American Volunteer Group flying fighters for Chiang Kai-shek against the Japanese in China, had become the China Air Task Force after the United States' entry into the war against Japan, and was now in the process of being built up into a powerful offensive and strategic weapon. The efficiency of Chennault's air force is attested by the fact that, in 1944, the Japanese launched a series of very large offensives to deprive him of his airfields. It should be noted, however, that as yet Chennault's bombers had struck only at targets within China, and as far afield as

Left : **Boeing B-29 Superfortress strategic bombers crowd one of the giant airbases built by US engineers on every available area in the Marianas after their capture. These bombers quickly devastated Japan's industries.**

Formosa to the east and Manchuria to the north-east.

In May 1944, though, the first B-29s arrived in India *en route* to China, and from the latter's bases these were at last able to strike at targets in southern Japan. The headquarters for this new and rapidly growing strategic force was XX Bomber Command. The first B-29 raid was made on 5 June, the objective being railway communications in the Bangkok region of Thailand. Further exploratory missions followed before the B-29s made their first raids on Japan on 15 June. Although based on airfields in the Calcutta area of India, the B-29s staged through some of Chennault's airfields in China. Here the runways had been lengthened by means of Chinese labour, and fuel brought in by the thousands of tonnes. Striking from this forward base area, the B-29s raided Japanese steel production in Kyushu, the island at the south-west end of the chain of Japanese islands.

Commanded by Major-General Curtis LeMay, XX Bomber Command went from strength to strength between June and December, 1944. The main trouble lay in the fact that there was still no adequate land route to China, which meant the B-29s had to remain based in India, too far from Japan for raids to be launched directly. The bombers still had to stage through China, refuelling from aircraft that had arrived with fuel instead of bombs. Even from China, the B-29s could range only as far as Kyushu, where they met with determined Japanese fighter opposition. Armed with 12.5-inch machine-guns and one 20-mm cannon, however, the B-29s were able to give a good account of themselves. Well streamlined and fitted with four powerful engines, the B-29s were also very fast, giving the Japanese fighters little time to get into the attack, their speed superiority being marginal.

The main weight of the strategic bombing campaign was not to come from China, but rather from the Marianas, the final objective of Admiral Chester Nimitz's central Pacific offensive. As soon as Saipan, Guam and Tinian had been captured in July and August, 1944, Boeing B-17 and Consolidated B-24 bombers of the army air forces moved into the captured airfields. The objectives of these bombers were not targets in Japan, but Iwo Jima and the Bonins further to the north, in preparation for the landings soon to take place. But whilst these raids got under way, engineers were hard at work lengthening and strengthening the existing runways, and building a vast complex of bases wherever

room could be found for one. As soon as adequate facilities were ready in October, the first B-29s of XXI Bomber Command moved in and set about preparing for the assault on Japan.

At first exploratory missions were undertaken, the B-29s from the Marianas blooding themselves in a raid on Truk on 28 October. By November all was ready, and the B-29s of XXI Bomber Command launched their first sorties against Japan on 24 November: over 100 bombers raided an aircraft production facility on the outskirts of Tokyo. For the rest of the year the B-29s continued to raid Japan, building up a store of experience under combat conditions. About four times every three weeks the bombers set off, between 100 and 125 strong. They climbed the whole way, so that when they crossed the Japanese coastline they were at altitudes in excess of 9,145 metres (30,000 feet). As with earlier raids from China, fighter opposition was very strong, the Japanese having deployed their best pilots in the most modern aircraft to meet this dire threat. The fighters over Japan were tough opposition, but the bombers also had to run the gauntlet of other excellent fighters operating from Iwo Jima. This gauntlet naturally had to be run twice, once on the way in and once on the way out. Many bombers, damaged on the way in, were shot down over Japan, whilst others damaged over Japan were dispatched by the Iwo Jima aircraft on their way back to the Marianas. Worthwhile results were being achieved, but losses were too high for the campaign to be continued indefinitely: by the end of 1944 XXI Bomber Command was losing B-29s at an average of six per cent per mission. Only losses under five per cent were acceptable in a prolonged campaign such as this.

In January and February 1945, the American joint chiefs-of-staff met several times to try to sort out the problems of the strategic campaign against Japan. The results had been quite good, although not as good as had

Above : **The industrial sector of Tokyo was completely burned out by American incendiary raids.** *Right :* **Superfortress bombers unload their clusters of bombs over Japan.** *Below right :* **Smoke pours up from Kobe's industrial area, ineffectively masking targets.**

been hoped and expected, but losses were too high, and the weather at high altitude over Japan was very poor, throwing many bombers miles off course and making optical bomb-aiming a chancy business. Radar bombing was of course a possibility, but this did not offer the same degree of accuracy as optical bombing, and it was small but vital defence facilities that XXI Bomber Command was trying to hit. And although production had dropped as a result of civilian dislocation during the bombing, Japan had profited from the small scale of the first raids to the extent of appreciating the problem and dispersing her armament industry.

The joint chiefs finally decided that what was needed was greater concentration of effort, and that the best way of securing this was the transfer of XX Bomber Command from India to the Marianas, so that the whole of General Nathan Twining's 20th Air Force could strike together. Until the move could be effected, LeMay was moved to command XXI Bomber Command which, it was felt, could profit from his experience.

The arrival of LeMay led to a complete change in tactics. Gone were high-level attacks with high-explosive bombs, to be replaced by low-level runs with incendiaries, carried out at night when the Japanese fighter arm was all but impotent. The new tactics were initiated with a fire raid on Tokyo on February 25, 1945 but it was on the night of 9 and 10 March that LeMay's tactics really proved themselves. Some 334 B-29s raided Tokyo, flying quite low and dropping 1,667 tonnes of incendiaries. The effect was devastating: a vast firestorm was started, in which the centre of the city was gutted, 83,000 people were killed and 100,000 more were

injured. Some 51 per cent of Tokyo was destroyed in this and four other raids during the next ten days. Bomb tonnage dropped was 9,365, the B-29s carrying three times the normal load when operating at medium to low altitudes. Only 22 aircraft, or some 1.4 per cent, of the 1,595 sorties dispatched were lost.

Meanwhile, Iwo Jima had been captured, and the B-29s were able to make emergency landings there. At the same time, the problem of Japanese fighters had been removed, and the fighters of VII Fighter Command installed in their place. Flying Republic P-47 Thunderbolt and North American P-51 Mustang fighters, VII Fighter Command was now able to provide escorts for the bombers right over Japan, further reducing the Japanese fighter arm's ability to harm the bombers. Daylight raids could now be made again, and as the Japanese fighters were grounded for lack of fuel (the result of the American submarine offensive against Japa-

nese tankers) or shot down by the escort fighters, the B-29s could dispense with most of their defensive armament, the weight thus saved being used for extra bomb load.

The campaign reached its climax between May and August, 1945, with the arrival of XX Bomber Command. The B-29s were able to roam at will over Japan, and the heart of industrial Japan was burned out. The five largest cities after Tokyo (Kobe, Osaka, Nagoya and Yokohama) were all almost entirely destroyed, and superb American target intelligence work enabled virtually every worthwhile target to be wiped out. HE bombs were dropped in industrial areas to break up the concrete foundations on which machine tools sat and the B-29s also undertook mining operations offshore.

By 1945, the strategic bombing campaign had brought Japan to her knees, and it was a pair of strategic bombers which finally toppled the crippled giant with the two atomic bomb raids in August.

Victory in Burma

WHEN the battles of Kohima and Imphal were over, the Allied high command was able to resume its strategic offensive and, characteristically, this was three-fold. The Americans had only one objective in Burma: to open the road to China in order to supply and mobilize the myriad Chinese armies against the Japanese occupying mainland China. The British were motivated by the liberation of imperial territory, and one school of thought believed that instead of an endless campaign in jungle and mountain, an air- and seaborne invasion of Burma to capture Rangoon would be quicker and cheaper. The third view, strategically very orthodox, was held by Slim, commanding the 14th Army. He believed that he had the measure of the Japanese, and if he could persuade them to stand and fight in central Burma he could destroy them there. Privately, he resolved to take Rangoon from the landward side, not for vainglory, but because he thought that he could do this more quickly

234

than an amphibious force short of many of the necessary craft, and hampered by all the delays imposed by special training and complicated staff planning. This is how the final campaign turned out in Burma in 1945.

The difficulties were formidable. The units of the 14th Army were tired physically, and the 1944 battles and the pursuit through the steaming jungles in the monsoon rain, which had chased the Japanese back across the Chindwin, had cost 45,000 casualties, although many of these would recover. The 14th Army would have to advance over the same desperate communications that had frustrated the Japanese, with a much more modern force making heavy demands on artillery ammunition and petrol. The first

calculations of Slim's logistic staff indicated that he could bring no more than four and a half divisions to bear because of the difficulties of supply. While in Burma the Japanese had, admittedly widely deployed and deficient of modern weapons, some ten and two-thirds divisions and as much as 100,000 service troops, who could function effectively as infantry on demand. This still formidable force was being rebuilt after defeats by the newly appointed commander of the Burma Area Army, the able Lieutenant-General Hoyotaro Kimura.

These logistic difficulties were overcome by fantastic feats of engineering and improvisation: hundreds of miles of new roads were built and surfaced with sacking dipped

in bitumen; transport ranged from elephants to aircraft; the engineers built rafts big enough to float ten tonnes of supplies each along the rivers, pushed by outboard motors; the longest Bailey bridge in the world (351.75 m or 1,154 feet) was built across the Chindwin at Shwegyin; and locomotives to restart the Burmese railways, wrecked by bombing, were flown up in bits for re-assembly or brought up whole on tank transporters from distant India. If ever a victory was won by logistic staff and the Royal Engineers, it was in Burma. In the event they enabled Slim to deploy six infantry divisions and two tank brigades.

The Japanese, numerous and still fired with suicidal patriotism, were to fight very

Above: **Men and machines of the British 14th Army press on towards Mandalay and the climactic battles for central Burma.** *Right:* **Lieutenant-General Sir William Slim, commanding the 14th Army, was one of the most brilliant and popular British commanders of World War II, despite first assuming command in Burma in the disaster-laden year of 1942.**

hard until the end, but they had had the stuffing knocked out of them in 1944. Their diversionary attack in the Arakan in February 1944 had been smashed, and the Chinese Army in India had written off the 18th Division by August. The 14th Army had been attacked by 115,000 men and had killed (or caused to die of wounds, sickness or starvation) 65,000 of them. Casualties fall hardest on junior leaders – captains, lieutenants and sergeants – and no army can take punishment on this scale and remain the same. As for morale, the spirit of the Japanese had changed from the exhilaration of conquering a third of Asia to a feeling of impending doom and determination to die in the service of the Emperor. It made them dangerous opponents, like the Germans, whose emotions were very similar, but it was not a war-winning attitude. By contrast, the British, Indians and Gurkhas, tired as they were, were cheered by victory. Each success in the ensuing campaign spurred them on to the next.

The plan laid down for 1945 was a compromise. In the north the CAI (now under the US Lieutenant-General Dan Sultan, Stilwell having been relieved) with the all-

British 36th Division was to clear northern Burma up to the Chinese border as far as Lashio. The British XV Corps was to embark on a web-footed operation in the Arakan, among the islands and creeks, and keep the Japanese forces there occupied. The 14th Army was to advance up to the line of the Irrawaddy river and take Mandalay.

Slim's own plans went rather further than this. He had two corps: XXXIII (2nd, 19th and 20th Divisions with a brigade of tanks) and IV (7th and 17th Divisions with a brigade of tanks) plus the 5th Division in reserve. XXXIII Corps was directed on the Irrawaddy from the north and north-west to cross the river 80 km (50 miles) downstream and 160 km (100 miles) upstream and close the pincers on Mandalay so, Slim hoped, attracting the bulk of the Japanese defence to that area. Then, when this was under way, IV Corps was to move with great secrecy down the Gangaw valley (which meant building a completely new first-class road, and the RAF holding off every Japanese reconnaissance aircraft) and thrust for Meiktila. Meiktila and Thazi, on a nodal point of the central road and railway system, comprised the main Japanese supply base,

strategically more important than Mandalay, or even Rangoon, because if the Japanese armies in central Burma were starved and defeated Rangoon would be indefensible. However, while the battles of central Burma were at full blast Slim's staff were working on the advance, the 'SOB' or 'sea or bust' plan, with Rangoon as the objective. (No one knew the war was to end so suddenly, and Rangoon was wanted as supply port for the British forces who would be going on to liberate Malaya.) All went according to plan, something unusual in military history, which almost always indicates that the defence was disorganized and resistance feeble. This certainly was not true of the Japanese, who 'fought without hope, but without fear'.

Slim and the 14th Army achieved this largely alone. Credit must be given to the contribution of the Chinese 5th and 6th Armies and the 36th Division, who started south as soon as Myitkyina had fallen in August 1944, but their efforts relaxed by mid-March and the Chinese were diverted home just as the main clash in central Burma was at its height. XV Corps cleaned up the Arakan, but there was no way of developing its further thrust. It was the 14th Army who

Above left: **In a short but vicious fire-fight near Prome, the Japanese ambushed an armoured column but were quickly beaten.** *Top:* **The largest Bailey bridge in the world was built over the Irrawaddy, a river 1,600 m (1 mile) wide in places with strong currents.** *Above:* **British and Gurkha infantry follow up an armoured thrust across one of Burma's many river lines.**

took on the hard Japanese core and destroyed it.

The final battle for Burma was a complex affair, involving an advance up to and across the Chindwin; the secret move of IV Corps so that it arrived to threaten Meiktila from a totally unexpected direction; the crossing of the Irrawaddy, a river 1,600 m (1 mile) wide in places, with shifting sand banks and strong and treacherous currents, in four places 240 km (150 miles) apart; followed by a number of operations with the aim of provoking the Japanese into counterattack and then destroying them.

XXXIII Corps advanced in the north, the 19th Division crossing the Irrawaddy north of Mandalay in January and turning south along the east bank. The 20th Division

crossed 65 km (40 miles) downstream of the city on 12 February and the British 2nd Division on 24 February, on their left. The crossing points were cunningly concealed, but were not unopposed. Japanese reaction was prompt, but true to their doctrine they attacked immediately, as soon as any force could be brought up to the 14th Army's bridgeheads, and they were defeated piecemeal. One counterattack by 1,200 Japanese infantry cost them 953 killed, and in one of the rare Japanese tank attacks Hawker Hurricane fighter-bombers destroyed 13 of the meagre Japanese stock. Then, with all the freedom conferred by air supply, the three divisions fanned out to cut the routes south of Mandalay to Rangoon and east to Maymyo, while inside this envelopment two pincers closed on the city itself.

Kimura reacted satisfactorily, pulling in his forces for a battle round Mandalay, only to find he had been fooled by an elaborate deception plan to make him believe that all the weight of the British offensive was in the north. IV Corps, tanks and all, had been secretly marching down the Gangaw valley, protected by the RAF from Japanese reconnaissance aircraft, to force a passage across the Irrawaddy 160 km (100 miles) south-west of Mandalay and only 80 km (50 miles) from the vital depots at Meiktila. Seeing the danger, Kimura switched his forces there, but he was too late. By 1 March, Major-General 'Punch' Cowan's 17th Division, with the 255th Tank Brigade, had surrounded Meiktila, which fell in four days. Almost the whole Japanese garrison, strongly dug in and amply provided with artillery and ammunition from the depots, was killed. The Japanese immediately counterattacked, and now the armoured/mechanized columns were able to take toll of them in the open, so that a continuous series of battles was fought across the entire front. At the same time, Mandalay fell after much bitter street fighting. On Mandalay Hill, converted to a fortress and taken by British and Gurkhas in hand-to-hand fighting, the defenders had to be burned out finally by rolling drums of petrol into their bunkers and setting fire to them with tracer bullets. However, a sign of the times was that the ancient Fort Dufferin, the keep of the city and proof against heavy artillery and bombing, was tamely evacuated. By the end of March, the decisive battle of central Burma had been fought and won, and Slim was anxious to advance on Rangoon.

At this point there was almost a serious setback. The sudden withdrawal of the Chinese/American forces was tolerable, but what was totally unexpected was the decision to use the USAAF element of the air transport force to ferry them out, as the whole mobility of the 14th Army depended on it. Fortunately, the US chiefs-of-staff relented after appeals came from Admiral Lord Louis Mountbatten and the British chiefs in London, and rescinded the order until 1 June or the fall of Rangoon, whichever was the earlier. In fact the real deadline was 15 May, as the monsoon rains could be expected on that date, and these would slow down or stop

all armoured operations and interfere with air operations, and therefore Rangoon had to fall in 40 days – with some 400 km (250 miles) to cover as the crow flies and against Japanese resistance.

Slim ordered IV Corps to drive straight down the Meiktila–Rangoon road, using one division to leapfrog through another, with armoured battle-groups leading without any regard for the flanks. They would get to Rangoon first and then turn back to mop up or consolidate, should any Japanese resistance flare up behind them. At the same time, Operation Dracula, at Slim's request, was reduced in size so that it could be expedited and Rangoon attacked from the sea to coincide with the last stages of the land advance and thus pin any reserves. On the other, longer route to Rangoon through Prome XXXIII Corps was to advance from the west. The Japanese forces who attempted to come in from the east were checked by a resistance movement carefully fostered in advance by the Karens, and by a technique developed in Burma by the Chindits: clandestine ground observers with radio sets calling for strikes by the RAF. By 22 April, Slim's advance had reached Toungoo. On 1 May, the day before the Dracula force was to land, a reconnaissance aircraft flying over Rangoon saw painted on the roof of a jail, which was known to hold many British prisoners of war, the words: 'Japs gone. Exdigitate' (RAF wartime slang meaning 'get a move on' – 'pull your finger out').

The Japanese had indeed gone, in a panic, and the landings were unopposed. The pilot of an RAF de Havilland Mosquito decided to land on the Rangoon airfield, where he damaged his aircraft, walked to Rangoon, hitched a lift downriver in a sampan and brought the news that Rangoon was empty.

The Japanese had yet to surrender, and the last phase of the war was both cruel and unnecessary. For the field army surrender was impossible; in fact Japanese-speaking liaison officers could not persuade some to do so even after the order to cease-fire from the Emperor himself was broadcast from Tokyo; it was believed to be a propaganda trick. The surviving Japanese, without ammunition or supplies, were lying up in the hilly tract – the Pegu Yomas – west of IV Corps' route and were now cordoned off by a belt of strongpoints down the road. They were ordered to break out and cross the dangerous Sittang river by raft, or by swimming, and then make for Thailand to continue the struggle. The weather was bad, the river in flood, many were ill and all were starving. They were shot like animals in a game drive by the 17th Division as they crossed the road, or from Bren gun posts along the banks when they were in the river. Many were drowned and many more killed by the villagers on the east bank. At last, a few survivors gave up. For the Japanese it was a sordid ending to a desperate venture. For the British-Indian Army, of the Raj, who were never to fight another war as such, it was a triumph, and for Slim and his commanders it was a military masterpiece.

The War in China

JAPAN's interest in China, principally as a market for her growing industries, was of long standing. However, from 1931 onwards Japan had stepped up her pressure in China, especially in the military sense. Various incidents in the 1930s culminated with the 'Marco Polo Bridge Incident' of July 7, 1937 when Chinese and Japanese troops clashed just outside the city in an affair carefully engineered by the Japanese. Here at last was the excuse they had been waiting for, and the Japanese wasted no time in launching a full-scale invasion of China.

Although Generalissimo Chiang Kai-shek's Chinese forces numbered some 2,000,000 men, their quality was poor, and both armament and leadership were sadly deficient. Chiang's main interest at this time, and in the years to come, was the problem of the communist guerrillas of Mao Tse-tung, although the two sides in the civil war had nominally dropped their differences in the face of the foreign threat. The Japanese Army, on the other hand, was a small but formidable force, well equipped and led, and full of fighting ability and skill. Unlike the Chinese, moreover, the Japanese had excellent army and navy air forces, and these played important strategic and tactical rôles until the advent of the American Volunteer Group checked their activities. China's most powerful weapon, it could be argued, was world opinion, or rather American opinion, of the Japanese invasion. Almost total condemnation led to a gradual increase in the supply of money and modern weapons to Chiang's government.

At first, however, the Japanese had it all their own way. Between July and December 1937, forces from Manchuria made large gains to the north of the Yellow river. Large areas of Chahar and Suiyuan were taken, but the main effort went into a drive south down the railway towards Hankow, Nanking and Sian. Civil unrest behind them combined with problems in logistics to halt the drive of the North China Area Army in December.

Further south, the China Expeditionary Army had invaded Shanghai on 8 August. The Chinese put up a surprisingly effective resistance, and it was not until 8 November that the Japanese were able to clear Shanghai. By the end of the year further reinforcements

cut to pieces the Japanese 5th Division in the Battle of P'inghsinkuan in northern Shansi.

On 12 December, the Japanese made a grave strategic error, divebombing British and American gunboats on the Yangtze river, sinking the American *Panay*. The attack was quite unprovoked, and caused enormous anger in Britain and the United States. Although Japan immediately paid a large indemnity, American public opinion was now firmly against the Japanese.

Determined to link up their two areas of control, the Japanese launched renewed offensives in January 1938. The North China Area Army struck south again after securing all of Shantung, and although its progress was steady, a nasty shock was in wait. During April, some 60,000 Japanese were cut off at Taierchwang by 200,000 Chinese under General Li Tsung-jen. After a desperate struggle, the Japanese hacked their way out to the north again, but only at the cost of 20,000 dead. After a swift regrouping, however, the North China Area Army renewed its advance in May, taking Kaifeng by 6 June. By the end of the month, the whole of the Nanking to Peking railway was in Japanese hands. Then, advancing west from Kaifeng to take the key junction of Chengchow on the Hankow railway, the Japanese were rebuffed when the Chinese breached the Yellow river dikes, flooding large areas and causing considerable loss in men and *matériel* to the Japanese. The offensive was cancelled in July.

The Japanese then shifted their main line of advance further south, and once again made progress towards Chiang's capital of Hankow. The city finally fell after very bloody fighting on 25 October. Chiang again moved his capital, this time to Chungking, further up the Yangtze river in the province of Szechwan.

On 12 October, meanwhile, the 23rd Army, part of the 6th Area Army, had landed near Hong Kong and moved quickly on Canton, China's most important port after Shanghai. Canton fell on 21 October, but the Japanese then felt that a reappraisal of their overall strategy was called for.

It was now decided that instead of the rapid advances of the previous 18 months, a war of attrition would be waged. With civil unrest and guerrilla operations rife in the areas they had conquered, the Japanese thought that additional conquests would be futile, and so decided instead to concentrate on destroying Chiang's forces wherever they could be found. Only after the Chinese armies had been destroyed, the Japanese felt, could the rest of China be occupied and pacified. In 1939, therefore, the Japanese confined themselves to securing a number of ports previously left untouched between Shanghai and Canton, taking the island of Hainan, and straightening their line in the Hankow and Wuchow region of central China.

Activities in 1940 were limited to the communists' so-called '100 Regiments Offensive' between 30 August and 30 November, when guerrillas attacked Japanese posts in Shansi,

Above: **The Japanese seemed invincible in the early years of the Sino-Japanese War. Only China's vast size seemed to prevent them from gaining outright victory.** *Above right*: **Moving south towards Canton, these Japanese troops pause for a hasty meal on the road.**

had allowed the China Expeditionary Army to move inland along the line of the Yangtze river to take the Chinese capital, Nanking, by 13 December.

By the end of the year, therefore, Japan had taken two large and strategically important areas of China. With Chiang's attention drawn more to this threat than to themselves, the communists had also profited, securing most of north-west China for themselves. Nevertheless, it should be noted that the communists' 8th Route Army, under the command of the able Chu Teh, had helped the nationalist cause considerably with raids on the Japanese. Indeed, in the only major battle against the Japanese fought by the communists, on 25 September the 8th Route Army's 115th Division had ambushed and

Chahar, Hopeh and Honan, disrupting the Japanese rear areas very successfully. For their part, the Japanese devoted 1940 to Indo-China, which they began to occupy in September. This proved the first link in the chain of events that was to take Japan to war with the United States.

In 1941, the Japanese launched a series of reprisal raids for the '100 Regiments Offensive'. The series continued into 1943 and cost the communists some 100,000 dead. Now, preoccupied with the events that led her to the world war, Japan's activities in China slumped considerably.

1942 was also marked by the continued lull in operations, with Japanese attention turned towards the consolidation of her conquests in South-East Asia and in the Pacific. The Japanese therefore remained on the defensive in China, and Chiang confined his efforts to supporting the British in Burma. For only here, via Rangoon and the Burma Road, could American *matériel* aid reach him. Within China, acute command problems arose between Brigadier-General Claire Chennault, commanding the China Air Task Force (lately the American Volunteer Group), and Lieutenant-General Joseph Stilwell, Chiang's chief-of-staff and military adviser. With the cutting of the Burma Road and the institution of the airlift of supplies 'over the hump' of the eastern Himalayas, there were not enough supplies to go round, and each commander wanted the majority of what did arrive for his own forces. Concerned with the security of China on land, Stilwell wanted the supplies for the Chinese army. Chennault, on the other hand, thought that the war could only be taken to the Japanese by his growing air forces, and requested priority for his needs. The eventual allocations satisfied neither party, although as Stilwell had believed in a near parity of supplies for each party, he was the better satisfied.

In 1943, China's position was desperate. Her isolation from western sources of supply had profound effects on her armed forces and had the Japanese been interested in major offensives, the Chinese would have found it hard, perhaps even impossible, to check

them. But the Japanese were content to launch instead the first of their series of 'rice offensives'. With many of their combat veterans having been shipped out to active theatres, the Japanese armies in China now had large numbers of raw recruits. The rice offensives, local attacks with limited objectives, were an ideal means of blooding them. The idea behind the offensives was for the Japanese to drive into a hitherto untouched area of China just after the rice crop had been harvested. The Japanese would advance swiftly, seize the harvest to feed themselves, and then pull back. In one of these offensives, however, the Japanese suffered a sharp rebuff at the Battle of Changteh, when American air support enabled the Chinese to throw the Japanese back in an action that lasted from 23 November to 9 December.

Roosevelt had meanwhile arbitrated in the Chennault/Stilwell controversy in favour of the former, who was now promoted to major-general and appointed to the command of the new 14th Air Force in China. Chennault was thus able to increase the scope of his attacks on the Japanese rear areas.

Chiang's efforts in 1943 were restricted mainly to the establishment of a blockade of the communist-controlled areas of north-west China, despite the truce between the two parties.

In 1944, the Chinese communists and the Japanese came to an unofficial truce, although

it is still not known whether this was negotiated or merely allowed to happen. The result was that the Japanese were able to deploy troops from this area in more important zones, and the communists were able to consolidate yet further their hold on north-west China.

Most of the Japanese forces from the north were shifted south for an offensive against Chennault's airfields. Built by hundreds of thousands of Chinese coolies, these were now numerous and well placed to make strategically significant raids on Japanese positions as far afield as Formosa and Manchuria. The most important of these bases were Nanning, Liuchow, Kweilin, Lingling, Hengyang and Chihkiang, all but the last being on the old Hanoi to Changsha railway, and at Laohokow and Ankang on the upper Han Chiang river. The Japanese now decided that these must be eliminated, the northern pair by an attack from Kaifeng, and the southern bases with a three-pronged offensive from Indo-China in the south, Canton in the east and Changsha in the north-east. Throughout the period from January to May 1944, the Japanese planned their offensives carefully and gathered in supplies. At the same time, General Yasuji Okamura's China Expeditionary Army undertook a series of attacks intended to clear the rail lines of north-east China of the guerrillas plaguing them and so ease the problems of

Far left : **In Shanghai the Chinese put up an unexpectedly fierce resistance, and the Japanese had to fight hard to gain their objective. Here Japanese marines have loopholed the banister of the steps to gain protection from Chinese fire.** *Above :* **Allied leaders visit the Flying Tigers' headquarters in Chungking. From left to right the first four are Field-Marshal Sir John Dill, Brigadier-General Claire Chennault, Lieutenant-General 'Hap' Arnold and Lieutenant-General Joseph 'Vinegar Joe' Stilwell.** *Left :* **A Japanese infantry support howitzer in action.**

the Japanese logistical staffs.

Not foreseeing what was to come, Chiang allowed Stilwell to use the best Chinese formations for an offensive in Burma, starting in May. Four days before this Chinese Yunnan offensive started on 11 May, the Japanese launched their east China offensive. In fierce fighting the Japanese advanced steadily against patchy opposition. Most of Chennault's airfields were lost by the end of November, by which time the Chinese position was desperate. The Yunnan offensive in Burma was called off and the two best divisions flown back to China by American aircraft. Chiang, whose relations with Stilwell had been poor for some time, finally had him replaced with Major-General Albert Wedemeyer on 18 October. Wedemeyer reorganized the Chinese defence, and in a counteroffensive east of Kweiyang on 10 December finally brought the Japanese to a halt.

In January and February 1945, however, the Japanese again went over to the offensive in south-east China, making great conquests on each side of the Hanoi to Hankow railway. In March, the offensive was extended into central China. The region between the Yangtze and Yellow rivers was seized, together with its major rice crop. For the Americans, the important air base at Laohokow was a major loss when it fell on 8 April after a sterling defence beginning on 26 March. The Chinese counterattacked on 10 April and halted this central offensive, and later managed to do the same with renewed offensives against Changteh and Chihkiang.

With the tide of war now running very strongly against them, the Japanese realized that they were overextended in China, particularly at the expense of the Kwantung Army in Manchuria, where the Russians now looked distinctly threatening. From May onwards Okamura began to pull his horns in and rationalize his positions. He was not fast enough. Chinese offensives had cut the Japanese links with Indo-China by the end of May. The Chinese offensives continued, and by the beginning of July some 100,000 Japanese troops were cooped up inside a defensive perimeter at Canton. Ably supported by American air power, the Chinese drove north-east, pushing the Japanese before them towards Kaifeng. The great airfield complex at Kweilin fell back into Allied hands on 27 July.

The Chinese drove on into August, when the armistice came and the Japanese laid down their arms, most of which were gladly seized by Mao's communists and Chiang's nationalists. With the Japanese threat removed, the Chinese civil war resumed activity.

Russia's War Against Japan

Above left : **Soviet units cross the Great Khingan mountains in north-east China during the lightning campaign against the Japanese.** *Above :* **Russian troops come ashore during landing operations carried out as part of the offensive to secure Manchuria, Sakhalin and the Kuriles.**

ON April 13, 1941 the Russians and Japanese signed a non-aggression treaty, and yet just under three and a half years later Russian forces invaded the Japanese puppet state of Manchuria as well as Inner Mongolia and Korea, and even parts of Japan in the form of the Kurile islands and Sakhalin. The reason was quite simply that Russia wished to regain the portions of the tsarist empire lost in the Russo-Japanese War of 1904 and 1905. At the Yalta Conference of February 1945, between Churchill, Roosevelt and Stalin, the two western leaders had agreed to allow Russia's ambitions in the east if Russia entered the war against Japan within three months of the conclusion of the war against Germany. Great Britain and the United States wished for Russian intervention so that Japan's forces would be yet further weakened before the Allies launched their great invasion of Japan in November 1945; and Russian intervention was almost certainly sure to destroy Japan's Kwantung Army.

A large part of Japan's heavy industry was based in Manchuria, or Manchukuo as it was known to the Japanese, and it was from here that Japan's invasion of northern China in 1937 had started. At its peak, the Kwantung Army had been a mighty force, but relative peace on this front, coupled with the constant and growing demands from other fronts as the war progressed, meant that the best formations and equipment had been bled off to supply the needs of other Japanese forces. In the middle of 1945 the Kwantung

Army was still formidable on paper, but its *matériel* was obsolete, and its understrength divisions were mostly manned by reservists.

For his invasion, however, Stalin assembled powerful forces, with the best of modern equipment, and with men and commanders well versed in the techniques of modern mobile warfare after their titanic war with Hitler's Germany. Three large fronts, or army groups, were gathered for the offensive, although only two were to play major rôles. West of Manchuria was Marshal R Ya Malinovsky's Trans-Baikal Front of five armies, one of them a tank army. These would strike south towards Peking in China, and south-east towards Tsitsihar, Harbin and Changchun. In their south-east thrust the armies of the Trans-Baikal Front were to link up in Manchuria with the armies of Marshal K A Meretskov's 1st Far East Front, striking west with four armies from eastern Siberia. In the north was the 2nd Far East Front, under General M A Purkaev. This front's forces were to take the great northern bulge of Manchuria, only lightly held by the Japanese. Other formations of the 1st Far East Front, notably the 16th Army, were to invade the Japanese half of Sakhalin island from the north. Finally, a mixed force of marines and infantry was to invade and take the Kurile islands from Kamchatka, with the aid of the Pacific Fleet. Overall command was exercised by Marshal A M Vasilevsky, and once the Trans-Baikal and 1st Far East Fronts had linked up, the Russians were to drive on Port Arthur, one of the most important objectives of the campaign.

On the whole, the problems the Russians would have to face were geographical and climatic, especially in the west, where Malinovsky's forces would have to cross large parts of the waterless Gobi Desert. But in the east, on the Ussuri river front, the Japanese had long realized that in a war with Russia this area would be very vulnerable, and had accordingly built fixed fortifications in great depth. To deal with these, the Russians deployed forces experienced in dealing with German fixed defences.

Two days after the first atomic bomb had been dropped on Hiroshima on 6 August, Russia declared war on Japan. The powerful air forces gathered for the Manchurian campaign struck out at Japanese targets as the armies rolled over the frontiers swiftly and irresistibly, with the exception of some of the 1st Far East Front's formations. On the Mongolian front, the Japanese fell back in good order and dug in on the slopes of the Khingan mountain range. But Malinovsky's

armour burst through in the south, outflanking the more northern Japanese positions. Thereafter, the Russians pressed on swiftly and ruthlessly, crushing or bypassing Japanese centres of resistance to ensure the greatest speed. Changchun had fallen by 20 August, as had Mukden. The 6th Guards Tank Army rolled on to Port Arthur, which fell on 22 August. The lightning advance of these forces had broken the back and the will of the Kwantung Army, in a display of dazzling mobile warfare rarely seen before or since. Great credit must go to the Red Air Force, which kept the tanks supplied with fuel, and the men with water and food.

Further to the south, more of Malinovsky's forces had struck down through the Gobi Desert towards Kalgan and Chengteh, the latter of which fell on 18 August, allowing the Russians to press on to the coast. Both Kalgan and Chengteh were taken, with the aid of the Chinese Communist 8th People's Army.

In the east, Meretskov's forces at first had considerable trouble with the fixed defences between Lake Khanga and the sea, the Japanese even going so far as to launch counterattacks which the Russians found very dangerous. By 14 August, however, the 1st Far East Front had broken through the fortifications and appalling terrain to open

country. The advance on Harbin now got under way in earnest. Aided by the Pacific Fleet, operating from Vladivostok the Russian land forces had also probed far into Korea. In the far north the 2nd Far East Front was making steady progress against moderate opposition, and the 16th Army was moving well down into Sakhalin.

On 14 August, the Japanese surrendered unconditionally, but not the slightest notice was taken by the Russians, who were determined to secure all their objectives before halting. The Russians claim, however, that in defiance of their government's surrender order, many Japanese units, especially in the Kirin and Harbin areas, continued to offer stiff resistance. On 17 August, the commander of the Kwantung Army got in touch with Vasilevsky and tried to arrange a ceasefire, but the Russian commander refused on the grounds that Japanese forces were still fighting after the previous surrender. The reason was probably that Japanese communications had broken down and the relevant formations did not know of the surrender, or if they did, their commanders had ordered them to fight on regardless. The major industrial city of Harbin was taken by the 1st Far East Front on 18 August, and elsewhere the Russian advance continued apace. By the time all the Japanese forces in

Manchuria had laid down their arms on 27 August, the Russians had seized all their objectives.

An assessment of the campaign must take into account the weakness of the Japanese, but nonetheless the Russians' performance was a staggering one. Battle-wise and tough, they had also clearly learned much from the Germans' manifest ability with armoured and mobile forces. Although their casualty figures are probably too low, it cannot be by too much: 8,219 dead and 22,264 wounded. The Russians claim also to have killed 83,737 Japanese, wounded an unknown number, and taken at least 600,000 prisoners. Most of the latter were shipped off to Russia, and as with many of Russia's German prisoners, a great number were never seen outside Russia again.

If the performance of the Russians was a good one, that of the Japanese was odd. Even allowing for the fact that it was at the end of the war, and that morale was low, some units had quite uncharacteristically given up without a fight. Other formations, however, fought with the old Japanese bravura, despite the obsolescence of their equipment and the poor physical condition of most of their men.

At minimal cost, Russia had secured for herself a vast slice of eastern Asia, together with an excellent all-year port.

The Atomic Bombs

WITH the conquest of Okinawa completed, the Americans were faced with the appalling prospect of invading Japan. Plans were drawn up for Operation Olympic, a 6th Army landing on Kyushu on November 1, 1945 and for Operation Coronet, 1st and 8th Army landings on Honshu on March 1, 1945. Judging by the past performance, the Japanese would put up a powerful and fanatical defence, and American planners estimated that the invasion forces would suffer at least 1,000,000 casualties before the back of the defence was broken. What else could the Americans do? It seemed unlikely that the Japanese would surrender unconditionally, and so the Allies would have to invade the Japanese home islands in order to bring the Pacific war to a successful conclusion.

Unknown to all but a very few high ranking officers and politicians, another solution was being worked upon. For some time, the possibilities of radioactive materials for explosive purposes had been suspected, and a large team of Allied scientists had spent a great part of the war trying to develop a weapon based on uranium or plutonium. At last, the scientists were ready for their first practical test at Alamogordo in New Mexico. An atomic device was triggered off by remote control on July 16, 1945 and a light 'brighter than a thousand suns' burst over the desert. Seconds later an enormous blast shook the ground and the air. The atomic bomb was feasible.

The problem for President Harry S Truman was now to decide whether or not to use the new weapon. The bomb was there, and so was the means to deliver it (the 509th Composite Group, USAAF, which had been training in the deserts of Utah with its B-29 bombers). The debate was a heated one, but in the end most senior commanders consulted, and Secretary of War Henry Stimson, thought that the new weapon should be used. Japan still had enormous military strength, they reasoned, and why should American lives be lost in their hundreds of thousands when a means of preventing it was available? Truman agreed with reluctance. At the Potsdam Conference in July, Truman told Clement Attlee, Prime Minister of Great Britain, about the weapon and his decision to use it. In the Potsdam Declaration of 7 July Truman and Attlee called on Japan to surrender, warning that refusal to do so would entail the 'inevitable and complete destruction of the Japanese armed forces and . . . the utter devastation of the Japanese homeland'. When Japan failed to reply, Truman gave his

Left : **Colonel Paul Tibbetts poses beside his B-29** *Enola Gay.* *Right :* **Tibbetts' bombing contributed materially to the Japanese surrender.**

authority for the first atomic bomb to be dropped.

The target selected was Hiroshima, a city of some 300,000 people, which was an important military objective but, as yet, little affected by conventional attacks. On 6 August the B-29 'Enola Gay', named after the mother of pilot Colonel Paul Tibbetts, took off from the Marianas and headed for Japan. The air-raid warning was sounded in Hiroshima, but seeing that there were only a few planes overhead, most people failed to take cover. The bomb was dropped, and exploded at exactly the right place and height, with a force equal to that of 20,000 tonnes of TNT going off. Exact figures are still not available, but it seems that 78,150 people died almost immediately and another 70,000 were injured. Most of the centre of Hiroshima was completely destroyed.

The impact of the bomb on Japanese politicians and military leaders was profound, but tinged somewhat with incredulity. The dropping of a second bomb on Nagasaki, on 9 August, altered that and convinced Japan's leaders that the war must end. The Nagasaki explosion, also of some 20 kilotonnes, killed 40,000 and injured 25,000 people out of a population of some 250,000. Luckily for the Japanese, the country on which the city is built is hilly, and this diverted much of the blast.

Emperor Hirohito at last made a firm decision and insisted on peace. There were inevitably dissenters, and a coup had to be put

down in Tokyo. Following discussions by radio, Japan agreed to an unconditional surrender, which in fact had several conditions for the benefit of the Japanese: the emperor was to remain, and Japan was to remain undivided.

A cease-fire came into effect on 15 August, although many Japanese refused to believe the emperor's broadcast and fought on for a few more days. They imagined that it was an Allied trick, for none of them had ever heard the emperor's voice before, so great had been his apolitical seclusion. Gradually, however, peace fell over the battlefields of the Pacific and Asia during the next few days. On 28 August General Douglas MacArthur and the first American occupation forces arrived in Japan, and the real impact of defeat began to be felt by the average Japanese.

The formal end of the war against Japan came on 2 September, in a ceremony on board the great battleship *Missouri* in Tokyo Bay. Each side was attended by many functionaries, a number of those in MacArthur's party being released prisoners of war, including Lieutenant-Generals Wainwright and Percival from the Philippines and Singapore. The Japanese Foreign Minister, Mamoru Shigemitsu, signed for the Imperial government, and MacArthur for the Allies as the Supreme Commander. MacArthur closed the ceremony with the historic words: 'I declare these proceedings closed.'

After perhaps some 50,000,000 people had lost their lives, World War II was at last over.

THE WAR LORDS

FROM an early age, Winston Churchill had been fascinated by war, and this emotional attachment was to remain with the energetic British politician throughout his life. Following in his father's footsteps when he decided on politics as a career, Churchill soon found that the control of the services as a minister was what suited him best: between 1911 and 1915 he was a successful, if idiosyncratic, First Lord of the Admiralty. However, his constant energy and enthusiasms went far beyond this, and Churchill was instrumental in hurrying along the development and introduction of the tank, for example. It was at this point, in World War I, that Churchill's main fault as a war leader became apparent: he had so much involvement and interest in his task that he could not stand by and watch the professionals get on with their job. He constantly meddled, came up with suggestions, some practical and others definitely whimsical, and constantly prodded his subordinates into the investigation of any device that he thought might be of use. This last factor was especially the case with strange 'war-winning' weapons, for Churchill was fascinated by technical devices.

Out in the political wilderness for much of the period between the two world wars, Churchill's warnings of Germany's ambitions were seen to be justified in the late 1930s, and Churchill once more began to regain credence as a politician. In 1939 he was recalled as First Lord of the Admiralty, and in May 1940, became Prime Minister on the resignation of Neville Chamberlain.

From this time, until he was ousted in the general election of early 1945, Churchill combined the jobs of Prime Minister and Minister of Defence with indefatigable energy. A stream of memoranda poured from his office to every conceivable department, the majority of them headed 'Most Secret' or 'Action This Day'. Like Hitler, Churchill had a passion for details, and was constantly on the lookout for these. Unlike Hitler, Churchill was prepared to abide by the professional advice of his senior commanders, at least most of the time. Churchill's relations with his senior service leaders were frequently stormy, but always aimed at getting Great Britain nearer to final victory.

Seeing himself as the embodiment of the British will first to survive and then to prevail, Churchill made himself a flamboyant personality with his dazzling rhetoric, siren suits, constant cigars and famous V-sign. Yet underneath he was something more – totally implacable, and realistic about how the war was to be won. Churchill realized that Britain alone could not hope to defeat Germany, and so his long-term strategy was to hold out at any cost until the United States was drawn into the war. Thus his country would become the springboard from which the reconquest of western Europe from the Germans would begin. Although this always remained his long-term plan, in the short term Churchill wanted action, anywhere and

Below : **In August 1942 Churchill visited the Middle Eastern theatre, where he conferred with Field-Marshal Smuts, the South African Premier.**

by any means that the British could strike at the Germans. Hence his preoccupation with special forces such as the commandos, and occasionally his diversion from the main effort in order to strike a quicker blow.

HITLER presents a puzzling picture as a war leader. Superficially, he was an amateur of considerable gifts, as his adoption of the von Manstein 'Sickle' plan for the invasion of France and the stand before Moscow indicated. But as a leader of a nation in arms Hitler had great faults, particularly in view of his 'sleepwalker's assurance' about the correctness of all that he did. It was this attitude that was to lead him to ruin: Hitler felt rather than thought out his plans, and was convinced of their essential correctness despite the fact that he did not really know what he was doing.

Nowhere is this more evident than in Hitler's overall concept of his war plans, or rather in his lack of them. In Russia, for example, the German armies were to carry all before them, with the primary objectives of Moscow and Leningrad. But Hitler had absolutely no idea where this was to lead him. He hoped vaguely that Russia would surrender, but made no plans for establishing a German defence line for the inevitable counteroffensives should she not do so. There was not even a definite stop-line for the first offensive, in 1941.

Although he railed at them constantly, Hitler was at first prepared to accept the advice of his generals in the overall conduct of operations. However, as soon as things began to go wrong, the true nature of Hitler's opinion of the military professionals became clear. He himself would take over personal command of the armies. He considered that the professionals were a group of aristocratic bunglers, who had risen in prestige by means of their position rather than any innate abilities. Hitler, in fact, despised the German generals as a class, and nowhere is this more

Adolf Hitler ist der Sieg!

Above left : **Hitler was ecstatic about the fall of France, whose surrender was signed in the carriage in which the Germans had capitulated in 1918.**
Above : **'Adolf Hitler is Victory!'**

evident than in his personal entourage, especially the nonentities he appointed to posts in the Armed Forces and Army High Commands (OKW and OKH), having rid himself of the last able officers from the Weimar Republic days. A constant meddler, with the dictator's usual fascination for minutiae, Hitler wished to control everything himself. He did this by having no able, aggressive subordinates, and keeping the command structure as fragmented as possible. Thus no overall high command, so essential to the running of vast and complex operations, was set up, and the senior staff officers were kept at work trying to run the great German war machine which had no real head and little coordination between the parts. Hitler himself interfered increasingly with the actual command of operations, as Stalin did, but lacked the other dictator's singleness of purpose and harsh grasp on reality. Hitler saw what he wanted to see; if reserves were needed, there was always a pin on the map board available. It did not concern Hitler that although the pin might represent a corps, this formation might be down to below divisional strength as a result of previous operations. With a complete lack of formal military training, and no real control of his emotions and desires, it was inevitable that Hitler should become the worst sort of 'mapboard general', with disastrous results for Germany.

BENITO Mussolini had been the first fascist dictator, and in the early stages of his career Hitler had looked up to this elder statesman with admiration. However, by 1939 the roles of Hitler and Mussolini had been reversed. No longer was Mussolini the forceful leader of a new political philosophy, but

rather a pompous man more interested in showiness than in real progress. The trains may well have run on time in Italy, but the farmers and working classes were still as backward as ever, and industry had advanced little in the decade and a half of Mussolini's rule.

Although heralded as a great victory, Mussolini's invasion and conquest of Ethiopia from 1935 on had been a shallow victory against negligible opposition, and had revealed serious flaws in the equipment and training of the Italian armed forces. The Italian experience in the Spanish Civil War had further reinforced this impression. Thus when he was informed of Hitler's decision to go to war, Mussolini begged not to be included. Italy had not got the strength for it and, more significantly, had few of the stocks of raw materials such as oil and rare metals needed for a prolonged war.

Having avoided involvement at the beginning of hostilities, Mussolini was not at all averse to picking up the scraps, and so in June 1940 he decided to take over some of southern France and Britain's North African possessions, as well as invading Greece. In all three areas the Italians were held or repulsed with some ease by inferior forces. It was a shock from which Mussolini was never to recover, and his immediate reaction was to call for help from Germany, embroiling that nation in military excursions into the Mediterranean: an area it had not before

Right : **Benito Mussolini,** *Duce* **of Italy, was the world's first fascist leader.**
Below : **Disgraced and captive, during autumn 1943, Mussolini had to be rescued by German raiders.**

considered. From this time on, Mussolini's Italy slipped slowly into obscurity. Mussolini was able to do little but rely on Hitler. His own grasp of military realities was scant, and his senior service advisers proved little better. Having entered the war in the belief that quick pickings were there to be had, Mussolini now found that his forces were totally inadequate for a sustained campaign. After his ousting in 1943, when most of Italy changed sides, Mussolini was rescued by the Germans and placed at the head of the puppet Salo Republic. He was killed by partisans in 1945.

FRANKLIN D 'Roosevelt, like Churchill, had a long acquaintance with military matters, having been Assistant Secretary of the Navy during World War I. Unlike Churchill, he had never served in the armed forces, and so was able to keep a clear distinction in his head between the overall direction of the country's war effort, and the actual conduct of operations. This had perhaps been Churchill's besetting weakness, and a pitfall that Roosevelt was careful to avoid.

In his second term as President, when World War II broke out in Europe, Roosevelt early on felt that the United States would inevitably be drawn into the conflict. Thus, in the face of a powerful isolationist lobby, he pushed through measures designed to step up the United States' war industries and armed forces, while at the same time providing as much material aid as possible to the United States' natural partners in Europe: France and Great Britain, although only Great Britain was left in the field after June 1940. Roosevelt's policy led to the supply of weapons and food, and also involved the straining of international law in such matters as the use of American warships to escort convoys near the American coast.

The American war machine was already moving into top gear by the time Japan's attack on Pearl Harbor in December 1941, brought the United States into the war. Roosevelt was content to leave production in the hands of the various boards he had set up earlier, and the conduct of operations to

his professional military advisers: General George C Marshall for the army, and Admiral Ernest J King for the navy.

Roosevelt, therefore, concentrated on the overall running of the war in the grand strategic sense. As commander in chief of the US armed forces, only he in the long run could decide where and when operations were to be initiated. However, he was on good terms with his service chiefs and usually took their word for the right order of priorities. Only when there was disagreement, as between Nimitz and MacArthur over the future of Pacific operations in the middle of 1944, did Roosevelt have to choose between one side or the other. But this was unusual, for the American war effort seemed normally to run itself under the direction of King and Marshall.

Thus freed from day to day decisions, Roosevelt was able to give much of his

Below: **Franklin D Roosevelt was President of the United States from 1933 to 1945.** *Bottom:* **Stalin, Roosevelt and Churchill were the three great Allied leaders at the Teheran Conference in 1943.**

attention to the problems of the Allies as a whole, the 'Grand Alliance', and to the future of the world after the end of World War II. He saw a broader picture than either Churchill or Stalin, and so was more concerned with long-term planning. Roosevelt and Churchill had always got on well together, and it was perhaps this personal relationship that was one of the most important factors in British and American cooperation. It also played an important part in leading Roosevelt to adopt the 'Germany first' policy: of the Allies' two enemies, Germany was the more powerful, and so the United States and Britain would concentrate on defeating her first, and only then turn their full attention to Japan.

JOSEF Stalin, the dictator of Russia throughout World War II, remains an enigma. Like Hitler, he was a total dictator, but unlike the German leader he was able to deal with all the complex problems posed by the conduct of vast operations and by the great dislocation caused by the war.

An astute and ruthless man, there is no doubt that Stalin was surprised tactically by Germany's invasion of his country in June 1941. Recovering quickly, he soon learned from his lessons. In the late 1930s he had purged some 400 senior commanders from the armed forces for political reasons, and this had an immediate effect on the Russian conduct of operations: the newer commanders had been pushed up too quickly, and frequently proved unable to cope with the stresses and problems posed by the swift German advances. Stalin let these commanders find their own levels – if they were successful, he left them where they were or promoted them; if they were unsuccessful, they were eliminated and new commanders appointed. By the time of the great stand before Moscow, the dead wood had been cut from the Russian military tree, and Stalin had found most of the senior commanders who were to serve Russia so well during the

Below: **Ministers Ribbentrop and Molotov sign the August 1939 Non-Aggression Treaty for Germany and Russia; Stalin watches.**

Above: **Roosevelt, Churchill and Stalin dine together during the Yalta Conference that partitioned Europe.** *Left:* **By the time of the Potsdam Conference, the 'Big Three' had changed, Harry Truman (centre) replacing the dead Roosevelt, and Clement Attlee, Churchill.** *Right:* **General Hideki Tojo.**

rest of the war. Most important of these new men was Georgi Zhukov, Stalin's right-hand man in military matters. Undoubtedly the ablest commander produced so far by Soviet Russia, Zhukov was equally at home in the field or in Moscow planning the overall shape of the Russian campaign.

Yet Zhukov was not sole master of the day to day running of the Russian armed forces. Stalin was a prodigious worker, and was fascinated by detail. Everything had to be reported to him, and he proved well able to absorb the implications of the vast flow of information reaching him. Rarely stirring from Moscow, Stalin controlled the Russian campaign by telephone, and no commander could rest comfortably as long as he knew that Stalin was in all probability scanning reports from his sector and might at any moment phone and ask pertinent questions.

Right from the beginning of the campaign Stalin had decided what must be done, and this policy was then pursued with implacable ruthlessness: while the armies tried to slow the Germans, all Russia's heavy industry was to be uprooted from European Russia and transferred to safety deep in Russia. Only with this industry could Russia hope to build the weapons needed for final victory, and so any and every loss was to be tolerated in order that the heavy industrial plants might be moved.

Once these plants were running at full steam again, the Russian armies could be built up and then go over to the offensive against the Germans. Numbers and a vast quantity of standardized *matériel* would be sufficient to drive the invaders back, and then the armies could start looking for more – improved tactical and strategic doctrines, and territories that could be taken over by Russia as the Germans were pushed back. The hallmarks of Stalin's overall leadership, however, were his single-mindedness and absolute ruthlessness, combined with his great organizational abilities.

L IEUTENANT-GENERAL Hideki Tojo was War Minister in the government of Prince Konoye in 1940, and observing the success of the Axis forces in Europe urged that Japan ally herself with Germany and Italy. In September 1940, the Tripartite Pact was signed between the three countries, and Tojo was sure that Japan could only profit from the alliance.

In October 1941, Tojo became Prime Minister and virtual dictator of Japan thanks to the traditions of political non-involvement forced upon the emperor. Although Japan was already involved in a major war with China, Tojo decided that his country could undertake a successful military campaign to secure Japanese interests in South-East Asia and the Indies, known as the 'Southern Resources Area'. If a lightning victory could be achieved over the Americans, British and Dutch, Tojo felt that his forces would not be overstretched. An impregnable defensive perimeter would then be set up, allowing most Japanese troops to be sent back to the main war in China. In the event, the

Allies were not prepared to accept the Japanese conquests in the Pacific, and Tojo lacked the authority or even the will to try to rectify matters with sensible military solutions. The perimeter was far too large for Japan to hold, and strategic withdrawal would have been in order. The Japanese high command was hopelessly divided: the army and navy had equal authority, and there was no overall command body to implement the decisions of the government. Tojo was the army's representative in the government, as well as the Prime Minister, but should his navy counterpart resign as a result of an unpopular decision, the government would fall according to Japanese law. Tojo's hands were tied, and as a result the armed forces fought bravely against the Allies, but piece-meal, and were slowly pushed back.

Tojo's gamble had failed, and after the American landings in the Marianas had shown that the war must end in defeat for Japan, Tojo resigned. At the end of the war he was the only Axis leader arrested for war crimes, found guilty and hanged.

Index

Acknowledgment

The publishers would like to thank the following individuals and organizations for their kind permission to reproduce the photographs in this book.

Associated Press 19, 52 left and right, 238–239, 246 above, (US Army) 110 below centre; Bapty & Co (print from J G Moore Collection, London) 27 centre, 34 above, 88–89; Blitz Publications (J G Moore Collection) 72; Camera Press 160 left, 172–173, 230–231, 250 above, (Imperial War Museum) 136–137, 156–157, 190–191; Fleet Air Arm; Yeovilton (J G Moore Collection) 88; John Frost Newspaper Collection 15 inset, 67 inset, 105 inset, 184 inset; Fox Photos Ltd. 21; Fujiphotos 110–111 above, 111 above, 123, 216–217; Robert Hunt Library 12 above, 12–13, 12 below, 13 below, 26, 27 above and below, 28, 29 above, 32 left and right, 33, 49, left, 51 centre, 54, 58 below left, 59, 60, 78, 79, 78–79, 81 centre left and centre right, 84–85, 85 above and below, 86 below, 87, 107, 113, 114, 115 above, 116 below, 131, 148–149 below, 175, 197 above and centre right, 207, 222–223 above, 239, 240–241, 247 above right, 248 below right, 249 above left, 251 right, (Imperial War Museum) 117; Imperial War Museum 2–3, 6–7, 10, 29 below left and below right, 31 right, 36–37 above, 43, 44, 45, 46, 47, 49 right, 50, 51 above, 61, 62–63, 63 inset, 66–67, 74 below, 74–75, 82, 83, 84, 86 above, 92–93, 95, 97, 100–101, 102, 114–115, 119, 132 left, 132–133, 134–135, 142–143, 143 below, 149 above right and below right, 150–151 above, 152, 152–153, above and below, 154–155, 158 below left and below right, 160–161 below left, 166–167, 168–169, 170–171, 171, 183 above right, 188–189 below, 194 above, 195, 197 cut-out, 197 below, 208 below, 232–233 above, 234–235, 235 cut-out, 236–237 above and below, 240, 241, 246 below, 248 below left, 249 above left, (J G Moore Collection) 90–91, (Nautic Visual Services) 148–149 above; Institute of Military Science, Helsinki (J G Moore Collection) 20, 22–23, 23 above and below; Keystone Press Agency 13 above, 18, 54–55, 55 below, 64–65, 65, 68–69, 69, 70, 71, 99, 103, 134–135 below, 155, 157, 158–159, 160–161 above, 161 below right, 162–163, 176–177 above and below, 182, 182–183, 183 below right, 196–197, 201–202, 204–205, 205, 218, 219, 220, 221, 222–223 below, 232, 232–233 below, 236, 249 below left, (Air Ministry) 34 below right, (US Navy) 96; S L Mayer 150 below; J G Moore Collection, London 4–5, 14–15, 24, 48, 53, 56–57; Novosti Press Agency 77, 126–127, 128–129 above and below, 129 right, 136, 139, 140–141, 242 left, 242–243;

Popperfoto 17, 31 left, 36 above left, 36–37 below, 90, 91, 179; Radio Times Hulton Picture Library 34 below left, 34–35, 38 above, 38–39, 39 above and below; The Director, The Science Museum 40; US Airforce 151 above right, 244, (J G Moore Collection) 168–169; US Army, Washington 143 above, 144–145 164, 165, 167, 172, 178, 187, 188–189 above, 194 below, 200–201, 249 below; US Coastguard 124–125, 229 above; US Marine Corps, Washington 120, 122, 184–185, 186–187, 188, 191, 192, 192, 192–193, 193 above and below, 198–199, 200, 201, 229 below, (J G Moore Collection) 224–225, 226, 226–227 above and below, 228–229; US National Archives 11, 108–109, 109, 125 inset, 146–147, 208 below, 212 (US Army Collection) 244 (US Navy Collection) 98, 210–211, 214 left, 214–215 above and below, 215 below right (US Navy Collection, print from J G Moore Collection) 206–207; US Navy 42–43, 104–105, 116 left and right, 118, 208 above, 209 above, 210, 223 below (J G Moore Collection) 106–107; Ullstein GMBH 18–19, 25, 40 inset.